DESMOND TUTU

DESMOND TUTU

A Spiritual Biography of South Africa's Confessor

Michael Battle

WESTMINSTER
JOHN KNOX PRESS
LOUISVILLE • KENTUCKY

First edition
Published by Westminster John Knox Press
Louisville, Kentucky

21 22 23 24 25 26 27 28 29 30—10 9 8 7 6 5 4 3 2 1

Scripture quotations are from the New Revised Standard Version of the Bible, copyright © 1989 by the Division of Christian Education of the National Council of the Churches of Christ in the U.S.A. and are used by permission.

Michael Battle had extensive access to Archbishop Tutu's unpublished papers in the early 1990s. Excerpts are used here with permission.

Excerpts from Wilhelm Verwoerd, *Verwoerd: My Journey through Family Betrayals*, ©2019, Tafelberg Publishers, appear in Chapter 7. Reproduced by permission of Wilhelm Verwoerd.

Excerpts from Tinyiko Sam Maluleke, "Can Lions and Rabbits Reconcile? The South African TRC as an Instrument for Peace-Building," *The Ecumenical Review* vol. 53, no. 2 (April 2001): 190–201 appear in Chapter 6. Reproduced by permission of Tinyiko Sam Maluleke.

Every effort has been made to determine whether texts are under copyright. If through an oversight any copyrighted material has been used without permission, and the publisher is notified of this, acknowledgment will be made in future printings.

Book design by Sharon Adams
Cover design by Allison Taylor
Cover photo: Archbishop Tutu at the COP 17 "We Have Faith: Act Now for Climate Justice" Rally on Nov. 27, 2011, in Durban, South Africa (Photo by Kristen Opalinski/LUCSA)

Library of Congress Cataloging-in-Publication Data is on file at the Library of Congress, Washington DC.

ISBN-13: 978-0-664-23158-3

Most Westminster John Knox Press books are available at special quantity discounts when purchased in bulk by corporations, organizations, and special-interest groups. For more information, please e-mail SpecialSales@wjkbooks.com.

Contents

Foreword

HIS HOLINESS THE 14TH DALAI LAMA OF TIBET

Since I am trained in compassion, I will be brief to allow you quick entrance into the marvelous life of my dear friend, Desmond. It is my firm belief that very few individuals practice dialogue as a means to resolve problems better than Desmond. And indeed, this prowess comes out of his spiritual life. Desmond is an avowed campaigner for the revelation of love all over the world. Because of this, I wholeheartedly welcome you to read this book to discover Desmond's own foundation of such a campaign to love. I applaud Desmond's disciple, Michael Battle, for writing this book. May his efforts here encourage further endeavors to know more about spiritual leaders who impact the world with joy and who aim to bring about genuine and lasting peace in our world.

One must know that the spiritual life requires action in the world. Desmond knew, for example, that to hold power at the barrel of the gun rather than through elections is immoral and outdated as well. He understood that a single ruler is not good and that a democracy is better. In my public teaching at Tsulagkhang, the main temple, in Dharamsala, India, on the morning of 19 March 2011, I concluded that it is also not at all good if the Dalai Lama keeps on holding ultimate power. The Dalai Lama as both the spiritual and temporal authority of Tibet in the twenty-first century had to change. I am the fourteenth in line of that institution of Dalai Lamas and it is most appropriate if I on my own initiative end the dual authority of the Dalai Lama. Nobody except me can make this decision, and I have made the final decision. The leadership democratically elected by the Tibetan people should take over the complete political responsibilities of Tibet. I will continue to take spiritual responsibilities for the remaining part of my life.

Like Desmond, I receive many invitations from different schools and universities around the world. They are not asking me to come to preach on Buddhism as such, but to teach how to promote compassion and happiness. So, to claim spiritual responsibilities does not mean my retreat from the practical concerns of living this life. Here, I think, is the great value of Michael Battle's book. Michael understands that the spiritual life is vital to the earthly one. I hope this book goes out into the international community who supports the Tibetan cause. I hope

Desmond's spiritual work will display my own spiritual sincerity for a democratized Tibetan polity. Such a polity raises our prestige in the world. So, too, Desmond's work to apply his joyful spirit to the ills of South Africa has raised his prestige in the world.

Although the world knows better, both Desmond and I are retired of sorts. If some problem arises that necessitates our help, we know that we are not alone in working for compassion and joy. We have you to help. I have not given up, and neither will Desmond.

Preface

It is a rare person who arrives at that state of perfect spiritual serenity. I suppose they are saints of sorts, not necessarily beatified and canonized saints, but the kind of people in whose presence we intuit the nearness of God, because they bring their best friend everywhere with them. God does not accompany them as a bodyguard or go in front of them like a Soviet tank clearing a path. He accompanies them as a soprano's pure voice accompanies a song, as a dewdrop sits on a rose.[1]

On one of my Tutu Travel Seminars to Cape Town, South Africa, in which Desmond and Leah Tutu kindly hosted theological students and clergy, one of my white students honestly but naively asked them, "How dangerous was it in South Africa during apartheid, and how did you deal with fear?" In the desert traditions of Christian spirituality, the question was more important than the answer. As the professor, I was nervous because my student certainly could have asked a better question—or at the very least, could have asked only one question at a time. But Tutu graciously answered both questions in one response: "God looked after us."

Indeed, in those dangerous times, Tutu's passionate concern for God and God's passionate concern for Tutu overrode fear. There were occasions when people would have been killed, had Tutu not stepped in, wearing his purple bishop's cassock. When I taught at Duke University, my colleague Peter Storey, a major Methodist leader from South Africa, told me about a time in the early 1990s in Soweto when he saw a teenager put a gun to Tutu's head. In that dire circumstance, Storey said to the youth, "Are you going to kill your bishop?" The kid backed down. God did look after Tutu.

Tutu also looked after God. When he was an active bishop, Tutu kept a rigorous schedule. At four in the morning he would wake, and then be on his knees in prayer for an hour. At five thirty, Tutu would walk and be silent. He would shower and be at his desk around six—often reading but also doing some desk work. At seven forty-five there would be morning prayer followed by the eight o'clock Eucharist. Breakfast would come around eight thirty.

Then he would formally begin his day at nine. So he would essentially have four hours of silence at the beginning of each day. In the middle of the day he would be back at chapel, then to a light lunch, then a siesta until three. So he would spend another two hours in silence in the middle of the day. At the end of the day he would spend half an hour in the chapel, then go to evening prayer. All told, each day would bring about seven hours in silence with God.

John Allen, Tutu's longtime friend, communication director, and biographer, told me that when he used to travel with Tutu, international organizations tried to pressure Tutu to do things morning, noon, and night. Allen said to them, "What kind of Tutu do you want? And why did you invite him here? Well, if you want him for his communicative skills, ebullient personality, and that kind of thing in which he thrives in big groups . . . if you want that Tutu, you need to respect his need for chunks of silence."[2] For Tutu, it was like two sides of a coin. If you want the spirituality, communication, and ebullience, you need the other side—silence, contemplation, and stillness with God.

Great stories about Tutu, like the ones above, have already been told; so why should you read this particular book? Much has already been written, filmed, and recorded about this important figure. Since theology and spiritual matters are ephemeral and, to some, even irrelevant, why should anyone be interested in looking at a historical figure like Tutu through a theological worldview? And personally, why should I write this biography, especially with the existence of my other books on Tutu's theology and my friend John Allen's expansive Tutu biography?

One answer has to do with my personal relationship with Tutu. I lived with him for two years in the early 1990s, and we have remained close since. Indeed, he ordained me to the clergy, married my wife Raquel and me, and baptized all three of our children. I will discuss this close nature of our friendship in the Introduction.

A further reason for this book is the fact that Tutu was a major leader of the antiapartheid movement in South Africa and frequently led demonstrations and spoke out on the world stage in support of democracy and civil rights. Even those who do not know the details know about the major events in Tutu's life: serving as the general secretary of the South African Council of Churches (SACC) from 1978 to 1985, receiving the Nobel Peace Prize in 1984, serving as the first black archbishop of Cape Town[3] and primate of Southern Africa 1986–96, and chairing the Truth and Reconciliation Commission (TRC) (1995–98). But even though many may know these facts, the tensions of racism, politics, and short-term memory may have caused amnesia.

Many may not know that when other black[4] South African leaders were jailed or exiled, Tutu was pressed into action to lead the opposition to apartheid South Africa. For example, by the late 1970s, around the time of the Soweto uprising, Nelson Mandela had been in prison for around fifteen years. For the younger generation of South African youth, Mandela had become increasingly unknown.

The Roman Catholic archbishop of Johannesburg, Buti Tlhagale, who grew up in Soweto, told John Allen that in the late 1970s the name Mandela was almost unknown to the younger Soweto generation. After the Soweto uprising of 1976, Tutu became one of the major figures to stand up against the apartheid government, along with people like Percy Qoboza (an influential black South African journalist and editor of the major black newspaper *The World* in Johannesburg), Nthato Motlana (Mandela's medical doctor who later became a prominent businessman), and Winnie Mandela (a major antiapartheid activist and Mandela's wife at that time).[5]

All of this occurred as Tutu was rising in the Anglican Church hierarchy, becoming bishop of Johannesburg in 1985 and archbishop in 1986. Here was a spiritual leader rising in a political world, with a complex set of constituencies. As a Nobel Peace Prize winner, he served all South Africans as their unofficial ambassador to the world at large. The form of protest he was able to engender on an international level was groundbreaking, as he pushed the point that sanctions offered the last hope of avoiding a "holocaust" in South Africa. Tutu also presided over the political miracle of South Africa's Truth and Reconciliation Commission (TRC) from 1995 to 1998, and subsequently acted as a global Elder counseling many parties' conflicts around the world. If many people already know all of this, why another biography on Tutu?

In short, I have two answers. First, in his senior years, as Tutu has moved off the public world stage and worked more quietly as an Elder, younger generations may not have learned of these major contributions that Tutu made in facilitating South Africa's democracy. There were many reasons why Tutu actively decided to move off the world stage, including his wisdom to cultivate new leadership, as well as the fragility of his health. Tutu's decisions to become lesser so that someone else could become greater, such as when he pulled back from the limelight when Nelson Mandela was released from prison, were not accidental. These were habits that he learned from the biblical narratives of spiritual people. The Anglican priest Francis Cull, who was Tutu's spiritual director at Bishopscourt, the residence of the archbishop of the Anglican Church of Southern Africa, served as Tutu's confessor. Cull would hold Tutu accountable to go on retreats at least once a year, do a seven-day silent retreat when appropriate, say his prayers, and confess his sin.

I remember Cull telling me about Tutu's spiritual disciplines when I lived with Tutu at Bishopscourt. Tutu had an intense awareness of his faults, Cull said, and was deeply introspective. Cull and I talked about how most people would never have believed this about Tutu, given his outgoing and buoyant personality. Cull used to say that you could not understand Tutu unless you understood Tutu's spiritual struggles as well.

So here in my first answer as to why this spiritual biography is important. Tutu may not be as well known to today's younger generations, just as Mandela was not known by the younger generations in the 1970s. But in Tutu's case, his seclusion has been self-imposed.

My second answer is the real reason for writing this book: Tutu is a saint. This point requires a deeper explanation, because I do not make such a claim out of sycophantic glory. What I mean here is that Tutu's maturity toward union with God provides a contrast to the alternative universe of apartheid, in which white separation from other races represented white holiness, in which true heroes and saints were only those of European descent and, even more particularly, Afrikaner.

The Hebrew word for holy is *qodesh*, which on the surface shares the same meaning of holiness or set-apartness. In the Hebrew Bible (Old Testament), to be holy meant to be transcendent and totally other, because God is this way. The concept of being holy carried the connotation of the weight of glory that only a select group, chosen by God, could carry. In the New Testament, the word for holy is *hagios*, which also means to be set apart.

In a horrific sense, "apartheid" also means to be holy. Afrikaner theology in support of apartheid was rooted in a misguided interpretation of Calvinist doctrine. Such Afrikaner theology was developed to inspire Christians to keep going on the "Great Trek," an eastward migration in 1836 of Dutch-speaking settlers who traveled by wagon trains into the interior of South Africa to escape the Cape of Southern Africa's British colonial rule. The Cape's original European settlers, known as Boers, were in constant clashes with the British Empire. The Boers became oppressors of black people as they sought to legitimize the subordination of other South African ethnicities by laying the theological foundation for modern Afrikaner nationalism and apartheid.

The Boer Wars, in which the British Empire tried to vanquish Afrikaner resistance, left many Afrikaners desperate as they tried to survive in Africa. Poor white Afrikaners lined the highways trying to sell whatever they had to survive. Eventually four South African colonies united politically into the Union of South Africa and relinquished control to democratic elections. When this occurred, a group of young white intellectuals called the Afrikaner Broederbond formally adopted their version of Calvinist theology based on the work of Abraham Kuyper, prime minister of the Netherlands (1901–1905). Kuyper was also a theologian who articulated the theological concept of pillarization, which advocated for political and denominational segregation of a society. Human beings should consciously divide into different hierarchies purposely set apart from one another, he argued. The Broederbond believed in such pillarization to separate blacks, colored, and whites.[6] Such a theological framework of "set apartness" was directly responsible for the establishment of apartheid in 1948.

The argument here and in much of this biography is that the worldview of apartheid was really one of hagiography (determining the criteria for sainthood), in which "separate development" was a euphemism for being holy. Apartheid was de facto a different version of the spiritual life, in which white people saw themselves particularly as saints. Apartheid was conceived and nurtured within the Afrikaans Reformed churches and was theologically justified as a political policy. No one can effectively argue that apartheid was simply about politics, because it was inherently a spiritual enterprise that justified white power over darkness and black people.

My premise of Tutu becoming an alternative kind of saint turns apartheid's hagiography on its head and requires a spiritual and theological perspective. This may raise the hackles of those who are disassociated from religious, spiritual, or theological discourse. Even if it does, we still need saints. If human communities want to stop repeating the mistakes of history, we need to understand the errant uses of religion. *The brilliance here of Tutu's sainthood is in how he leads us to see how we are all saints—not just the set apart.* Tutu states, "In my theology there are no ordinary people. Each one of us, because we are God's representative, God's viceroy, God's stand-in, and a God-carrier—each one of us is a very special person."[7] Few can argue against Tutu's positive impact on the world in this regard.

There are those who believe that spiritual discourse is often only about the subjectivity of personal salvation—so much so that there is often no substance to whatever is being described as spiritual. A brief word, then, may be in order as to my interchangeable use of "spiritual," "mystical," and "theological."

For me, mysticism denotes a spirituality lived out in those seeking the tangibility of divine presence. For example, there is the story of a mother trying to comfort her son, who is resisting bedtime. "Son, don't be afraid," she says, "God is with you." The boy, now crying even harder, says in between sniffles, "But mom, I need someone with skin on." Spirituality is the skin of mysticism. Theology is a manner of thinking about mysticism, which is present in all our world religions but is often relegated to otherworldly pursuits. In Christian mysticism, however, there is not a sharp distinction between mysticism and theology or between personal experience of divine mysteries and the church's theology. As the renowned Eastern Orthodox theologian Vladimir Lossky states, "We must live the dogma expressing a revealed truth, which appears to us an unfathomable mystery, in such a fashion that instead of assimilating the mystery to our mode of understanding, we should, on the contrary, look for a profound change, an inner transformation of spirit, enabling us to experience it mystically."[8]

So, in keeping with this balance of mysticism, spirituality, and theology, this biography uses these terms interchangeably. It is true, however, that mysticism in particular holds an apolitical connotation among many, as an inaccessible realm hidden from mortals. Tutu's spiritual life changes all of this as he states, "As I grow older, I am pleasantly surprised at how relevant theology has become in my perception."[9]

My biography of Tutu offers more explicit attention to a remedy for this, as I believe Tutu's political life is actually illumined by deep spirituality—the kind of spirituality that is usually noticed only in crises or after death. In many ways, Tutu's spirit is akin to an artist who is known and valued only after death. Tutu's art looks like expensive grace (as opposed to cheap grace), restorative justice, and Ubuntu (the African concept of interdependence)—all pieces of work sold at high value when the community realizes that a great soul like that will never be seen again.

So I come clean in the outset of this biography with my mystical assertion that Tutu is a saint. Those who are saints work in the nexus between human and divine realities. This may come as little surprise to some who have critiqued my perspective on Tutu's life—claiming that my theological work on Tutu is akin to hagiography, with little critique. What I write here will be of little surprise to such critics. To my surprise, however, most of these critics still honor Tutu's spiritual acumen.

Christian hagiography still remains the domain of a white, European world-view in which the literary genre of spirituality seldom includes black folks. Yes, Tutu is honored as a political agent. For example, Tutu was among sixteen people honored with the Presidential Medal of Freedom, presented by President Barack Obama in 2009. "With unflagging devotion to justice, indomitable optimism, and an unmistakable sense of humor," Obama said, Tutu "has stirred the world's conscience for decades" and "continues to give voice to the voiceless and bring hope to those who thirst for freedom."[10]

Of course, I agree with Obama and thank him for honoring Tutu in the United States in this way. But Tutu is much more—and even much deeper. In many ways, Tutu's invaluable witness in the twentieth and twenty-first centuries reminds me of a humorous story told about a kindergarten class. A kindergarten teacher was observing her classroom of children while they were drawing. The teacher would occasionally walk around to see each child's work. She asked a little girl named Susan what she was drawing. Susan replied, "I'm drawing God." The teacher paused and, being theologically correct, said, "But Susan, you can't do that. No one knows what God looks like." Without missing a beat or looking up from her drawing, Susan replied, "They will in a minute."

Tutu's life demonstrates God. Few individuals take on such an impossible task. Even fewer demonstrate the impossible. Tutu falls in this category of someone defying the odds. As a biographer, I seek to be like little Susan and write what God looks like in the world. Although this may be critiqued by some who say that Tutu does not represent God, the work intended here is not to diminish the ineffable God, even as Tutu—an ecumenist who believes in interreligious dialogue—still adheres to the essential revelation of God in Jesus Christ. As I display in the latter chapters of this biography, such revelation never gets in the way of deep friendships with other saints, like the Dalai Lama, whose revelation of God is much different. Again, Tutu's constituencies are complicated. But the revelation of the incarnation provides a basis for Tutu's purchase on sainthood: God's incarnational ways of laying down bridges between worlds on which humanity may cross into God's divine life. My premise of sainthood, therefore, does not mean Tutu is God or that he is perfect; rather, I lay out a narrative of Tutu's life in which God is present and vital. Tutu is the first to admit his failings and shortcomings, the first to long for what he would do over if he could. Such admissions and longings, however, are signs of Tutu's genius as a confessor.

THE DEFINITION OF A SAINT

In the language of Christian spirituality there are the categories of confessor and confessee. A confessor is one who hears the confessions of others, while the confessee is the one who provides the confession. As any good spiritual director worth her salt would admit, to be a good spiritual director, you have to be in spiritual direction. In the same way, when one thinks about what it means to be a saint, one must be aware that saints know that their holiness comes from the reference point of God, who naturally reveals that, for human beings, holiness exists on a continuum. In other words, by virtue of the fact that we are created, our holiness will always look like a cartoon compared to God's holiness. The very definition of holiness—to be set apart—thus looks different for a human than it does for God. That Tutu is holy (saintly) does not mean he is Jesus, but that given the circumstances of Tutu's life, he offers a discrete life set apart, demonstrating God in the world. So how will I go about displaying Tutu as saint?

Describing Tutu as a saint is controversial both in the sense of writing on him as a living figure and explaining the deeper meaning of the word "saint." The concept of "saint" is often never fully explained, or is used in a superficial way to describe a nice person. When I describe Tutu's spiritual life here, I do so with the intent of describing a complex life in a controversial time. Thereby, Tutu's life as saint is used in the traditional theological sense but also as the literary foil to the concept of apartheid.

As we will see in this book, Tutu does display the exemplary character of a saint, but his power is in how he helps us to see God's purpose to make us all saints. In the confusion of those in power claiming apartheid's holiness in setting apart a supreme white people, Tutu's spiritual life sheds light on how to see apartheid for what it truly is: sin. Rather than a vapid sainthood, Tutu's life represents the foil to dysfunctional understandings of apartheid as "being set apart (holy)" and even "ordained by God." This spiritual conflict between apartheid's image of God and Tutu's image of God prompted me to settle upon the deeper need to look at Tutu's life through the three Christian mystical stages of maturing in the life of God—purgation, illumination, and union—which I will discuss in the Introduction. It is because of these mystical stages that I describe Tutu both as a mystic and a saint.

Through the framework of these stages I will describe Tutu as a person modeling a sane contrast to the spiritual forces of apartheid. My motivation here is not to exalt him in some artificial way, but to show how religious exemplars like Tutu can make the world a better place. It is in these three mystical stages of purgation, illumination, and union with God that I will seek methodologically to explain more fully this concept of Tutu's sainthood. Tutu does not achieve something called sainthood; rather, a holy life is thrust upon Tutu. This will help all of us see similar spiritual physics occurring in our own lives as well. Instead of using religion dysfunctionally as a political means, as in the case of apartheid, reading about Tutu's spiritual life should motivate us to accept what God is trying to do in our particular lives and in humanity as a whole. There can be no separation of one from the other.

In this receptive spirit, I preface this spiritual biography of Tutu as a prayerful response to the many current challenges facing the world, for which leaders like Tutu are needed all the more. It is in this prayerful response that I think Tutu ultimately teaches us how to understand the character of a "saint" differently than the hagiography that is often used to describe heavenly minded leaders of no earthly good. In other words, Tutu's life displays how, in God, we are all saints. Even though you may come from different spiritual traditions or no spiritual tradition at all, I hope that, when reading this book, you might stay open to the need for sane religious leaders like Tutu, who, as history continues to be written, will be found on the side of truth and reconciliation, rather than deceit and conquest.

In such history I seek to elucidate Tutu's spirituality, humor, character, and political impact through his speeches, sermons, lectures, and media statements, but most of all through my personal relationship with him. I had the unique opportunity to live in Tutu's household during the two years (1993 and 1994) in which South Africa gave birth to its first real democracy by electing Nelson Mandela as president. Although I met Mandela on a couple of occasions, I had the sustained experience of watching Tutu up close and sharing some of South Africa's historical moments with him—even standing next to Tutu as he cast his first vote as a South African citizen.

So another value of this biography is that it is not written from a displaced writer's viewpoint, tracking down secondary resources to create a piecemeal narrative; I both display Tutu's miraculous life witness and help the reader make real connection to this extraordinary figure, who helped a nation-state confess its sin of apartheid.

Finally, let me spell out four key benefits to reading this biography. First, readers of *Desmond Tutu: A Spiritual Biography of South Africa's Confessor* will be able to recognize a great discrepancy in Western culture—namely, how spirituality is more intelligible through communal experience than individual experience. Second, I help the reader participate in the difficult work of thinking through how to make spirituality relevant again to political structures. Those who care about institutional structures like government, mainline religions, and the business world—whether through deep commitment or great concern—will find this work on Tutu of great value. Third, those individuals who will not settle for the routinized spirituality of dying institutions will be able to understand a better strategy of personal fulfillment as intelligible through Tutu's life and witness. Last, in light of increasingly violent events around the world involving refugees, immigration, white supremacy, and much more, this book offers a means of thinking through spiritual practices that may address systemic causes of violence. To this end, my bibliography highlights as many as possible literary responses by Tutu to the root causes of human violence.

Writing a book like this inevitably leads the writer to acknowledge appreciation for those who helped to make it happen. The list here is impossible to name completely. Naturally, Desmond and Leah Tutu must be named initially, as they gave me access to published and unpublished work and generous hospitality in which I got to know them as dear friends. I am grateful for getting to know their children: Trevor, Thandi, Naomi, and Mpho. My brother in ministry, Edwin Arrison, has been coleading our Tutu Travel Seminars in January and August. Edwin, Desiree, Layla, and Laura have become my family as well. Piyushi Kotecha, CEO of the Desmond & Leah Tutu Legacy Foundation, provided vital assistance to me in the process of publishing this book. John and Liz Allen were shepherds for me as I initially navigated the world of South Africa. I am indebted also to John for his friendship and helpful insights in making this biography coherent. Roger Friedman and Benny Gool served in situating this biography for its most potential. John de Gruchy and his work at The Volmoed Trust retreat in South Africa inspired me throughout my writing. I am also thankful to Kurt Dunkle for patiently supporting my writing at General Theological Seminary in New York. Eric Tuttle and Ellen Taylor did magnificent work as my work-study students. Grants from the Louisville Institute and Conant Grants from The Episcopal Church were extremely important in providing the necessary resources to be able to write this biography. And to the president and publisher of Westminster John Knox, David Dobson, a big thank-you for not only sticking with me through two books at WJK, but for also honoring me with your time in editing this book. Thank you, Julie Mullins, for picking up the baton and seeing this through the finish line, which was no small feat considering the COVID-19 pandemic. And I am grateful to Hermann Weinlick for his final read of the text. I am also in debt to Tony Gerritsen, principal of St. John's Theological College in Auckland, New Zealand, for providing the space and community to finish this book. The spiritual creativity in New Zealand is fantastic! Lastly and importantly, to my wife, Raquel, and our three children, Sage, Bliss, and Zion—thank you for seeing me through this significant work that will allow subsequent generations to learn about the spiritual life of Desmond Tutu.

Abbreviations

AACC	All-Africa Conference of Churches
ANC	African National Conference
BCM	Black Consciousness Movement
CI	Christian Institute of Southern Africa
CPSA	The Church of the Province of Southern Africa
CR	Community of the Resurrection
DRC	Dutch Reformed Church
NGK	Nederduitse Gereformeerde Kerk
NHK	Nederduitsch Hervormde Kerk
PAC	Pan Africanist Congress
SACC	South African Council of Churches
SACP	South African Communist Party
SPCK	Society for the Propagation of Christian Knowledge
TRC	Truth and Reconciliation Commission
UDF	United Democratic Front
UN	United Nations
WARC	World Alliance of Reformed Churches

Michael Battle with Archbishop Desmond Tutu in 1994, Bishopscourt, Cape Town. Author photo.

Introduction

I will begin this introduction to the fascinating life and witness of Desmond Tutu in an unusual way, by pointing out for the reader the potential weaknesses in my approach, two in particular. First, there is a lack of objectivity in my approach. A good friend of mine at a major university once told me that "objectivity is not all it's cracked up to be." After we both shared a laugh, I learned that through the current movements in literature and academic life, objectivity is always interpreted. What this means is that I need to be transparent as to who I am as the biographer when engaged with the subject matter of the life I'm studying. In fact, I believe my relationship with Tutu will even be beneficial to the objectivist types who long for parameters, causes, and effects. In other words, I offer Tutu's biography in the relationality of having lived with him, and even having been ordained a priest in the Anglican Church by Tutu in Cape Town at St. George's Cathedral on my birthday, December 12, 1993.

I consider myself as part of the study of objectivity here. As stated in the preface, much of what I write here is from my first-person observation of the life and character of Tutu each year since 1993. I have been blessed to have Tutu perform most of the major rites of passage in my adult life. His friend and biographer John Allen joked once that I better outlast "the Arch," otherwise he would have to do my funeral service as well. For me to write any way other than out of such a relationship with Tutu would be disingenuous and ahistorical. After all, there are many critics of Tutu who can offer a balanced approach, if that is desired.

What concerns me here, however, is that such forces have not sought such balance; rather, there seems to be a norm of quietude toward Tutu's accomplishments. In other words, it seems as though there are those who have intentionally blocked credit due to Tutu for his accomplishments. I believe this is because of the implicit spiritual nature of his work, something secular society finds difficult to fathom.

Therefore, I offer my twenty-five-plus-year relationship with Tutu and subsequent primary research on him as a good thing rather than a methodological hindrance. Also, as an African American[1] focused on the intersection of Christian spirituality and nonviolence, I offer a different paradigm in which to situate Tutu. There are very few black writers who are explicitly known for their work in Christian spirituality. In fact, I would argue that, perhaps outside of Howard Thurman, who influenced Martin Luther King's spirituality, there is no such black "contemporary voice" on Christian spirituality. I believe this dearth of writing about black spirituality is due to the lack of effort to associate Christian spirituality with communal concepts, Celtic Christianity perhaps being an exception.

I also believe that racism plays a part in controlling the discourse of who can be classically described in the discourse in Christian spirituality. For many in the Western world, "black spirituality" is an oxymoron. Often Christian spirituality is perceived in terms of light and darkness, thereby implying that blackness cancels out an orthodox understanding of what is spiritual. This is an unfortunate association, since in Christian mysticism, darkness is a key component in knowing God. For example, Dionysius the Areopagite, mentioned briefly in the Bible (Acts 17:34) and known as the pioneer of Christian mysticism, describes Moses' encounter with God as Moses' not actually meeting God's substantial nature, but meeting the place where God dwells. Dionysius puts it this way:

> This means, I presume, that the holiest and highest of the things perceived with the eye of the body or the mind are but the rationale which presupposes all that lies below the Transcendent One. Through them, however, [God's] unimaginable presence is shown, walking the heights of those holy places to which the mind at least can rise. But then Moses breaks free of them, away from what sees and is seen, and he plunges into the truly mysterious darkness of unknowing.[2]

Dionysius's genius is in exposing the incomplete human bias about God. No doubt the associations of light and whiteness encouraged many European Christians to transfer their identity more readily onto divine things—so much so that black people were cursed with blackness. Dionysius helps us see that most human perceptions of spirituality are self-contained or focused on one's personal perspective. In any case, the medieval canon of European persona can no longer serve as the only perspective of spirituality. Much more work must be done to enhance the Western tradition of spirituality in light of what the church looks like in this new millennium. My book offers such a work to the reader. This biography's most valuable contribution may be in my unearthing of Christian spiritual and mystical sources from an unusual source for many in the Western world: the continent of Africa.

The second weakness of my approach could be diplomatically described as this work's being too contemplative (meaning confessional or religious). To write a spiritual biography on Desmond Tutu as confessor, however, I cannot help but be confessional and religious. Paul Brett helps me explain through his observations of a Tutu speaking engagement:

> Here was no dry academic lecture for publication in a learned journal, [by someone] who would review evidence, quote research, qualify in footnotes. Here instead was someone speaking out of years of struggle in one of the most inhuman, and tense, political situations of modern times. Here was a Church leader personally involved in a situation commented on almost daily in the international press, and well-documented in the lives of millions of black people longing for the basic political and economic freedoms.[3]

I totally agree with Brett's assessment of Tutu. (In fact, I grieve not being able to write a complete work just on Tutu's sense of humor and profound contagious laughter, both of which contributed to his lectures being anything but dry. In many ways, I think this sense of humor was Tutu's greatest God-given weapon as a confessor, because humor disarms pretension and deceit.) Even though I am a theologian, my intention as his biographer is to present Tutu's life not as a "dry academic lecture," but as a life seen through both deep admiration and my personal relationship with him as a father figure.

Through field research and analysis of primary documents, I will argue that Tutu's life and work are crucial for both the well-being of the world and the survival of the church that seems equally bent toward crisis and culture wars. I am also afforded the perspective of studying Tutu's continuing impact, especially his role as chair of the Truth and Reconciliation Commission,[4] his subsequent leadership role with the United Nations' Millennium Development Goals, and lastly his relationship with the Dalai Lama and other global leaders. Most of all I seek to show the reader Tutu's spiritual life. Tutu invites us into the spiritual life as he realizes the centrality of worship, meditation, the Eucharist, quiet days, retreats, and the life of prayer. This realization is not so much by precept as by example, pointing to the fact that this aspect of the Christian life, as Tutu once told me, is caught much more than taught.

My assumption is that many do not realize the deep spirituality of Tutu. For example, it brings rich excitement to Tutu to see monks engaged in the regular round of daily prayer—matins, midday prayer, evensong, and compline. As Tutu remembers his early experiences with monks, he laughs when he says, "We lesser mortals were engaged in more mundane pursuits such as study in theology."

Such spiritual formation happened early for Tutu, because his context of apartheid needed well-formed spiritual masters to challenge it. Tutu was particularly impressionable in the spiritual world, and it has remained as an indelible mark in his own consciousness to realize that he was being sustained by these faithful acts of worship, adoration, confession, thanksgiving, and intercession. He was forever changed to discover Christian monks who prayed so faithfully and so often. The chapel where Tutu trained as a seminarian, he said, "was hardly left empty outside of service times. . . . It is at this seminary, St. Peter's Rosettenville, Johannesburg, that I learned the nature of an authentic Christian spirituality."[5]

The reader will also sense that this biography is not written from a journalistic perspective, in which linear events are outlined by which to chronicle the political life of Desmond Tutu.[6] Instead of such an approach, I have chosen to take advantage of my own relationship to Tutu and my life experiences with him. I am a Christian, and I care deeply about this identity. Likewise, I am black, and I care deeply about this identity also. In order to understand the perspective from which I write, the reader needs to understand how these two identities are interrelated. Most of my life has been spent in the discovery of how black identity and Christianity help us better see practices of peacemaking and reconciliation. I started this discovery with Tutu, an exemplar of someone who brings black and Christian identity together.

In white society, Tutu profoundly negotiated how Christianity helps us better see practices of peacemaking and reconciliation. Such an exemplar has led me to think that one of the unnerving issues of human spirituality is how many people believe that spirituality separates us and disconnects us from our actual, political lives. In other words, spirituality (or religion, for that matter) is forced into the private domain and bears little traction to help us live as connected communities.

Tutu announced in July 2010 that he would retire from public life later that year. His retirement would begin on October 7, 2010, on his seventy-ninth birthday, he said, and he looked forward to spending more time with his family rather than at airports and conferences. Tutu told a media briefing at St. George's Cathedral in Cape Town that the time had come to "slow down, sip Roobios tea with my wife," and "visit children and grandchildren," instead of traveling from convention to conference to university campus. He added he would honor all existing appointments but would not add any new engagements to his schedule.[7]

When I learned that Tutu had set his own perimeters for his retirement, I was relieved to discover the structure of this spiritual biography. Not only did I now have the scope of time to measure his public witness, I was also convinced of how I saw his essential impact on the world through Christian mysticism. My intuition had always been that this book should be in the genre of a spiritual memoir; hence I was happy to learn from John Allen, Tutu's longtime communications director, that John's important biography on Tutu left space for my spiritual biography. Talking to me in a driveway in Stanton, a suburb outside of Johannesburg, John said he was pleased with his book's public reception, but I wanted to find out how he saw my work on Tutu complementing or competing with his own work. John told me that in many ways he ended his own work on the spiritual theme I present here and that more work was essential on

Tutu's spiritual impact. John writes in his epilogue, "Tutu's understanding of an omnipresent spiritual world, in which the ancestors and saints are as much part of one's experience as people now living, helped him to break down the barriers in modern Christianity."[8] John told me not to worry, that our two works on Tutu should complement each other. John's words in the driveway encouraged me. It was as if I could pick up where he left off. In John's epilogue he writes, "The foundations of Tutu's stature and his moral authority are to be found in his spirituality and his faith. It is in these also that his legacy can most clearly be discerned."[9]

John's genius comes from his journalistic background, as he recounts the historical framework in which Tutu acted. My biography, on the other hand, is more akin to Athanasius's work on the *Life of St. Anthony*, the African saint who founded monasticism. My problem, however, is that the general public does not care about Athanasius or the *Life of St. Anthony*, a work written around the year 356 CE. So why should a spiritual biography matter? I learned from Athanasius that spiritual biographies are just as vital as historical pieces, because they provide a metanarrative of the central character's life and work. This biography of Tutu provides a lens to see what often goes neglected in our own lives, because the spiritual life is hard to see. Even more, the work of reconciliation is hard to perceive, especially if one does not know something needs to be reconciled.[10]

METHODOLOGY

As mentioned in the preface, I will display Tutu's spiritual life in this book through the three stages of Christian mysticism: purgation, illumination, and union. This may seem like an odd construct for a political leader like Tutu, but as I try to display in Tutu's life, Christian mysticism is in fact essential in understanding his life. I will show how purgation exemplifies Tutu's formation as an institutional church leader, illumination exemplifies Tutu's role as confessor, and union exemplifies Tutu's elder years as sage. Although this is not a chronological biography, I seek to provide a framework for readers to figure out where in Tutu's life they are. So the ordering of this book follows Tutu's life through his three stages: (1) ordained public ministry (purgation); (2) chair of the Truth and Reconciliation Commission (illumination); and (3) designation as a global Elder and sage (union).

The first part of this book, Purgation, traces Tutu's formation into becoming a complex public figure.[11] In this first part I expose the reader to how Tutu becomes a man of intense spirituality. This formation occurs through significant relationships and his formation as a priest of the Anglican Church, which has often been described as the handmaiden of the oppressive system of apartheid. This contradiction between deep spirituality and the institutional church leads to the second part of the book, Illumination, in which I discuss Tutu's ability to act as South Africa's and the world's confessor through the TRC. Lastly, in the third part of the book, Union, I glean from Tutu's role of confessor how he naturally is unable to retire, due to the church and world's constant need to confess sins and mistakes. This is the period in which I describe Tutu as sage.

So why this threefold division: Purgation, Illumination, and Union? The reason is simple. I think Desmond Tutu is a Christian mystic. As Tutu's life proceeds through purgation, illumination, and union, not only does mysticism describe Tutu's life; it also prepares him to counter apartheid's concept of holiness. These three parts of the ancient Christian practice of Christian mysticism, originating in Dionysius, also display Tutu's maturation in the spiritual life as a saint. Hence my argument that Tutu is both a mystic and a saint.

Mystic and saint become synonymous as the human pilgrim participates more fully in the relationality of God and creation. Tutu becomes a mystic and a saint as he participates in God's holiness that transcends the concept of holiness in apartheid. Evelyn Underhill, an Anglican mystic (1875–1941), in her book *Mysticism* defines mysticism as "the expression of the innate tendency of the human spirit towards complete harmony with transcendental order, whatever be the theological formula under which that order is understood." She envisions such harmony as union with God, in whose presence human beings become holy. For Underhill, at the end of the day mysticism is practical, not theoretical.[12]

Christian mysticism is often controversial among Protestant sensibilities that envision a contradiction between mysticism and the gospel message of salvation through faith.[13] This is complicated further by what is described as the negative or iconoclastic theology of Dionysius. Although scholars differ on the true identity of Dionysius, his impact on the discourse of Christian mysticism is unquestioned. He envisioned Christian mysticism as how we move into the life of God without restriction and mediation. This sets the stage for why it may seem strange for some that Tutu is associated with Dionysius and the Christian mystics; however, much of my work on Tutu in the past has made these connections already.

In my other work on Tutu, I received resistance to and disbelief about my premise that Tutu is a mystic. Some felt this could not be true because Tutu was an African freedom fighter, while others felt my take on Tutu was naive and idealistic. My premise of Christian mysticism has yet another obstacle to overcome: Tutu is political. For those who think of Tutu primarily as a political actor on the world's stage, this notion that Tutu is a Christian mystic, a saint, and a political leader may seem impossible to accept. But it will come as no surprise to others that the church is just as political as secular governments. In fact, Tutu in no small part was discovered by a Christian monk, Trevor Huddleston, whose work was deemed just as political as Tutu's.[14] My teenage children often laugh when I inform them that Tutu was discovered by a monk. They joke, "Dad, you'll make Tutu into a superhero, because most superheroes have a monk trainer!"

I base this spiritual biography not upon such comic-book formation of a hero but upon my primary knowledge of Tutu and my research on his life over the years. In 1995, when "biography as theology" was popular, I submitted a chapter of my PhD dissertation on the topic "Archbishop Desmond Tutu's Biography as Theology." However, my supervisor at Duke University at the time, Stanley Hauerwas, and I decided to allow the biography to stand on its own. A quarter of a century has passed, and you are now reading the manifestation of this plan—allowing for a more substantial and longitudinal work on Tutu as a distinct text of theological intelligibility in a violent world. During this time, my thinking and writing on Tutu has fermented in such a way as to be manifested in this overarching spiritual biography.

In some ways I understand my kids' assessment of Tutu as the quintessential hero, as I would pray at dawn and sunset with him. Serving as Tutu's chaplain in those years, praying, driving, and even jogging with him, I learned not to talk too much, to allow Tutu to be contemplative in the midst of his hectic schedule. I recall one such trip to St. James Church, a white church in Kenilworth, a suburb of Cape Town. The day before, the church had witnessed a massacre, perpetrated by four black members of the Azanian People's Liberation Army (APLA). Eleven members of the congregation were killed and fifty-eight wounded. Tutu had been called out of morning prayer to make the emergency trip, and as we set off on the journey, I heard him resume his prayers from the back seat. It was at that moment I realized the insight of Tutu's deep spirituality: the hardest thing for him in the midst of a turbulent world was to keep saying his prayers every day. We all needed such prayer as we approached the driveway of St. James Church.

Again, this may seem strange to those who extrapolate a kind of extroverted political character for Tutu, based on his powerful speeches and defiance against apartheid. Nonetheless, this is who Tutu is—a man of deep prayer influenced deeply by the traditions of Christian mysticism derived from Christian monasticism. It may seem strange for Western educated folks to associate Tutu with such seemingly esoteric speech and Christian mysticism, but we gain further insight from Dionysius as to why Tutu belongs among Christian mystics. The role of a prophet in Christian mysticism is important, as Dionysius explains:

> Foolish is my word for those who are attached to knowledge and who love things that can be known and have beginnings: they believe there is nothing supernatural beyond these. They recognize they know him "who has made darkness his dwelling place," in much the same way as they know themselves. And since, as the *prophet* [my emphasis] says, the divine teaching of these secrets is beyond them, what are we to make of those even more foolish folk, who live not only by their mental powers and their own natural philosophy, but descend lower still, beneath them, and live by those bodily senses they have in common with animals?[15]

Tutu agrees as he explicates further the deep call of the prophet. Tutu believes that the prophet is God's spokesperson. Such a person is not simply a communications officer or a puppet of a ventriloquist; rather, a prophet is made in this threefold mystical way of purgation, illumination, and union. The prophet especially knows the first stage of purgation, as suffering inevitably occurs for prophets. The Christian prophet heeds Jesus' admonition that unless a person takes up the cross and follows him, such a person cannot be Jesus' disciple. Suffering is the essence of prophecy.

So how does one know whether God has taken hold of a person to be a prophet? Herein, Christian mysticism becomes all the more important. Since a human being cannot always know what is of God, self, evil, or chance, the process of maturation in the Christian life takes on the three stages of the mystical life. Human beings depend on the metrics of Christian mysticism in which to discern closeness or distance from God; and the church is used to validate such journeys. Tutu speaks to such potential prophets:

> Are you ready to speak up boldly, criticizing evil without fear or favor, ready to bear the consequences? Are you ready for the suffering that is almost inevitable—the taunts that you were mixing religion with politics, that you were unpatriotic, the scurrilous attacks on your integrity, on your person and those you love? Are you ready for the sake of God's word to risk detention without trial, banning, deportation and even death? It all sounds melodramatic but look at what happened to Bishop Reeves, to Beyers Naude et al. Are you ready to suffer being unpopular. . . . Do you have a sense of humor not to take yourself seriously remembering whatever the evidence apparently to the contrary, that this is God's world and He is in Charge? If you don't fill this bill, then count out prophecy.[16]

For some, it may seem strange that prophecy is somehow involved in Christian mysticism. But if you think about it more closely, it makes sense. Tutu explains further, "Those who would speak must do so out of a personal experience of God borne of a life of prayer, meditation, Bible Reading, retreats, and regular participation in the sacramental life of the church, people for whom the spiritual is absolutely central. They must then proceed to say 'Thus saith the Lord' and speak out of a deep and passionate love for the land and the people."[17]

When I was a professor of spirituality and black church studies at Duke University, one of my chief concerns was to bring spirituality together with other kinds of discourse. What this question implied for me was the difficult matter of measuring what it is that I do when I teach and research "spirituality." Am I a dispenser of information? Do I disciple others? Am I a coach, coaxing the less enlightened into maturity? Or am I simply a mentor? Parker Palmer's insight into these matters is helpful as he states,

> Then I ask the question that opens to the deeper purpose of this exercise: not "What made your mentor great?" but "What was it about you that allowed great mentoring to happen?" Mentoring is a mutuality that requires more than meeting the right teacher: the teacher must meet the right student. In this encounter, not only are the qualities of the mentor revealed, but the qualities of the student are drawn out in a way that is equally revealing.[18]

My answer to making sense of "spirituality" came to me in Palmer's advice. I had to focus on practices of mutuality. The best kinds of spirituality are always about mutuality. This is why Christian mysticism's threefold process of purgation, illumination, and union ends the way it does—finding mutuality with God. From such insight I also focused on Tutu's beautiful concept of Ubuntu theology, in which the goal of human identity is mutuality. It is in this way of being human that Tutu helped to dismantle apartheid. In sum, I make sense of the structure of this book and my own autobiographical context of this biography through how I have been formed to be black in the world while also being focused on Christian spirituality.

In order to understand how my formation is important to understanding the life of my mentor, Tutu, one must also understand two other particular and relational identities: African and Anglican. In my African American identity, I challenge some of the divisions that characterize theological and religious discourse today. One may see this challenge in my books on Tutu or his theology.[19] Tutu's thought is grounded in religious experience in which God creates what is good by creating what is different. Consequently, there is no legitimacy in an apartheid narrative (itself a homogeneous theology) that forms people into believing that otherness, that is, racial difference, is the foundation by which one race may dominate another. As I lived with Tutu, he became my teacher of such insights, and I became his student. I learned from Tutu in the deeper contexts of learning, by being with him. Being is crucial for a theological teacher, because such subject matter cannot be easily measured by the typical empirical standards.

Again, as Tutu would say, such things are caught, not taught. For example, mathematics teachers may observe the progress of their students through how well they reason out a particular formula. In biology, a professor will see the results of a student's lab. In theological/spiritual discourse, however, what results could ever satisfy the quest to know God? Herein is my claim for this biography, that my "being" with Tutu carries a deeper authority in which he produces mutuality between student and teacher—between me and him.

I made this claim once at a conference on teaching and learning, and it was interesting to note the responses to my claim. The primary response was refutation, namely, that the theological teacher should not seek mutuality with a student, because there are necessary dynamics in which certain boundaries are conducive to learning. The further argument against the claim was that to assume the goal of mutuality is to exacerbate hegemonic relationships between teacher and student, especially as the student can never be in an "equal" relationship to the teacher.[20] This is a strong refutation that demands a careful response.

What do I mean by mutuality? Frederick Buechner helps me explain my meaning of mutuality through his definition of vocation as "the place where your deep gladness and the world's deep hunger meet."[21] In the context of a biography written by a student of Tutu, the concept of vocation proposes a kind of mutuality, in which teacher and student's behavior are congruent not only with words and ideas but also with commitments and practices. The theological teacher helps the student see the world differently by learning to see "what is not there." By learning to see "what is not there" in the world, we learn to see "what should be there." Besides Mahatma Gandhi, Simone Weil, Martin Luther King Jr., and Mother Teresa, there is no one better suited in the twentieth and twenty-first centuries to teach us this lesson than Tutu.

As an African American Christian theologian, I argue that how I continue to see "what is not there" is informed by my commitment to God's interrelational image of Trinity. From this perspective of God's mutuality, I practice "what is not there," namely, my vocation of being African American and Christian. This leads me back to Buechner's definition of vocation. Those who teach theologically have an opportunity to develop "the place where your deep gladness and the world's deep hunger meet." By Tutu's being mutual with me as his student, I also facilitate the revelation of Buechner's concept of vocation to the reader of this biography. This revelation of vocation honors the theological student who innately knows that God is known through vulnerability. This is a counterintuitive process, however, because we often come to mutuality first through conflict and disorientation. We know mutuality by first knowing what it is not. Therefore, to move out of this introduction into part 1 of this book, we do well to see that Tutu's formation requires his own mentors of mutuality. Tutu's own formation as a student of other spiritual masters helped him to understand how to go about the impossible of task of bringing about the miracle of mutuality in the hostile world of apartheid.[22]

How then do I understand myself as a theological teacher in this biography? One can synthesize an answer only through the mutual search for communal ways of knowing. In other words, Tutu's life and witness are meant for diverse communities. Unfortunately, since Tutu is African and Christian, he is often pitched to limited communities. In the 1980s, conservatives (including conservative Christian leaders) tried to spin the media toward the contradictory image of Tutu as both radical and fake. Jerry Falwell stated, "If Bishop Tutu maintains that he speaks for the black people of South Africa, he's a phony."[23] And more radical communities wanting to exact revenge on those benefitting from apartheid claimed that Tutu was a "sell-out." Tutu being seen in these contradictory ways speaks well to his integrity, to his never giving in to easy solutions that benefit certain groups at the expense of others. Tutu's life shows us how to do more than charity work. His spiritual formation helped him to discern between charity work and community service. Charity work implies "detached beneficence," whereas community service conjures up images of doing good deeds in impoverished, disadvantaged communities by those who are wealthier and more privileged.

I hope in this biography to show how Tutu's mystical sensibilities challenge the perceptions of both community service and charity, replacing them with spiritual and human responsibility in a pluralistic but unequal society. By doing so, community service and charity shift from an individualistic experience into a social responsibility.[24] Another quality of genius possessed by Tutu is in his charisma to call individuals to become community. Although descriptions of such community appear to be politically neutral, such practices of becoming community in a multicultural world demonstrate a deeply political reality. All of this points toward Tutu's spiritual formation. What moves him beyond "charity" work is the intentional and disciplined focus of his spiritual life. Such focus begins with his adoration of Jesus.

Addressing South African Methodists, Tutu said:

> Jesus was forever a man of prayer, who sat the spiritual unequivocally at the center of His life, and it is from this vertical relationship with the Father that He drew the resources for His ministry of healing, feeding, preaching and forgiving. We could well say that Jesus was a man for others precisely and only because He was first and foremost a man of God, a man of prayer. If it was so for the Son of God Himself how should it be otherwise for us? He is our paradigm. Our resources can be ultimately only spiritual for we cannot be conformed to the world but must be transformed and have our minds renewed. Our struggle is not just with flesh and blood but against the powers and principalities, with supernatural forces in the heavens so that we must needs put on the whole armor of God as we seek to satisfy the deep longings of the human heart; for a great African saint has said, "Thou hast made us for thyself and our hearts are restless until they find their rest in thee"; as we seek to assure God's children that they are of infinite value in the Father's sight and nothing can change that fundamental fact about themselves; that they don't need to amass material possessions or behave like bullies, throwing their weight around to prove who they are for their value is intrinsic to their being created in God's image; as we seek to assure them of God's forgiveness of their sins, the sins of uprooting millions and dumping them as rubbish in resettlement camps, destroying flimsy, plastic covers under which hapless women crouch . . . for true spirituality is not a form of escapism. Authentic relationship with God is tested and expressed in a loving relationship with neighbor; therefore, the vertical and the horizontal belong together. Christianity knows no false dichotomies. Politics and religion speak of life and all life belongs to God who is Lord of all life. Love of God and love of neighbor are two sides of the same coin, how can you say you love God whom you have not seen when you hate your sister and brother whom you have.[25]

Although this is a spiritual biography, I aim to provide as much context as possible in the confines of this space and genre. We now turn to an overview of Tutu's life and the beginnings of his church work. Hopefully, this will help ground the reader for what follows, as Tutu faces the challenges of purgation, illumination, and union. I am keeping in mind that many readers will not know the details of apartheid in South Africa. Indeed, many students reading this book will have been born after the movement. So we will begin with a brief and basic historical context in which to understand this spiritual biography.

PART 1
PURGATION

"I hope the normal pressure of the accord will lead them to undergo a Damascus experience of conversion and come to see that their best chance of success and survival lies in aligning themselves with their fellow South Africans."[1]

—Desmond Tutu, *Star Sun*

Tutu anoints Michael Battle's hands with oil at Battle's ordination to the Anglican/ Episcopal priesthood at St. George's Cathedral, Cape Town, on Battle's birthday, December 12, 1993. Author photo.

Chapter 1

Diving in Troubled Water

Here in part 1, before getting into the theology of purgation, I will present a brief overview of Tutu's formative experiences growing up. Such formation I name as purgative in the sense of how Tutu was shaped to be an unusual institutional church leader. Many of the traditional markers of a self-contained institutional church leader were eventually burned away or purged from Tutu's style of leadership, as he was forced into a primary role of resisting the evils of apartheid. Before we see Tutu's tour de force in this regard, a basic biographical overview of Tutu's life may give the reader better traction in navigating the difficult terrain in which Tutu traveled.

The first difficult terrain that purged Tutu's leadership was in the synthesizing of African and Anglican identities in light of colonialism. As we will see, Tutu chose the Anglican Church as his spiritual home. The Anglican Church is one of the largest Christian denominations on the global stage, behind Roman Catholics and Eastern Orthodox. Interestingly enough, the Anglican churches formed into the Anglican communion around 1867 in London, England, when John Colenso, an English bishop sent to South Africa, got into trouble for his progressive theology among the British colonies. The English bishops made Colenso go back to the principal's office in London like a naughty child to face charges of excommunication. The first Lambeth Conference to bring Anglican bishops together was convened in order to deal with Colenso. The current Anglican communion has more than eighty million members around the world. Based in London, the archbishop of Canterbury acts as one of the instruments of Anglican unity, but unlike the pope in the Roman Catholic Church, cannot exercise authority in Anglican provinces outside of the Church of England.

In light of the above, it is important to see how Tutu's church formation cannot be divorced from his African and ordained Anglican identity. Colonized African identity is particularly charged from the outset as to whether or not to accept negatively imposed identities, especially identities caught in the ambiguity of legitimate or illegitimate humanity. To work against this ambiguity, I believe that there can be no concept of African and Anglican identities without full disclosure of their contingent, politically oppressed histories. In other words, to understand Tutu, one will also need to resist seeing African Christian spirituality as illegitimate discourse. Tutu helps me see this when he states, "Who you are affects and determines to a very large extent what you see and how you see it."[1] By looking at Tutu's Christian mystical sensibilities, I think Tutu's life displays how spiritual convictions need not lead to civil wars but can actually help sustain healthy political witness.

Tutu's spirituality is highly significant precisely because one cannot distinguish its theory from its praxis, because both toil synchronically toward the desired effect of reconciliation and transformation. Those close to Tutu often said they didn't know anyone more comfortable in his own skin than Tutu. When you meet Tutu, you cannot help but meet his spirituality. You can speak only about what you observe. In the years I lived with him, observing his strict regimen of prayer and silence, and in all the years since, I have indeed observed Tutu's integrity of theory and praxis.

There is an unfavorable history of the church's complacency in the face of racism and apartheid. Although apartheid was formally constructed as a legal system in 1948, when white Afrikaners vied for power through their emerging National Party, South Africa's history is one of deep racism and white colonial oppression.[2] Tutu believed that the white right-wing party in apartheid South Africa would have to undergo a Damascus-road conversion experience. This is a biblical allusion to Paul, who once persecuted Christians, before God put Paul, then known as Saul, through the purgation of change. On the road to Damascus, he was hit by light and thereby forever changed. The experience was so dramatic, so expansive, that he changed his name. Once Paul completed his purgation process, he was illumined with the vision to be an apostle and witness for Christ. Purgation, however, had to happen first.[3] Here, in part 1 of Tutu's spiritual biography, we look at the change process that occurred in South Africa as well as in Tutu's own life leading into his leadership in the church.

FORGING TUTU'S IDENTITY

Desmond Mpilo Tutu was born in South Africa on October 7, 1931. Tutu's grandfather had been a minister of an African Ethiopian church. His father, Zachariah Tutu, was of Xhosa ethnicity and his mother, Aletta, was Tswana, short with a prominent nose. Tutu states, "I resemble her physically and perhaps inherited her trait of standing up for the underdog."[4] Tutu's mother fiercely loved him. The disability of polio from an early age may have played into the need for such a fierce love, although they never really knew what was physically wrong with Tutu as a child. To this day he has a weak grip with his right hand, but he still loved to play rugby as a fourteen-year-old. He also had tuberculosis as a child, at one stage believing he was dying because he was coughing up blood.

That Tutu's mother loved him deeply cannot be taken lightly. because his father used to drink too much and sometimes beat his mother. Tutu survived these experiences, which were so profound and so formative that, as we will see later in this chapter, at one point he thought he should become a doctor.[5]

Tutu recounts that his earliest memories are of Christmastime in a black township in South Africa. It was a time that he recognized even then as something quite special. There was always a flurry of activity even in the poor homes, some of them like matchboxes, some of them more like hovels, in the squalor of the black townships. But to Tutu they were homes nonetheless. A special purgative activity that Tutu referred to was the spring cleaning, when "people put a fresh lick of paint on peeling walls and there was a peculiarly African way of plastering walls with soil and with kraal manure, with some women being very adept at producing intricate patterns in different colors on the walls and floors of the houses." Tutu can still remember even after these many years the clean and fresh smell in the homes that had all been done up.

Tutu recalls that he looked forward to this special time because even in the poorest home parents bought their children something new to wear, though this might be nothing more exciting than a pair of cheap tennis shoes or a pair of khaki shorts or a pink dress for the girls. It might be the only time in the year when he would be lucky enough to get something new that was his own and not have to wear yet another hand-me-down. So it had to be a special time, for in nearly all the homes, where most parents had their work cut out just to make ends meet, they would have baked tasty little cakes and brewed a delicious ginger beer, because "the township urchins went round to every house to ask for a 'Christmas box.'" Many in Tutu's community growing up wanted to have something to give away, and many could afford at least to give as gifts a few of their cakes and ginger beer.[6]

Zachariah Tutu pushed education in the mission schools and was headmaster of a Methodist Church primary school, which caused young Desmond to be baptized in a Methodist church. Tutu recalls, "The Methodist church has certainly mothered me in the faith because it was in this church that I was baptized."[7] (Nelson Mandela also was baptized in a small Methodist church in the

Eastern Cape village of Qunu.) Tutu had two sisters, Sylvia and Gloria (two brothers died in infancy). Zachariah allowed him to read comics: Superman, Batman and Robin. Tutu states, "I had a huge collection."[8]

Tutu recalls that he first discovered that there were black people in the United States when he was young, when he picked up a battered copy of *Ebony* magazine. Tutu said that he grew inches taller with pride as he read the magazine, especially as he read about Jackie Robinson breaking into Major League Baseball. "That did wonders for me as a person." He also remembered seeing the film *Stormy Weather*, featuring an all-black cast. Tutu could not recall whether it was a very good film, but he did remember that it made a theological statement depicting how we are all made in *imago Dei* (the image of God).

Tutu laments that he did not have positive role models as a young person searching for an identity. He says that one way to destroy a person's self-esteem is to tell them that they don't have a history, and that they have no roots. The narrative in Tutu's youth was how white people came in the seventeenth century. "Whenever the Dutch or English colonists went over into black territory and got the blacks' cattle, the word used was the colonists 'captured' the cattle. But . . . the Xhosas always 'stole' the cattle. And we were very young, but I mean we began to scratch our heads."[9]

Tutu spent five years of his childhood in Ventersdorp, a town in the North West Province of South Africa. One day Tutu saw some black children scavenging in the dustbins of the white primary school. The white children received school lunches but had thrown away the prepared lunches. These white children came from homes that were uniformly better off than those of their black counterparts. The logic behind the free school-feeding for white children baffled Tutu. Those who needed feeding most and whose parents could least afford it were denied it, while those whose parents could afford it and who did not really want it had it forced on them.

At the time, the apartheid South African government was spending about ten times more per annum educating a white child than it was spending educating a black child. This gross disparity in economic resources also displayed itself in the education facilities that were available to the different race groups. The white school was attractive, with well-laid-out and well-maintained grounds, airy and well-lit classrooms, adequate sports grounds, well-stocked libraries, and well-equipped laboratories. White schools had qualified teachers with moderately sized classes. "We in contrast were using a church building as our school with several large classes sharing the same room; this situation was unbearable." Black teachers were not all fully qualified. White counterparts lived in well-appointed residential areas, with bright street lighting, paved streets, waterborne sewage, hot and cold running water, public swimming pools and libraries, as well as other facilities that the well-to-do have come to take for granted.

Tutu fetched water from a communal tap in the street and used the bucket system of toilets. His township had dusty unpaved streets, no street lighting, and hardly any sports or recreational facilities. "What I am describing was not exceptional," Tutu remembers. It was uniformly the case throughout the Union of South Africa. "South African people had to make do with 13 percent of the surface of the land of their birth, whilst the white minority, no more than 20 percent of the total population, rattled about like a tablet in a box over the vast 87 percent of the land available to them. That was a few decades before World War II."[10] Tutu would often reminisce about these statistics and often state in his mature years of resisting apartheid that this inequity remains. Although the black middle class has increased slightly with the end of apartheid, the economic scale continues to tip heavily in favor of the white population in South Africa.

For Tutu, the point of this reminiscent stroll down memory lane is to say that even though generations of black South Africans were subject to gross violations of their human rights, had their human dignity trampled on, and were turned into victims of a vicious system of injustice and oppression, these very same black South Africans grew up with faith intact that the world could change. Many white South Africans in Tutu's childhood thought they could ignore black folks, because they lacked that vital commodity, the political power represented by the vote. For example, Tutu lists the black and colored townships under this assumption when he states, "How many Sophiatowns, District Sixes, Pageviews, Vrededorps, etc. . . . should we point to as evidence that the basic human right to a secure and inviolate home has been grossly violated?" Tutu witnessed these inequities time and again as he grew up in Minsieville, Krugersdorp, Roodepoort, in Western Native Township and in Sophiatown—all destroyed by apartheid's juggernaut of racism and political power.[11]

TREVOR HUDDLESTON

As Tutu grew up in the context of apartheid, two major influences emerged from his early youth. They are Trevor Huddleston and, perhaps most vital, Tutu's mother.[12]

Trevor Huddleston was an enlightened white Anglican monk who became a legend in the black community of Sophiatown, where he lived and preached for twelve years in the towering Church of Christ the King. Huddleston, a member of the Anglican Community of the Resurrection (CR), touched the lives of many in South Africa. Tutu recalls that the

> Grammy-nominated jazz trumpeter Hugh Masekela got his first trumpet from Father Huddleston, who had got it as a gift from Louis "Satchmo" Armstrong, as only he could. . . . And if blacks still talk to white people, an extraordinary miracle in present-day South Africa, then it will be in large measure due to people like Trevor who made us realize that we too count, we too matter in the sight of God, we too, even when we are black, are people to whom hats ought to be doffed.[13]

Tutu recalls that when Huddleston, a tall white monk dressed in his black clerical dress, would walk past the Tutu home, he would always raise his hat to Tutu's mother, a washerwoman. At the time, Tutu had never seen a white man do anything like that before for a black woman who was not educated.[14] "When did I first meet Father Trevor Huddleston?" Tutu asks. "Oh, he was father to so many in Sophiatown. I thought it was when I started school in 1944 in what was called Western Native Township; it is now Western Colored Township in our country obsessed with color and race. It was a high school started by Father Raymond Raynes when he was priest in charge of Christ the King in Sophiatown, a position in which Father Trevor succeeded him. This would have been in 1945, at the end of World War II."[15]

Tutu made his first good confession to Trevor Huddleston, the beginning of a relationship that would shape Tutu for the rest of his life. Tutu lived in a hostel that the CR fathers opened for young men who were working or at high school and had problems with accommodation. Tutu states, "I made my first real sacramental confession to [Huddleston]. . . . He was so un-English in many ways, being very fond of hugging people, embracing them, and in the way in which he laughed." Tutu humorously recalls how Huddleston did not laugh like many white people, only with their teeth, he laughed with his whole body, his whole being, and that endeared him very much to black people. If he wore a white cassock, it did not remain clean for long, as he trudged the dusty streets of Sophiatown with the little children with grubby fingers always wanting to touch him and calling out "Fader" with obvious affection in their little voices. Huddleston could move between playing marbles on the floor with street children to next moment meeting ambassadors, high-placed officials, and leading business people. For example, Huddleston had a very close relationship with the famous South African writer Alan Paton, who at the time was running the Diepkloof Reformatory. Tutu states, "The white priest in *Cry, the Beloved Country* is probably modeled on Trevor Huddleston."[16]

Trevor Huddleston had come to Johannesburg in 1943 and continued Raynes's work but he had done something that Raynes had never been able to do; he worked well with many whites in Johannesburg. Even though CR was associated with socialism and radical fringes, white South Africans began to give Huddleston money for his churches and schools. It must be noted that two kinds of white people were firmly established by this time in South Africa: those whites from the British Empire and those from Europe who now called themselves Afrikaners. The whites who supported Huddleston were from his own British background and did not support the Afrikaner Nationalist government. Huddleston opposed the racist policies of the Afrikaner government (including the Group Areas Act, the Population Registration Act, the Suppression of Communism Act, the Criminal Law Amendment Act).

Trained well in his monastic community to be unafraid of politics, Huddleston wrote speeches and letters to the press, as Raynes had done, about local government. However, the whole South African struggle was now transferring

itself to the national and international levels, so that Huddleston found himself in front of a wider audience. In all this he was following his own advice to
Nelson Mandela. Huddleston states, "[Mandela's] got to be a diplomat. But he's
leading a revolution. It's a very difficult combination."[17]

Formed in CR, Huddleston was an ideal spokesperson against the policies
that the church thought evil, because he was clear about his own convictions and
well informed about his opponents. He was also brave, a virtue that he would no
doubt pass on to Tutu. As time went on, the leadership of the African and liberal
forces became more and more focused upon Huddleston himself—as did his
opponents' anger. Then two actions of the government brought this struggle to
a crisis. The first was the Bantu Education Act, passed in 1953, which took away
control of all schools from church missions. St. Peter's School, Rosettenville, the
most famous African secondary school, where Huddleston was superintendent,
closed. St. Cyprian's School, Sophiatown, which CR had rebuilt and which took
over fifteen hundred children, closed.

Most missions decided to accept the Bantu Education Act, reasoning to
themselves that a bad education for Africans is better than no education at all.
The Anglican Diocese of Johannesburg, however, decided to close down the
schools, on the grounds that a stand had to be made now about something so
fundamental as equal education for children. The battle was an accident waiting
to happen, especially for Huddleston, trained by CR. This unavoidable battle
was made more difficult by a second action, the Western Areas Removal Scheme,
a government-sanctioned policy that gave permission to destroy the African
renaissance, Sophiatown.

Huddleston fought the government policy to destroy Sophiatown with the
weapons he had. This monk became chairman of the Western Areas Protest
Committee; kept in touch with the ANC and the Transvaal Indian Congress;
warned the press of his activities by providing them with detailed copies of his
itinerary. Huddleston did this because there was no legal appeal against what was
happening; he had to appeal to public opinion. We will come to see that these
tactics were also instrumental for Tutu, who used these means to bring attention
to corrupt government authorities. But it meant also that the authorities fought
Huddleston more ruthlessly.

Tutu states:

> The vigorous opposition to the removal of Sophiatown was spearheaded
> by none other than Trevor Huddleston. Perhaps you should read of his
> exploits in South Africa in his book, *Naught for Your Comfort*. He was here,
> there and everywhere, tirelessly organizing and addressing a protest meet-
> ing here, a vigil there, appearing in court to seek a court interdict to frus-
> trate the Government's intentions. He was a fully engaged Christian. . . . It
> was surprising at first to see a priest so heavily involved in political affairs.
> But it became clear that he was doing this not in spite of the fact that he
> was a priest and a religious to boot, but precisely because he was these
> things. Later he was to tell me just how he relied very heavily in his public
> campaigns on the fact that his brethren were very closely identified with

what he was doing through their intercessions, through the daily offering
of the Holy Sacrifice of the Eucharist. I came to learn that not from him,
for, as it should be, this was a hidden part of his life about which he was
properly reticent to speak. . . . It was because of his encounter with God in
the spiritual life that he was constrained to be a man for others. . . . But this
public life was only a part of a far fuller life, a life shot through and through
by the realities of a higher and spiritual realm.[18]

Added to all this were the mundane (and not so mundane) difficulties that
surrounded the Community when Huddleston became famous. People would
ring up Rosettenville at all hours of the day and night. Not so mundane was
the fact that Huddleston's life was threatened, the tires of his car slashed. Police
followed him wherever he went, and there were always secret police at his meetings. It boiled to the point in 1955 that they ransacked the priory office and took
away Huddleston's personal papers.

All this disrupted the life of the Community. For CR it was not the political
engagement that mattered to their concerns; what became urgent was the physical and emotional strain on Huddleston. He was fighting so hard and it seemed
he would break. It seemed like he would have been arrested and then disappear
for years among the torture of apartheid law. Huddleston had to take a break
before he himself broke. Only a few months after he left the country, the treason
trial started, in which Mandela was imprisoned. Huddleston certainly would
have also been one of the accused.

It must be noted here, lest I am accused of holding up a patronizing model
of the white man's burden to save Africa, that by no means do I seek to imply
that Huddleston was somehow the messiah for South Africa. Rather, I seek to
display a somewhat detailed narrative here to show that Huddleston's spiritual
formation facilitated a vision for Tutu to respond effectively against apartheid. In
short, Huddleston was not the only one to resist apartheid. Resistance erupted
among peasants, the petite bourgeoisie, intellectuals, government-appointed
leaders, women, students, industrial workers, shebeen queens, and those who
clung to the fringes of the new urban and industrial areas.

Resistance incorporated rural as well as urban constituencies, and often
crystallized around the local community issues and seemingly apolitical events,
sometimes dismissed by historians as evidence of social irresponsibility and
unqualified criminality. These events ranged from trading disagreements, agri-
cultural campaigns, women's legal right to brew beer, rumors that shops were
selling poisoned goods, religious schisms, food boycotts in schools, and resistance to mission education. In many ways, apartheid South Africa had spawned
a resistance culture.

There were early broad-based and varied forms of resistance that constitute
the historical background to the more intense, better organized, and overtly revolutionary charter of resistance in South Africa that Tutu came to ride the crest
of. Most famously, Mahatma Gandhi himself learned his famous satyagraha,
nonviolent resistance, in South Africa. Such organized resistance historically

emerged largely in response to the racism inherent in the constitution of the Union of South Africa, declared in 1910, and in the 1913 Native Land Act. In short, Huddleston's resistance must be understood in relation to the more hesitant and cautious actions of earlier times. The more radical responses of South African resistance against apartheid constitute a "last resort" by the oppressed in asserting their unquestionable right to be free. It is this hermeneutic that underlies Tutu's theology, in which the identity and responsibility of the church is held accountable.

TUTU AND THE MONKS

Community of the Resurrection, a monastic community that remains today, proved to be important for the formation of the young Tutu's spiritual life. Even though Tutu himself never became a monk, he did associate with several monastic communities such as Franciscan Anglican Order, Julian of Norwich Anglican Order, Taizé, and more. This kind of formation that started in his childhood helps to explain Tutu's communal spirituality and theology. For those in the secular world who may not be familiar with Christian monastic communities, there may also be a lack of understanding of how Tutu's spirituality became integral with his political leadership.

Tutu's formation among Christian monks explains how one may see Tutu himself as a political priest, a tradition most associated with Latin American spirituality and liberation theology. Tutu's encounter with monastic spirituality, however, displays that this tradition of spirituality and political witness really goes back much further in the Judeo-Christian history to Jesus, John the Baptist, and the Hebrew prophets. From spiritualities that seek human liberation we learn that the goal must always be the restoration of relationality with God.

In Christian spirituality in particular, monastic communities formed to guard against becoming an impotent abstraction of God's creation, by growing in the relationship between creature and creator. In short, this relational spirituality later became Tutu's theological strategy: to model the divine life in the corrupt society of apartheid. Monastic community in Christian asceticism (meaning to exercise or train) is a lifestyle defined by specific disciplines for the purpose of pursuing deeper connection with God and creation. Often such ascetics withdraw from the world in order to fulfill such disciplines and renounce material possessions and pleasures. In such withdrawal it is easy to see how Christian spirituality could develop an apolitical reputation.

The ascetic tradition of monks and nuns that has influenced Tutu, however, provides Tutu a practical if not a political resource by which the primary goal of human beings is no longer racial identity, but community. In this light, the particularity of physiognomic differences defined by race can be seen as God's good creation and cannot be used in dysfunctional political worldviews to oppress any human identity. The new identity purged through Christian baptism now becomes one's primary identity, capable of ordering all other God-created identities. As we will discuss later, any attempt at defining human identity as less than God's created good is now deemed as heresy. The word "heresy" originally meant taking a side or making a choice. The word turns pejorative in the New Testament as the action of a person who causes division by leading people in the wrong direction. Heresy ultimately came to mean something even stronger, namely, purposely distorting the truth revealed in Jesus Christ and leading both those in the church and those in the world to a lack of any witness of truth.

To counter such distortion, there was a need for a more balanced form of Christian spirituality, as practiced by Pachomius of Egypt (ca. 292–348). In Pachomius's cenobitic (communal) monasticism, there was no withdrawal from the world. This is important to Tutu's spirituality, in that the charge against apartheid as heresy meant that heresy was no longer an antiquated discussion. So too Tutu inherited a spiritual worldview in which direction to God's presence must be practiced not only in solitude but also in human relationships. How could white Christians claim omniscience of God's whereabouts and then create a theology in which black people could not live fully in God's presence? This led Tutu to embrace another kind of political spirituality.

Huddleston as a monk influenced Tutu's understanding of the Christian vocation as one of reconciliation and the restoration of relationality. The ascetic model of sacrifice and commitment in religious communities offers a contrast to secular power structures of division and conquest. The aim of Tutu's spirituality is always about moving beyond perceived categories of oppressive identity to those of human and divine flourishing. Tutu states:

> I was greatly blessed to have been trained for the priesthood by a religious community, the Community of the Resurrection, sometimes called the Mirfield Fathers after the Yorkshire town in which their mother house is located. I learned much more from these wonderful CR Brethren by example than by precept. Life with them taught me that prayer, meditation, retreat, devotional reading, and holy communion were all utterly central and indispensable to an authentic Christian existence. You could not but be impressed that they really lived by what they taught, when you regularly saw members of the Community on their knees in the chapel, outside of service times. We saw the same people deeply involved in the struggle for justice in South Africa.[19]

The CR taught Tutu that what was required was not simply a political program of material improvement or an identity as black or white, but a whole new understanding of society. Tutu states, "It is at this [CR] seminary, St. Peter's Rosettenville, Johannesburg, that I learned the nature of an authentic Christian spirituality."[20] And this spirituality makes Tutu work from theological commitments derived on a deeper and more mystical level than racial classification.

ST. PETER'S COLLEGE

It was at St. Peter's Theological College, Rosettenville, that his upbringing with the CR had even more influence. "We learned then that religion is more *caught* than *taught*." Tutu discovered what he called holy people who could have out-done James in possessing camel's knees from their dedication to a life of prayer. He was impressed times without number to find these people of God on their knees in chapel. "And today what we learned then has I think come to be woven into the warp and woof of our lives."[21]

From all of these spiritual sources Tutu learned that spirituality—prayerful Scripture reading, meditation, the use of sacraments, the Offices (daily prayers), and retreats—must be central in his life, lest he lead a distorted and defective life. Tutu qualifies, "I don't claim to do all these things well (in fact I know I don't) but still I try to grow. That is why I have said that it is my commitment to a relationship with our Lord and Savior Christ which constrains me to be what I am and to do and to say what I say."[22] A relevant and authentic Christian spirituality then leads to an involvement in the sociopolitical sphere. Our vertical relationship with God is tested out and flows into our horizontal relationship with our fellows. It is obedience to the imperatives of the gospel that demand a so-called political involvement. The love of God, said Jesus, embraces love of neighbor. How can you love God whom you have not seen when you hate someone whom you have? If Jesus is Lord, then he is Lord of all life and not just of segments of it. For Tutu, the priority will always be spiritual, authenticated by a vigorous concern that God's will be done in politics and economics.

Tutu's understanding of how spirituality leads to politics developed from his sense of community and how our dependence on others leads to growth in the spiritual life—the greatest "other" being God. To make this point, Tutu has referred to an old two-volume work, *The Faith of a Moralist*, in which A. E. Taylor describes why there will be no jealousy in heaven. Tutu reflects on Taylor's insight and concludes that this lack of jealousy in heaven is due to our laser focus on God, who is infinitely our creator, while we always remain the created. By focusing on God, community naturally flows back upon the created. In one of Tutu's Lenten retreats before Easter, he describes how some people will be in advance of others in their love for God, and nothing will delight them more than to point out what for them will be yet undiscovered depths in the being of God. To seek God is to seek community in which there will be no time for the pettiness of jealousy. And so it will go on unto the ages of ages.[23]

In addition to Tutu's monastic influence, there was exceptional freedom in Sophiatown to allow for white monks to enter Tutu's life. In Sophiatown, in the 1930s, 1940s, and 1950s, there existed the closest thing to a free society in South Africa. Here, if only for a moment in history, a new kind of black Africans—a group of second- and third-generation urbanite, detribalized, working-class Africans—was able to flourish. But all this came crashing down when the government used the Group Areas Act to declare Sophiatown a "white" area. In 1955 the bulldozers flattened Sophiatown and transported its residents to Soweto. And a new suburb was laid out for white families appropriately called Triomf.[24]

The Tutu family switched churches when their children switched mission schools. From Methodists, they became African Methodist Episcopal (a distinct church denomination growing out of the Black church in the United States), and finally Anglicans when Tutu's sister Sylvia enrolled at St. Peter's, a racially mixed school run by Huddleston and the Community of the Resurrection. The CR had a mission in Sophiatown, Christ the King, which was a complex with a convent, church, nursery and primary school, nursery teacher's training college, and monastery. They also had a hostel for male students and workers. Tutu came to stay in the hostel to be near school and the influence of the CR. Huddleston's fame grew as he supported black South Africans against the depredations of the apartheid authorities. He fought against the demolition of Sophiatown. And his politics flowed naturally from his devout Anglo-Catholic worship, which was deeply incarnational and sacramental. Tutu marvels that he used to sit on Huddleston's lap as a child.[25]

Tutu contracted tuberculosis and was in the hospital for nearly two years. We learn from Tutu that almost every week Huddleston visited him. Tutu never quite got over how a white man could care so tenderly for a black ghetto boy whom the doctors announced was dying. It inspired him, to receive care from so many compassionate people. He wanted to become a doctor to "end the TB scourge. I was so idealistic, but it was not to be."[26] Instead, Tutu became a seminarian.

In one of his sermons, Tutu recalled his first year as a theological student at St. Peter's College in 1959 in Rosettenville, preparing for ordination to the diaconate at the end of the year. It was during that year that Bishop Ambrose Reeves came back after fleeing to Swaziland. He was kept under surveillance when he returned to South Africa and came to stay at St. Benedict's House in Rosettenville, with a police car dogging his every movement. Tutu said, "We laughed at what seemed an inept way of trying to intimidate him. So we were not ready for the news shock on the Monday when he was deported to England."[27]

At an early age, Tutu learned from Christian examples like Ambrose Reeves and Huddleston that the command to love God involved more than going to church on Sundays. He learned not to accept the normalcy of how the church mimicked the dysfunctions of a racist society. This learning would be a kind of purgative experience, leading Tutu to resist the identity offered by a corrupt society and to recognize the image of God offered in all persons. For the CR and Tutu, however, the image of God is relationality, an image of *kenosis* (self-emptying) that destroys the false identities that deny God's image of the fullness of relation. Therefore, an ascetic account is necessary in order to understand Tutu's function in South Africa and his own authentic Christian spirituality. Instead of perpetuating practices of racial discrimination, Tutu operates within a spiritual tradition that challenges any force that seduces persons toward adopting finite identity as though it was the very image of God.

In Tutu's formative years he struggled to know God in an apartheid society. The struggle had to do with our discussion above, namely, relationship to the established white church. Tutu states, "I can't myself compute what I learned about God and the things of God from my associations with, for instance, the family of the late Pastor Makhene of the AME Church. . . . Perhaps it is just as well that we do not know these mysterious things to save us from an arrogance of certainty. I do know what I most cherish about my association with Canon Z. Sekgapane. I remember that he was my first Anglican Priest. (You will note that I was ecumenical from an early age—having been baptized in the Methodist Church, going on to the AME and linking up with a relative who was a minister of an Independent Church.)"[28] Tutu recalls being quite a spectacle as he carried his banner in a revival service of a black congregation. He remembers a host of children who enjoyed ridiculing him process in his newly discovered Anglican procession. The strange thing for Tutu was that many of these same children ended up becoming Anglicans themselves.

His identity as an Anglican is owed in large part to Canon Sekgapane. The thing Tutu remembers most of all about Canon Sekgapane was just how he cared for his acolytes, especially when they went to outstations. It is extraordinary the things that remain indelible in one's mind, Tutu recalls. "He never himself sat down to eat until he was satisfied that the servers who had come with him had been adequately catered for."[29] In large part, Tutu reflects upon how that gentleness and caring nature of this black Anglican priest played a large part in making him think about becoming a priest one day. There was such a complex of factors in this question of vocation for Tutu. Did he want to become a priest because he had been touched by an attractive person such as Canon Sekgapane? Tutu concluded that the ordained priesthood must be something special if it could have people like this man.

Tutu wrote in 1979:

I have never in public before spoken about what can only in my view be described as a vision. This is so with a deep sense of reticence knowing just how easy it is to be deluded and fearful that people might perhaps think maybe a little better of me and quite wrongly. I must have been perhaps eight or nine years of age. And I was lying on the stoop of our home in Ventersdorp. I don't know whether I had fallen asleep or what, but I recall quite vividly that I experienced as it were a great light shining and somehow it seemed that Jesus and the devil were having a tug of war over me. And I heard Jesus saying (speaking in Xhosa) "This is my child." And the vision or the dream ended. Perhaps I have done wrong in telling this—it could appear as so much like a kind of showing off. So please forgive me and I hope God forgives me if it puts obstacles in the way of those who may be coming to Him.

The next point in my pilgrimage I remember equally vividly. I had written my Standard VI Exams and everybody expected me to pass. . . . Well, I *failed*. You can't imagine just how much I cried that night. I was quite inconsolable. But that traumatic experience seems to have taught me that I wasn't self-sufficient at all, that I was always dependent on God. It was painful when it happened, but it was a salutary lesson which I hope I have not forgotten.[30]

As South Africa's confessor, Tutu was deeply influenced by CR. The beauty of CR's own struggles and tensions to be a relevant spiritual community in the world inspired Tutu to embrace the African concept of Ubuntu as the worldview of persons in community. Not only does Tutu's African culture determine Tutu's Ubuntu theology, but Tutu's self-avowal to be a product of a *religious* community is also important for understanding his theology of Ubuntu.

Tutu learned from Huddleston and CR that there should be no effort to ease the tension between his religion and his political activity. Being around Huddleston, Tutu learned that here was someone who was fundamentally at peace with himself, not torn in different directions. Huddleston's sociopolitical activity flowed naturally from his worship, from his religion. Tutu learned from Huddleston that being a member of a religious community, with its disciplined life of worship and adoration as part of the regular round of existence, could also sustain him. Tutu is often fond of saying that he is particularly glad to know that monks and nuns were upholding him in their prayers as they said the monastic offices.

For Tutu,

> All this made eminently good sense to me, so I faithfully tried to emulate my illustrious mentors. For me, the spiritual, almost as matter of course, has become central in my life. Let me put it in a slightly different way, and perhaps more modestly. I try to make the spiritual central in my life, mindful as I am of our Lord's injunction that we should not parade our religious activity before men and women, but that it ought to be kept in the closet. Otherwise people might think you are better than you really are.[31]

Tutu puts all of this in the strongest of terms: "Without what I hope is an encounter with God, without the Eucharist, without meditation, I could not survive. I might just as well try to get along without oxygen. It is almost as physical as that."

The influence of the Community of the Resurrection on Tutu engenders a political spirituality in which the continuity of liturgy, devotion, and practical affairs are all equally played out, especially as Tutu is given the onerous task to lead nonviolently out of political crises. From the Community of the Resurrection, which has produced activist priests such as Archbishop Trevor Huddleston, Tutu experiences a theological model of Christian community that remains aware of its responsibility to the needs of the world. In 1987, Tutu explains his debt to CR in his visit to a centenary celebration of the Society of St. John the Divine in Pietermaritzburg, South Africa:

> [I]t is interesting to note quite a few significant occasions when a person was healed and the faith (an indispensable ingredient) was supplied, not by the patient, but faith that came from someone else who was somehow related to the patient. The father of the boy who had a demon healed after

the transfiguration "Lord I believe help thou my unbelief," the Syrophoeni-
cian woman's daughter, healed at a distance after her mother had watched
our Lord repartee and drew His admiration, the nobleman's son and then
of course the story of the paralytic whose friends tore open the roof to let
him down before Jesus because of the crowd.[32]

In this address, Tutu continues to talk about the concept of vicariousness,
standing in on behalf of others. Tutu speaks of vicarious suffering such as that
experienced by Jesus, as a lamb standing before the shearers dumb—by whose
wounds we were healed—suffering on behalf of others so that others may benefit from that suffering. Tutu states, "You know how as parents we often have
to prompt our offspring to say, 'Thank you,' and find that we end up being the
ones who really say thank you to Uncle Peter for the sweets." Tutu's debt to CR
is similar. An important principle of Christian faith is how the few often exist for
the sake of the many. This image is not so much a utilitarian debate about means
and ends, as it is the practice of Jesus, who declared that he had come to serve
rather than to be served. Jesus teaches us how to ultimately live. Tutu concludes:

> What a wonderful relief. What a tremendous thing it is to know that we
> have religious communities. We are meant to gather for worship and ado-
> ration, but we do this feebly, and often irregularly. What a [thing] to be
> thankful for to know that you are these dear brothers and sisters providing
> on our behalf. We who are so remiss, so [unmindful] of the first cause of
> our existence. You provide that regular round of worship and adoration,
> you uphold our world before the mercy seat of heaven. . . . We would be
> in a pickle if you ceased to exist. We would forget that we were meant to
> be poor, to be chaste, to be obedient; we would fail to offer to God this
> threefold sacrifice of poverty, chastity and obedience and you my dear Sis-
> ters of the Society of St John the Divine have been doing this faithfully
> and devotedly for 100 years. I wonder just how many you have helped to
> penitence, to conversion, to health, to forgiveness and for how many you
> have said thank you to God when they had failed like little children to do
> it. Also, you do tremendous work through schools, but the greatest work
> is done here. We will never know the full extent of our debt to you and we
> just know it is inestimable and we come to you to say Thank you to God
> and to yourselves.[33]

TUTU'S BRIEF CHRONOLOGICAL FRAMEWORK

As Tutu matured, he chose the name Desmond for its English meaning of "courageous." Mpilo, his name of preference before, was a Sotho word given by his
paternal grandmother through Tutu's miraculous recovery as an infant from an
illness that still leaves him with a slightly paralyzed right hand, making him a
southpaw. Tutu's first high school classes were in a Full Gospel church. Tutu
shared this hall with perhaps two other classes and recalls that he could listen
in on the other classes if his teacher wasn't being particularly interesting. Tutu's
class did not have any desks. They sat on benches and then knelt beside them

when they needed to write on their desktops. In those days, Tutu recalled the excitement when World War II came to an end. During a school holiday, Tutu and his classmates waved Union Jacks to welcome King George VI and his family. He fell in love with Queen Elizabeth with her marvelous smile. Tutu still admires her today. "She is my favorite Royalty."[34]

Although Tutu was admitted to medical school, he could not enroll because his family could not afford the fees. So Tutu went to the Teacher Training College. It was at that time that Hendrik Verwoerd (1901–66), the architect of grand apartheid and eventual prime minister of South Africa, introduced Bantu Education in 1953, a segregation law that legalized disparate and separated educational facilities. Because of the severity of Bantu Education, Tutu had no other option but to go to theological college; so he pursued the priesthood out of necessity rather than high ideals.

After studying at Bantu Normal College in Pretoria and at the University of South Africa, he obtained a bachelor of arts degree in 1955. In 1958 he went to St. Peter's Theological College, Johannesburg, where he received his licentiate in theology. Tutu obtained his next formal degree when he went on to study for his bachelor of divinity and master of theology degrees in theology at King's College, London, in 1962.

Those subsequent years for Tutu were rated as some of his most formative experiences as he negotiated a new frame of reference of being international and trained in a prestigious British college. Tutu thrived in those years as he states, "Of all my academic honors, I prize my F.K.C. most."[35] This meant in 1978 that he was made Fellow of King's College. "I studied for four years in King's College University of London. I mention this not to boast. It is in order to pay a warm tribute to some of the most outstanding teachers it has been the privilege of any student to have." Tutu studied with Denis Nineham, who wrote the Pelican Commentary on the Gospel of Mark; Christopher Evans, the eminent Johannine scholar; Eric Mascall, the Anglican theologian on Thomas Aquinas, and many others. "I valued my time at King's for it was a time for me of much growth," Tutu concludes.[36]

Only someone who has been a victim of discrimination and injustice could ever savor what it must have meant for a black person from South Africa to enjoy this atmosphere of academic freedom, where people were free to think. It was an opportunity for a young black man to think what, in a repressive setting like apartheid South Africa, would have been regarded as subversive thoughts. "It was almost intoxicating to be treated as what one knew oneself to be, a person created in the image of God, perhaps for the very first time in my life when the color of my skin was really a total irrelevance making not an iota's difference to any assessment that my professors might seek to make of me."[37] And yet Tutu writes:

> About 10 years ago I told my professor at King's College London who had supervised me for the M.Th. degree that I now wanted to go on to a Ph.D.

He was delighted until I told him that I wanted to write on Black Theology. He is very sympathetic to the Third World and eminently fair. But he was flabbergasted and said he did not think there was enough material to research into Black Theology for a doctoral degree. I suspect that he really meant that Black Theology was not really academically respectable. I have no doubt at all if my dear professor were to see this work being reviewed, his anxieties on both scores would be removed.[38]

It is important that Tutu provides this caveat in his Western education, because it displays the ubiquity of bias against black persons. As we shall soon discover in Tutu's more formal leadership, this bias incubates into full-blown racism, as the European colonial model refused to franchise governments of both black and white constituents, and was often adamantly opposed by white leaders who developed their stronghold in the apartheid era, a period begun by D. F. Malan's National Party in 1948 and lasting until Nelson Mandela was elected president of South Africa in 1994.

The Malan administration fully assumed the tenets of apartheid, the legal separation of the races, and used coercion to ensure both a constant supply of cheap black labor and complete control over land rights. This was done through a parliamentary procedure formed for representatives of white voters only, a political process that slowly eliminated black participation in a centralized government. In 1956, *colored* voters in the Cape Province could elect only whites as representatives to Parliament, and four years later, the final stages of the evolution of the African's lack of political control can be seen in the deletion of parliamentary seats of the white representatives of both black and colored voters.

In short, the following time line of Tutu's meteoric rise in Anglican Church leadership may prove useful to the reader as this biography deepens its methodology of viewing Tutu's life through purgation, illumination, and union.[39] In 1954 Tutu became a schoolmaster in Johannesburg, and the next year he went to teach at Krugersdorp. As seen above in Tutu's change in formal education from school teacher to ministry, Tutu began to train for the Anglican priesthood at St. Peter's. He was ordained on December 18, 1960, and served curacies at St. Alban's, Benoni, a city in the East Rand in South Africa (1960–61) and St. Philip's, Alberton, a city in the East Rand (1961–62), and then at St. Alban's, Golders Green, in London, England (1962–65), and at St. Mary's, Bletchingly, in Surrey, England (1965–66). In 1967 he returned to South Africa to be appointed the first black lecturer at St. Peter's Theological College, incorporated into the Federal Theological Seminary (Fedsem) in Alice in the Eastern Cape.

Fedsem was ahead of its time as it conducted the experiment of ecumenical theological education, namely, church leaders from different Christian denominations studying together. Fedsem opened in Alice, Eastern Cape, in 1963, to counter apartheid's Group Areas Act, which forced black theological colleges situated in white communities to close. Fedsem was built next to Fort Hare University College, as progressive South African spiritual leaders opted for the model of English collegiate universities like Oxford, Cambridge, and Durham, that shared resources like the chapel, faculty, staff, and libraries. In 1970, Tutu accepted a teaching post at the University of Botswana, Lesotho, and Swaziland (UBLS) in Roma, a settlement in Maseru District of Lesotho, and then moved again to become associate director of the World Council of Churches' Theological Education Fund (1972–75), working from a base in England (Bromley, Kent, and serving a further curacy at St. Augustine's, Grove Park).

From then on, Tutu's rise in leadership was meteoric. During these times, wise Anglican leadership put Tutu on a fast track to church leadership. Tutu became dean of Johannesburg in 1975, bishop of Lesotho in 1976, general secretary of the South African Council of Churches (1978–1985), combining this post with those of assistant bishop in the diocese of Johannesburg (1976–78) and rector of St. Augustine's, Soweto (1981–85). In 1985 he was elected bishop of Johannesburg, in the following year archbishop of Cape Town, and metropolitan of Southern Africa in 1986. Tutu also became president of the All Africa Conference of Churches in 1987. In terms of emerging on the world's stage, Tutu won the Nobel Peace Prize in 1984.

During all of this, Tutu and Leah formed a family. Their first child was Trevor (named after Trevor Huddleston). Tutu states, "Much later we were to name our son Armstrong as his middle name, after Satchmo."[40] After Trevor, Leah and Desmond had three daughters: Theresa Thandeka (Thandi), Nontombi Naomi, and Mpho Andrea. All three daughters entered the Anglican Episcopal priesthood.

Perhaps Tutu will be remembered most by his position as chairman of the Truth and Reconciliation Commission (TRC), appointed by Nelson Mandela in 1995. As we will see in subsequent chapters of this biography, Tutu's role in the TRC was both controversial and invigorating. Lastly, in 2007 Tutu became the founding member and chair of the organization known as the Elders. They are an independent group of global leaders working for peace, justice, and human rights with the vision of a world where people share a common humanity and responsibility for each other on behalf of future generations.

BEGINNING TUTU'S SPIRITUAL FRAMEWORK

We began the first chapter with a brief display of Tutu's chronological changes. It is important to note the context of these changes in Tutu's life. We will now focus upon a spiritual framework of Tutu's life and thought. Although I realize Tutu's chronological frame of influence does not stop as of the writing this book, I remain convinced of the importance of framing this book as a spiritual biography. More specifically, we begin here with purgation. As stated above, the *first purgative element* in this spiritual biography is to resist spiritual discourse that says the "real" world is insignificant. In other words, otherworldly religion that is no earthly good must be purged from normal associations of spirituality.

This is the case because early in his life Tutu began to develop a political spirituality. Spirituality is real but difficult to reveal.

Biographical discourse is much more alluring through the realities of gossip and intrigue. The same is the case for politics and religion. Tutu's life counters these realities in that he learned to see politics and religion as interdependent. So I seek biographical material here with purgative (cleansing) elements that reveal Tutu's significance and deeper realities that often lie dormant in the public arena. This reminds me of Athanasius's biography of Antony.[41] Athanasius (ca. 296–373), one of the most important Christian theologians and bishops, wrote about Antony (ca. 251–356), the founder of the Christian monastic movement, but struggled to have an attentive audience for the biography. His struggle is similar to my own. Superficial typecasting of Tutu as either a politician or bishop lessens the real impact he has had on the world. In spite of such categorization, I seek to make this biography as public as possible, because this spiritual biography provides an overarching story aimed at God's restorative powers of union in diversity. After all, this is how many religions describe how God created the world.

I focus in this biography on Christian mysticism, wrought in monastic societies, because my guiding idea is that Tutu's Christian mystical identity orders his complex persona in negotiating with and resisting the normalization of apartheid. What may seem obvious here is not. One may think Tutu's spiritual identity would naturally buoy him through the horrors of apartheid, but many people around the world are unaware that *apartheid itself was a spiritual movement.*

This is crucial to understand, in light of the seemingly incommensurate discourse between politics and religion. Most people around the world look at Tutu as essentially a political agent whose spiritual identity is somehow ancillary. Certainly, I have a lot of sympathy for this perspective, in light of the "Monty-Pythonesque" nature of how the church often behaves and more tragically how religion often fans the flames of violence. So it is natural to want the spiritual to be void of politics and become a mere private affair—relegated to the personal and interior spaces of life. But this does not capture the life and work of Tutu.

A *second purgative element* is to see through false dichotomies. Religion and politics are a false dichotomy for Tutu. I believe God formed Tutu to ultimately become a global confessor—that is, he elicits truth-telling that heals souls. In the current political climate of "fake news" and "post-truth" societies, practices of spirituality such as confession show how religion and politics work hand in hand to provide cohesion and coherence. In the ancient arts of spirituality and asceticism, this was known as the cure of souls. I display this prognosis of the cure of souls through Tutu's life as he facilitates both South Africa's confession that apartheid is evil and South Africa's repentance never to let it happen again. In turn the mimicking behavior of confession and truth-telling happened around the world.[42]

This was an extraordinary accomplishment that many fail to see, because most of us have learned about apartheid as a political movement. Apartheid, however, was just as much religious as political. To get the religious zealot to confess any error of worldview is a miracle. Only a few achieve this. One who did was Paul, who was first zealous about destroying Christianity but ended up becoming one of the greatest articulators of it. To get a religious person to confess sin and become conscious of the sin is no small feat. It is a miracle.

Confession of sin purges the soul of false realities and persistent hypocrisies. Confession is a purgative practice in the church, meant to remind the disciple that evil is not the ultimate reality of creation. It takes an extraordinary person with powerful spiritual formation to facilitate confession. It takes a person who sees an expansive picture of God as the God with us (not against us). God's kind of power of love, mercy, restoration, and forgiveness is such that God never gives up on creation. Tutu states, "Injustice, evil and oppression cannot last forever."[43] In fact, well-known Western theologians like Karl Barth think that the very knowledge and consciousness of sin means the victory over sin has already occurred. To acknowledge or name something as sin means that sin's power and nihilism have diminished. To name sin provides the reference point from which to control it and move away from it. Knowledge of sin provides the reference point not to normalize its existence. One gains this reference point as one moves through the mystical threefold method of purgation, illumination, and union with God.

To understand confession in a more proactive way, confession is the practice of the presence of God amid humanity. This is vital to understanding Tutu's life and work in the midst of the complex narrative of apartheid, which had its own god. Getting the oppressor to see God in common with the oppressed was Tutu's greatest contribution and what Tutu will be known for throughout human history. For the oppressor to confess that their god was ultimately diminished in the hegemonic religion of apartheid is a miracle that we all need to replicate. Outside of the first four centuries CE, we have very few Christian leaders as great as Tutu in this respect of facilitating a common vision of God while still adhering to the particularity of Christian faith.[44] So it is in this understanding of confession in the midst of Christian mysticism that we begin the threefold mystical life of Tutu, starting with purgation.

More specifically, understanding the life of Tutu requires an understanding of the relationship of confessor and confessed. This leads to the context of Christian mysticism in this biography, in that the spiritual role of a confessor orders Tutu's complex persona as he negotiates even more complex South African societies that are seduced to normalize the evil of apartheid. As Tutu has said, had churches not justified apartheid theologically, it might never have existed.[45] This guiding idea of Tutu as confessor and the acknowledgment of an apartheid society as confessee lead to the conclusion that his life and work affect inquiry concerning not only the South African context of apartheid, but the Western world's religious context as well. Of course this even goes beyond the Western world to countless global contexts in which forty or so wars are currently waged, 90 percent fought in the name of God or religion. So I make the case here for why Tutu's life invites deeper reflection upon what needs to be clarified and purged in the world, our communities, and selves. How Tutu practiced such purgation occupies our attention in the next chapter.

Tutu sitting with religious leaders (left to right) Moulana Faried Esack, Allan Boesak, and Colin Jones, the dean of St. George's Cathedral. Courtesy of African News Agency (ANA) Archives.

Chapter 2

Tutu and Christian Mysticism

In this chapter we will begin to explore Tutu's rise in church leadership through the lens of the first stage of Christian mysticism, purgation. My goal here is to show how Tutu's spiritual leadership in his public ministry and ordained life contained purgative elements that prepared him to lead in his subsequent roles as chair of the Truth and Reconciliation Commission (TRC) and later as Elder. With this in mind, chapter 2 investigates the mystical theme of this book further in order to make the case for how Tutu is a Christian mystic. In this regard, we will explore one of the central themes of Tutu's theology, Ubuntu. In short, chapter 2 sets the stage for a theological discussion situating Tutu's life in the complex world of apartheid.

PURGATION

As we have seen in the introduction, the first stage of Christian mysticism is purgation. Herein a person's pilgrimage to God must confront purification in order to eventually dwell in God. Such confrontation is as simple as reflecting upon what behaviors prevent a deeper love of God. From such reflection develop ascetic practices such as repentance, humility, and self-denial, which are vital to begin the journey to God. This is why the first part of this book displays the harsh context in Tutu's life, including the profane world he grew up in called apartheid. Tutu's intuition was to defy the socialization of apartheid, which would have one believe that black people are inferior, no longer belonging to God and the African land. Indeed, it requires a firm grasp of God's presence to resist the contamination of an apartheid world. For Tutu to venture deeper toward God was fiercely contested in the sinfulness of apartheid.

For the Christian mystic, purgation is the renovation of character in which to begin the journey toward God. For Tutu, this was not only aimed at an individual's character but at the whole of a nation-state called South Africa. Evelyn Underhill is helpful here in understanding what Tutu was up against: "False ways of feeling and thinking, established complexes which have acquired for us an almost sacred character, and governed though we knew it not all our reactions to life—these must be broken up."[1]

The world of apartheid South Africa was rife with false ways of feeling and thinking, and Tutu spoke often of his struggle to overcome this debilitation. In order to move toward a true way of feeling and thinking, Tutu experienced purgation that set him on his path toward God at an early age. Through Christian faith, he learned how to know himself for who he really was: God's child. The mystics would see this occurrence of purgation in Tutu's life as God's taking hold of Tutu's intellectual faculty of reason and imparting true wisdom. This could not be only God's unilateral action; Tutu had to agree and reciprocate this "taking hold." Tutu would have to learn how this true wisdom was not only in God's domain but in Tutu's as well. In other words, God would represent Tutu, and Tutu would represent God, in the world of apartheid.

God's wisdom displayed in Jesus Christ now sat in judgment of a world of apartheid and was reciprocated in a black boy living in the township of Soweto. Living in this purgation, Tutu would learn to give correct reverence to God, with whom he became inextricably linked. This would become purgative (if not terrifying) as Tutu's God acted differently than the god of apartheid. Tutu's God would act as prosecutor, witness, and judge against apartheid and return the verdict of guilty upon that apartheid world. This linking to God over and against apartheid is important to help us understand why Tutu early on participated in the Christian monastic life of the Community of the Resurrection and the virtues that resulted from a life of poverty, chastity, and obedience.

It is in this context that we understand the spiritual life of Tutu. For Tutu the spiritual life is a means to an end, communion between God and creation (including political life). In other words, it is not enough just to be spiritual. Those who say they would rather be spiritual than religious should be aware that apartheid had its own spirituality. What matters here is that we need a metric of maturity as to which road to take in the spiritual world, because some roads indeed lead to hell. The necessity of spirituality is therefore a purely practical question of how to navigate toward God. Mysticism is distinguishable from spirituality, in that spirituality is about practicing the presence of God, and mysticism is about communion in which spirituality is often thrown aside when the actual end of communion with God and creation is attained. In other words, for mystics spiritual practices are not ends in themselves; rather, they are means toward God.

Through disciplined practices of the spiritual life known as asceticism, someone may fast and develop a focused concentration on God and thereby control unruly instincts. But these same acts may make another so hungry and sleepy that they can think of nothing else.[2] Thus all spiritual practices undertaken in the first stage of the mystic way are aimed solely at achieving enough of an open heart and mind to recognize the true goal of this life: communion. For Tutu, the mystery of communion and the community of the saints cannot be forgotten by Christians who believe in a supernatural reality. He explains:

> It is wonderful to have the angels and the archangels to remind us that reality is more than just that which we can apprehend with our senses, and who can assist to become more truly human for we are so the more worshipful and adoring when we can be the more sensitive to the mysterious. The more we grow, the more we can be surprised by the beautiful, the good, the true, by the sheer wonder of it all, when we are not blasé and dull-witted, unpoetic, literal minded souls.
>
> We will soon in this service join the angels and the archangels in what they do ceaselessly, worshipping and adoring God as they sing "Holy, holy, holy, Lord God of Hosts. Heaven and earth are full of thy glory," as we discover more and more of that divine glory often in unlikely and unexpected places. The angels and archangels help us in our warfare against the powers of evil, spiritual forces beyond our strength to overcome and we know that the war has already been won even if the battles seem to be so fought. We are on the winning side. Injustice, oppression, evil, exploitation have already been routed and we are God's fellow workers with the angels to establish His Kingdom of righteousness, of justice, of love and peace and reconciliation, of laughter and joy, of compassion and caring, of fellowship and sharing in which we know that each individual person is of infinite worth, not just to be respected, but to be held in awe and reverence, to abuse this person makes us guilty of blasphemy.
>
> I am reading a book that invites us to cultivate the angel of death, not in a morbid fashion, but as those who recognize a fundamental fact about us, that we are mortal. We are going to die. . . . If you were suffering from a terminal disease you would have a totally different perspective to life; you would regard every moment as a gift, a precious unrepeatable gift. You would regard many things as if of little consequence such as taking part in the rat race which makes stomach ulcers into status symbols. You would want to have your affairs in order and so far, as possible, you would want to be reconciled with all and would hardly want to leave a bad impression as a person difficult to get on with. Your value system, what you regarded as important, would undergo a radical change. Well, the author of my book reminds us that it is breathtaking in its simplicity and obviousness, and you wonder why you had not thought of it before. The author concludes: We are all terminal cases.

But it is wonderful that it does not matter for even as we fall into this abyss of the unknown, there we will find the everlasting arms which can never let go of us, of the eternal love that created us because it wanted us as part of creation that is moving towards its fulfilment when God will be all in all and all manner of things shall be well. . . . what rapture it will be as we lie prostrate before thy throne to fall and gaze and gaze on thee . . . surrounded by the angels and the archangels that worship and adore God, Father, Son and Holy Spirit, from eternity unto the ages of ages, forever and ever. Amen.[3]

With the concept of Christian mysticism, Tutu invites us too into a journey toward God. Depending on the context from which you read this book, this journey may look like movement also toward communion, or it may resemble more of a discourse of political ends in which justice is ultimately desired. In any case, Tutu's life invites the reader to imagine more than meets the physical eye. Tutu is no mere political actor on a world stage. Similar to the life of the Dalai Lama, his life is more of a portal into how we may seek communion with that which is greater than ourselves. Tutu invites us into a process of growing up as human beings in the hope that we are more than animals.

In short, Christian mysticism's start of purgation seeks to move persons in the right direction, away from contamination and toward the true life created for us by God. Bernard of Clairvaux is helpful here in his third sermon on the Song of Songs. Bernard deals with the verse, "Let him kiss me with the kisses of his mouth" (Song 1:2), and compares the three stages of the mystical way (*via mystica*) with the three kisses. The first stage of purgation is called "the kiss of the feet," with reference to Mary Magdalene kissing the feet of Jesus: "It is up to you wretched sinner, to humble yourself as this happy penitent did so that you may be rid of your wretchedness. Prostrate yourself on the ground, take hold of his feet, soothe them with kisses, sprinkle them with your tears and so wash not them but yourself."[4] The strong language of "wretchedness" may seem off-putting to twenty-first-century sensibilities, but without such shocking language we miss the gravitas of how and where to move away from dysfunctional spiritual worldviews. Herein, Tutu's brilliance is in showing the wretchedness of apartheid.

MYSTICAL EMBODIMENT

As I discussed earlier, I have observed Tutu's devout spiritual life since 1993. The early morning contemplative prayer, morning chapel, Eucharist—all continued, even when he was traveling. Lavinia Crawford-Browne, Tutu's personal assistant for over twenty years, recalls that Tutu would continue his cycle of prayer in cramped office space or on an airplane. It would not matter where he was, he would pray.[5] For the service of the Eucharist, he would somehow always find bread and wine. Such a service might be performed in an airport with everybody walking past observing the festivity as Tutu and staff were focused on God. For Tutu it was absolutely essential to contemplate the love of God in silence, as well as share a eucharistic worship service every day except Saturday.

Tutu also practiced spiritual retreats and quiet days with his spiritual director, Francis Cull. For spiritual retreats, Tutu's routine was to be on retreat the week before Easter and then at some other time of the year when he could get away and go to a convent or monastery. These contemplative practices provided Tutu his strength and support through the difficult days of apartheid. Intentional time with God gave him the courage and the capacity to make extremely difficult decisions.

For example, in the peak of apartheid in the 1980s when he was archbishop, Tutu would be at prayer in the chapel. When chapel finished, he would come out and say, "We will march tomorrow." Tutu would be so inspired that he would not wait to schedule this with other church leaders, because he simply knew what God was calling him to do. Crawford-Browne recalls during such moments that for Tutu to consult with others was simply not necessary, since God had told him to march. "That was Tutu's great gift to us in South Africa."[6] Tutu had the strength, the conviction, and the commitment to do what God called him to do. This was also courageous, since Tutu was on numerous death lists and certainly could have been assassinated by the clandestine security police. Nevertheless, Tutu was convinced that God would protect him.

Even when Tutu traveled around the world, one of the first questions Tutu's staff would be asked was why there were no arrangements for Tutu's security detail. "Well, we say God is looking after him," Crawford-Browne recalls. Tutu did not use security, as he traveled with only family and assistants to help him with logistics. Of course, Tutu would be concerned that his family and staff not be put in situations that might endanger them. At the same time, if Tutu was going to lead a march against apartheid or participate in a political funeral for a black leader who had been killed, he expected his staff to support him. In the 1980s, this was especially true in South Africa's states of emergency. Crawford-Browne remembers that Tutu and staff would often in the 1980s go to public funerals, which usually turned into opportunities for black activists to release their stress from living in apartheid. Tutu's white staff members, like Crawford-Browne and John Allen, were also courageous, as they would stand side by side with Tutu in the midst of the crowds.

Tutu's daily disciplines and asceticism were not his means to appear holy or to follow some kind of perfunctory religious ritual; instead, they provided him the ongoing energy and creative impulse to face the monumental moments that were in his daily, ordinary routine. In other words, Tutu had somehow to normalize the extraordinary challenges he faced every day.

It is helpful here to understand the wisdom of Wyatt Mason's article on the artist's life. Mason as an American journalist, essayist, and critic articulates the stereotype of the artist who believes that hedonism is a meaningful part of their creative production. "There's boozy Faulkner, banging out novels and screenplays while pickled, and Dorothy Parker and Jackson Pollock, producing their poems and paintings alongside the empty bottles," Mason writes.[7]

This association with artists is nothing new, since the description of hedonism comes from fourth-century BCE Greece. In this early context, however, there was a belief that something divine occurred in the mortal creative activity. The early Christians were aware of this Greco-Roman worldview of creativity and instead of hedonistic gods, they adhered closer to ascetic practices to unearth such creativity. This would have especially been the case, given that these early Christians would not have come from the elite classes. For these early Christians, who set in motion their understanding of how to live creatively in the world, no such relationship between hedonism and creative energy is necessary. For them, spiritual discipline and creativity became the new paradigm.

Mason's article on the contemporary artist is helpful here in that ascetism still remains in the activity of creation. Asceticism, he writes, "is a regimen that evolves out of the need to do something unreasonable that an artist can't be reasoned out of doing: work, demanded by no one but the self that makes it, because making is what the artist needs and knows."[8] "Asceticism" comes from the Greek word *askein*, "to exercise," like an athlete training for a major sporting event. Paul writes, "Do you not know that in a race the runners all compete, but only one receives the prize? Run in such a way that you may win it. Athletes exercise self-control in all things; they do it to receive a perishable wreath, but we an imperishable one. So I do not run aimlessly, nor do I box as though beating the air; but I punish my body and enslave it, so that after proclaiming to others I myself should not be disqualified" (1 Cor. 9:24–27).

So *askein* is a word that grows into the Greek word *asketes*, which means to become a monk or holy person. The stereotype of such a person was either that she would withdraw from the world or that, because of rigorous spiritual training, she was very different from many other people. "The old saw about boxers, that they wouldn't expend a certain kind of energy before a bout—sexual energy, which would need to be hoarded if the fighter wanted to be at peak strength—aligns nicely with this notion, one in which the ascetic isn't starving herself so much as harnessing her powers, because power is a finite thing."[9] The point here about Tutu's life is that his spiritual disciplines and daily asceticism were not for show or ostentation but for productivity in the dysfunctional society of apartheid. Tutu's spiritual disciplines were his weapons, with which he could be bold in defiance of the spiritual counternarrative of apartheid—that white people are God's only chosen, holy people.

Mysticism and asceticism may be far from the minds of those who know Tutu as a political agent on the world's stage. After all, mysticism and asceticism are often associated with escapism from the real world. And belief in God and a transcendent reality has often been considered by some of the best intellects in human history as delusional. Mystics are also associated with suffering. Many have advocated that one must endure suffering in order to one day experience heaven or another kind of beatific world. In Christian mysticism in particular, mystics are often known to be like this, as they would often obsess about sin and discipline themselves in so severe a manner that it appeared to be more masochistic than spiritual. For example, the early major Christian mystic Origen is known to have castrated himself to prevent sin. In so doing, these mystics were anachronistically criticized as neurotic, thereby keeping their followers in a state of obsessive submission never to sin again.

There is an obvious difficulty with this kind of mystical approach when it comes to describing the spiritual life of Desmond Tutu. Indeed, if one deems the mystic as an inane spectator in the real world of violence and struggle, then this framework of mysticism will seem unintelligible for Tutu's life. After all, at least in the Western world we already have too many who have lost confidence in our political, cultural, and religious institutions. We also, however, have many people who self-identify as "spiritual but not religious" and yet often feel morally paralyzed to do anything significant with their lives. These people are often criticized as naive in the belief that social ills can be cured through the spiritual life. In response to refugees, gun violence, or human trafficking, we see apathy, with what seems to be the inevitable triumph of evil on a global scale. After all, what can any one of us do to change such a world?

Some early Christian mystics tried to find cosmic solutions by withdrawing into the desert to pray. When Christianity was declared by Rome a state religion in the fourth century, the Jesus movement became the mystical monastic movement, as Christians grew disillusioned with the institutional church and its civil religion. Their retreat was not from an evil world but from corrupt religion, in which evil seemed to flourish and many felt powerless to combat it. A new mystical movement formed in Christianity to meditate and contemplate ways in which the evils of the world could change into the flourishing of God's people. These Christian mystics entered into existential space to combat evil while all along forming alternative communities to a corrupt state religion. Christian mystics who followed this path into the desert were not seeking selfish escapism, nor were they seeking the twenty-first-century obsession of Western Christianity, personal salvation. Instead, they were seeking an authentic contemplative space in which to ebb and flow between the spiritual and natural world. In other words, these mystics were not escaping social action; rather, they were creating it.

It is from this context of mysticism, that the reader of this biography is meant to learn more, not just about the effects of Tutu's life and work, but also about prior questions that inevitably arise concerning Tutu's motivations and passions. Tutu in many ways was a pioneering spiritual leader, helping his own natural world move out of the sinful conditions of racism. Many reading this may not have specifically associated racism in a spiritual context like sin, but this sinful context was the underlying premise for Tutu. How one comes to understand Tutu in this context will be instructive not only for his context, but for future contexts in which human beings seek to understand how human beings can actually be transformed from sinful existence.

Indeed, transformation is the ultimate desire for Christian mystics, but such a desire needs to face paralysis not only in the dysfunctions of masochism or apathy. For example, Tutu describes actual transformation in his own pioneering journey. It was sometimes amusing, he says, in his early days of public ministry to be a black leader in a white congregation in South Africa. He commended the white South African bishops in 1975 for the courage to appoint him dean of the Anglican cathedral in Johannesburg and then have him succeeded by yet another black person, Dean Simeon Ilkoane. It was a time of a "transfigured church," because in turn Tutu was also succeeded by the first so-called colored dean, Merwyn Castle.[10] (In the racial caste system of apartheid, to be labeled "colored" connotated mixed race.)

To show how Tutu was a pioneer in this succession of white ordained leadership in the Anglican Church, he recounts how he had to get a government license to solemnize marriages as a government-appointed marriage officer. The complication here was that Tutu had to explain in an apartheid South Africa how a black man like himself was able to perform wedding ceremonies for whites and other races. So Tutu, an ordained clergy person who normally would not have to do the following, purposefully got a civil-government marriage officer's license that authorized him to solemnize marriages in which the couple could be any race except where the husband was an African. In Tutu's own words, he writes:

> Isn't that something? I had to get another license from a different Government Department. When I wanted to visit my parishioners in hospital, I had to find out whether the hospitals would agree to my visiting. Most were welcoming, but clearly the patients were surprised to have a black in the ward who was not cleaning the ward or being a servant in one way or other.
>
> It was even more fun visiting my flock in their apartments, when I would often be told I must use the servant's entrance at the side or back of the building. Sometimes I would stand on my dignity. But it was interesting once when the Prime Minister had called for a National Day of Prayer because of some assumed threat to South Africa or other. I had said we should not have any such service in the Cathedral. . . . I had gone earlier and announced that there would be no service and a white woman sitting next to the son of our suffragan bishop said, "That boy must be wrong." I eventually had to produce an address which they had not quite expected.[11]

I cannot imagine the countless stories in Tutu's life in which his pioneering social location as a black South African leader in a white church led to awkward if not dangerous situations. It took a toll on Tutu, as white South Africans believed one reality about him while he was living another reality.

Tutu's Christian mysticism must also be qualified by a different reality. His pioneering leadership in the public arena was not as an aloof desert mystic living in isolation; rather, much of Tutu's emergence on the world's stage could also be categorized as pastoral or compassionate. Such a sensibility may be why Tutu's life led to such a deep relationship with the Dalai Lama, who also embraces a life of compassion. Such compassion was important to me when I first met Tutu in 1992 in Atlanta as a beleaguered, young PhD student audacious enough to ask Tutu if I could write my dissertation on him.[12] Despite my preconceived notions about Tutu from the media before I actually met him, I was pleasantly surprised to learn about his truer nature: "First and foremost Bishop Desmond is a pastor."[13]

I learned this fact firsthand while living in residence with Tutu during the period of South Africa's first democratic election.[14] There is great compassion in this man who rose up from a shanty town. A pastor essentially is a leader who has compassion and facilitates community. All else builds upon this virtue of compassion. Tutu, as an archbishop and head of the Truth and Reconciliation Commission, successfully negotiated the political mire of his South African context by remaining true to his spiritual conviction that no one should be a thing; rather, we are all children of God and made in God's image.

The blending of Tutu's disciplines spawned from Christian mysticism and his natural pastoral acumen is what leads to the second part of this book, illumination. Tutu's life, however, first had to navigate the purgation of social realities that never intended for him to control as a public leader. Tutu, through his life and work of reconciliation, as South African confessor, played a vital role in shaping the social conscience of South Africa and its response to apartheid.

A simple example of Tutu at work as South Africa's confessor was when he challenged an apartheid government to imagine the world as it should be. Tutu imagined:

> You know on the day before I was ordained a priest by Bishop Stradling, I accompanied him when he went to confirm at Christ the King Church in Old Sophiatown which lay in ruins as if devastated by the bomb, but the Church shell stood on the hill just as St Mark's Church stands overlooking the scene of desolation. I thought then of the lines in the hymn: "In vain the surge's angry shock, in vain the drifting sands; unharmed upon the stressed rock the eternal city stands." And it is true that God is our rock and strength as the psalmist puts it. Nothing can prevail against that rock. Evil cannot prevail ultimately—oppression and injustice cannot win against God. St Mark's is a symbol that this is God's world. He is in charge. . . . You have first the people of District 6 grievously. You can make amends. What a wonderful 21st birthday for District Six it would be and what a beautiful 100th anniversary present for St Mark's it would be if the Government were to say, we are reversing our policy on District 6. We made a mistake. We are allowing coloreds to return to their old home. We will help them to reestablish themselves there. It would pour oil on wounds harshly inflicted 21 years ago. It would remove a source of anguish. It would cover up an ugly scar. . . . I call on Mr. Botha to hear this cry, this plea.[15]

As Tutu recounts the tragedy of the removal of so-called colored people out of District Six in Cape Town in 1966, Tutu's life and work in an apartheid society represent a distinct narrative in which Tutu displays a complex set of attributes or descriptions.[16] Here is an African community leader who facilitates the emergence of his peoples from under the ravages of colonialism, and an ecumenical

Christian leader who claims catholic authority against apartheid structures. As I have sought to articulate here, however, there are other realities seldom seen in the larger world concerning Tutu's life. These realities are spiritual and mystical.

To understand Tutu as a spiritual agent (and not simply a political one) is vital, in light of the incessant need to learn from exemplars who point humanity as a whole toward solution rather than destruction. Also, more particularly, Tutu's life provides a powerful leadership model for my own North American context, which still struggles with the contradictory issues of inclusion and particularity, spirituality and religion, religion and politics, and affinity versus other. The value of this biography is that by seeing through Tutu's life, we are all able to nurture inquiry regarding the character of synthesizing differences without diluting them, and through such inquiry make inclusion and particularity confluent rather than contradictory. Unashamedly, as someone who imprints upon Tutu, like a hatchling imprints upon an adult bird, I am especially interested in displaying Tutu's life so that current and future leadership will have a creative, healthy, and vital reference point called God.

UBUNTU AND CHRISTIAN MYSTICISM

In much of my past work on Tutu, I focused on the concept of Ubuntu as his theology of God and community.[17] A brief word is in order here, to build on what is meant by this concept that I have used so frequently to describe Tutu's theology. (For more detailed analysis of Ubuntu, see my previous works.) The meaning embodied in Ubuntu is too important to African culture to define it simply as just another communitarian model. In any consideration of the political implementation of Ubuntu, its ultimate meaning must stress that human means must be consistent with human ends. In other words, the freedoms of individuality and community are so strong in African culture that it should be difficult to tell them apart. In short, Ubuntu means human beings need each other in order to be human. This interdependence is just as true in the divine life of God.

However, on a political level, this does not mean that one should suffer at the expense of the other. A profound lesson of South African history is that the racial means used in pursuing political ends determined the nature of community in a way that was antithetical to the ideals of African culture. I have claimed that this ideal of the nature of community is Ubuntu, a profound concept in Bantu ontology that certainly warrants extensive research by theologians, social scientists, and philosophers. Where Ubuntu merges with Christian mysticism is through the African worldview of interdependency, which illumines Tutu's life as confessor and Christian mystic.

To my knowledge, outside of an edited volume written in 1978,[18] no one has attempted to construct what is unique to the character of African Christian mysticism that pertains specifically to black people. In particular, no one has attempted this in a manner intelligible to an African epistemology of community. In light of the spurious use of the term "mysticism" and the disparaging view of African Christianity as the byproduct of colonialism and European missionaries, our discussion should prove instructive to many who long to make sense of African Christian spirituality in more beneficial ways. In other words, such study is important in light of exemplars like the African Desert Fathers like Antony and Pachomius and Desert Mothers like Syncletica of Alexandria, Theodora of Alexandria, and Sarah of the Desert. More contemporary black exemplars in Christian spirituality are Archbishop Janani Luwum (martyred in Uganda), Howard Thurman, Verna Dozier, and Desmond Tutu.

Hence, despite the association of Christian mysticism with Western European discourse, one cannot dismiss African Christian spirituality from Christian mysticism. Ubuntu provides an African worldview in which human and divine identity may find mutuality in the concept of community. In this way ultimate community with God follows through the mystical procession of purgation, illumination, and union. The last stage of union is when a person experiences direct apprehension of God, an experience that is rare but possible. Since God's nature is to be three persons in common substance, union with God occurs solely from God's initiation upon human persons, who then discover transformation into God's life through purgation and illumination from impoverished singularity to the flourishing state of communal generosity.[19] Tutu illustrates such generosity:

> We know by divine revelation that God is fullness of being, pulsating love from all eternity because God is a fellowship, a community, God is a society from all eternity in which God the Son, who is coequal, coeternal with the Father pours forth in return His entire love and being on the Father. The love that binds them together is so immense that this love flowing between Father and Son is God the Holy Spirit. And so God created us wonderfully, not out of necessity. He did not need us; but gloriously, He wanted us. . . . We are privileged to be God's . . . eucharistic persons who hold everything in trust for God and who are forever saying thank you God for your generosity. We return to you what you have entrusted to us temporarily—our time, our money, our talents, our future lives. We are but responding to and seeking to reflect only your own lavish and magnificent generosity.[20]

Christian consciousness is formed by this narrative of God's interaction with creation, whether persons acknowledge God or not. Salvation comes in the turning toward God in community.

Having set this theological context, we begin toward God's community through the concept of purgation. Living in community creates a worldview to seek where God is acting in the world. Living alone makes such a worldview harder to perceive, given the temptation to believe that one's self-contained consciousness is already God. Moving into communal awareness cleanses self-awareness to be able to contain the awareness of the other. This is why Jesus constantly taught a golden rule: love God with all of who you are and in so doing you cannot help but love your neighbor as yourself.[21] Purgation is this process of being cleansed by God's presence. Therefore, spiritual practices such as forgiveness are not so much what we choose to do as what we practice in the purgative experience of becoming like God. Without forgiveness there is never the opportunity to rise above the affliction of irreconcilable persons. In forgiveness, the wound between Creator and creation is cleansed so that the wound can no longer fester. As John of Patmos writes in the Bible, he experienced such purgation stranded on the island of Patmos. In so doing, his imagination eventually developed to see the transfiguration of a new heaven and earth. Tutu also had a similar experience.[22]

For Tutu, heaven is the environment of personal vulnerability, that is, a set of relationships in which persons are able to recognize that their personhood is bound up in the other's humanity. Particularly appealing to his South African environment, Tutu imagines the kind of heaven that moves beyond racial distinctions as determinative of human identity. As Tutu states further, "We have in this land a pyramid of power and privilege based on color—the lighter you are of pigmentation, the higher you stand on the pyramid of privilege and power. In this pyramid blacks are the broad base of the exploited and oppressed. Next is the so called coloreds and then next Indians and right at the top Makulubaas [white boss], white. It is a pigmentocracy."[23] Through Tutu's own purgative experiences of learning to forgive, his imagination for reconciliation increased, allowing for a heavenly imagination in which human identity is elevated as persons find communion with others and God.

Ubuntu's definition that "person is a person through other persons" makes sense of how South Africans should then proceed to operate on the basis of more than racial identity. People need not kill each other because they are black or white but should instead rejoice in how God has created persons differently, so that new meanings and identities are always possible. Tutu's worldview of Ubuntu was criticized as idealistic and vulnerable to white hegemonic systems that may have wanted such "rhetoric" from Tutu to pacify a black revolution. My own work on Ubuntu was criticized as idealistic and uncritical of reified racism. What is missed, however, in such criticism is how Tutu was never naive in his exhortation of Ubuntu. In the same way that heaven is idealistic, Ubuntu's ideal provides human beings an African cultural imagination to see the world differently. Just as heaven can be interpreted in dysfunctional ways—such as suggesting that life on earth does not really matter—so too can Ubuntu, peacemaking, and reconciliation.

In many ways, Tutu's Ubuntu worldview becomes a major concept of African Christian spirituality, providing a purgative reference for European Enlightenment worldviews that deductively seek to "establish" who a person or community is. Tutu's Ubuntu excludes Western tendencies to grasp competitive claims of authority that limit and define infinite personhood.[24] Ubuntu is purgative in that instead of warring factions, when one lives in Ubuntu, one resists being manipulative and self-seeking and "more willing to make excuses for others"[25]

and even discover new meaning in other persons. Therefore Ubuntu is a purgative element that critiques the effort of European intelligentsia to distinguish
which primates are more human. Human beings are more than mere animals,
as Tutu concludes, "If you throw a bone to a group of dogs you won't hear them
say: 'After you!'"[26]

Most explicitly for Tutu's context, the purgative aspect of Ubuntu provides
an alternative to violence. Since perspective determines actions, Tutu's heavenly
perspective provides invaluable insight into justice, in which white and black
people may see themselves as more than racial rivals. "When you look at someone with eyes of love," Tutu believes, "you see a reality differently from that of
someone who looks at the same person without love, with hatred or even just
indifference."[27] One's gaze of the other without love is the opposite of Ubuntu.
Cleansing one's negative perspective of the other is vital also in seeing oneself
more clearly. The awareness of self-hatred is invaluable in also seeing the natural
trajectory in hating others. Therefore, Ubuntu serves as a purgative element in
both revealing and cleansing the contamination of how apartheid forms persons
toward violence and competition. Ubuntu also displays how apartheid seeks to
legitimize legal and social structures by which victimization becomes a normative worldview of the common good.

Tutu's worldview of Christian mysticism counteracts this system of apartheid.
His Ubuntu incorporates the African Bantu perspective of personhood with a
mystical image of God's diversity in unity. Such a mystical image is in the Christian understanding of how the triune God (Father, Son, and Holy Spirit) is the
persona of love itself spilling out to love creation into being. This is Christian
mysticism in that no one person can claim control of life. The consciousness of
what life is comes through the interdependence of knowing. In other words, if
all that existed was a solitary self, such a self would not know it was alive without the reference point of the other. Any claim of singular control or power is
delusory and foolish. In the Bible, Jesus knew this as he continually taught his
power-grabbing disciples to relinquish power and control to God. In characteristic humor, Tutu explains this in one of his sermons: "Jesus gave a new, a
very important responsibility to Peter. He said, 'Feed my sheep.' It's almost like
asking a thief to become your treasurer."[28]

Through purgation of power and control, the Christian concedes to the need
to be transformed into a new consciousness, one in which human beings exist
because of God's interpersonal love symbolized by the relationality of Father,
Son, and Holy Spirit. Tutu states, "God does not love us because we are lovable,
but we are lovable precisely because God loves us. God's love is what gives us our
worth. . . . So we are liberated from the desire to achieve, to impress. We are the
children of the divine love and nothing can change that fundamental fact about
us."[29] Yet, as the mystical concept of purgation denotes, God's love is vulnerable
in human reciprocity to in turn unfold love in others. Here, this vulnerability
plays out in Tutu's political spirituality of leading a nation-state to a new identity
for all South Africans (black, white, colored, Indian, et al.). For Tutu, the unity

of South Africa has to include the mystical elements of how such unity necessarily contains difference. This mystical discussion, for Tutu, does not stop with the unity of racial identity.

Purgation's goal is ultimately toward union with God. Such union looks like a transformed world in which all manner of things will be made well. Caught up in this end, Tutu calls upon all people of faith, whether or not they are Christian, to participate with God in this purgative enterprise of transfiguration, so that what is in bondage to corruption will be liberated as it groans to be made complete. This interreligious and multiracial enterprise is such that the whole of creation groans in expectancy of a new creation. Although Tutu's ecumenism is such that particularity of his own Christian faith matters, he also advocates that other faiths also matter. Therefore, in keeping with the methodology of Ubuntu, Tutu speaks from his own particularity, not in a way to deprive other religious faiths, but to invite others to do the same. This is especially true among the Abrahamic faiths of Judaism, Christianity, and Islam, which share the narrative of a common origin. Tutu states:

> Clearly the entire situation cried out for atonement, for re-unification. . . . And so we could say that the story of the Bible, which is the story of our deliverance, is the story of the quest for that primeval unity. It is a deep yearning for integration, for harmony, for fellowship, for unity, for communion. Consequently, the descriptions of the end time, the time of the consummation, the eschatological time when the kingdoms of this world would become the Kingdom of our God and His Christ, we hear echoes of the descriptions of the beginning times recorded in the Pentateuch, the paradisal times when Adam lived in harmony with all creation. (Gen. 2:8–20; cf. Isa. 11:6–9)[30]

SIMONE WEIL, MODERN CHRISTIAN MYSTIC

Tutu's methodology of maintaining his particular faith commitments (e.g., "the Kingdom of God and His Christ") does not mean for Tutu that other interpretations of how God reigns on earth are necessarily wrong. This brings us back to my language of political spirituality, that is, the effort of seeing how diverse divine worldviews can exist in concert or symphony rather than dissonance. A good symphonic example of a worldview of diversity in unity that would complement Tutu's concept of Ubuntu is that of the French Christian mystic Simone Weil (1909–43), for whom the concept of creation was an incessant problem. Stephen Tomlin states, "Weil was a mystic, ostensibly the most antisocial of all identities, who was also engaged in the heart of society. She had a strong sense of community in an age which has replaced this sense by mass-mindedness: which is to replace a conscious, responsible sense by a mere sensation, unconscious and irresponsible. She always sought to relate private and public morality."[31] Like Tutu, with his mystical bent of purgation, Weil described creation inevitably moving through purgation. For example, she describes two kinds of suffering in creation: pain (i.e., suffering that can be alleviated) and affliction (i.e., suffering in which victims are permanently marked). She states, "When we talk of the problem of pain we make a distinction between suffering and affliction. The problem of suffering or mere pain is how to bear it. When the crisis is over, as in a bout with a headache, the problem disappears. We have a great capacity to be indifferent to this kind of pain. Affliction, on the other hand, is a kind of suffering which marks you indelibly, not merely on the body but on the soul. It is the 'mark of slavery,' signifying an uprooting, a permanent estrangement."[32]

Tutu recounts such affliction in South African history with the example of antiapartheid activist Steven Biko's death in detention in September 1977. For black people, South Africa was an evil place, full of fear, in which those sanctioned to protect them were in fact sanctioned to kill. The final outrage was that they drove Biko eight hundred miles from Port Elizabeth, comatose and naked, on the back of a jeep. The officer in this case responsible, far from being severely dealt with, was actually promoted from colonel to brigadier.[33]

The government had become so callous to human identity in black people that the minister of justice, Jimmy Kruger, drew applause from a contingent of the Nationalist Party Congress when he said that he was indifferent to Biko's death. Biko's death was so gruesome that he was left lying in his own urine on a soaked mat for at least one night. Police and doctors did not protest against this inhumane treatment, and those who said they would have intervened claimed they did not because Biko pretended to suffer. Tutu asks rhetorically, how could someone pretend to have red blood corpuscles in his spinal cord, and nerve damage that indicates brain damage? I would hear Weil answering Tutu in the following way, "Affliction hardens and discourages us because, like a red-hot iron, it stamps the soul to its very depths with the scorn, the disgust and even the self-hatred and sense of guilt and defilement which crime logically should produce but actually does not. Evil dwells in the heart of the criminal without actually being felt there. It is felt in the heart of the man who is afflicted and innocent. . . . Everybody despises the afflicted to some extent."[34]

Weil's purgative vision is helpful in explaining the South African situation in that she discusses the "blindness" of mechanistic structures in society as analogies between affliction and mere pain and makes interesting distinctions. If, for example, oppressive people in power, thereby creating oppressive structures, were not blind, there would not be an affliction. In other words, if Biko were actually a human person to Kruger, there would be spiritual nerve endings in Kruger that would prevent afflicting any human being in such a way.

Biko's black theology was extraordinary in that he called black people away from the abyss of affliction. For Biko, black is beautiful. This is extraordinary because those who are afflicted often see themselves as anonymous before all things, victims and deprived of their personality as they are being turned into things rather than human beings. As Weil concludes, affliction "is indifferent; and it is the coldness of this indifference, a metallic coldness, which freezes all those it touches right to the depths of their souls. They will never find warmth again. They will never believe any more that they are anyone."[35]

Another key mystical insight that Weil provides is that suffering permeates creation in which evil is so complete that evil destroys itself. This enigmatic goal of evil is the most dangerous state of being, because beyond evil's turning on itself is the stage at which evil is perceived as innocence, thus blind. Tutu explains,

> Then there is the mystery of evil. Why should there arise a Hitler, an Amin—why should there be a holocaust perpetrated by those who appeared to be quite normal human beings, why should apparently decent human beings not be incapable of the horrors of apartheid, why should apparently normal people engage in necklacing? Why should there be those who are not appalled by a Crossroads, who can carry out the destruction of a District Six, who can torture to death a fellow human being as part of their normal daily life and return home to embrace their wives and children, to eat birthday cake and be to all intents and purposes normal—why should there be evil at all in the universe of a good God?[36]

Again, Weil is helpful here in that she makes conscious that the greatest affliction ultimately is death itself. Both Tutu and Weil offer mystical imagination for how true spirituality cannot maintain quietism with evil. In Christian mysticism, the context is even deeper than evil in that death is the ultimate foe. Tutu's Ubuntu is helpful here, as he used the concept of relationality as the opposite of death. Through Tutu's vision of Ubuntu, God's love is such that God gives space in creation for persons to become fully alive. In so doing, God respects human reciprocity and freedom in such a way that God expects persons to accept the vulnerable consequences of living in a universe made for freedom. In Christian spirituality, God incarnated a way to negotiate the finality of death through Christ. In Christ the two extremes collide—the finality of death and the eternity of God. In this collision, a door opens. Tutu observes:

> Perhaps the greatest paradox then was the one of life coming as a result of death. If one denied oneself and did not seek to preserve one's life then paradoxically one found it enhanced the opposite to occur. A grain of wheat, He said remained alone if it did not die, but if it fell to the ground and died then life would come. . . . Has it not been wonderfully paradoxical that the way in which those whom the rulers of the world put to death because they were Christians had a way of haunting their killers for they seemed to live on after death, perhaps more potent in death then if those put to death had been alive. Just look at the impact of the death of Steve Biko has had. Just think of the death of other Christians, e.g., Dietrich Bonhoeffer, Archbishop Luwum in Amin's Uganda, Archbishop Oscar Romero in El Salvador and now Pakamile Mabija. They are witnesses to Christ and to the power of the resurrection over death.[37]

Weil is helpful to Tutu's Christian mysticism when it comes to death, in that human beings are God's creations in the void of nothingness. Such a void could be considered as death. God's grace fills this void, however. Grace is attracted to the void as to a vacuum. The operation of grace is therefore equivalent to a form of *decreation*. For since the act of creation is an act of withdrawal on the part of God to allow for that which did not exist, human salvation from death lies in the humility of God to create that which did not exist. This is Christian mysticism in the sense of the paradox of purging nothingness to allow for substance. For Weil this paradox is akin to a "falling upwards," a kind of being rooted in the sky.[38] Although this mystical speak may be too esoteric for some, it is helpful in the attempt to be as fully conscious as possible to premises of religious faith such as Christian mysticism. This means for Tutu that when he addresses the sin of racism or apartheid, his spiritual premise is much deeper—that if we continue in such sins, we increase the propensity for concepts like affliction and death.

Christian mysticism provides a corrective vision to delusion and wish fulfillment so readily transparent in apartheid. Instead of such delusion, proper attention to God should produce the desire for goals other than death, such as reconciliation and justice. In short, true attention to God disallows the treatment of others as means to the ends of the powerful and ruthless. Tutu understands that

> at the heart of things is an ultimate reality that is good and loving, concerned to see that justice and goodness and love will prevail. This ultimate reality I believe to be personal, a being with whom I can enter into intimate personal relationship. Despite all appearances to the contrary this ultimate reality, God, is in charge, but in charge in a way that does not cancel out our autonomy as persons. God gives us space to be persons who are moral agents, with the capacity to respond freely, to love or not to love, to obey or not to obey, free to be good or to be vicious. God has such a profound reverence for our autonomy and freedom that He had much rather see us go freely to hell than compel us to go to heaven. As they say, the doctrine of hell is God's greatest compliment to us as humans.[39]

My intention in this chapter has been for the reader to briefly explore Tutu's rise in church leadership through the first stage of Christian mysticism, purgation. My goal here was to first show how Tutu's spiritual leadership contained purgative elements that prepared him to lead in his subsequent roles as chair of the Truth and Reconciliation Commission and later as Elder. The mystical theme of this book was explored further in order to make the case for how Tutu is a Christian mystic. In this regard, I suggest Tutu's theology of Ubuntu is really a purgative element of apartheid's propensity to separate as opposed to unify. In short, the theme of purgation initiates how to situate Tutu's life in the complex world of apartheid.

In my previous books I have tried to show how Tutu's theology offers theological discourse a much needed corrective to individualistic kinds of spirituality that often catch on in the Western world—and even worse, are used in dysfunctional ways. As we will learn later in this biography, such Western practices of spirituality and politics go hand in hand in the Western world until they bump up against Africa. Tutu explained this crash during his European tour after he received his Nobel Peace Prize in 1984. Tutu's context is his use of the nonviolent means of sanctions against South Africa's apartheid regime, which seemed to be an abhorrent tactic to many white people in the Western world. Tutu pointed out to a group in the United States the contradictory policies of the US, which applied sanctions against Poland when it threatened the Solidarity movement, but balked at doing the same when black trade unionists in South Africa experienced similar treatment: "They say, no, no, no. Sanctions don't work. Sanctions don't work. We must instead have a policy of constructive engagement."

It was not as if Tutu was trying to be provocative for rhetorical effect. Rather, he was saying to the Western world, we depend on you. "We depend on you because our liberation is your liberation," he said. "For the God whom we worship is the Exodus God, the God who leads his people always out of bondage into freedom."[40]

So what does all of this have to do with Christian mysticism? What is claimed in this book is that there is a different way of knowing God. I name this as Christian mysticism. Purgation is the initial stage of "unknowing," or cleansing dysfunctional ways of knowing God. This approach to God carried the methodology of removing from one's mind those concepts both negative and positive that described God. Such practiced removal was necessary because God would always be much more than a person could conceive. This had to be practiced because of the human tendency to cling to such incomplete perspectives of God. Therefore, Christian spirituality produced Christian mysticism and the methodology of purgation, illumination, and union. As I seek to display in Tutu's spiritual life, this Christian mystical tradition can be extremely helpful in methodologies toward reconciliation. In Tutu's spiritual leadership, he relies on the mystical tradition of destroying idols and hypocritical constructs in which only Europeans are powerful or can live in the double standards of power.

Reconciliation, at its heart, is a concept articulated in mystical terms. The Christian rite of reconciliation (contrition, confession, forgiveness, repentance, and reunion) mimics the threefold process of Christian mysticism (purgation, illumination, and union). The ultimate reconciliation is with God, who imparts to creatures connatural relationship. In other words, human beings can actually live with God. Mysticism is the claim of immediacy of contemplative intuition. How mysticism becomes relevant to our discussion here is through African concepts like Ubuntu, in which not only individuals but whole communities seek such immediacy. In short, the definition of Ubuntu is that personhood is always interdependent. A person is a person through other persons. For Christians this is congruent with how God is a Trinity of persons. Such a concept, that a community can be mystical, is strange to Western notions of self-contained spirituality.

For even as we attempt a description of something called spirituality, even more particularly Tutu's spirituality, often we find ourselves bringing our cognitive, categorizing faculty of knowing into operation, as opposed to communal ways of knowing. During the past several hundred years, religious belief, practice, and experience have become an option for Western persons, rather than a core way to organize life experience. For those who remain believers, too often religion is a separate compartment of life, with various religious duties to be "done," but with little influence on ordinary life, other than the vague desire to do good and respect the rights of others. One attends church on Sunday and then gives little thought to religious commitment the rest of the week.

Organized religion in the West has seen its influence decline in many ways, as this dichotomy between the religious and the secular has become more pronounced. Even the rise of various fundamentalist groups has not challenged this, since personal faith is seen as operating in a fairly narrow, restricted sphere with social or political implications favoring one's own affinity group. The Western person brings much of this perspective to spirituality, when the matter to be discussed is only that which is "religious" for the kind of people "I" want to be around. Hence the dichotomy arises in how prayerful experience is important, but one's involvement with local politics is not, as long as "my" affinity group is not threatened. Any approach or suggestion that reinforces this dichotomy in Western experience between "religion" and "life" lessens the chances for any healthy political spirituality to emerge.

Tutu's African spirituality is radically different, for "religion is seen as inseparable from African culture."[41] Herein the last stage of Christian mysticism is important, that of unification with God. In African traditional religions, formal distinctions between the sacred and the secular, the spiritual and the material dimensions of life, do not exist. In South Africa this integration between the spiritual and material is complicated by apartheid, itself a religious worldview in which the Afrikaner feels chosen by God.

In Tutu's worldview, life and religious expression are one, since the invisible world of the sacred is so intimately linked with ordinary life. The universe is basically a religious universe. African spirituality is thus a daily affair, permeating every aspect of life: rising, getting water; cooking food; going to the farm, office, or school; attending a funeral or wedding; drinking beer with friends. Certain religious ritual surrounds specific life events in Western contexts, such as birth and death, but the African spiritual worldview is broader, since it encompasses all that is human and part of life. The African who becomes a Christian or Muslim or follower of any other world religion looks for an experience of spirituality that also encompasses their whole life: language, thought patterns, social relationships, attitudes, values, desires, fears. It is not enough to "do religious things" regularly, since their desire is for a spiritual worldview that will fill the world with meaning and be especially sustaining in times of fear and crisis.

African Christian spirituality offers a cosmology not just for the continent of Africa but for the whole world to participate in recovering spiritual sight for how we all relate to each other and to creation. In Tutu's spirituality, the African person brings her or his desire that experience of God be found in every facet of life, without exception. Western spirituality, formed in the pattern of religion as one part of life, can be disconcerted by the wholistic view presented by Tutu's spirituality, but the Western world has much to gain from Tutu's African Christian spirituality.

At the same time, as we have seen with Tutu's formation in London, England, the distinct values of African and Western worldviews can enrich each other, the Western person learning the value of communal experience as formative of the person, and the African person coming to a deeper awareness of her uniqueness. Tutu states, "I have said before that when I have seemed to stand out in a crowd, it has only been because I was standing on the shoulders of others—many, many others, humble and unknown and unsung who by their courage and dedication have refused to let go of their vision of a free South Africa."[42]

The reader will discover through a comparison of the Western and African views of spirituality that all persons are "like some others," since they are formed in the worldview of their culture. Through this similarity of discovering sight through our particular cultures, we gain the hope that we may all one day see a common vision of God in our midst. This is the Christian hope for heaven in which there will be community enough for all persons to discover their destiny together. Purgation of dysfunctional religion and hegemonic worldviews sets Christian mysticism in motion to get to this heaven. Tutu's influence of Christian mysticism is such that he is able to imagine in intelligible ways how those who are different may find a common destiny. In the same way, sensitivity to the difference of worldviews relating to the spiritual life is thus a prerequisite for fruitful, grace-filled sharing and discernment of the fullness of what spirituality can come to mean. What is helpful to Tutu is that in African mystical sensibilities, one is most truly one's self in community.

Tutu's spiritual life carries with it the daily need of habits and skills given through communal practices. For Tutu there can be no experience of God solely as an individual's experience per se, as if God's presence resides only in the personal realm. Indeed, I make the controversial claim in several of my other writings that it is foreign to African worldviews that becoming a Christian involves only a personal relationship with Jesus as "your Lord and Savior." Tutu's spirituality does not separate personal and communal notions of salvation in this Western manner. Neither does he accept the cosmology often preached that if you were the only one alive, God would still come and die for you. God's communal nature cannot be separated in this way. These ways of naming relationship with God through Western individualism are unintelligible to African ways of knowing. In the end, Christian mysticism helps Tutu articulate a communal image of God as diverse persons in a unified nature. Community, understood through Tutu's sensibilities, becomes the image of God. It is from such community that one can then understand this African proverb: The reason that two antelopes walk together is so that one might blow the dust from the other's eyes.

As we turn toward the next chapter, we will see that the demands of Tutu's spirituality extend not only to people who naturally agree with Tutu, but to his enemies as well. We see more of Tutu's application of Christian mysticism in his public ministry as he serves as titular head of the Anglican Church in Southern Africa. Such public leadership becomes a tremendous challenge to Tutu's spirituality in light of the disruptions of apartheid. It is inevitable that Tutu's spirituality hits bumps in the road, as Tutu navigates both the institutional church and the public societies that extend beyond South Africa. This further complicates how South Africa is changing in response to the Western and now Asian world (i.e., China is now moving into the continent of Africa is an expansive way).

Especially for Tutu's spirituality, as people move from rural to urban environments, community life can no longer be taken for granted. The challenge for African communities is in the increasing negotiations that exist between the individual and the community. The natural challenge to the African communal worldview then becomes whether or not African communal sensibilities are intelligible apart from Western notions of the individual. In other words, since the end of apartheid, South Africa has increasingly become the gateway of the Western and Asian world to know the African world. This is a vital challenge, for as we see in Tutu's leadership in postapartheid South Africa to befriend spiritual leaders like the Dalai Lama, Tutu became just as much a thorn in the side of the dominant black South African government as he did in white apartheid. Tutu's Christian mysticism was both consistent and dynamic, as he negotiated a complex polity like apartheid as well as the postapartheid scramble for leadership and direction in Africa.

Tutu at the World Council of Churches Central Committee Meeting in Johannesburg, South Africa, January 20–28, 1994. Author photo.

Chapter 3

Purging Scales from Eyes

In chapter 2 we began to see how purgation informs Tutu's own life. With this in mind, chapter 3 moves from the theological conversation of purgation into the purgative experiences of Tutu's ordained and public life. This also includes a more contextual discussion about how South African society's view of black and white identity caused him to experience purgation, helping ground the reader for the later stages of illumination and union in Tutu's life. In this chapter I will explore how Tutu rose in church leadership in such a way that he helped the scales to fall from the eyes of both South Africans and global citizens concerned with the evil of apartheid. In many ways, as Tutu's public leadership grew more turbulent, so did the resistance of apartheid leaders to Tutu. With the concurrent motion of Tutu's rise and the fall of apartheid, people began to see the system as evil rather than holy.

Because of this concurrent motion, it proves difficult to parse out Tutu's political leadership from his spiritual leadership. Hence, I coin the phrase *political spirituality*. The word "politics" comes from the Greek word *polis*, "city-state." Such a city was more than New York City or Kansas City; rather, *polis* referred more to an *ideology*. To speak of the *polis* was like speaking of a religion, because it referred to faith in human institutions and political leaders. My goal here is not to raise a false dichotomy that often appears between spirituality and politics. One of the church's most prominent saints, Augustine of Hippo (354–430), an African who lived in what is now known as Algeria, describes the two realities of the city of God and the city of the world. They cannot, he says, be neatly separated, because people who live in both are contaminated by original sin. In other words, sinners live in both the city of God and the city of the world.[1]

Tutu's political spirituality resisted this contamination as apartheid grew to become the state religion of South Africa. The Afrikaans word "apartheid" means "to be holy" or "to be set apart." The brilliance of Tutu's spiritual leadership contained purgative elements that helped him expose the evils of apartheid, as well as lead his own city-state in resistance to seeing an apartheid state as the city of God. So we continue the theme of purgation in order to situate Tutu's life in the complex world of apartheid. Tutu's powerful political witness to the world is characterized by his holy orders of the priestly life.

Part 1 of this book exemplifies this paradox in which Tutu's spiritual formation (purgation) prepares him for powerful political witness. The tension in this paradox is in how such spiritual formation never released him to follow a political or business career. Even though one seldom makes such an acknowledgment, the nation-state of South Africa owes a great deal to Tutu's spiritual formation. Such formation became a catalyst for disparate communities to make public confession of evil done by perpetrators against victims. Tutu's spiritual formation gave people the vision to see how to disrupt these cycles of politico-spiritual abuse. And such formation makes people celebratory and thankful (the literal meaning of the Christian concept of Eucharist).

Despite the tension between religion and politics, I fail to see anyone better than Tutu model how religion and politics need not be antithetical, but can be purged in such a way that human communities benefit from the symbiosis of the two. This point has become all the more apparent to me as an African American writing this book. Religion and politics are very much on the minds of United States citizens after the historical circumstance of having elected a black man as the president of the United States and then elected a racially provocative white man, Donald Trump. It is not accidental that while Barack Obama had to articulate how religion and politics fit together as he weathered the storms of being associated with Jeremiah Wright and the black church, Donald Trump was helped to the presidency by the white evangelical vote, despite Trump's failure to display a morally integrated life.

Both examples are not accidental, because religion in many cases has been the catalyst for political change (e.g., the black church in civil rights, Buddhism in Tibet). Tutu realized the spiritual power of religion to stop violence and abuse; avoiding the all too frequent result of civil war, which many religions have helped ignite. Religion is similar to holding the tail of a tiger. Tutu knows this and works hard in his spiritual life not to tame the tiger, but to release it in a (super)natural habitat. Such a habitat for Tutu is God's ultimate reality of creation in which all of us (not just one's affinity group) are meant to flourish together. The prophets in the Bible envisioned the same. Isaiah describes a wolf lying with a lamb and a lion with a calf (Isa. 11:6). This vision of the prophets is why, I think, Tutu told an American crowd seeking political comfort: "The greatest memorial to Bobby Kennedy would be if you made it impossible for any US administrator to collaborate with apartheid. Please do that before it is too late. We shall be free, and we will remember who helped us to be free."[2]

When I lived with Tutu, I learned firsthand about how hard he works in his spiritual life to release the tiger. Tutu taught me the strange lesson about what our deepest relationships can look like, that a foreigner could actually love and commit to me more than those who are most familiar to me. This is the strange thing about Jesus' kingdom of heaven (supernatural habitat), that our primary relationships will look different as they expand beyond natural and biological groupings. In the spirit of Tutu's sense of humor, the following story I overheard years ago helps to illustrate my point here.

An old country doctor went to a rural area to deliver a baby. It was so far out, there was no electricity. As the story goes, when the doctor arrived, no one was home except for the laboring mother and her five-year-old child. The country doctor instructed the five-year-old to hold a lantern high so he could see, while he helped the woman deliver the baby. The five-year-old did so as his mother pushed in travail. After a little while, the doctor lifted the newborn baby girl by the feet and spanked her on the bottom to get her to take her first breath. The doctor then asked the new five-year-old brother what he thought of his new sister. "Hit her again," the five-year-old said. "She shouldn't have crawled up there in the first place!"

This is the kind of humor Tutu uses to open our eyes to the sibling rivalries in which we live. Through the horror of apartheid, Tutu's spirituality teaches him that no longer will we be centrally related through our biological families of mother, father, sister, brother, aunts, uncles, and cousins. Jesus even says, "Whoever loves father or mother more than me is not worthy of me; and whoever loves son or daughter more than me is not worthy of me" (Matt. 10:37). For Jesus, whoever does the will of God in heaven is his brother and sister and mother. Tutu emulates this understanding of Jesus. Jesus is constantly reorienting our relationships to look like heaven—to look supernatural. As we see in much of the New Testament, it was foreigners—those who were not naturally connected to Jesus—who paid the most attention to him.

To find God's supernatural habitat, Tutu is also influenced by those famous words of Ruth, a foreigner to Naomi and Israel—

> Do not press me to leave you
>   or to turn back from following you!
> Where you go, I will go;
>   Where you lodge, I will lodge;
> your people shall be my people,
>   and your God my God.
>   (Ruth 1:16)

Tutu used such exemplars as Ruth and Naomi to preach about how God forms new relationships and bonds among humanity. I often heard Tutu preach on these texts, expressing his belief that God wants to surprise us in the kingdom of heaven—for us to see who our friends really are. We will be surprised to understand that those most different from us can actually be closest to us. When we see God, a whole new reference point will be given to see more clearly. As I recounted in the preface of this book, the following story, again in the spirit of Tutu's storytelling, illustrates how God provides a whole new frame of reference.

A kindergarten teacher was observing her classroom of children while they were drawing. She would occasionally walk around to see each child's work. As she got to one little girl, Susan, who was working diligently, the teacher asked Susan, "What did you decide to draw?"

Susan replied, "I'm drawing God."

The teacher, being theologically correct, paused and said, "But no one knows what God looks like."

Without missing a beat, or looking up from her drawing, Susan replied, "They will in a minute."

Tutu frequently uses this kind of humor to illustrate how one's vision of God creates a trajectory toward a new kingdom, one in which a supernatural habitat can form. Although it may indeed be idealistic, when we seek God, a new kingdom comes to mind. As mentioned above, here is Isaiah's specific vision:

> The wolf shall live with the lamb,
>   the leopard shall lie down with the kid,
> the calf and the lion and the fatling together;
>   and a little child shall lead them.
> The cow and the bear shall graze,
>   their young shall lie down together,
> and the lion shall eat straw like the ox.
>   (Isa. 11:6, 7)

These are some of Tutu's favorite words of Scripture, for they expand our imagination to see instincts and natures changed so that we exist as more than predators and victims, more than eating or being eaten, more than a violent reality we call life. Tutu's spiritual formation makes him wise enough to understand that the goal of spiritual leadership is not to control religion and politics; rather, the goal is to become the catalyst in which both religion and politics lead to (super)natural outcomes.

Spiritual leadership is akin to the Cherokee parable in which an old Cherokee tells his grandson about a battle that goes on inside people.

> The old man said, "My son, the battle is between two 'wolves' inside us all. One is Evil. It is anger, envy, jealousy, sorrow, regret, greed, arrogance, self-pity, guilt, resentment, inferiority, lies, false pride, superiority, and ego. The other is Good. It is joy, peace, love, hope, serenity, humility, kindness, benevolence, empathy, generosity, truth, compassion and faith."

The grandson thought about it for a minute and then asked his grandfather: "Which wolf wins?"
The old Cherokee simply replied, "The one you feed."

South Africa (and the rest of the world) owes a great debt to Tutu's spiritual formation for helping him to envision a reconciled reality that most of us cannot imagine. As stories and parables are meant to teach, human cultures are called to learn from history. Surprisingly, such an obvious fact takes leaps of faith that almost seem irresponsible, even subversive of whatever the world calls justice. To see the world as God intends the world to be, however, is to inhabit these biblical, utopian visions of vegetarian wolves and lions. As to what this utopia looks like, Tutu, like the US politician Bernie Sanders, favors the redistribution of wealth. Sanders is fond of pointing out that 1 percent of wealthy people control 99 percent of US resources. "The oligarchy in this country, whose greed is insatiable," Sanders said, "is destroying Lincoln's vision of America, is destroying our vision of America, and is moving us toward a government of the few, by the few and for the few."[3]

Tutu's vision of unity does not have such a hierarchy, as he is on record saying, "The gap between the so-called affluent West and the poor . . . is not being narrowed. Instead it is increasing alarmingly and could very well be the cause of a genocidal war."[4] This is important in that he also knows the existential crisis of the rich. Tutu states, "I never cease to be amazed that there are so many white people who genuinely want fundamental change in South Africa, i.e., political power sharing in a nonracial, democratic and just South Africa. I am amazed that they should want this to happen when the present dispensation ensures that they enjoy quite substantial privileges simply because they are white. I would I am sure have needed an extraordinary access of grace to want to overturn a system that provided me with such privilege and power."[5]

Tutu is a founding trustee of the Equal Opportunity Foundation, started in 1987 with a grant from the Coca-Cola Export Corporation. The Equal Opportunity Foundation has worked exclusively with small, grassroots communities, particularly in the rural areas of South Africa, funding projects in both urban and rural areas. These projects included health care, early childhood learning, education training, skills training, university outreach, African culture, scholarships, and the provision of resource centers in rural areas. Tutu states, "The Equal Opportunity Foundation is a wonderful example of an organization which is working for the good against interminable odds. It is a beacon of hope, showing us that the way to expel the darkness in our land is to begin by lighting a few small candles."[6]

However, the problem in South Africa remains that whites maintain considerable political weight, and the few control enormous resources. The security apparatus and the civil service remain dominated by whites. Mining and agriculture, which account for 95 percent of South Africa's exports, are also white domains. As a result, the legacy of economic recession and a stagnant economy

have plagued South Africa's new nation. A unified South Africa requires the wisdom of the elders. It will take wise leaders to figure out land reform and housing
policy in such environment, in which apartheid set the rules for almost fifty
years.[7] Tutu concludes:

> We have held the USA in high regard. I used to teach English and History
> at High School before I went for ordination training. We were inspired by
> the American war of independence. I made my students learn Abraham
> Lincoln's Gettysburg speech about government of the people, by the peo-
> ple and for the people. I made them learn the idealistic preamble to the
> Declaration of Independence. We have believed perhaps naively that your
> land was the home of the brave and land of the free, a fearless upholder of
> justice, freedom and democracy. We have considered it as self evident that
> you would be automatically on the side of justice, freedom and democracy
> supporting those who were seeking to achieve these for themselves. Brutal
> reality has been sadly disillusioning, and we have been rudely awakened.[8]

For Tutu, the issue of equal distribution of wealth is really the task of learning
from history.

> We seem to be hell-bent on proving that "we learn from history that we
> don't learn from history." We do not learn from Afrikaner history that
> there is no way in which a people can be forever subjugated. We do not
> learn from 1976 that we have a new breed of young people who are quite
> unafraid and who are determined that South Africa will be free, whatever
> the cost to them. We do not learn from Zimbabwe that we must negotiate
> whilst there is still time, and not arrive at a non-racial society only after
> needless bloodshed, hatred, and destruction.[9]

Tutu's context of learning about an inequitable wealth distribution was from
an apartheid culture determined to keep significant political power in the hands
of a white oligarchy, because this political power gave access to other kinds
of power. At that time, South Africa had the most inequitable distribution of
wealth in the world. In 1924 the whites, who made up 21 percent of the population, received 75 percent of national income, whereas the blacks, 68 percent of
the population, received only 18 percent. In 1970 the whites, reduced by then to
17 percent of the population, got 72 percent of the income, while blacks, 70 percent, had progressed to 19 percent of national income. Tutu knew it was unlikely
that there would be any significant redistribution of South African wealth without a significant shift in political alignment.[10]

For Tutu, the spiritual response to this economic inequity was the concept of
Jubilee. In the Bible, Jubilee stipulated that the land be fallow during the Jubilee
year. Jubilee is closely related to the concept of sabbatical, rooted in the story that
God rested upon finishing creation. In Jubilee, however, we are called to realign
inordinate ways in which human will is no longer God's will. This realignment,
described in Leviticus 25, has profound implications for how we should order
our political, economic, and social relations. Here the criteria of Jubilee are

release of slaves, relief for debtors, and the return of stolen land. In South Africa many black homelands were simply stolen in the European scramble for Africa. Concerning the tragedy of forced removals in District Six, mentioned above, Tutu believes that such occurrences were standard practice in European colonialism. For Tutu, there were spiritual underpinning of such sin, not only in South Africa but in the rest of the world's history concerning colonialism. In order to stop such cyclical evil among human beings, Tutu thought we should invest as much passion and zeal in calling for the cancelation of the foreign debt of economically developing countries, as was done in the antiapartheid movement. For him, this is the new moral issue to which we must be committed.

Economically developing countries pay out exorbitant costs to service their debt. In some ways they are subsidizing the affluence of the West. Tutu also has a critique of the so-called "third world," in that they may have been brainwashed to consume a great deal of Western aid because of the corruption of a decadent elite. Tutu states, "And so we can't just say 'cancel the debt' when the resources so released may not serve the majority of the people. I suggest that there should be a twelve-month moratorium on repayments and there should be a strict condition to uphold human rights and the democratization process as well as using resources for appropriate development clearly benefitting the majority of the people. If these conditions are met, then the debt should be cancelled, and the people given an opportunity to make a fresh start (the Jubilee principle) unhampered by entails of debts."[11] Tutu's call to justice here in economics stems from his experience of how the Western world is represented in South Africa. In his mind it seems as if there is a conspiracy among certain Western countries and big businesses to keep blacks in South Africa forever in bondage. Tutu concludes:

> I hope the US is not embarking on a dangerous course in Africa. Blacks who have worked for freedom peacefully and who have prayed and waited for it will despair when they see the leader of the free world hobnobbing with their oppressors. They will despair and take to fighting. They will despair and then say, blood is thicker than water, and they will despair and turn to the communists who will provide them with arms and support. Please America, you are a lover of freedom, be true to your great history. Dear friends it is our children who are being detained, it is our children who run the gauntlet of police dogs, and bullets and tear gas. It is our children who must go into exile, it is our children who must starve in the resettlement camps, it is our children who must see their migrant father once a year. They are just not pawns in an international political chess game, they are our children like your children. Is it nothing to you who pass by? Is there any sorrow like unto this sorrow?[12]

The 1960s and 1980s contained the heat of South Africa's states of emergencies in which the apartheid government sought to neutralize dissent rising from townships. In 1986 Tutu's authority increased dramatically as he became archbishop, the titular head of the Anglican Church of Southern Africa (ACSA), known until 2006 as the Church of the Province of Southern Africa (CPSA).

As archbishop, Tutu oversaw geographical areas called dioceses in South Africa, Mozambique, Angola, Lesotho, Namibia, Swaziland, and Saint Helena. In South Africa alone there were about 4 million Anglicans out of an estimated population of 45 million. The current archbishop is Thabo Makgoba, who succeeded Njongonkulu Ndungane in 2006.

During Tutu's tenure as archbishop, South Africa experienced the climax of international pressure against apartheid. The registration of black trade unions and the lifting of job restrictions signaled a move away from obvious racial discrimination. Tutu knew, however, that such positive moves were usually a ploy of the apartheid government to offer small rewards to contain the masses. This was important as resistance to Tutu's call for international sanctions against the apartheid government began to take root. As archbishop, Tutu voiced strongly how all South Africans were being brainwashed to believe that the country was facing a "total onslaught" from outside, Communist from the East, liberal-inspired sanctions from the West.[13]

The Cold War was brewing during this time. There was no doubt in Tutu's mind that Mikhail Gorbachev, with his perestroika and glasnost, was a critical catalyst for encouraging change to take place in South Africa. The South African government tried to promote themselves as the last bastion against the depredations of a rampant Communism. They knew that especially in the USA, Americans were guaranteed in a Pavlovian conditioned response to be anti-Communist. The South African government knew how to play American sentiment in this regard, so as to overlook apartheid South Africa's horrendous human rights violations. White South African leaders, Tutu knew, need only mention the word "communism."

In the media, this apartheid government was equally smart in insisting on certain terminology, knowing again that the right words would evoke appropriate responses from the West. So invariably, the liberation movements were described as terrorist organizations and their members as terrorists. This South African government called on liberal English newspapers in South Africa to avoid using even reasonably neutral terms such as "insurgents" or "guerillas" to describe the antiapartheid movement. So Tutu's legitimate liberation struggle was easily vilified, because Westerners equated it with that of the IRA (Irish Republican Army) and PLO (Palestine Liberation Organization), and the disapproval and condemnation were then assured.

Tutu recounts that when some Westerners tried to point out that there was a hallowed tradition in the West and in Christianity that upheld the validity of a justifiable insurrection, and that the doctrine of the just war was applicable in the case of South Africa, he and other antiapartheid leaders were flabbergasted to discover that the West and its church by and large had suddenly become pacifist when it came to declaring war against apartheid.

Tutu describes returning from Moscow in 1988, where he had been among about six hundred guests of the Russian Orthodox Church, which was celebrating their thousandth anniversary. While there, Tutu asked the Soviet deputy foreign minister what he said to those who accused Russia of engaging in a policy of Soviet expansionism by using Cubans as surrogates in Southern Africa. The foreign minister's response would surprise those with stereotypical knee-jerk responses to the Soviets. He said they think problems of injustice should be solved nonviolently, that one cannot establish justice by using violence. Tutu thought it would surprise some to know that Russians had no selfish interest in the African region; instead, they had an interest in seeing that the apartheid crisis here was solved equitably. What matters, he said, is that peace is served.[14]

In Tutu's international travel, he sought to ensure that countries would exert political, diplomatic, but above all economic pressure on the South African government. Tutu needed to be this international voice because so many of South Africa's black leaders were in jail or exile. His message to the international world was that apartheid must not be made more "comfortable," must not be "improved." It must be eliminated. Investors should invest in South Africa only provided certain strict conditions were met, including that black workers be housed as family units in family-type accommodations near the place of work of the breadwinner. International communities should have no alliance with the migratory labor systems or the Bantustan policy of separate territories for blacks, a lynchpin of apartheid. Also, black workers, Tutu said, should be unionized. The South African government did take a few steps in this direction, with a policy in which black trade unions were officially recognized for the first time. More momentum was needed, however, in order for black workers to sell their own labor in free commerce and movement, thereby opposing another important element of apartheid, the rigid internal passport system known as the pass laws. Tutu also called for massive investments in black education and training. Lastly, he said specific pressure needed to be placed on the South African government for eighteen to twenty-four months in order to force them to implement these conditions. Tutu concluded, "The onus would be on them. If they failed to implement this code, then the pressure would become punitive. In effect we are saying invest of course, but only if apartheid has been or is being dismantled."[15]

Tutu felt that his international work was worthwhile, since it would one day vindicate the antiapartheid movement by showing the world what could eventually happen in South Africa. Unity could be captured in the dramatic moment when the world watched Nelson Mandela step out of prison. This unity would no doubt be a giddy moment when humanity experienced exhilaration. When this did eventually happen, in 1990, Tutu said, "We were all proud to be human. There was a nobility we all shared then. . . . We are all waiting with bated breath for the end of apartheid and the establishment of a new dispensation in South Africa, democratic, non-racial and non-sexist."[16] Before Tutu actually rejoiced, however, in seeing Mandela released and South Africa's first democratic government installed, Tutu had to continue to work to purge the brainwashing system of apartheid that tried to force its citizens to live under the delusion of "us against them."

Because of the perceived onslaught of communism and the growing unrest in the liberal Western world, in 1982 Pieter Willem (P. W.) Botha, the South African prime minister, called for a "'total national strategy" outlined in twelve points. Tutu states, "Today we know, from the Prime Minister himself and other government sources, that this 12-point strategy is really a slightly disguised apartheid, being a modernized reformulation of Nationalist Party principles. Anyone opposed to the total strategy is labelled a traitor and a part of the total onslaught. We are really being asked to protect exploitative capitalism, to assist in our own oppression and exploitation."[17]

Tutu believed that the South African government provided substantial privileges and concessions to certain blacks in urban areas, thereby co-opting them to form a buffer between the white capitalist "haves" and the other black "have-nots." Since they would benefit so singularly as part of what Francis Wilson terms the "core economy," they would be some of the most vociferous supporters of the status quo. But those who do not qualify for inclusion in the core economy will be condemned to the outer darkness.

The Riekert Commission's report, a government document released in 1979 that had the stated goal of improving economic conditions for blacks, was initially welcomed as a step toward liberalizing pass laws and supposedly eliminating discrimination. But it was eventually seen as an instrument of injustice and oppression,[18] a tool the South African government used to its own advantage. Tutu's charge to the South African government was to stop shuffling the chairs on the *Titanic* and see that systematic change—not technical fixes like those in the report—were needed. Apartheid was still in place, he said, and it continued to relegate thousands to starvation and death in the teeming, eroded homelands.

In the face of this, Tutu believed the church must do more than just talk. The survival of South Africa was at stake. The church could no longer sit around watching the death of District Six, a forced removal of so-called colored people from Cape Town, and just shrug its shoulders or pass pious resolutions. The church could not sit around while people were systematically destroyed through population removal schemes. The church could not sit around while people were detained without trial in the name of a nonexistent justice and for an alleged law and order that was long ago subverted by the erosion of the rule of law. Black family life was being deliberately destroyed by the migratory labor system. Ridiculous practices still existed, as black people were banned for publications that promoted community building and black self-esteem. Organizations and assemblies were outlawed by the apartheid system, as a critical mass of black people became a greater threat. Even white Christians like antiapartheid bishop David Russell were penalized for attending church conferences.

Tutu was more specific, as he believed that Jesus Christ called all people to freedom—not just some. Jesus' gospel (good news to the poor) demands that we struggle for justice and peace, compassion and reconciliation, for laughter, joy, and life, which belong to the kingdom of God. Even in these public pronouncements of faith, in the late 1980s, Tutu made the prophetic prediction that South Africa would have a black prime minister within five to ten years, but cautioned that South Africa learn from history to prepare for that event. For Tutu, white South Africa had a choice: whether change would happen peacefully, or only after more death and destruction, as happened in Zimbabwe. Tutu concluded, "And that black Prime Minister will almost certainly be Nelson Mandela; so let us support the Free Mandela Campaign."[19]

CHANGE AS PURGATION

President Barack Obama ran his first presidential campaign on the theme of change, but many people became ardent advocates of change only if it meant that things remained the same. In fact, we experienced the phenomena of US politicians whose raison d'être was none other than to make Obama a one-term president.[20] Representatives were supposedly elected by the people of the United States to address the needs of the people. But in our two-party political system, half of these representatives interpreted their mandate as nothing more substantive than to get rid of Obama. This was a phenomenon due both to the unanimity of this party in this endeavor and the fact that the object of removal was the first black US president. The context of purgation helps us see this pernicious phenomenon honestly. Many people deemed blackness to be the contamination of the US presidency. In public, however, most of these people claimed that their opposition to Obama was not about race but about Obama's birth certificate, or universal health care, or government funding of what they saw as a welfare state, or the economy.

This context of the United States is important in seeing Tutu's own task in purging the wily forces of an apartheid state. Tutu's spiritual leadership did not have the luxury to patiently wait for this contradictory knot to unravel. White South African leaders were acting like racists while at the same time advocating publicly for a gradualist end of apartheid. For example, the apartheid South African government claimed that it was committed to the principle of change through self-determination for what it called the various peoples of South Africa. This would in turn be determined through balkanized reservations (Bantustans) for each of the twelve black ethnic groups. Only with those restrictions did the apartheid government allow for self-determination. In light of such mendacity, Tutu's spirituality was paramount in unveiling the deceit of apartheid.

In the context of this political entrenchment by the government, Tutu had to find ways to advocate for real change. Black people did not want apartheid made more comfortable, with minor fixes and technical changes; they wanted it dismantled. The spiritual and political solution was not in concessions to corrupt powers and principalities but in power sharing. In saying his prayers through the daily office of prayer, Tutu would have read the following scriptural passage numerous times: "For our struggle is not against enemies of blood and flesh, but against the rulers, against the authorities, against the cosmic powers of this present darkness, against the spiritual forces of evil in the heavenly places" (Eph. 6:12). Tutu's problem of change as purgation was how to bring about peaceful, godly change in a violent world. There was the rub.

Tutu believed fervently in peaceful change but also knew the purgative affects called for in Christian mysticism. This required fundamental change, meaning political power sharing and transformation, rather than technical fixes. Tutu's methodology, he believed, would be the kind of change that occurred through truth-telling, negotiations, and discussion. He often said, "Anything that can be done peacefully to persuade the South African authorities to go to the conference table would get my support. We have asked the international community to exert pressure—political, diplomatic but above all economic—on the South African Government to urge them to come to the conference table before it is too late. We must learn from the example of Rhodesia. Zimbabwe could have been born without the trauma of a racial war and 20,000 deaths."[21]

From Tutu's spiritual training, he knew that purgation often included the concept of suffering in change. People would say to Tutu, "If economic pressure was applied against the South African government, blacks would be the first to suffer." Tutu responded, "Blacks are suffering now! Is it not better to have suffering with hope than suffering without hope?" Then through his sharp wit would ask, "When did everybody suddenly become so altruistic anyway?" Tutu relied on change through the purging of economic boycotts, explaining how sports boycotts had worked to capture the attention of white South Africans. Tutu continued, "It depends on the effectiveness of applications. Others will say, 'If we apply pressure, others won't,' and so their pockets might suffer. The moral turpitude of this argument is breathtaking. It is on the same level as 'Your car will be stolen. If I don't steal it, someone else will. So, I will steal it.'"[22]

Tutu heard many tautologies to this effect, implying that what black folks need is more prosperity, because by simply having wealth, those who are unemployed will eventually find employment and apartheid will eventually fade away. Tutu rejects this, "I wish that were true. South Africa has experienced boom after boom, but nobody can say that the effect for Blacks has been an easing of their sad lot."[23] From South Africa's first encounters with European colonialism, the tautology existed of poor black people moving out of poverty by depending on white people's wealth to trickle down. This tautology was more than a philosophical methodology; it was also a theology or theo-political vision. For example, one of South Africa's first prime ministers, seminary-trained Daniel François (D. F.) Malan (1874–1959), states, "The history of the Afrikaner reveals a determination and definiteness of purpose which make one feel that Afrikanerdom is not the work of man, but a creation of God. We have a Divine right to be Afrikaners. Our history is the highest work of art of the Architect of the centuries."[24] Malan, a Dutch Reformed Church minister, is known to have coined the term "apartheid." In keeping with his theological training, no doubt he understood such a term in the positive connotation of holiness and purity. This is especially true in keeping with our theme of purgation, as Malan initially formed the Purified National Party. In Malan's mystical stages, purgation literally meant the purging of black folks from South Africa's divine call to inherit their promised land.

Each European people developed a theo-political nationalism, placing each of their identities at the center of consciousness as God's chosen people. The Old Testament's understanding of how Israel carried God's select destiny of a promised land was usurped by European worldviews of Christianity in the name of mission to the heathen. Special destiny meant that each European nation combined God's providence of favoring them with a national historical legend. For example, the Afrikaners' "Great Trek" across Southern Africa was combined with Israel's conquest of the promised land. This Great Trek named Afrikaners as Voortrekkers in the period that led to the balkanization of South Africa in the nineteenth and twentieth centuries. During this time, a kind of Afrikaner liberation theology formed in which God favored the Afrikaner against the onslaught of being placed in British concentration camps (the Anglo-Boer War 1899–1902) and ongoing battles of Vegkop, Kapain, and Blood River against the black Bantu peoples. F. A. van Jaarsveld states, "For the Afrikaners the parallel with the chosen of the Lord grew into a form of mysticism; by their sufferings in fulfilling God's calling they would be purified. Furthermore it led to the predilection for the Afrikaner 'volks'–leaders to see themselves as men with a calling, or to fulfill the will of God."[25] During this time, their slogan was "Africa for the Afrikaners."

Apartheid actually became more entrenched and more vicious in this trickle-down theory. In 1980 the government banned four black newspapers and affiliated black journalists at a time when the economy, unlike elsewhere, was flourishing because of the price of gold at that time. At one point, one in every forty-three blacks in South Africa swelled the average daily prison population to almost 100,000, making South Africa the Western nation with the highest proportion of people in jail, many of whom were simply arrested for not having their apartheid pass identification.[26] From apartheid's formal beginning in 1948 to the states of emergencies in the 1980s, the South African government uprooted over two million black and colored persons, putting them in resettlement camps. This was all done in pursuit of the theo-political vision of the founders of apartheid, that it was God's will to put black folks on reservations. The intent was that there would be no black South Africans, only truly white South Africans. So black family life was assaulted by this apartheid policy. Black children were starving in these resettlement camps by deliberate apartheid policy. With his sharp wit, Tutu joked, "We were told that apartheid is dead. We would like to see the corpse and be invited to the funeral."[27] This theo-political assault of apartheid made Tutu pray, "God, please help us to know that we matter, that we are creatures of your love, from all eternity, for you chose us in Christ even before the foundation of the world. . . . if we really could believe that, the world would be revolutionized."[28]

PURGATION OF BLACK IDENTITY

As South Africans increased in their awareness of how apartheid sought to brainwash people into submission of a theo-political mindset, Tutu spoke more and more to black South Africans about the effects of apartheid. Blacks in South Africa had far too frequently been objects whom others discussed and talked about. Blacks were talked about excessively but were seldom engaged in dialogue. Martin Buber's concept of I-Thou, in which conversation could occur through the intimacy of dialogue, was an unknown concept of mutuality in apartheid South Africa. Black people were treated in a manner befitting objects, not subjects. This was not only the case with white Afrikaners; the history of British colonialism was just as horrific. Villa-Vicencio states:

> The heresy of racism, separatism and apartheid is all-pervading in South Africa. In spite of the declarations of principle and belief (important as these are at the level of prophetic witness and as ideals to be striven for), separate worship, segregated holy communion services and racially constituted fellowship and service organizations (whether in youth work, women's associations or men's fellowships) are also the hallmarks of all the English-speaking Churches in this country. In this respect the English-speaking Churches are almost as racially divided as the Afrikaans Reformed Churches.[29]

Tutu knew this and often had to appeal to the great angels among us. "I appeal to you to be true to your traditions, biblical and historical, true to the kind of Christian of William Wilberforce. We shall be free and want to say that the British helped us to be free."[30]

Nevertheless, it became possible for a South African government to claim to be Christian, invoking the name of God in the preamble to its constitution, while at the same time in that apartheid constitution excluding 73 percent of the population from any meaningful participation in political decision making. Is it really possible for a government to uproot three and a half million blacks from their homes and settled communities and dump them as if they were things, and still call itself Christian? It was as if black folks were trash. Black children suffered by deliberate government policy. Black families suffered through the migratory labor system, in which black fathers had to leave wives and children to eke out a miserable existence in a single-sex hostel for eleven months of the year. Black people were dehumanized and stripped of their essential personhood and humanity in an I/It relationship.[31] Spiritually, Tutu tried to console his people that God was different from the white god of colonialism, that the living God revealed in Jesus is always about connection and relationality. Tutu states:

> We have such a God . . . who cares that people are oppressed . . . who is concerned about injustice . . . who cares because people are hungry and homeless and naked. I must say that if God did not care I would not worship Him because he would be useless for me and our people. . . . God cares that people are detained without trial. . . . There are nearly 2000 people detained just now. I am proud that our church is witnessing in this way against injustice and oppression. The problems of our country cannot be solved by locking up the leaders of our community like this. Our country's problems will also not be solved by our killing one another [or necklacing]. The problem of our country will be solved when we sit down and talk as fellow South Africans. I know that we are going to be free. I know because our cause is just. We don't want to oppress or boss it over others. We don't want to drive anyone into the sea.
>
> Black people want only what white people want for themselves, freedom to live wherever we want, to have men and women live as many white families, wherever they want, freedom for our children to be educated wherever we want, freedom to be involved in all political and other decision making which affects us, yes freedom to be truly citizens of South Africa with all that that means. We want freedom from [want], from fear, freedom to be truly human. We know we will get this because God is with us and if God be for us who can be against us? I pray that tomorrow will be peaceful and that we will observe it now.[32]

Tutu ends this sermon in this way because he knew the next day, June 16, 1986, would be the tenth anniversary of the black South African youth uprising in the township of Soweto. This was no isolated occurrence, in which Tutu spoke with spiritual resolve to anchor his people against the storm of apartheid. Tutu recounted one such storm, "The crowd lining the road on the edge of Phola Park was the signal that—yet again—something was wrong. As we drove through the crowd, a woman shouted: 'Tshis'inyama' ('Braai [barbecue] the meat') and we knew we had stumbled across a necklacing."[33] Herein the purgation of black identity cut both ways, as the dominant white culture sought to strip back people's self-esteem, and black people acted out of such violence.

Such black-on-black violence further complicated Tutu's spiritual role, as he had to negotiate both black liberation from white power and black liberation from internal oppression. Tutu continues, "We look out and we realize that there have been over 1400 deaths related to unrest since 1984, . . . and most of these have been of people killed by the security forces of this country. There has been an escalation of so-called black on black violence in the townships, necklacing and petrol bombing. . . . Just imagine when apartheid is gone you won't need to listen to Bishop Tutu deliver such speeches. What relief!"[34] Anglican leaders like Tutu, the Methodist Church head Mmutlanyane Mogoba, and SACC president Khoza Mgojo made impassioned appeals to a sad and bleeding nation to end the violence. Tutu said that this ecumenical witness—built as a result of the struggle against vicious apartheid that had wreaked havoc among people's lives—gained collective credibility.

On another occasion when similar black-on-black violence occurred, Tutu addressed black hostel dwellers who belonged to the Inkatha Freedom Party (IFP) during a visit by religious leaders to the troubled Tokoza township.[35] He encouraged the crowds to wipe the scales from their eyes and see the ugly and evil system called apartheid for itself, namely, the force causing black people to mutilate corpses in burnt-out cars. Apartheid was the worldview in which women attorneys and freedom fighters met gruesome deaths. Then through his sense of humor, Tutu took a strange turn in his speech to these black people. It was a turn to encourage his people to be resilient and imaginative:

> I know there are very deep feelings in the black community. I wanted to be able to arouse deep feelings in those that I love very deeply, the white community. My brothers and sisters, they report all kinds of things that I say overseas, the things that they think the white community would like to hear that Bishop Tutu said. They don't report that Bishop Tutu, standing up in London, two weeks ago, at the Royal Commonwealth Society, says, "White South Africans are not demons. It would be a wonderful thing to dismiss them, it would be easy to dismiss them and say, oh! They are all demons. If you look carefully you can see the horns and if you look even more carefully, you will see that they can't even sit comfortably, because they have got tails." No, no, no, white South Africans are ordinary human beings. Most of them very scared human beings and I ask the audience, wouldn't YOU be scared if you were outnumbered five to one? They don't record that because if they reported that, then some white people in South Africa would begin to think that Bishop Tutu, actually, is not such a ghastly ogre as they try to make out that he is. Now my brothers and sisters, let me tell you something. I am the bishop of the Diocese of Johannesburg. My flock is black, my flock is white. One has got to say to our people, "I love you, I care for you, enormously." And when I care about black liberation, it is because I care about white liberation . . . until about April this year, I was not using a South African passport. Now look at me! I am as South African as Biltong. . . . Can you imagine what this country is going to be like without Apartheid! . . . I just want to stop and say to you, my friends, I am looking forward to the day when I invite you to the celebration of our liberation.[36]

In Tutu's attempt to purge both black and white South Africans from violent points of view, one begins to see how apartheid South Africa was destroying all of its residents. It would have been easy for black South African leaders to give up on their nation-state. In his essay "Reflections on Gandhi," George Orwell wondered whether the nonviolent resistance Gandhi advocated would be possible in a totalitarian state. The premise of Gandhi's strategy was that nonviolent resistance would "arouse the world" and prick its conscience. Yet Orwell noted that it is only possible to arouse the world if the world hears what you have to say: "It is difficult to see how Gandhi's methods could be applied in a country where opponents of the regime disappear in the middle of the night and are never heard of again."[37]

In early 1985, when black leaders in South Africa tried to control the extent and targets of violence, they were working under premises similar to Gandhi's. They enjoyed a certain amount of freedom of association, they could be quoted in the newspapers and could appeal to their fellow blacks as well as their oppressors. But as political "spaces" narrowed, and it became increasingly difficult to make protest heard, as the South African government wielded the implements of an Orwellian state, more and more blacks would wonder whether nonviolent resistance was futile.

Individuals within South African institutions such as the church, the press, community groups, unions, and the African National Congress (ANC) questioned the wisdom of restraint as they too fell under the government's repressive measures. The ANC began in 1912 as the South African Native National Congress, a black political organization seeking black voting rights. It evolved into a formal political party, initially utilizing nonviolent means to end apartheid under the leadership of such figures as Albert Luthuli, Walter Sisulu, Oliver Tambo, Mandela, and many others.

Mandela joined the ANC in 1943, shortly before the National Party's white-only government officially established apartheid in 1948 as a system of racial segregation. Mandela and the ANC committed themselves to overthrow the apartheid government, although initially through nonviolent protest and just war criteria. In 1961 Mandela cofounded uMkhonto weSizwe (translated from Xhosa: Spear of the Nation) as the militant branch of the ANC. Because of such leadership, Mandela was arrested and sentenced to five years in 1962 for plotting to overthrow the apartheid state following the Rivonia Trial in 1963, and Mandela was given a life sentence in 1963.

Some ANC leaders would urge the ANC to abandon its just war criteria and simply wage war on the white population. The ANC military leadership, that is, the uMkhonto underground, with a politically tailored strategy suitable for guerrilla warfare, continued to emphasize that attacks, even in white areas, should be directed only against combatants: soldiers, police, and civilians such as border farmers directly integrated into the government's defense structure. Stephen Davis, a political scientist, thought that the ANC, having been consigned to political antiquity by most blacks prior to the Soweto uprising, must finally be judged by its developed powers of persuasion in the late 1970s and 1980s.[38] What is most significant about ANC progress is that it succeeded in implanting an underground network sufficient to ensure the escalation of rebellion.

Elements within the church establishment would push black clergy toward a more understanding attitude toward violence. As these pressures increased, international leaders like Tutu felt more and more pressure from all sides. As the highest-ranking black clergy figure, Tutu was pressed to lead opposition to the government. Yet as he rose in the Anglican Church hierarchy, becoming bishop of Johannesburg in February 1985, he had to answer to more and more white members of his flock. As a Nobel Peace Prize winner, he also served as black South Africans' unofficial ambassador to the world at large. The outside world and many white South Africans had been repulsed, not aroused, by the violence in South Africa. Such violence included police and military executions of black leaders, township homicide of those who were deemed police informers, bombings, and torture. To which a weary Tutu said, "It's clearer and clearer to me that the West doesn't care about black people. All they spend time on is the violence of the ANC, yet [the government's] shooting [of] children is not violence. I'm tired, very tired of the hypocrisy. I'm sick and tired of trying to persuade white people that our people don't like violence."[39]

In October 1984 the Nobel Committee awarded the Nobel Peace Prize to a South African for the second time in its history. The Committee said that Tutu wielded "the weapons of the spirit and reason" and that he was "an exponent of the only form for conflict solving which is worthy of civilized nations."[40] He was just fifty-three years old, and was recognized in part, as the first black general secretary of the South African Council of Churches, for turning the Council into a force against apartheid.

Tutu earned this recognition. For example, while leaving a political funeral in Duduza with Bishop Simeon Nkoane, a portion of a black crowd seized a suspected black informer and began to force a tire around the suspected informer's shoulders. This was done as part of the horrific practice of necklacing, which leads to the victim being burned alive when gasoline is poured into the tire and set aflame. Tutu and Nkoane jumped into the middle of the mob and protected the suspected informer with their own bodies. They hustled him into a waiting car and the car sped off with the informer, leaving Tutu to confront the frenzied crowd. On another occasion Tutu lay down on the body of a suspected informer and told a mob that it would have to kill him first if it wanted to kill the informer.[41]

A few days after the Duduza incident, Tutu addressed a hostile crowd at a political funeral in KwaThema, another destitute black township. Tutu said, "Our cause is just and noble. That is why we will prevail. You cannot use methods to attain the goal of liberation that are used by the 'system.' Why don't we use methods of which we will be proud in years to come?" Sensing the audience's cool response, Tutu theatrically stretched his arms, as though offering himself in Christlike sacrifice, and said: "I understand when people are angry or hurt and want to take it out on those we think are collaborators. But I abhor all forms of violence. I want to condemn in the strongest terms what happened in Duduza. Many of our supporters around the world said then 'Oh, oh. If they do those things, maybe they are not ready for freedom.' Let us demonstrate the discipline of people who know that they are ready for freedom. At the end of the day, we must be able to walk with our heads high!"[42]

Many blacks lacked Tutu's moral pronouncements but shared his trepidation about the tactics of popular violence.[43] Yet Tutu believed that there were circumstances, such as those named in Augustine of Hippo's theories of just war, that could validate when violence could be necessary. Behind his pleadings for the government to negotiate a solution to the conflict was the veiled threat that someday even Tutu might conclude that a violent war against apartheid might be justified. But in the violent years of the 1980s, he kept trying to find a way to placate the ANC's military wing (uMkhonto weSizwe), which advocated for a stark "submit or fight" formulation of blacks' choices. Tutu went to Lusaka, embraced ANC leaders, and urged negotiations. He went to the presidential residence in Cape Town and urged then-president P. W. Botha to enter into negotiations. The form of protest he favored was international economic sanctions, hammering at the point that sanctions offered the last hope of avoiding a "holocaust." Speaking in favor of sanctions, Tutu stated in 1981:

> Tell our black brothers and sisters—sports people and artists—not to come to South Africa. They are lured by fat fees. But when they come here they live in the white part of town. They don't share our misery usually. They give comfort to the perpetrators of an evil system by letting them have international contracts. Let your labor unions help ours and let them use their muscle to assist us to be free. Help by providing educational opportunities for blacks from South Africa (both those in exile and from inside the country) to help equip us for the day of liberation. I have no doubt at all in my mind that we will be free.[44]

Thus Tutu raised the specter of international isolation less than a year after President Botha's triumphant tour of Western Europe. But even as Tutu pleaded his case, he doubted whether his message was getting through. The government's resolve was stiffening, and young blacks were growing more militant. Tutu himself even said that if he were a young black person, he wouldn't follow a man named Bishop Tutu.[45]

Many militant blacks had dismissed Tutu's position, saying that Tutu was an international figure and had to be seen as nonviolent, but ordinary youths were not apologists for the dictates of the international community. Many blacks thought that Tutu should consult political organizations instead of preaching to them. "Clerics want to come from above the struggle," one United Democratic Front (UDF) leader complained. "They say don't do violence because we know what's best for you." The UDF was a conglomerate antiapartheid organization that Tutu would naturally listen to and then take its critique to heart. Tutu also encountered great tension at the KwaThema funeral. Tutu was said to threaten to "pack my bags" and leave the country if blacks did not restrain from using violence. "Go to where?" a UDF leader asked with disdain. "Does he think he is doing us a favor by being here?"[46]

PURGATION OF WHITE IDENTITY

Those who hold a white identity in South Africa are complicated by the fact that there are at least two white identities in the country: Afrikaner and English speaking. (This is true even though most white Afrikaners also speak English.) The implied distinction here is that those of both Dutch and English backgrounds fought, against each other, to own South Africa. White identity is further complicated by apartheid's legal category of "honorary white status." Strangely enough, an African American or an Asian person could be given such status when applying for a visa or when entering South Africa with a US passport. All of this is to say that white identity in South Africa is difficult to purge of racism, unlike the United States' more uniform category of white identity. (The caveat here is that white identity in the US can be stratified into economic or geographic levels, such as poor whites or those with an Appalachian identity.)

Obviously, US white people feel a strong attachment to their racial group. In Ashley Jardina's 2017 survey in the United States, respondents were asked how important being white was to their identity. Over 40 percent said it was very or extremely important, 54 percent said that whites have a lot or a great deal to be proud of, and 43 percent reported that whites in this United States have a lot or a great deal in common with one another.[47] During the 2016 US presidential election, Donald Trump mobilized a sizable subset of the white American population to vote for the Republican Party. In South Africa the key party for many white South Africans postapartheid is the Democratic Alliance (DA), composed predominantly (80+ percent) of Afrikaans- and English-speaking white South Africans.

It is an educated guess that the majority of white South Africans and the majority of white US residents do not advocate for the extreme positions on white identity held by groups like the Ku Klux Klan (KKK) in the US or the Afrikaner Weerstandsbeweging (AWB) in South Africa. At the same time, white identifiers share some of the same views associated with supremacist groups, about black retaliation, immigration, redistribution of land and wealth, and so on. For example, white people in the US are much more likely to rank illegal immigration as their top concern, rather than the economy, health care, unemployment, outsourcing of jobs to other countries, abortion, same-sex marriage, education, gun control, the environment, or terrorism.[48]

Jardina's survey also discovered a new phenomenon in the United States (which would not be new to white Afrikaner identity): aggrieved white identifiers, who believe American society owes white people much more than they believe they have. They want the same benefits of identity politics that they believe other groups enjoy. Jardina states, "For instance, white identity is strongly associated with support for Congress passing a law which would designate one month of the year as White History Month." We learn from political scientists like Jardina that white identity politics no longer draws its gravity from hooded Klansmen or disaffected white men marching with tiki torches. Jardina concludes that "white identity politics is packaged much more decorously and clearly part of mainstream opinion. Any condemnation by Trump or others of white nationalism might reinforce the already negative views most Americans have of these extremist groups, but it will likely do little to change the broader and more pervasive role of white identity in American politics."

Tutu's white world has made a similar turn, but only recently. In Tutu's lifetime he was a target of white hostility, often referred to as "the black bishop." For many white South Africans, Tutu had committed the sin of expecting to live and be treated like a white man. That such a thing as imitating white identity was possible first occurred to Tutu in the 1950s, when Tom Huddleston passed by on the street and tipped his hat to Tutu's mother. "I couldn't believe my eyes," Tutu said later. When the government introduced Bantu Education, Tutu joined the church. The Bantu Education Act of 1953 was such that the apartheid state tried to control Christian schools, who up until this point had relative autonomy as to how to structure education and formation outside of the apartheid state. For example, although Tutu had originally wanted to go to medical school but was too poor to go, the teaching profession was good to him.

Tutu built himself a sound house in an area of Soweto known as Beverly Hills. As Tutu's institutional church career ascended, his children were educated at private schools, such as in Swaziland, and they dressed stylishly. Tutu had traveled extensively outside of South Africa, notwithstanding the government's refusal to give him a passport from 1979 to 1981. Tutu remembers, "I have lost my passport on a few occasions, once for two years because I was accused of advocating sanctions."[49] Tutu was indignant that his fame served as little protection from "a whippersnapper of a policeman" who stopped him at a roadblock and asked him for identification. "Any policeman who says he does not know me does not deserve to be in the police force."[50] On another occasion, Tutu's wife and daughters were strip-searched at a police station. "If they treat me [and my family] like that, what do they do to so-called ordinary people?"

By the time Tutu gave his Nobel Peace Prize acceptance speech in December, the death toll in antiapartheid protests since the 1984 Vaal uprising just three months before had risen to 150. Although Tutu did not endorse violent resistance to apartheid, it was clear to him, as it was to South Africa's previous Nobel laureate in 1960, Albert Luthuli, that black South Africans had been patient, "peace loving to a fault." In his Nobel speech Tutu said, "We understand those who say they have had to adopt what is a last resort for them. Violence is not being introduced into the South African situation *de novo* from the outside by those who are called terrorists or freedom fighters, depending on whether you are oppressed or an oppressor. The South African situation is violent already, the primary violence is that of apartheid, the violence of forced population removals, of inferior education, of detention without trial, of the migratory labor systems."[51]

As we've seen before, the Christian mystic Simone Weil is helpful in understanding the irony of feeling sorry for such a perpetrator of the violence of apartheid, even when such a person could not feel sorry for himself or herself. I earlier quoted Weil as stating that affliction hardens people's souls with the scorn of guilt. I think Weil would accept my definition of white guilt as also representative of affliction. Weil's insight is helpful in explaining the dangers of white identity in the "blindness" of mechanistic structures in society. Affliction is anonymous before all things; it deprives its victims of their personality and makes them into things. Tutu concedes Weil's insight that, at times, he feels overcome by the evil emerging from the TRC.

One story that particularly haunts Tutu is the police murder of Siphiwe Mtimkulu in the Eastern Cape. Mtimkulu was drugged, shot behind the ear, and burned. While his body burned, states Tutu, the police had a barbecue off to the side. "I can't actually get over it!"[52]

As we will see in illumination, the second stage of Christian mysticism, Weil's insight into affliction helps us understand the first stage of purgation. This is why Tutu sees the need for catharsis in making a full and public disclosure of past crimes. To admit guilt, even in the secrecy of the bedroom, is not easy. It is "facile" to say that confession is only between a penitent and God. Tutu states, "If I quarrel with my wife and I say to her, 'It's between me and God,' that marriage is not going to last very much longer." The relationship is both vertical and horizontal. "The Bible is quite clear about it when it says: Love God and love thy neighbor. The two are linked together."[53]

How much more difficult must it have been to reveal the most heinous crimes right before the eyes of the nation! And how difficult it must have been to name superiors and colleagues and thereby to "betray" the "comrades" and the entire organization! It took considerable determination to break rank and to resist the circle of subtle threats and compensations; such people will appear to the system as traitors and deserters. Despite Tutu's spiritual argument for the TRC, it seems that a considerable portion of the implicated police and security forces were still trying to protect the "system" and themselves, with the hope that they would somehow manage to avoid the TRC and the courts.

It is reasonable, of course, to admonish citizens to live with compromises. On the other hand, it must be understood why the anger of black victimized human beings against white identity increased before things got better in South Africa. If victims of apartheid experience that their oppressors escape their evil acts, while they themselves continue to wait for decent houses, jobs, and professional training, there will be no true community.

The full acceptance of white identity capable of being African will largely depend on the measure in which the needs of black and white identity become more symmetrical and in balance. There must be a clear willingness on the part of white South African society to make amends in unequivocal terms. This is called repentance. If such repentance is not forthcoming, white identity might well appear as the incessant oppressor. This means that, as a Christian and as a person who is a member of the church, processes of dehumanization cannot be tolerated. In this light Tutu reasons, "Is it not revealing how when we meet people for the first time we soon ask, 'By the way, what do you do?' Meaning, *what gives you value?*"[54]

In this chapter we moved into Tutu's purgative experiences of his ordained and public life. Such purgation was primarily the result of apartheid's states of emergency, in which white political leaders desperately tried to justify why white identity rose to the top of a spiritual hierarchy. Therefore, Tutu's society of black and white identity caused him to call for the purgation of what it means to be black and white. My intention for the reader is to understand how Tutu's rise in church leadership gave him the authority to deal with these deeper and moral spiritual issues. Tutu is owed a great deal of historical credit for navigating the race wars of South Africa. In such navigation Tutu facilitated a way for the scales to fall from the eyes of both South Africans and global citizens. We now turn to our discussion of purgation, to how Tutu prevented the extremes of the purgative process, namely, a nation boiling over.

Partial view of crowd gathered at Chris Hani memorial and march, April 14, 1993. Author photo.

Chapter 4

A Boiling Nation

Our previous chapter alluded to our entry point for chapter 4, namely, how did Tutu facilitate the purgation of apartheid South Africa while helping it avoid the chaos of civil war? Many believe it was a miracle that South Africa escaped such war before and after its first democratic election in 1994. It is this miracle that guides us through this chapter, as we see how Tutu became an important element in how this miracle manifested itself, not only in South Africa proper, but in the country's churches. Here we explore why Tutu's spiritual life mattered so much in how South Africa and the South African churches moved from apartheid to a free, democratic South Africa.

In Tutu's view of this new society, South Africans would have to realize that the miracle of freedom was the beginning of the real journey and not its end. In this thought, Tutu was coming to grips also with his ordained and public life to understand that in South Africa's newfound freedom, certain habits and disciplines must be established to ensure a better future. I hope that this exploration of how Tutu's spiritual life engaged the birth of the real nation of South Africa will help ground the reader for what is to come in the second part of this book, Illumination. Before we get there, we first turn to South Africa and Tutu's spiritual life on the verge of South Africa's democracy.

Those who constructed apartheid envisioned the crescendo of South Africa's power to include the fullness of apartheid and not its purgation. In fact, as we have seen, apartheid for these political architects was a holy enterprise, blessed by God. But by setting whites above other races, apartheid caused South Africa to boil over into chaos. Though the 1980s proved to be the most openly violent stage of apartheid, in many ways South Africa had begun to boil in the 1960s and 1970s.

Tutu's rise as a spiritual leader in the 1970s and 1980s occurred after the 1976 uprising and its suppression, when a growing number of South African activists had begun to move away from the racial focus of the Black Consciousness Movement (BCM) toward a more active strategy of opposition and an inclusive national ideology. BCM, a grassroots antiapartheid movement, emerged in South Africa in the mid-1960s due to a void of black leadership created by the banning of the African National Congress (ANC) and the Pan Africanist Congress (PAC) after the Sharpeville massacre in 1960. As many activists shifted away from BCM, Tutu's rise as a spiritual leader occurred simultaneously with South Africa's climax of apartheid rule. Tutu states, "Since 1976 I have appealed to the government to heed our *cri de coeur* [passionate appeal]."[1] By late 1979, the economy showed signs of recovering from the recession of the mid-1970s.

More significantly, mass militancy and state repression abated, allowing activists to begin to pursue the pragmatic approach they had been discussing. Eager to encourage this turn away from mass militancy, the state did not impede the development of these local organizations or their negotiations with local authorities and businesses, which granted concessions. The state also relaxed regulations controlling the legal growth of black trade unions and enacted a new, more inclusive constitution. In the space provided by these state reforms, national African leaders formed the United Democratic Front (UDF).

They set out to form local organizations of civil society to press for material gains and, later, further political reforms. By the time of the early 1980s, mass participation, rekindled in the 1970s, had been channeled away from outbursts of anger and into more structured forms of mass organization, following a national agenda consistent with that originally set forth in the ANC's Freedom Charter. The Freedom Charter was established in 1955, when the ANC went into townships and rural areas to record demands such as "land for all landless people," "living wages and shorter hours of work," and "free and compulsory education, irrespective of colour, race or nationality." All such demands were compiled into a final document by ANC leaders. Subsequently, a broad alliance of these Charterist groups, loosely coordinated by the United Democratic Front, rode the wave of mass activism to the forefront of opposition. Those that retained a less pragmatic focus on shaping ideas and racial or class identity, such as the Azanian Confederation of Trade Unions (AZAPO: founded 1977–78, heir to BCM after the 1977 banning) and others that came together to constitute a National Forum (NF: founded 1983 as coalition of AZAPO and others,

BCM and socialists), found themselves caught in the undertow of a decline in mass support.

By late 1984, the conditions that had kept the South African state and its opposition in dynamic equilibrium had changed again. South Africa had slipped back into a recession, suffering from the continued structural constraints of apartheid and the delayed impact of the West's decline in fortunes, leading to reduced governmental incentives to provide further material concessions. Buoyed by the recent success and the encouragement of the still-exiled ANC, however, popular expectations and mobilization continued to build, exploding first as unrest in the Vaal triangle near Johannesburg in 1984, after the ratification by whites of the new constitution. Anxious to head off a crisis, the state moved to close the space it had opened and to discourage popular organizations, declaring a state of emergency in which both local and national leaders were detained, and mass meetings and other forms of publicity were curtailed. But this unrest was not easily contained. Earlier strengths became vulnerabilities as the movement's purposeful avoidance of divisive issues left it open to conflict, once the leaders were cut off from the local organizations, and then further constrained by the effective banning of the UDF in February 1988.

This period is important to see the significant political context for Tutu's rise and apartheid's climax. These are apartheid's prominent years, between the banning of the ANC and the PAC in 1960 and the lifting of the ban in 1990. As we will see in part 2, Illumination, this time frame between the 1960s and the 1990s became the illuminating years in which the TRC would create the metric in which South Africans could give their confession. As Anthony Marx in his book *Lessons of Struggle* states about this period, the central issue is the internal dynamics that have shaped the opposition to apartheid, particularly its shifting ideology and strategy.[2] During this period many blacks kept up no pretense of loyalty to the government. When the former ANC leader Walter Sisulu and his comrades were freed from jail in October 1989, blacks (and a few thousand whites) held a rally in a soccer stadium and openly flew the flags of the outlawed organization. The size of the crowd rivaled that of the 1938 white gathering that galvanized Afrikaners and led to the first National Party government.

Throughout the period during which BCM and UDF were seen as the most popular internal opposition movements in South Africa, industry steadily grew, and an increasing number of urban black workers formed their own unions. With the effective banning of the UDF and many of its major affiliates in February 1988, these groups' public activities were curbed, though some church-based supporters did remain active. Union activities were less severely restricted and, according to Marx, emerged publicly as the leading form of popular organization and expression. The unions have been both "identity oriented" like the BCM and "resource mobilizing" like the UDF. By combining these two approaches, the unions tried to incorporate both of the movements' strengths.

Underlying each of the approaches of recent opposition movements in South Africa are distinct assumptions about whether the established social order is based on persuasion, institutional coercion, or their interaction, and about whether to challenge that order primarily by posing alternative ideas, mobilizing protests, or both. Such differences correspond to the theoretical and historical debates over how regimes collapse and why their opponents succeed or fail in gaining power. All of this was illustrated in how Nelson Mandela was finally released from prison by the leadership of Frederik Willem (F. W.) de Klerk. In an interview, Tutu praised de Klerk as someone who had gone through a Damascus-road experience, an allusion to Paul in the New Testament. In view of everything that happened subsequently with Mandela's release from prison, Tutu was asked how he finally saw de Klerk. Tutu responded honestly with the ambivalence many black leaders had toward de Klerk, by addressing what black people felt about the apartheid security forces. Each time de Klerk confronted these matters, police violence was never confessed.

THE 1960S AND 1970S

In the 1970s South Africa was 78 percent Christian, with most of these people attending church regularly. Yet most political analysts have difficulty placing the churches' role at that time as a significant opposition movement in apartheid South Africa. This may be understandable, given the premise that apartheid itself was constructed from a theological point of view. Even though the church was not technically seen as significant opposition to apartheid in South Africa until the late 1970s, some churches in South Africa very much opposed apartheid. The complicating factor here of course is that the Afrikaans Reformed Church in South Africa fought internally to the point of dividing itself based on race.

Let us look at the spiritual geography of the churches in South Africa. There are three white so-called sister Afrikaner churches.[3] There are four churches in what is called the Dutch Reformed family of churches.[4] Then there are seven churches among the World Alliance of Reformed Churches (WARC), in which the NGK was suspended.[5] Lastly, the four main English-speaking churches are also represented.[6] These distinctions of geography of churches are important as we later come upon yet another South African church organization, the South African Council of Churches (SACC), of which Tutu was once secretary general.

The church in South Africa could easily be seen as of little significance against apartheid, since it looked so divided itself. Chris Loff is helpful here as he states: "The 'final solution' to the 'problem' was the establishing in 1881 of the racially separate NG Sendingkerk. Instead of the church committing itself to overcome the sin of racial pride, black people were asked to be the least and to leave the church. In Mossel Bay there was an extreme case where it was insisted that black members should rather join the Lutheran Church or the Anglican Church."[7] As the Afrikaner church walked in lockstep with the National Party, the colored and black Reformed churches were alienated. Therefore, the Afrikaner church saw itself against, by and large, the rest of the church.

From the rest of the mainline church in South Africa (e.g., Anglican, Methodist, Roman Catholic, Lutheran), a moral mission emerged to tear down the idolatry of apartheid's emphasis of white superiority. This was led by dynamic clergy who made this a part of their work. For example, in the UDF, leaders such as Smangaliso Mkhatshwa, a Catholic priest from the Pretoria township of Shoshangkuve; Frank Chikane, a young Pentecostal Soweto clergy person who ran the Institute of Contextual Theology, South Africa's center of liberation theology; and Rev. Mcebisi Xundu, the leader of community organizations in the Durban townships, mounted strong protest against apartheid. This was complicated by the fact that such protest inevitably had to occur against other churches in order to fully address apartheid. In other words, these clergy had strained relations with the church establishment. For example, the Catholic church was wary of Mkhatshwa's political activity, especially in light of the pope's tepid attitude toward Latin American liberation theology.

All of this occurred during the period of Tutu's days as general secretary of the South African Council of Churches (SACC), from 1978 to 1984. Because of the SACC's resistance against apartheid, the National Party officially declared the SACC to be a "Black organization," even though it was racially diverse and ecumenical. From the SACC platform, Tutu carried more authority in the 1970s than from his Anglican denomination, because at the time the SACC included 63 percent of the country's 19 million Christians within its member churches, with 85 percent of the membership having an authoritative black base. Formed in 1968, the SACC had a radical reputation of opposing apartheid, but its standing faltered because in its early years its leadership consisted mostly of white liberals.

The situation changed steadily in the 1970s as Tutu was appointed general secretary, confirming the SACC's status as a genuine focus of black opposition to the South African regime. Peter Storey, a white Methodist Christian leader against apartheid and president of the South African Council of Churches, stated, "Bishop Desmond Tutu's task is to carry out the policies of this Council. . . . If Mr Le Grange [opponent of Tutu and member of Parliament] thinks that he can in some way alienate the member churches from the Council, I would remind him that 80 percent ... are victims of the apartheid policy."[8]

Another major white leader against apartheid who worked with the SACC was Beyers Naudé, perhaps the leading Afrikaner cleric and antiapartheid activist. For Naudé the boiling point had already occurred with the Sharpeville massacre on March 21, 1960, when white South African police killed sixty-nine black demonstrators. Naudé could no longer justify his NGK's position on apartheid. He states, "I made an intensive study of the Bible to prove that those justifications were not valid. I concluded that the passages that were being used by the white DRC to justify apartheid were unfounded. In some cases, there was a deliberate distortion in order to prove the unprovable!"[9] After Naudé resigned from the NGK, he became a crucial agent in the boiling effect and upheavals in his Afrikaner church.

Tutu also remembers the Sharpeville massacre as a touchstone historical moment in South Africa's history. Tutu's spiritual work was cut out for him after Sharpeville, because not only did he have to convince a white power-grabbing government to be contrite and repent; he also had to convince black South Africans who felt justified to take up arms that this was the wrong response. It was an impossible task, because unarmed black people who had been demonstrating peacefully against the pass laws had been shot by the police. Many of those killed had shotgun wounds in the back, indicating that they were running away from, not attacking, the police. Tutu tried to hold back the tide of black violence as he asked the question, "Is South Africa a better place by resorting to violent demonstration?" Tutu's genius was in how he could appeal to common sense while at the same time shouting the radical message of repentance.

For the government, such repentance as Tutu sought meant an understanding that black nonviolence would reach its limit. At that time the ANC and the PAC were both seeking to help the white rulers know the plight of black people through petitions, delegations, peaceful demonstrations, and pressure resistance campaigns. They had no constitutional means of doing this legally, because the ANC had been denied any means of legal protest during apartheid. These nonviolent efforts seemed to no avail. The authorities increased their intransigence and banned these two organizations, virtually forcing them to take up the armed struggle. It is odd that they should be condemned for doing something they were forced to do. In such conundrums, Tutu was thankful that white spiritual leaders like Naudé emerged.

Immediately after the Sharpeville massacre, Naudé facilitated the Cottesloe Consultation, a meeting of representatives of the World Council of Churches (based in Geneva, Switzerland, the most ecumenical representation of the global church) and eighty South African church delegates, in Cottesloe, a Johannesburg suburb. From the Cottesloe Consultation emerged major resolutions that rejected race as the basis of any kind of exclusion, especially by the church. Even more radically in the face of apartheid, this consultation affirmed the right of all people to own land and have a say in how they are governed. Naudé fought against any theological basis for apartheid, even after the university-professor-turned-prime-minister, Hendrik Verwoerd, forced Naudé's DRC delegation to repudiate the consultation. The Dutch Reformed Church was no longer part of the World Council of Churches.

In 1963 Naudé founded the Christian Institute of Southern Africa (CI), an ecumenical organization facilitating interracial dialogue, research, and publications. The DRC forced Naudé to choose between his status as DRC minister and the directorship of the CI. As a result, Naudé lost his status as minister in the Dutch Reformed Church. Tutu later said, "Beyers became a leper in the

Afrikaner community."[10] Later, after his unbanning in 1985, he succeeded Tutu as general secretary of the SACC.[11]

In the 1960s and 1970s, there were other major spiritual leaders like Naudé going through their own purgation. Most Black Consciousness followers spurned Christianity as a white man's religion. However, other black leaders embraced the tenets of Christian faith. For example, while studying for a science degree at the University of the North in 1972, Frank Chikane, a future general secretary of the SACC and prominent member of the ANC, had attended church services even though students had barred services from the campus. Chikane would be suspended by the Apostolic Faith Mission in 1980, the year he was ordained, because of his political involvement. In 1981 he was suspended again by his conservative church, and afterwards he was never posted to a congregation. So it is understandable why young black leaders had little patience with the Christian church, even if they remained Christians. Each of them bucked opinion within black politics, as well as within their churches, and often paid the price.

Chikane wanted to make clear that violence was a major issue to the people in the black townships, because they were constantly confronted by white troops invading their townships. For many black Christians in South Africa at that time, there was no such thing as a "violent option." It was simply the necessity of the situation in which you fight or die. It was a logical consequence of what apartheid South Africa was doing to the people. Christian leaders like Naudé, Tutu, and Chikane could indeed discover nonviolent options, but faith was required. Faith was especially required in knowing that both violent and nonviolent means seemed to meet the same reaction in apartheid South Africa. After Chikane was released on bail in early 1985 during a treason trial, his house and family were attacked with gas bombs. Because of his faith, Chikane continued to preach nonviolence, although he knew others were prepared to use violence against him.[12]

Chikane later headed the Institute for Contextual Theology (ICT), which had helped formulate the Kairos Document, a statement on the role of the church under apartheid. The statement urged churches to openly oppose the government and participate in the struggle for liberation. The Kairos Document ("kairos" means God's time) addressed the question of violence head on. "When Jesus says that we should turn the other cheek he is telling us that we must not take revenge; he is not saying that we should never defend ourselves or others."[13] The Kairos theologians also criticized churches that pretended to be neutral in an apartheid society. How could Christians be neutral and condemn all violence, when such violence included guerrilla bomb attacks killing children as well as the shootings and beatings by the government? These theologians said churches should not sidestep tough moral questions by issuing such blanket condemnations. "How can acts of oppression, injustice, and domination be equated with acts of resistance and self-defense? Would it be legitimate to describe both the physical force used by a rapist and the physical force used by a woman trying to resist the rapist as violence?"[14]

Spiritual leaders like Naudé, Chikane, and Tutu had to navigate the new waters of black leaders commanding the authority of not only black people, but now white, colored, Indian, and all the diverse makeup of South Africa's population. Tutu recalls worrying at the time that it might lead to another Pharaoh-Moses situation. Tutu recalled how Moses kept going back to Pharaoh to warn him that God said unless he let the children of Israel go free, then all kinds of disaster would befall Egypt (see Exod. 7–11). Tutu remembered how Pharaoh became more and more obdurate, even hardening his heart. Like Pharaoh, those who wielded power, mainly the white community in South Africa, were set on a collision course with history. Tutu warned white political leaders that unless the oppressed black, colored, and Indian people were liberated, the oppressor would also be enslaved. It was as if the oppressed and the oppressor were on an imprisoned chain gang, walking together on a slippery slope.

It was really in the 1970s that Tutu found his voice as the purgative prophet, warning those in power that their intransigent and godless law would reap destruction. Tutu anticipated that the end of apartheid would come in one of two ways: civil war or peaceful transition. Unless a change of direction took place, they were headed over a cliff. Anyone who adopted more draconian powers was dangerously unaware that the law of diminishing returns applied in this area of human relations. Tutu warned those in power that what they had hoped for as outcomes in the regimes would never occur if they "became more and more ruthless, unjust and repressive, gaining ever less and less security and peace, law and order."[15] Tutu articulated these dire circumstances to a nation-state that could be appealed to on the common ground of Christian faith. Tutu concludes, "Please, will somebody realize that the man who shot the Krugersdorp Municipal officials was issuing a serious warning that this is how most blacks feel. . . . I am frightened but that is just the plain truth—when a black confirmation candidate aged 16 years can say 'I don't want to be confirmed by a white bishop' then we have reached a very serious state of affairs. God help us."[16]

Although Tutu appealed a great deal to the Moses-Pharaoh analogy, he also appealed to the Israelites wandering in the wilderness. Tutu constantly acknowledged that they were led out of the wilderness of apartheid by the goodwill and guidance of the international community—receiving prayers and concerns from sisters and brothers around the world. Being led out of the wilderness created a deep level of community that could share the life of the Spirit at an intimate level. Tutu needed such community to see him through the persecution he would endure. Even though Tutu's work was still as a Christian leader of the SACC, the South African government in 1981 appointed a judicial commission, the Eloff Commission, to investigate the SACC. The purpose was to discredit Tutu and the SACC so that, as Tutu states, "none of their overseas friends and partners, nor South African member churches, would want to touch them with the proverbial ten-foot pole."[17] The South African government was intimidated by the SACC, which had assembled an impressive array of overseas church leaders and delegations to descend on the country. As these leaders flowed in and out of South Africa, they formed solidarity with those fighting apartheid inside the country, and the South African government ended up with egg on its face. Tutu wrote to those leaders once, thanking them for their prayers, and for supporting economic sanctions "which have brought us to this point when a new South Africa is about to be born."[18]

THE 1980S

As we see with the Eloff Commission, Tutu constantly faced the binaries of the Western world such as church or state, individual or community, and denomination or church. Ubuntu became Tutu's clarion call to move beyond such binaries for the sake of a unified South Africa. African church history is complicated by the Christian churches of Europe and the Americas that moved into Africa, bringing their Western worldviews with them. When Western persons, formed in a worldview that favors the individual and her or his rights and responsibilities, encounter African spirituality, they meet persons whose experience of the self is distinctly different.

In contrast to the Western worldview, the African individual does not exist apart from the community; hence Tutu's worldview of Ubuntu could even help unite the divisions among the churches.[19] In both God's Trinitarian identity and God's methodology in creation, a person is part of the whole, and personal identity flows from corporate experience and never in isolation from it. God therefore defines who one is created to become, and who one becomes defines God's created community. Tutu's mission was to apply Ubuntu in all aspects of his leadership, even with the difficult circumstances of dealing with a myriad of denominations. We discover evidence of Tutu's leadership in this respect during his SACC days. Tutu was proud of the ecumenical church, since church leaders refuted those trying to recover the theological justifications of apartheid. Tutu had to defend his leadership role during his SACC days against the unfounded allegations of General Johann Coetzee, chief of South Africa's security police, who testified at the Eloff Commission that the SACC was not representative of its member churches. This situation of being under investigation by the South African government was so contentious that Tutu requested during Holy Week the support of Robert Runcie, archbishop of Canterbury, Philip Russell, archbishop of the Province of Southern Africa, Bishop A. I. M. Haggart, archbishop of the Episcopal Church of Scotland, Archbishop Paul Reeves of New Zealand, and Clyne Harradance, a lawyer and lay person from the Anglican Church of Canada. They all came to Tutu's aid during the busiest time of the church's calendar, Holy Week.[20]

General Coetzee's critique against the church was against the sort of people who he felt had nothing better to do than sit around hoping to be invited to Pretoria to testify before the Eloff Commission. They were people such as the president and the secretary of the Methodist Church, the general secretary and chairperson of the United Congregational Church of Southern Africa, the general secretary of the Presbyterian Church of Southern Africa, the archbishop of Cape Town, the presiding bishop of the Evangelical Lutheran Church of Southern Africa, the scriba of the Reformed Church in Africa, and the Roman Catholic archbishop of Durban. Tutu felt honored that the churches rallied together, with the president of the World Alliance of Reformed Churches speaking up for the SACC. Tutu defended these church leaders who went to Pretoria at great personal inconvenience and at their own expense. The response to the Eloff Commission demonstrated solidarity among these churches and their commitment to the SACC.

The Eloff Commission was originally appointed in November 1981 to examine the financial affairs of the SACC, with Justice C. F. Eloff as chair. The Commission believed the SACC had difficulty raising funds from its own constituency in South Africa, but little problem receiving funds from overseas. The SACC, therefore, was distancing itself from its member churches and becoming an independent bureaucratic body. Later the Commission's scope broadened to investigate the SACC as a whole, in order to dismantle the organization all together.

At first, the Eloff Commission was not favorable of Tutu's work. Eloff's 451-page report charged that the SACC's original work was to spread the gospel, but that it was also concerned with political, social, and economic issues. The Commission said that not only did the SACC condemn the government, but it also gave practical effect to this stance by adopting and pursuing "strategies of resistance to the government." The report quoted strategies of resistance to the state such as civil disobedience, evasion of military conscription, and the international disinvestment campaign against South Africa, called "economic sabotage." The Commission declined to recommend that SACC be declared an "affected organization" (a euphemism for being a black banned organization), which would have cut off the foreign financial support that made up 97 percent of its budget, but recommended that the SACC be covered by the 1978 Fundraising Act. This act included a section allowing the minister for social welfare to "prohibit the collection of contributions for any purpose or in any manner . . . on behalf of any person or organization." The minister of law and order said member churches of the SACC should note that "if the Council persists in its tendency towards confrontation, the state might feel forced to use counter-measures." Interestingly enough, this political leader asked if member churches wanted to be members of a political pressure group or if they truly want to be members of the church of Christ.[21]

With the exception of the Dutch Reformed Church, initial church reactions to the Eloff Commission were supportive of SACC. Archbishop Philip Russell stated that he did not believe the findings would hurt the trust and support given by Anglicans to the Council. The Methodist president said he was disturbed that the secular panel had passed judgment on a church organization in its witness to the imperatives of the gospel. The Roman Catholic side said the Council was right to strive for the recognition of human rights. Tutu was strongly critical of the report, citing the immorality of forced population removals, the system of education of blacks as abomination, and the abuse of black migrant laborers. Tutu said the Commission had no competent theologian nor a single black member sitting in judgment of an organization that was 80 percent black. After the release of the Eloff Commission report, the newspaper *Beeld* had a cartoon of Tutu behind a machine gun. The ammunition boxes around him were labelled civil disobedience, economic sabotage, sympathy for terrorist organizations, and revolutionary road. A single bullet from the Eloff report had dislodged Tutu's bishop's miter (liturgical hat), and Tutu was asking, "Hey, who gives you the right to shoot back?"

In the end the SACC benefited from the Commission, since it was shown that whatever the past omissions of the SACC, Tutu had put its financial house in order. The thrust of the Commission was political and spiritual, since it vindicated the SACC's theological basis in its conclusion. Also, Tutu received the endorsement of the ecumenical support of the South African churches. In Tutu's purgative experiences with the Eloff Commission, Tutu believed the uniqueness of each person is affirmed and acknowledged, but one's own individuality and freedom are always balanced by destiny and community. Obviously, white political leaders who may have claimed to be Christians by knowing when to conveniently separate religion and politics lost to Tutu's resilient spirituality, which shaped his SACC work and changed the results of the Eloff Commission. As Tutu's voice as spiritual leader grew, so did his political authority. This unusual arrangement of the spiritual and political evolved as, increasingly, the only voices of protest within South Africa were those of church leaders, as black political resistance was stifled and black leaders were sent into exile. This made the church all the more important—and dangerous. The church more and more became a major threat to the apartheid government, which even began to ban certain church groups.

By 1983, black South Africans were subjected to detention without trial and the rule of law was undermined and subverted, with legal due process "becoming as rare as a dodo in the cases that most need it."[22] Political policies were now creating enemies rather than political stability. There were many political trials, and the maximum-security jails were filled with many who were first moved by the ideal of working for a new South Africa, nonracial and truly democratic. Many of those nonviolently opposed to apartheid had been arbitrarily banned, detained, and banished. Several families didn't know where their children were. Over eight million blacks were no longer South African citizens, but aliens in their land of birth; and over two million had been uprooted from their former homes and dumped like rubbish in poverty-stricken ghettos of misery euphemistically called resettlement camps.

In a sermon in 1983, Tutu turned to the topic of political legislation. Tutu preached that God's children were made to starve by deliberate government policy in a land of plenty, that God's children were told they didn't qualify to be in an urban area because an all-powerful bureaucrat had decided that they were not human enough. Tutu states, "The Pass Laws which caused Sharpeville are very much with us. The *Dommpass* has survived Dr Pieter Koornhof's declaration of war on apartheid which had been pronounced dead but is painfully alive and kicking."[23]

South Africans representing many contexts (e.g., Afrikaner and black) realize that freedom, which is inevitable, is not cheap. The Bible says those who have died are not glibly comforted. But the same Bible tells us the kingdoms of this world will become the kingdom of our God—a kingdom of justice, compassion, peace, love, and prosperity, where God will wipe away all tears, where there will no more be weeping and mourning. For the kingdoms of this world, powerful kingdoms of injustice and oppression and exploitation, will become the kingdom of our God, who shall reign for ever and ever.[24]

In 1983, Tutu also prayed that the World Council of Churches event might come to South Africa in the future, "so as to dispel the horrendous misconceptions that especially white South Africans have of the WCC."[25] It was not until January 1994, after the WCC Central Committee met in Johannesburg, that Tutu could say the age of miracles has not ended.. Who would have believed that the South African government would be welcoming the Central Committee of the World Council of Churches (WCC) to South Africa? The WCC had been virtually a swear word and certainly anathema to many (mostly white) South Africans for its "scandalous" grants to "terrorist" organizations from its "notorious" Special Fund, administered by the "much hated" Program to Combat Racism. The presence of the WCC in South Africa was testimony that much had happened since Cottesloe, when WCC member churches tried to take stock together after the aftermath of the Sharpeville massacre of peaceful anti–pass law demonstrators in March 1960.

For nearly fifty years since 1948, when the Nationalist Party won its first election on a blatantly racist policy, one had found South African Christians on one side or the other of the great divide created by the apartheid policy. Instead of the church's ancient Nicene Creed, one's attitude to apartheid became a test of orthodoxy, a status of confession. Consequently, institutional bodies such as the WARC and the Lutheran World Federation suspended those South African member churches thought to be guilty of the heresy of apartheid. Tolerance had ended for apartheid's theological justification.

For Tutu, this was an exhilarating time, as he saw ecumenism come alive. Of course, such demonstrations had occurred in the past, but those were led mostly by black South Africans and a few white leaders who tried to articulate God's love for all human beings. To be free is to be human. The church's work was invaluable in this period, as new theological perspectives emerged to explain why apartheid was wrong and why Christians around the world had a responsibility to resist the evil of apartheid's theological justifications. Tutu states that international support left the South African government "with considerable egg on its face in its attempt to discredit the SACC with the Eloff Commission which

I am reliably told was what persuaded the Nobel Committee to award the 1984 Peace Prize to the then General Secretary of the SACC."[26] Of course, this general secretary was Tutu himself.

WHY DID TUTU WIN THE NOBEL PEACE PRIZE?

Tutu received the news that he had been awarded the 1984 Nobel Peace Prize when he was on sabbatical at General Theological Seminary in New York, praying several times a day with seminarians in the monastery-like setting of the campus. Tutu said it was with more shock than surprise that he received the news. Tutu told a gathering after receiving the award, "I don't want to boast, but it is important for our black people to know that we were given outstanding VIP treatment everywhere. . . . It is interesting to note that not a single South African university has yet thought us fit to get their honorary degree. . . . In my own city, Johannesburg, hardly any white run organizations (apart from the Black Sash) congratulated me on the Nobel Peace Prize nor welcomed me as Bishop of Johannesburg." Tutu goes on to say that he had yet to hear from the mayor of Johannesburg welcoming him back or congratulating him. Tutu jokes, "And world of wonders, my contact with the traffic police in my city was when they towed away my car from the Cathedral when I was parked in a restricted area as I rushed to a service. And even when I explained [who I was], I still paid R100, and the world wonders."[27]

Tutu won the Nobel Peace Prize in 1984, but his name had been before the Nobel Committee since 1981, when he was nominated by the American Friends Service Committee. When Tutu eventually won the prize, the office of the prime minister in South Africa had "no comment." These were strange times; instead of feeling proud that one of its citizens won the most prestigious Peace Prize, South African state television gave the first report on Tutu's accomplishment in six seconds, and editorials called Tutu a troublemaker and expressed outrage that such a man should receive a Peace Prize.[28] The same week Tutu's prize was announced, Archbishop Denis Hurley, president of the South African Catholic Bishops' Conference, was in court to answer charges under a security law that makes it a crime to disclose certain activities of South African police and troops. Allan Boesak was being threatened with similar charges. Both in 1961, when Albert Luthuli won the Nobel Peace Prize, and in 1984, the South African regime acknowledged its black Nobel Peace Prize winners with a "no comment" and more repression.[29] This would change only when both Nelson Mandela and F. W. de Klerk won the Nobel Peace Prize in 1993. This story ran incessantly.

Tutu responded to Mandela and de Klerk's award in one of the daily South African newspapers, *The Argus*: "I was going to nominate [de Klerk] and Mr Mandela for the joint award if things went well." He congratulated both men "most warmly." The award was "a fitting climax to the struggle to dismantle apartheid." Talking about his own Nobel Peace Prize, Tutu said it had "helped to focus the world's attention on what was happening in the country."[30] The complexity of this award could be seen in the mere fact that it is doubtful de Klerk's own father would be proud of him receiving a Nobel Peace Prize. The *Argus* article went on to report that Jan de Klerk cast aspersions on the award when it was won by Chief Albert Luthuli. His son's winning the prize with Mandela, whom the elder de Klerk had helped imprison, would not have sat well.

In a historical sense, South Africa's three prizes represent the three phases of the struggle against apartheid. Luthuli won it as his organization exhausted peaceful resistance and took up arms; Mandela won it for ending the armed struggle he had begun; and Tutu won for his campaign in the intervening years for international pressure as an alternative to violence. Although Tutu's commitment to peace could not be questioned, it was a moral victory for his campaign for international sanctions against South Africa; perhaps it is even more realistic to see it as a political decision to intervene in support of a peacemaker or peace process, as defined at the time. Tutu received it when he was the most vocal and influential representative of the view that sanctions, though difficult, were a lesser evil than armed struggle. His award was a huge boost to the campaign to isolate Pretoria.[31]

For Tutu, the Nobel Peace Prize gave hope to many in a world that has sometimes had a pall of despondency cast over it by the experience of suffering, disease, poverty, famine, hunger, oppression, injustice, evil, and war—a pall that has made many wonder whether God was loving, omnipotent, and compassionate.[32] Philip Russell, a previous archbishop of Cape Town, comments that Tutu's focus on making God's love for all relevant to politics and economics speaks not only to South Africa but to a world in turmoil: "As a Christian . . . I rejoice that a fellow Christian has been so honored, for—as he himself, in his humility, will insist—it is really to the unique role of Jesus Christ as mediator that our thoughts, and praise, are being directed."[33] By and large, church members came around to see how important this designated prize to Tutu became.

In his acceptance speech, Tutu emphasized that the prestigious Peace Prize is given to honor all who are committed to struggle for justice, peace, and reconciliation—not just to him. For him this was not being conventionally modest. Tutu is the first to admit that he is not excessively modest. Tutu, in his profound sense of humor, recounts a time at Howard University in Washington, DC, when he was awarded an honorary doctorate. They asked him for his measurements, his body weight and size. These Tutu was able to give them fairly easily. But they also wanted to know the size of his head. "I told them this would be more difficult to give. It was changing every day."[34]

From Tutu's spiritual base, and now from his secular authority on a world stage of receiving the Nobel Peace Prize, Tutu began to lay the groundwork for his understanding of the substance of peace for a new South Africa. One of the concepts Tutu immediately articulated was that there could be no peace in South Africa as long as there was no justice. There can be no real peace and security until there is first justice enjoyed by all the inhabitants of that beautiful land. For Tutu spiritually, the Bible knows nothing about peace without justice, for that would be crying, "'Peace, peace,' where there is no peace" (Jer. 8:11 and Ezek. 13:10). God's *shalom* inevitably involves righteousness, justice, wholeness, fullness of life, participation in decision making, goodness, laughter, joy, compassion, sharing, and reconciliation.[35] In a twenty-first-century world Tutu notices the deep discrepancies of having the capacity to feed ourselves several times over, and yet we are daily haunted by the spectacle of the gaunt dregs of humanity shuffling along in endless queues, with bowls to collect what the charity of the world has provided.[36]

Why did Tutu win the Nobel Peace Prize? An aspect of the answer is certainly that the Nobel Committee was sending a message to an apartheid government that the world was watching. I think, however, the larger reason was that the Nobel Committee saw that Tutu would be a long-lasting figure in South Africa, who could bring systematic patterns of peacemaking to a nation in dire need. Such a strong character of peacemaking was vital to South Africa in the 1980s as the birth pangs were felt that a democracy was about to be delivered. For example, some five years after Tutu won the Nobel Peace Prize, in 1989 the Mass Democratic Movement, a coalition of mainly ANC-aligned organizations, engaged in the Defiance Campaign to disobey apartheid's discriminatory and unjust laws. The SACC-affiliated churches undertook a related "The Standing for the Truth Campaign," when it was declared that unjust, immoral laws do not require obedience. Banned organizations flouted the law and unbanned themselves. The government and its cohorts realized then that they would have to raise the levels of repression to an intensity they well knew the Western world would find unacceptable. That was a price the government was no longer willing to pay, for they were feeling the brunt of isolation.

For Tutu it was exhilarating to witness the resilience of South African people when by rights they should have long ago been "cowed and dispirited." They were ready to run the gauntlet of tear gas, whips, police dogs, water cannons, rubber bullets, and even death, as they declared that enough was enough. In Cape Town, on September 6, 1989, about twenty people were shot and killed as they participated in nonviolent opposition to a racist election that occurred before the first democratic election in 1994. Black South Africans were properly incensed and called for a demonstration of Cape Town's sense of outrage and revulsion. That is how the mammoth march on September 13, 1989, happened in Cape Town, involving over 30,000 people calling for peace on our streets in Cape Town. It was impressive, it was peaceful, it was dignified. It was to be the mother of demonstrations, for soon thereafter marches happened all over the Republic of South Africa.

In addition to Tutu's leadership in nonviolent demonstrations, Tutu's eventual role in spearheading sanctions against his own country played a large role in his nonviolent leadership. Tutu believed that some enjoyed the luxury of the academic debate about whether sanctions worked. Tutu himself was not prepared to indulge in such a waste of time. The more vilification he got from the government, the higher his stock rose in the black community and overseas. For example, the South African government stopped fighting in Angola during its conflict with Namibia, not because they underwent a change of heart, but because they could no longer fund that war, in part because of an arms embargo by outside nations. So, for Tutu it is because of sanctions, a nonviolent strategy against the brutality of apartheid, that Namibia is independent today.

The acclaim that Tutu received for his peacemaking skills grew because of such nonviolent strategies and how he approached politics in general. One example can be seen in how he dealt with a disagreement with one of his archrivals, President P. W. Botha. Tutu told a joke during this time about a fictional figure named Vander Merwe. This was a buffoonish character that many South Africans make fun of, just as Americans might make fun of Forrest Gump or the Beverly Hillbillies. One day, Tutu said, Vander Merwe was upset that the US and Soviet Russia alone were getting the praise for their space program. So he announced that South Africa would send a spacecraft to the sun, no less. When someone remarked, "But Vander Merwe, that craft would be burned to cinders long before it reached the sun," Vander Merwe rejoined, "You don't think that we South Africans are stupid, do you? We will launch it at night."[37]

Tutu gave credit to Botha's incremental repentance by going on to say that the future of South Africa cannot be decided by whites alone, as was the conventional wisdom. Tutu remained frustrated, however, with those who could not support the goal of this incremental repentance and go all the way to implement this politically. Tutu also gives credit to Fanie Bota, the minister of manpower, for establishing a new labor dispensation that recognized black labor unions. For Tutu, this represented a very significant step forward in the right direction. Then, as if trying to get his audience to implicitly recall the Vander Merwe humor, Tutu asked, "Can somebody tell me why all this positive action has been virtually nullified by the action of the SAP [South African Police], who have harassed black trade union leaders and generally made their lives uncomfortable."[38]

Tutu's approach to politics was indeed unusual. He possessed the unique gift of disarming warring parties and getting them to look more consciously at the dangerous situation at hand—and even to laugh at the ridiculous nature of how they got there. Apartheid had succeeded only too well in splintering the community of South Africa. The result of apartheid was that people living in the same country looked at what appeared to be the same thing, and yet perceived totally different things. Tutu's genius was in his ability to get them to see the same thing. For example, most whites in South Africa believed political violence was introduced into South Africa by neighboring countries, which many South Africans are taught to view as full of terrorists and communists. As stated earlier, they believed that there was a total communist onslaught from outside against South Africa.

On the other hand, most blacks believed that the real violence in South Africa was the legalized, institutionalized violence of apartheid, that totally evil system perpetrated against blacks every day of their lives. Tutu was puzzled when he looked at other international contexts of violence and civil war. Why were groups such as the contras in Nicaragua, or UNITA in Angola, both of which fought against popularly chosen governments, lionized in the West as being freedom fighters, while organizations such as the ANC and PAC, which had long used nonviolent methods against a vicious and thoroughly undemocratic and racist policy such as apartheid, were castigated as terrorists? After all, they were engaged in an armed struggle against a regime the world had consistently condemned.[39]

Here was a constant political theme espoused by Tutu, especially to the white powers that be: black South Africans have been wonderfully patient and peace loving. They have begged. They have pleaded. They have used every peaceful means possible, and at every turn they have been rebuffed. So many of them have said, "What must we do? What can we do to reclaim our lost birthright?" And these have opted for the armed struggle. Where Tutu became most dangerous to the National Party was when he would then conclude that he supports those who aim for a democratic South Africa. Tutu qualified his support, as he consistently condemned their violent methods. "We have said to the authorities we condemn all violence—the violence that seeks to uphold an unjust and immoral system such as apartheid and the violence of those who react to the legalized violence to overthrow it. We have appealed to the authorities and warned that once a people become desperate, they will use desperate methods. I want to warn South Africa, I want to warn the authorities that vicious penalties suffer very soon from the law of diminishing returns."[40]

In fact Tutu tried to warn the National Party government that those who opted for the armed struggle, those whom blacks regarded as freedom fighters, those who were prepared to make the supreme sacrifice, believe that they must perpetrate the worst possible damage, because they were going to hang anyway. For Tutu, the problems of South Africa could never in the end be solved by violence. Tutu asked, "Why don't the white South Africans hear the black South Africans when they say, 'Go to the conference table before we reach the point of no return when a bloodbath becomes inevitable?'" Tutu's genius was in getting opposite sides to see the validity of negotiating political power sharing while there was yet time to negotiate nonviolently. Tutu concluded this way: "Let me tell them quite seriously: Apartheid can't win. . . . South Africa will be free, either through bloodshed and violence or through negotiation, dialogue and discussion. I am committed to justice, peace and reconciliation and freedom, total freedom at whatever cost."[41]

As we will shortly see in part 2 of this book, Illumination, Tutu's role as confessor in South Africa is more intelligible today, since there is more of a reference point for how an apartheid government indeed adhered more to fear than to common sense. In the thick of things, Tutu undertook the impossible task of having to convince a political system, based upon the theology of apartheid, to be contrite about its racist and oppressive policies. Every institution of white power—from the National Party to the corporate boardroom to the editorial desk to the defense force to the white Afrikaner churches—would be tied into the theological narrative of apartheid, in which God had chosen the Afrikaner people to withstand insurmountable obstacles posed by the British and black Africans to bring about God's kingdom come on earth. While shutting channels of rebellion, the goal of Afrikaner leaders was to open doors to reform in which civilized, democratic people could fend off communism and what they saw as the savage rule of the day. Ultimately, in the mind of the Afrikaner, black violent resistance would be forced into political irrelevance as blacks realized the advantages of dialogue and the futility of warfare. I would imagine that many Afrikaner leaders thought that Tutu could be co-opted in such a strategy—after all, Tutu grew to become somewhat of a Christian in their minds.

This thinking became a flaw in Afrikaner strategy among the ruling elite, a group that proved so fractious as to be unable to muster the political strength to initiate reforms substantial enough to deter rebellion. The National Party could not even define accurately for itself the political complexion of South Africa's black population, a determination vital to the task of heading off guerrilla warfare. According to the landmark Rabie Commission report,[42] the insurgency evidently did not warrant political analysis by the government until the situation was out of control. Further weakness to this strategy was that the Afrikaner government saw communist agitators carrying orders from Moscow as behind most of the unrest. This distorted analysis of black politics justified the Botha administration's reluctance to adopt major reforms. Apparently, the thinking here was that most blacks could be won over by measures well short of power sharing. Yet these steps were to prove so ill matched to black grievances as to aid only marginally and temporarily in the government's struggle against rebellion.

The Afrikaner strategy thus evolved into a policy managed by generals rather than politicians. Moreover, the building of a bunker state without meaningful incentives for peaceful change meant that Pretoria would be waging a largely conventional war against a politically driven insurgency. The government's massive military power might allow it to slow the rebellion, but not to stop it. Most of all, the major point of the rebellion was being missed by incommensurate worldviews. As we will see, this made Tutu all the more important as South Africa's confessor, because he was one of the few national and international leaders who could appeal to a common worldview among the British, Afrikaner, and South Africans of color: that is, Christianity.

Tutu creatively stepped into a vacuum and slowly changed the strategy from what was in the best interest of the military to what was in the best interest of a nation-state that had strong Christian roots. Tutu, as South Africa's confessor, challenged the common worldview that militarization somehow makes a nation stronger. Tutu's genius here was in how such militarization even weakened the white power base, since it failed to offer a coherent vision of South Africa's national future or hopes for peace. Tutu tried to get Botha and others to see that this absence of mobilizing leadership sharpened the impact of attacks by militants designed to wear down the white will to fight. Instead of "rallying around the flag," white ethnic splits widened, morale dropped, and draft evasion soared. Emigration, while at one time low, reached record levels in 1985 and again in 1986, as black political unrest intensified. Professionals such as doctors and lawyers led the way.[43]

In conclusion, Tutu facilitated the purgation of apartheid South Africa, without the chaos of civil war, in several ways: by shining a light on how the church itself was not reconciled; through his international voice calling for nonviolent resistance through economic boycotts; and through his wisdom of supporting Mandela's release, to be discussed in chapter 5. It indeed was a miracle that South Africa escaped civil war before and after its first democratic election in 1994. With this in mind, in chapter 5 we look at Tutu's significant relationships and how they withstood the apartheid years. When South Africa experienced the climax of its purgation through both the release of Mandela and the first democratic election, some purgation remained as those in Tutu's circles experienced posttraumatic stress syndrome during their fight against apartheid.

TUTU AND DE KLERK

Tutu thought that up to February 1990, de Klerk was too clandestine in his politics and should not have been. But Tutu gave credit to de Klerk for the fact that de Klerk called on his senior officers to operate by more means than survival, than violence. This indeed helped give South Africa's transformation a chance to take place. Even though de Klerk appeared earlier on in an apartheid state not to understand quite what South Africa needed in terms of stability, due to a particular apartheid culture, he did realize in the end that stability would not happen without his role as state president.

South Africans and the world could see that despite the first democratic election in South Africa, many of the white leadership had not changed. For example, the police role at the Boipatong massacre in a township on June 17, 1992, when forty-six township residents were killed by local people living in hostels, was not one of incompetence, because the things that have been revealed are quite interesting. Tutu said black South Africans frankly did not believe that the police force, which during the state of emergency had been so efficient "that you could not scratch yourself without the police knowing,"[44] could suddenly have turned inept. This brings Tutu back to security issues during South Africa's first democratic elections.

Much of the important cause of violence was the "third force," those within the security forces who clearly wished to subvert the process toward democracy. At a news conference at Arlanda airport in Sweden, Tutu called for international peacekeepers for the first all-race elections on April 27. De Klerk had dismissed such an earlier proposal by Tutu as unworkable. Firstly, the police did not respond as quickly as you would have thought they would. Secondly, they did not know how to deal with the confiscated weapons to be used as evidence. Thirdly, they did not seem to be able to separate the inmates of the hostel (from where the attack came), although some had injuries, and some had not. Nor did they try to relate that to the blood that was found on weapons. Now, finally, Tutu felt South Africa discovered yet another element of so-called incompetence, the wiping off of the police tapes dealing with the period. Tutu states, "I mean one can say that one of these incidents was one of incompetence. But to say a second, a third and a fourth were also incompetence, I think you have to be very gullible."[45] Tutu began to see a kind of pattern. On the whole, the police were able in the past to get away with a great deal, "and they still want to get away with things." What Tutu was saying at that time was that it was strange that de Klerk was not able to see this. There was something fundamentally wrong with the security forces.

Tutu said to de Klerk, "Your experience of the police is not that of a black person." And yet de Klerk listened to Tutu. Tutu reflected that it was more pleasant to talk with de Klerk than with P. W. Botha: "He appears to take seriously the things you present to him although whether he then follows them up is something else." For Tutu, this meant that de Klerk could not easily extricate himself from his community. Tutu was the Anglican archbishop of a church body that has white, colored, Asian, and black. Those were Tutu's people: "That is my flock, those are what I care for."[46] For Tutu, if de Klerk had integrity as a political leader, he also should be open to all kinds of people—especially as a president of a nation-state.

Tutu concluded about de Klerk that he liked him, though de Klerk perhaps did not always receive the best counsel from his advisors. In terms of good and evil, an interviewer asked Tutu whether or not he saw de Klerk as an evil person? Laughing out loud, Tutu said, "Not yet."[47] Tutu concludes, "I take my hat off to Mr. De Klerk for the indispensable part he has played in setting in motion the revolution happening in South Africa. He deserves the accolades he has received. . . . God appears to have given Africans a remarkable capacity to forgive."[48]

In 1989, de Klerk became South African president and set in motion Mandela's release. First, de Klerk lifted the ban on the ANC and other black organizations and suspended executions, and then in February 1990 he ordered the release of Nelson Mandela. Since de Klerk's bold initiatives to release Mandela, Tutu was becoming embarrassingly respectable, and people were changing their views about him and his erstwhile apparently reprehensible conduct. However, Tutu said the press coverage of Chris Hani's assassination and other issues had left him "disillusioned"—that they had returned to the pre-February 1990 days in the reaction of some whites to what they call Tutu's undignified display at the Chris Hani funeral. Tutu states:

"We have had saturation coverage . . . of the killing of five whites in East London. . . . I am sure that massacres must be extensively covered, and yet 21 people were killed in Subking at the time of Chris Hani's assassination and that horrendous massacre did not get a fraction of the treatment."[49]

For Tutu, South Africa was a veritable roller-coaster ride as it anticipated Nelson Mandela's release from prison and the preparation for South Africa's first democratic election. This meant that February 2, 1990, was unbelievable, as Tutu watched de Klerk make his courageous, epoch-making address in Parliament. Tutu said that he had to keep pricking himself to be certain he was not dreaming it all up, because here was an Afrikaner state president speaking about unbanning popular political organizations that for decades had been fair game for the dirty tricks of the apartheid security forces. For Tutu, this was a miracle, as de Klerk incredibly spoke about releasing and actually did release Nelson Mandela from over a quarter of a century's incarceration for having had the audacity to claim that he and other blacks were really ordinary human beings. This was the release of someone who had come to be a symbol of opposition to injustice, oppression, and racist hegemony worldwide. And when February 11 came, and Mandela was indeed released, the euphoria much of the world experienced was boundless.

Chris Hani march in Cape Town, April 14, 1993. Battle is marching on the right of Tutu and Njongonkulu Ndungane, then the South African Anglican bishop of Kimberley and Kuruman, who succeeded Tutu as archbishop of Cape Town. Author photo.

Chapter 5

The Purge of Relationships

Throughout Tutu's life he has struggled with the ebb and flow of apartheid. In the previous chapter we looked at the crescendo of apartheid to highest tide in 1990, when Nelson Mandela was finally released from prison. In this chapter we look at the toll of those years on Tutu's significant relationships. Hopefully, the reader will reach a deeper understanding of Tutu's spiritual life as he struggled to stay related to both his enemies and his friends. With this in mind, chapter 5 demonstrates how some of Tutu's relationships weathered significant storms, while others ran ashore during the onslaught of apartheid. Tutu's struggle to mend such relationships around him should help ground the reader for what is to come in the later stages of Tutu's life. So, in a sense we encounter the dual meanings of purgation; as Tutu's relationships were tried by fire, some were washed away.

To help illustrate how the concept of purgation helps in understanding Tutu's context of his spiritual life and his political relationships, consider the first film in the series *The Purge*. In this film franchise, the setting is a future dystopian United States, where crime is legalized one day a year. On Purge night 2022, youth randomly target suburban families. One white family is targeted after rescuing a wounded black stranger who was once the primary target of the Purgers.

The white suburban family is told they will be murdered if they don't surrender the black man within an hour. Spoiler alert: the black stranger rescues the white family when the purging gang invades the household and attempts to kill them. Despite mixed reviews, the creative story in this film touched a raw nerve among many people around the world, as the film grossed $89.3 million during its run, far surpassing its $3 million budget.

Tutu's spiritual leadership was such that he anticipated how South Africa could easily become this dystopian future. After South Africa's long history of whites targeting blacks in a legalized criminal system of apartheid, Tutu worried about how he could in some cases restore, and in other cases begin, relationships with leaders who could prevent another purge in South Africa. No one was more aware than Tutu of the significant nature of the ANC and the tremendous power it wielded to bring South Africa into a land of flourishing.

Some ANC leaders, however, began to think that Tutu was overstepping his bounds when they heard him castigate African countries for their appalling human rights record. Tutu's stance was determined not by whether the perpetrators of injustice were white, but by whether injustice was being perpetrated and human rights were being violated. Tutu's authority and basis for being concerned about injustice of any kind was always based in his spirituality. Tutu made his hope clear that in South Africa's first democratic elections, momentum of freedom and justice would continue to be the case, whoever made up the government of the new South Africa.[1]

Perhaps Tutu was concerned about the desire for blacks to seek revenge or the impulse to dominate others, now that power had changed hands. Tutu's spiritual centeredness made him intensely aware that spontaneous violence was the crucial factor for South Africa's instability and political context. Such instability had always been the case, due to the European scramble to control the southern gateway into the African continent. For example, during the 1950s, Chief Albert John Luthuli, then president of the ANC, wrote in his book *Let My People Go* that "every so often the yoke becomes unendurable, something explodes, and for a while blind resentment takes control." Later Luthuli reflected that, given the black burden in South Africa, it was a wonder that the average black did not struggle more violently.

White South Africans, Luthuli said, saw the occasional bursts of black violence as evidence of blacks' violent nature. Before his death in 1967, he wrote that white South Africans persuaded themselves against the evidence that they shared South Africa with barbaric and hostile black hordes. In their minds, the black's amiability must therefore be a deception. Luthuli described the passive aggressive relationships whites had with blacks this way: "You keep out of reach and jab repeatedly at him to rouse him to anger. If you succeed, that proves he is a wild and savage creature. Now and then you do succeed—the best tempered animal gets sick of ill-willed pestering. Sometimes you do enrage him. Sometimes the chain made for him, snaps. Then there is a riot. Whites see only the riot."[2]

But the reaction of blacks to apartheid's chains was not only against the government, but against each other. Many in townships were shocked by the most brutal aspects of unrest, including the apparent arbitrariness with which many necklacing victims were identified as collaborators. Nonetheless the heightened militancy was widely supported. As in 1976, when parents had joined the uprising only after seeing the heroism of their own children, in the mid-1980s the initial fear and disgust of many township dwellers toward this brutal violence was often followed by respect and desire to join the movement.

Thus the uMkhonto weSizwe (MK), which means the Spear of the Nation, became the armed wing of the ANC. MK arose in the wake of the 1976 Soweto uprising. While previous ANC armed efforts managed to carry out just minor sabotage missions, the new MK had an arc of countries from which to draw resources. Three hundred poorly instructed saboteurs had been replaced by at least eight thousand well-trained guerrillas. Homemade bombs had been superseded by Soviet assault rifles and rockets. Lastly, a deep-cover intelligence service offered the ANC access to the republic's most sensitive installations.

Perhaps one of most important responses to the state's repression was the greater national focus of opposition. Whereas activism in the early 1980s had been directed to local demands, repression made it clear that grievances could only and finally be resolved by challenging national structures. Although the protests remained locally organized, by 1986 the demands associated with such protests no longer were confined to local issues; now they called for the unbanning of the ANC, the release of Mandela, and an end to all apartheid legislation.

One could argue according to Davis that the ANC was the most quixotic guerrilla organization of modern times.[3] Its leadership endorsed violence, but with manifest reluctance and an aversion to terrorists' tactics. ANC officials did shun overt symbols of war, such as PLO-style camouflage outfits, often preferring to resemble establishment attorneys. Instead of refining its ideology, the ANC acted as a consciously federal coalition with little consensus on basic principles, other than nonracialism and the overthrow of minority rule. Its main offices and bases previously lay as far as a thousand miles north of the South African frontier; yet through its underground movement it sought to influence daily events inside South Africa.

TUTU AND MANDELA

Even archbishops forgot their archiepiscopal dignity and "toyi-toyed" in the streets of Soweto when Mandela was released from prison. A like euphoria was being experienced in many capitals of the world, as people seemed to discern the demise of apartheid, one of the world's most intractable problems. And Tutu was most appreciative. He wrote, "Mr. Mandela spent his first night of freedom at 'Bishopscourt,' the official residence of the Archbishop of Cape Town. We could not quite relish his new-won freedom because he was disturbed frequently to take calls from the White House, from State House in Lusaka, and elsewhere. Yes, we savored the dizzy heights of euphoria then."[4] In his same response, Tutu goes on: "I had been a member of the Peace Facilitating Committee made up of Church and business leaders, and I must say I reckoned it was nothing less than miraculous to behold erstwhile enemies such as the then Minister of Defense, Roelf Meyer, actually on first-name terms with ANC's Thabo Mbeki, and pulling each other's legs."[5]

Tutu thought there is no doubt at all that South Africans should tip their hats metaphorically to de Klerk for his remarkable and courageous initiative of February 2, 1990, to release Mandela from prison. Whatever may have motivated him—whether he underwent a genuine change of heart about the viciousness and immorality of apartheid or, being a pragmatist, realized that apartheid had no hope of being viable—is in a sense totally irrelevant. What is of crucial importance is that he took the steps he did and made the decisions he made. He has usually been incensed by any suggestion that apartheid was evil or immoral, because, he claimed, those who conceived it were not evil or immoral men. Indeed they were devout, committed Christians. He knew this intimately, because his father had been one of them, and he knew his father to be a good man. Perhaps he has a congenital blind spot. When he has been asked to apologize for all the awful things wrought by apartheid, he has found it difficult to do this categorically and without qualification. Be that as it may, we cannot take away from him the credit for doing something that required very considerable courage.

Tutu pays tribute unreservedly to de Klerk for his courageous initiatives of February 2. It is difficult for Tutu to imagine that de Klerk's irascible, finger-wagging predecessor, P. W. Botha, could ever have brought himself to do anything so radical as release Mandela—and almost surely to destroy Afrikaner unity.

Nelson Mandela may be the most famous name ever associated with South Africa. Worldwide, his was the name most associated with the political movement to end South African apartheid. As befits a man with an outsized legend, Mandela's life was epic in the biblical sense of people who sacrificed for the sake of others.[6] Trained as a lawyer, a young Mandela joined the ANC in 1944. He became deputy national president of the organization in 1952, with the goal of leading nonviolent resistance to apartheid. The Sharpeville massacre in 1960 also changed Mandela's life, as it moved him away from peaceful demonstration, to form a paramilitary branch of the ANC to resist apartheid.

On December 5, 1955, Mandela was arrested for "treason" but acquitted. He was arrested again on August 5, 1962, in KwaZulu-Natal for illegally leaving South Africa, to visit Morocco, Europe, and London. This time he was convicted and sentenced to five years on Robben Island, the notorious prison for political prisoners. In 1963, while imprisoned, he was tried again for sabotage, and in June 1963 was convicted and sentenced for life. Like the biblical figure John of Patmos, who was sentenced to spend his life on an island, Mandela spent the next twenty-six years of his life there, confined to sleep on hard floors in a small cell without plumbing. He was also forced to work in a rock quarry, which caused him severe eye damage. Also like John of Patmos, Mandela wrote letters, and was able to receive one letter every six months. He could have one visitor per year, for no more than thirty minutes. On December 7, 1988, Mandela was moved from the island prison to house arrest in a cottage at Victor Verster Prison in Paarl, outside of Cape Town. Mandela sacrificed twenty-seven years of his life imprisoned, resisting South Africa's apartheid state. He was officially released on February 11, 1990, following de Klerk's speech.

Mandela and de Klerk would go on to jointly receive the Nobel Peace Prize in 1993. As in a biblical story, the onetime prisoner, Mandela, in 1994 became South Africa's first democratically elected South African president. Upon the completion of the Truth and Reconciliation Commission, Mandela retired from politics in 1999, but remained an iconic figure of truth and reconciliation for the world until his death on December 5, 2013.

Tutu deserves some credit for the successful transition of Mandela from prisoner to folk hero to president and icon. In fact, Mandela and his wife, Winnie, spent the night of Mandela's release at Tutu's residence at Bishopscourt. More importantly, Tutu never sought to take Mandela's place as the face of the anti-apartheid resistance while Mandela was imprisoned—despite the fact that Tutu's popularity had shot through the roof while Mandela was imprisoned. John Allen told me of a study that showed Tutu was more popular than Mandela at one point, yet Tutu never tried to take advantage of that or push Mandela out.

Tutu also helped set the stage for Mandela's release by telling de Klerk that he should not go down in history as having overseen the greatest bloodbath in South African history, a racial civil war. Tutu also told de Klerk that he should not further divide the Afrikaner "Volk" with fearmongering and so make them vulnerable to the machinations of the hostile world that, in their minds, always wanted to destroy them.

For Tutu, the crucial contribution to de Klerk's change of heart was Nelson Mandela himself. Had de Klerk encountered a bitter and angry person in their prison meetings, hell-bent on revenge for him and his people for the several decades of oppression and injustice, it is highly unlikely that he would have risked letting him and his colleagues out of prison. What de Klerk found, though, was what an eagerly awaiting world saw when Nelson Mandela, a free man, walked out of Victor Verster Prison on February 11, 1990, with his wife and fellow activist Winnie next to him. The world saw a man almost regal in his dignity, magnanimous to a fault, ready to forgive, loving South Africa and all her peoples, black and white, now with a communal love, and willing to work for South Africa's true liberation in a new nonracial, nonsexist, and democratic dispensation.

Mandela was someone who genuinely wanted reconciliation and peace. When the ANC met with the government later that year at Groote Schuur in Cape Town, it was not surprising that the ANC delegation was composed of the representatives of nearly all the races of South Africa: black Africans, so-called coloreds, English-speaking whites, Indians, white Afrikaners, men and women. That spoke volumes to their commitment to rapprochement and reconciliation in a land so deeply polarized by decades of apartheid repression and alienation. Tutu gave thanks to God that at the beginning, at least, there was a remarkable rapport between de Klerk and Mandela, which must have facilitated the many meetings they had. This was all really a small miracle, according to Tutu, in that the prisoner and his jailer, the oppressor and his victim, were able to sit at one table to negotiate the dismantling of apartheid and the peaceful transfer of power from a small minority to the majority. They would be negotiating a revolution, no less. South Africa's apartheid government must have believed that South Africa's purgative climax had taken its toll. Tutu saw that apartheid's repression and violence had "kicked the stuffing" out of the South African people.

TUTU AND MY AUTOBIOGRAPHICAL WITNESS

As I wrote earlier, I had the privilege of living with Tutu during the period of South Africa's first democratic election.[7] Ever since then, as noted in the beginning of this book, I have imprinted on Tutu like a disciple to a spiritual master. I learned firsthand by living with him that Tutu is above all else a pastor. By pastor I mean someone with the ability to lead people to nourishment and stability, and to do so in difficult times. All else builds upon this identity. The identifier of "pastor," which becomes synonymous with that of "shepherd," comes from the Latin verb *pascere*, "to lead to grazing lands." This term "pastor" also means "elder" within the Bible.

In the Hebrew Bible (or Old Testament) the Hebrew word רעה (*ra'ah*), is used as a noun to describe a shepherd, and as a verb "to tend a flock." For example, in Jeremiah 23:4, both meanings are used (*ra'ah* is used for "shepherds" and "shall feed"), "I will raise up shepherds over them who will shepherd them, and they shall not fear any longer, or be dismayed, nor shall any be missing, says the LORD." In the New Testament, "shepherd" as a Greek noun is *poimēn* and the Greek verb *poimainō* is "feed." A Scripture passage using this term is Ephesians 4:11 (the apostle Paul speaks to the "pastors" of the church in Ephesus). In Acts 20:28, Paul tells them that they are now overseers because of the Holy Spirit, and they are to feed the church of God. Although Protestant churches are more familiar with this expression of "pastor" for their spiritual leaders, Roman Catholic, Eastern Orthodox, and Anglican churches represent the role of pastor through bishops, who hold a formal crosier that looks like a stylized shepherd's crook. Tutu, as an archbishop and head of the Truth and Reconciliation Commission, successfully negotiated the political mire of his South African context by remaining true both to his spiritual convictions and to the authority given him to pastor the anxious nation-state of South Africa.

So, if Tutu is a pastor, how does the description of "confessor" fit in? One of the oldest uses of the term "confessor" is as someone described as a saint who suffers with the people. When Christianity emerged as the religion of the state in Europe, this description of "confessor" became the title given to the kind of saints who lived a holy life and died in peace. The definition of "confessor" also changed in church history, as "sinners" or defectors of the faith sought to be reconciled to the church. Such penitents needed to find confessors who had gained church authority to plead their case and reinstate sinners to the communion of the church. So the current definition of "confessor" formed from reinstating sinners. A confessor today is a priest who has the authority to hear confessions.

Through Tutu's life and work of reconciliation, it is my contention that he, as South African confessor, played a vital role in shaping the social conscience of South Africa and its response to apartheid. This role was especially important in creating access for both black and white people to reinstate a country that represented everyone, not just white people. Tutu's life and work in an apartheid society represents a distinctive narrative in which Tutu displays a complex set of attributes or descriptions, that is, an African community leader (elder) who facilitates the emergence of his peoples out from under the ravages of colonialism (pastor), and an ecumenical Christian leader who claims catholic authority against apartheid structures (bishop).

Through primary experience with Tutu and by undergoing field research and analysis of primary documents, I learned firsthand that Tutu's life and work were crucial to the survival of South Africa and its warring factions.

It was during the existential moments of South Africa's miracle of negotiating a revolution into peaceful transition that I flew to Cape Town in March 1993, not knowing exactly what would happen to a South Africa on the brink of its first democratic election. When I arrived, I stayed at a retreat home for retired South African clergy. While there, I befriended the retired archbishop of Cape Town, Robert Selby Taylor, the director of the retreat home. Archbishop Taylor welcomed me into the fold. He would take me on walks in the Kirstenbosch Gardens, have me attend events at St. George's Cathedral, and talk extensively with me at meals about his impressions of the Anglican Church. While I stayed at this retreat home, I would walk to Bishopscourt, where Archbishop Tutu lived.

Bishopscourt, adjacent to the Kirstenbosch Gardens, was one of the most beautiful places I had ever seen. The history of Bishopscourt was complex. It technically belonged to the Church of England and still caused somewhat of an awkward relationship with the South African government. In addition, Bishopscourt presented its own prophetic stance against apartheid in 1986, when Tutu was elected archbishop of Cape Town. Tutu puts it this way: "Even in death [racial distinction] might not be mixed in the cemeteries, hospitals, ambulances. When I became Archbishop I announced that I would live in Bishopscourt, the Archbishop's official residence in what was a white area under the discriminatory Group Areas Laws without first asking for Government permission to do so. In doing this I was at the time breaking the law and courting prosecution. Today, that law, as with apartheid's other obnoxious laws, has been repealed."[8]

So, even though the place was beautiful, my initial experiences in South Africa were those of uncertainty and loneliness. I felt very much like a fish out of water. Slowly, I got to know many in the Bishopscourt staff. John Allen was especially welcoming to me, as he would direct me to Tutu's files and archives. I was given complete freedom to roam through these files, and even the responsibility by Lavinia Crawford Browne to help organize them. I was especially drawn into the life of worship at Bishopscourt, in which morning prayer began at 7:15 a.m. and evening prayer at 5:30 p.m. Without fail, unless Tutu was traveling, you could find Tutu in his designated chair surrounded by prayer books, names to pray for, Bibles.

Then came the moment of Chris Hani's assassination. Hani was the leader of the South African Communist Party, a leader of the military wing of the ANC, and a fierce and vocal antiapartheid activist. He was gunned down on April 10, 1993, by a far-right anti-communist who got the pistol from a senior leader in the South African Conservative Party.

Tutu and other church leaders issued a statement expressing "shock and outrage" at the cold-blooded assassination, a callous and premeditated murder timed to shatter the Easter message of peace so urgently needed. No amount of political rhetoric could explain away this dastardly deed. The role of Hani in the delicate process of political negotiations was of vital importance, making his untimely death even more tragic. Tutu sent condolences to his family, offering this prayer: "May the Lord who understands human pain and suffering help you to bear this loss and assist you to discover ways to remember Chris with love and pride, without pain."

In the days following, Tutu did not hesitate to speak openly about the assassination. He said publicly that this assassination of Hani was a deliberate attempt to derail the peace process and that there were corporate, sinister forces at work behind this violent act. Tutu addressed a special word to the South African politicians, reminding them that Hani's death was a shock to the momentum toward South Africa's first democratic election. Because of these circumstances, urgency now made the political task all the more difficult to find political solutions to the internal conflict bent on taking the country to hell. Tutu warned politicians publicly to spare no effort to find a speedy settlement. He encouraged the South African public not to grow weary but to call for peace and an end to violence. He knew that South African society was fragile, as Hani's death made militant black groups feel justified in striking back.

In a way that only Tutu could do, he used spiritual force to call upon all not to do anything to negate what South Africa had already achieved. The struggle for peace, democracy, and justice required the disciplined channeling of our combined energies as a people, he said, and the resolute determination not to be sidetracked by tragic events in the objective to have a democratic election. "In our responses there should be no more loss of life. Let our pain and anger be like birth pains giving life to a society where democracy, justice and peace will replace totalitarianism, injustice and violence."[9]

I remember attending Hani's memorial service with Tutu at St. George's Cathedral. Hundreds of people had crowded into the cathedral for a midday service. Tutu gave the main address as mourners joined hands and waved them above their heads, shouting enthusiastically in response to Tutu's authoritative voice and applauding loudly in a manner probably unprecedented for stately old St. George's Cathedral. In this address, Tutu paid tribute to Hani's recent call for peace: "He was a person of very considerable integrity. When circumstances changed, he changed with them, despite the fact that to change in his position might have lost him support." Responding to the possible criticism of honoring a Communist in the cathedral, Tutu said that Hani had committed himself to peace, reconciliation, and the negotiation process. Tutu reminded the crowd that it was not Communists who created apartheid; it was Christians. Ironically, in the cathedral, the people applauded this archbishop's insight that Christians can oppress and Communists can redeem.

Tutu went on to list certain demands on this oppressive Christian government of apartheid—demands like peace, democracy, joint control of the security forces, and a firm date for democratic elections. Tutu said, "We call on the government and indeed on all political groupings—for goodness sake, we cannot afford any further delay." There was also loud applause and deep belly laughs when Tutu made an appeal for discipline, especially to those who, like himself, "have this wonderful complexion." With a mischievous grin, Tutu was referring to his dark skin. As though he were a symphony conductor, he moved the crowd from such laughter to the conviction of the lasting hope of freedom. "Does anyone doubt we are going to be free? We must be single-minded and disciplined. . . . Undisciplined actions put all leaders at risk—and we can't afford that. . . . We are going to walk the high road to freedom, all of us together. We will be free, black and white together." The congregation of political protestors stood to their feet at the end of Tutu's speech.[10]

The service was cut short so that leaders could get to the Grand Parade, where a crowd of several thousand were growing restless and violent. We proceeded out of the cathedral in an orderly fashion and marched to the Grand Parade in honor of Chris Hani. This was a surreal experience for me, because I was born in 1963, too young to experience firsthand the civil rights protests led by Martin Luther King Jr., John Lewis, Rosa Parks, and others. I could only watch on television these brave people withstanding bone-breaking water pressure from fire hoses and ruthless attack dogs. This event at St. George's Cathedral changed all that. I took my place in the history of civil rights protests as I locked arms with Tutu and marched with him through volatile crowds full of gunshots, police dogs, tear gas, military tanks, and nervous armed military officers. We had no protection except for the purple cassock that Tutu wore as archbishop of Cape Town.

During our march, a youth was shot dead and more than a hundred protesters injured as some in the crowd clashed with police in the city center. "They killed him, they killed him," a man shouted with tears on his face as he was dragged away from the police. The youth of about seventeen died when police opened fire with buckshot. Devastation was everywhere—torched and wrecked cars; storefronts smashed from looting; tires, motorcycles, and litterbins set on fire. As providence had it, I walked side by side with Tutu and Njongonkulu Ndungane, the bishop of Kimberley, who would one day succeed Tutu as archbishop of Cape Town. As the three of us walked, bottles and projectiles flew around us. Clergy, international marshals, and monitors tried to stop the looting by channeling everyone to the Grand Parade, where Tutu and others would address the crowd. These shepherds knew it would be the best hope for the crowds' survival if they would move toward Tutu. These marshals and monitors were deeply afraid of exponential violence, and tried to persuade police to withdraw from the volatile crowds.

One reporter heard the account of a bystander: "Babulele uChris Hani babulele isolja. Isimanga esingaka sokubulala isolja" ("They have killed a soldier—Chris Hani; what an incredibly frightening thing to kill a soldier"). Two angry older women had a youth by the arms and shirt, dragging him toward a police van while a third harangued him in Xhosa and slapped him about the head. The scene was chaos, like something from a Hollywood movie. Some protesters ran along St. George's Mall shouting slogans and singing as they hit and kicked anything that appeared breakable. They shouted, "Jy loop nou saam met APLA hond!" ("You are walking with APLA—Azanian People's Liberation Army now, dog!"). A youth shouted this in Afrikaans as he slapped a reporter in the face. APLA was the military wing of the more radical black political party known as the Pan Africanist Congress (PAC).

For a moment, attention was diverted to a luxury tour bus making its way through the crowd. It was Muhammad Ali, the boxing legend, headed for Tutu's public address. But as soon as Ali's bus made its way through, the chants intensified, and youth shouted "War, War, War." Trevor Manuel, the ANC head of economics, was hit in the face. Tutu, John Allen, Ndungane, and I made our way through back streets to the city hall dais where Tutu would speak. We heard shots ricochet off concrete and steel. Bystanders ran for cover. Some found comfort in seeing Tutu still marching in his purple bishop's cassock. But the crowd was so frantic that they almost knocked us over. We made it closer to the eye of the frantic storm, where Tutu faced the police, who were lined at the end of the street. Two cars were nearby with smashed windows. The police fired their guns into the air. Tutu pleaded with them not to use force. As I stood next to Tutu, I heard him say to the police, "There are hostile elements here who want to make use of this thing. Most of these people are being peaceful. So far, you have been reasonably good."

HANI'S FUNERAL

Unfortunately, I was unable to attend the funeral of Chris Hani on April 19, 1993. I was fortunate enough, however, to get the text of the historical political sermon that Tutu delivered there. Some say that this was the most intense sermon of Tutu's career. He started out greeting the eighty thousand people in the stadium in the name of Jesus Christ. He wished them a good day in Xhosa, repeated in seSotho, Afrikaans, Shangaan, and English. He told the crowd that they had come together to bury a great son of the soil. "Is there anyone here who doubts that Chris was a great son of the soil?" Tutu said. Tutu told the crowd that he loved Hani for his warmth and his laughter, recalling a time at Bisho when Hani stood next to Tutu as they were singing, "Lizalis 'idinga lako Thixo nkosi yenyanyiso" ("Fulfil your promise, Lord God of truth"), and he belted it out with a wonderful baritone, singing all the verses by heart. Then at the end Tutu asked him: "Hey, Chris, how can a Communist sing and sing so lustily a Christian hymn?" And he laughed as he alone can laugh.

In the very week of his death, Tutu told the crowd, Hani had been speaking about the peace corps, about how everyone must become a combatant for peace. Tutu tried to debunk the stereotype of Hani as a "crazy communist." He made the crowd laugh when he said, "If a communist were to say: 'Hey, it is raining outside. Don't go out, you will get wet,' then they expect everybody else to say, 'Ai, no, no, no, no, a communist has said you are going to get wet. We must say no you won't get wet because it is communist rain.'" The crowd cheered loudly as they laughed and whistled.

For Tutu, Hani was a hero and a great leader, irrespective of whether he was a Communist. After all, those who oppressed South Africans were not Communists but Christians. "We were oppressed by those who claimed to be Christians such as we are." This made the crowd cheer and whistle some more. Tutu pointed out that Hani died between Good Friday and Easter Sunday, Tutu recalling that God extracted out of the death of Jesus Christ a great victory, the victory of life over death, that God showed in the victory of Jesus that goodness is stronger than evil, that light is stronger than darkness, that life is stronger than death, that love is stronger than hate. God was telling South Africans the same message in the horrible death of Chris Hani, Tutu said. His death was not a defeat. His death became a South African victory in the unexpected outcome that gave this country yet another opportunity.

It was at this point that Tutu triggered the crescendo of his sermon. He raised his voice and cadence. "We demand democracy and freedom. When?" The crowd responded, "Now!" "We demand a date for the first democratic elections in this country. When?" ("Now!") "We want a transitional authority with multiparty control of security forces. When?" ("Now!") "We will be free! We will be free in this country! We are going to rule this country! We are going to be the government of this country. We, all of us, black and white, all of us are going to live in peace and justice and friendliness in this country!"

Tutu ended his sermon by urging the crowd to commit themselves to discipline, to peace, to negotiation and reconciliation. He reminded the crowd that nothing would stop them from moving to freedom, because God was on their side. At the end, Tutu led the crowd in a call-and-response. "We will be free!" ("We will be free!") "All of us!" ("All of us!") "Black and white together!" ("Black and white together!") "We will be free!" ("We will be free!") "All of us!" ("All of us!") "Black and white together!" ("Black and white together!") "For we are marching to freedom!"[11] It was said that at this funeral at a Soweto football stadium, no speaker present, including Mandela, touched the hearts of the crowd more than Tutu.[12] The genius of Tutu in this moment was his recognition that millions needed a cathartic moment to pour out emotions rather than other people's blood. Tutu committed himself to become that channel, to prevent uncontrolled violence.

One would have thought, with the assassination of Chris Hani, that the sky would fall or the end was near. What South Africans discovered, however, was that many black South Africans had developed the disciplines of civil disobedience on the way to their first democratic election that loomed large in the horizon. Tutu stated:

> You see, quite extraordinarily, the violence has been contained—it has been limited, mercifully, to only certain parts of South Africa—some parts of Natal and currently the East Rand. It is also quite amazing that the violence is mostly not racial. Now and again there have been instances when people have been attacked because of their race, but such instances have been exceptional and indeed almost aberrations that have been roundly condemned all round, e.g., the attack on St James' worshippers, Amy Biehl, the Heidelberg Pub.[13]

As South Africans approached their first democratic elections on April 28, 1994, they were aware of the wily forces trying to thwart this historical event from ever occurring. For the first time, the practice of seeing South Africa on the basis of geography rather than racial groups became established. Tutu was proud of his nation, as the violence subsided and moved away from racial and ethnic inference. Tutu astutely observed that despite the obnoxious label given to South African violence by the media, black-on-black violence, "I have never heard them describe Bosnia or Northern Ireland as the scene of white on white violence, and is the suggestion that it would be better to have black on white violence?"[14] A way forward for the myriad conflicts emerged. No longer was South Africa in intractable conflicts like Zulu versus Xhosa. Such a rivalry was largely politically motivated in colonial wars, to divide and conquer Africans. In the region of Natal, one could even see Zulu pitted against Zulu who had declared different political affiliations. When the ANC and Zulu-based Inkatha Freedom Party did not come together, Tutu played a crucial role in organizing a summit between Mandela and the Inkatha president Chief Mangosuthu Buthelezi. Tutu's role as diplomat in the regard was widely known in South Africa: "Archbishop

Desmond Tutu has brokered a long-awaited meeting between African National Congress president Mr Nelson Mandela and Inkatha Freedom Party leader Dr Mangoustu Buthelezi. . . . National Peace Secretariat chairman Dr Antonie Gildenhuys said Archbishop Tutu's 'excellent' news enhanced the prospects of peace significantly."[15]

To Tutu, one of the crucial factors in ensuring the success of the coming elections was to make them as inclusive as possible. This meant making great efforts in bringing Chief Buthelezi back to multiparty constitutional negotiations, a forum he had been boycotting for several months. He had warned of civil war and anarchy if his demands for an autonomous region for Zulus were not met.[16] South Africans were urged to stay calm in the face of violence on the eve of the country's first democratic elections. Tutu's role was to be the nonanxious presence as others tried to incite violence. One such instance was when there was a car bomb in Johannesburg that killed nine people and injured ninety-two. Tutu spoke up and said those responsible would not derail the elections, which would be "free and fair," despite those trying to subvert them: "As long as security forces show they are effective . . . we must not panic. . . . Let us say no to evil, no to corruption, no to hatred and oppression, no to intimidation and violence, disease and ignorance, . . . yes to forgiveness and reconciliation, laughter and joy, caring and sharing," he told a congregation at St. George's Cathedral.[17]

South Africa was on the brink of catastrophe when Chris Hani was assassinated. Yet it pulled back from disaster, because diverse people listened to the pleas of their leaders for peace. It was a miracle that a race war did not break out. All the more, this context right before South Africa's first democratic election in 1994 was rife with violence, as political agitators on both sides of the racial divide tried to influence when or if there should be such an election. Tutu was the South African confessor who helped his nation confess that which was wrong and needed change. In turn, he could encourage South Africa to shout after him, "We will be free, all of us, black and white together." Most would have thought blacks would be unforgiving of whites, that they would say, "To hell with white people," but, wonderfully, they chanted back, "We will be free, all of us, black and white together."

Tutu was also quick to give credit to the larger, global community who shined a light on the depravity of apartheid. Tutu stated, "You, dear friends in the international community, have a huge share in any victory we may be able to notch up. Most inadequately on behalf of our people I want to say a feeble 'thank you.' These hackneyed, fly blown, shop soiled words are meant to convey the utterly ineffable—the deep heartfelt appreciation and gratitude of millions. This is the one time I know I can say without fear of contradictions and without sounding presumptuous, I know I am speaking on behalf of millions."[18]

After my baptism of fire of marching with Tutu, he invited me to come and live with him at Bishopscourt, where I served in the role of his chaplain. On that chaotic day I saw how Tutu's spiritual leadership was vital in helping people see each other as human beings, rather than objects that purgers wanted to wash away. The concept of purgation is indeed one of positive connotation, rather than that of a dystopian future. Tutu's spiritual leadership was key to this definition of purgation, as he moved through his own equivalent baptisms of fire, eventually, as we shall see, into his stage of illumination. Before we move into that part of the book, Illumination, it is helpful to look at two more key relationships in Tutu's life that underwent purgation: Tutu and his clergy, and Tutu and his contemporary spiritual leaders.

TUTU AND THE CLERGY

The political tension was so thick in the days leading up to South Africa's first democratic election that Tutu had to address his clergy, who were becoming increasingly anxious about their roles in those days. This meeting, which I witnessed firsthand, serves as a microcosm of how Tutu related to the clergy under his care. Tutu spoke to his clergy the day after the march of peace in Cape Town after Hani's assassination. Tutu looked more like the conventional bishop, as he tried to put out the conventional fires in church politics, this time around the clergy's political involvement in the upcoming elections. Tutu started singing the Kyrie Eleison, then the Lord's Prayer. He proceeded to make wedding announcements. The whole scene of watching Tutu as the conventional bishop was surreal as I recalled police dogs and military tanks aimed at us just a day before.

Tutu then got into the touchy subject of being a political priest by addressing head-on those priests who were directly involved in organizing political elections. The clergy, according to Tutu, should make themselves available for roles as observers and monitors as the major elections approached, but they should first clear their roles with regional bishops and their parish. As Tutu was giving this pastoral instruction, he commended his priests for their passion and justice.

Then Tutu chastised some of the clergy for having signed a statement about how they would support the ANC in the coming election, and for doing so without consulting him. Tutu acknowledged that there were many reasons for the clergy to be excited about the upcoming election. He understood their enthusiasm to be prophetic. He also understood their need to give direction to their people at a grassroots level. And Tutu understood the need by his zealous clergy to condemn the racist tactics in the political campaign that led them to sign. Tutu then said he knew only three clergy who signed so far—the fourth, Tutu said, was his wife. There was great laughter among the clergy at that.

The Synod of Bishops made a clarion call to get people to vote. Then there was a paper presentation from a theological commission about the role of the church in constitutional matters and how there needs to be a concerted effort to bring this country together for this election. The diocesan council stated that all clergy should vote but that each had the right not to vote. They were quite clear, however, that the Anglican Church wanted qualified people to vote conscientiously.

To summarize the main point of disagreement between Tutu and his clergy: Some desired to take a political stand during the elections, while Tutu as arch-bishop demanded that his clergy remain nonpartisan. To discuss this, meet-ings were organized by Professor Charles Villa-Vicencio and Anglican clergy like Matt Esau, Barney Pityana, and Edwin Arrison. In such meetings Tutu did speak against the racist tactics in campaigning in the Western Cape by the white National Party: "We call on people not to vote for any party which uses such despicable methods." Clergy who wanted to go a step further than Tutu believed that the gospel values of an inclusive society committed to the care of the poor, the marginalized, and the oppressed were best represented in the political man-ifesto of the ANC. Anglican clergy explicitly stood up in such meetings to say that because of apartheid they would vote for the ANC. Tutu then said that in this election "clergy should still remain open to criticism in assessing the ANC if they should win, especially in the implementation of their policies."[19]

During clergy meetings Tutu mentioned the racist tactics used to prevent Africans to vote, like the use of a comic book. Tutu was instrumental in releasing a statement that condemned racist tactics and urged not to vote for any party using scandalous tactics. This leadership by Tutu produced a great impact to make others aware of how the church was implicated in racist tactics. Tutu told the clergy, however, that he was not playing games. He said, "Our people are dying," but warned his clergy that they were acting not as individuals but as representatives of the Anglican Church. Tutu stated, "We waste energy being divided."

The situation between Tutu and his clergy intensified. Someone told Tutu in mockery, now that his church supports the ANC, could he read a political statement from Tutu's pulpit? Tutu said, "I'm very upset. I think this is . . . quite publicly embarrassing to me, the church and the Synod of Bishops." What does the church gain from these actions? "If you think the Archbishop has gone soft or needs goading to take action, then this is superfluous. I have never done things to be in glory and don't need goading to speak out against injustice. I am very sad. I am probably angry, but I am much more deeply, deeply distressed. If there are contributions to help me understand your actions, we open now for discussion."

An Anglican priest, Keith de Vos, then stood up and called Tutu "your grace." De Vos proceeded to say that he appreciated the archbishop's role as a diplomat, but he still struggled about the boundaries of political involvement as a priest. The current role of the church seemed inadequate to de Vos, with the church having little impact. De Vos warned that many colored people have swallowed the National Party's line. "This is a most dangerous situation, your grace. Am I to be silent about who they should vote for because I am in obedience to you, or do I have the freedom to say who I will vote for in front of them?" De Vos concluded, "I told my son that if anyone votes for the National Party, then ask if they suffered from amnesia."

Another Anglican priest, Michael Weeder, stood up and said, "Your grace, I understand your anger, I want to speak as a colored. God didn't name me this, I have been legislated to this. We are still talking antiquated language of bondage. You said we must support a party with democratic values, so one thought we should vote for DP. Or when we can't endorse ANC, people are thinking the same." After Weeder finished his speech, a white Anglican priest stood up and said that he supported Tutu's position of impartiality.

In Tutu's closing remarks he said that there is a decree put out, and no one is deprived of the right to participate in the arena of politics, but not in the role as licensed clergy. This is clear not just in the most violent arenas. As a priest, Tutu warned, clergy must make the decision in good conscience, whether to be licensed or give up his or her license as a priest and speak out for a specific political party. Tutu spoke firmly against disloyalty. Yet he spoke about his own pain and need to unify the clergy. Tutu said, "None of us here want to see the NP win. Don't vote for a party who does this. . . . People can't be so stupid not to see the way to go. You can make your stand in different kinds of ways. Your stand doesn't just compromise me, but our ministry."

Tutu encouraged his clergy to schedule appointments and sit down with him to discuss the complexities around all of this; however, Tutu said that he could in no uncertain terms endorse any political parties without undermining the church. "I feel as deeply about the things you say, but I have to defend the church," Tutu said. Tutu reiterated that he loved his clergy but has the vocation to hold the church together and endorse the spirit of the bishops. "I'm not saying I like it. I don't say I agree with Fred on unity and diversity. There is diversity that is division. The minute where political indifference is OK, it certainly isn't. A great deal will be gained, from a simple statement that you endorse the statement against racism. I honestly don't see what more you have gained in comparison to the categorical condemnation and do not vote for this party."

He encouraged his clergy that they could be as specific as they liked in their condemnation of racist tactics in political elections. For example, he referred to an incident in which the pictures were used of the "station strangler" to scare voters about a black-led government. With regard to the communist question of political involvement, Tutu encouraged his clergy to notice his media interviews, in which he gave the kind of things they should say. He referred them to the magazine *Challenge*, in which he made statements about possible theological resolutions with communism. He concluded that he had just preached at a funeral of a Communist. Some may say this is wrong, but what must be clear to clergy is that we condemn outright all racist campaigns.

As archbishop, Tutu wanted the clergy to support a decision by their bishops preventing priestly endorsement of any particular political party and believed that clergy who have endorsed particular parties contravened the spirit of this policy. Tutu commended his clergy for their deep concern about racist campaigning tactics that motivated their action. He also noted their concern that their congregations perceived the church's nonaligned policy to be an anti-ANC stand. Tutu said the decision to prohibit clergy from belonging to political parties was in view of the fact that they ministered to members of all political parties in their congregation. Tutu called upon Christians "to exercise their vote with care and responsibility."[20]

Of course, the controversy was not solved overnight. Tutu had to deal with the question, "Why has the cry 'Don't mix religion with politics' such a long pedigree?"[21] I had a conversation with John Stubbs, dean of theological studies for the diocese of Cape Town, and he told me he was against the stance Tutu took on clergy's role in politics and thought they should be able to participate fully in the political arena. Stubbs questioned Tutu's distinction between authoritarian and authoritative. Stubbs thought my work would be valuable in bringing out why Tutu held his view of clergy nonpartisan participation. Tutu stated, "People in authority (whether home, school or government) obviously tend to prefer the character who is docile, eager to toe the line, hardly able to say boo to a goose, since it is more comfortable to deal with those who will not rock the boat." But this means dealing with highly regimented and often totalitarian states, where there is order and unanimity of wills because debate and dissent are frowned upon with a dull gray uniformity being the order of the day.

For Tutu, political authority is healthiest in a setting that is conducive to growth in independence, which will naturally be persuasive rather than coercive. Tutu's theology is such because God does not coerce but tries to persuade rather than dominate creation, as shown through the revelation of how Jesus negotiated powers and principalities. Human beings must "be respectful of the integrity and autonomy of others rather than undermining of them; friendly and sympathetic rather than threatening."[22]

Tutu would often say that he bristled when some people said he was too political while others said he was not political enough. The double messages in people tended to come either from those who wanted to maintain a status quo that was defending them and not other people, or from those unwilling to look down the trajectory of really wanting to scorch the earth with revenge. Tutu couldn't give in to either of these extremes, because he was trained to see that Jesus Christ came as a human being and thereby sanctified all of human life. "We therefore have to be deeply political in our involvement in life; that is imperative of our faith, but we should not be politically aligned. That doesn't make us apolitical; it makes us non-partisan."[23]

TUTU AND CLERGY DISSENT

During my time in South Africa, I got to know Barney Pityana, a major South African political activist and also an Anglican priest and friend of the famous South African martyr Steven Biko. Pityana at that time was a lecturer in religious studies at the University of Cape Town. I remember Pityana telling me he was "unrepentant" about signing a declaration stating that he would vote for the ANC. "It would have been criminal for the clergy in the Western Cape not to have made their position public, because the people of God require a moral lead." As the election approached, the climate became intense about how religion and politics mixed together. Tutu repeated his position in subsequent weeks that any Anglican cleric who appealed to the public to vote ANC was contravening the spirit of the decision of the Anglican clergy. Clergy should not belong to a political party, he said. Though not all agreed, Tutu's message began to take root among the clergy. For example, Anthony Langenhoven, whose name was included in the declaration, denied that he had signed it. "I'm furious. I never signed any declaration," he said.[24]

Those wary of Tutu's position feared that the churches would go back to religious matters only and miss the opportunity to show the world creative solutions to political problems. For Philippe Denis, a lecturer at St. Joseph's Theological Institute, based in the Roman Catholic tradition and located at Cedara in Kwa-Zulu-Natal, there seemed to be some evidence of this already happening. Denis pointed out that already the Anglican Bishops Synod led by Tutu had withdrawn in some ways from the political arena by forbidding Anglican priests to be members of political parties. Further, some churches had changed their position and were now strongly advocating the lifting of sanctions.[25] Other evidence of this trend seemed to be when the Southern African Catholic Bishops' Conference said the church fulfilled its role best by remaining independent of political structures. The provincial executive officer of the Anglican Church, Canon Rowan Smith, said the church's stand was well known and that no such trend was occurring. Smith stated, "A cleric who chose to accept public office would have to give up his or her license to officiate as a priest."[26]

Tutu would not compromise his position to let Anglican priests sign a statement that they would vote for the ANC. He continued to say publicly that licensed Anglican clergy who did so inevitably side with a political party and were acting in contravention of the spirit of their decision. Obviously, this was a struggle in Tutu's own heart, as Anglican clerics continued to say they would vote for the ANC. Even more of an internal struggle for Tutu was that it was now publicly known that the controversial document was also signed by Tutu's wife, Leah.

The Synod of Bishops in February decided to forbid clergy from being card-carrying members of any political party. This decision applied to ordained, licensed clergy and could be extended to cover full-time church workers. Tutu defended the measure in an address to the Anglican Students' Federation (ASF) at Imbali, Pietermaritzburg. The ASF had called for the decision to be reviewed, and Tutu, who acknowledged that "many of my young priests want to eat me up raw" because of the measure, had rejected this, John Allen said. Tutu told the ASF it did not mean the church would become politically neutral, because it remained committed to justice. However, it would be impossible for clergy to minister to parishioners of opposing political views if they were party members. Allowing party membership would prejudice church efforts to mediate in political conflict and might jeopardize, in particular, efforts to mediate between Inkatha and African National Congress aligned forces in Natal.

With all the goodwill in the world, Tutu thought, there is no way in which people who belong to a political party that is opposite to the one to which clergy have declared themselves to belong are going to be able to accept the spiritual authority of clergy.[27] It turns out that Tutu had wisdom as he guided his flock, but it was a wisdom born out of the purgation of becoming a free South Africa. He was willing to appear weak and compromised as he counseled clergy to maintain the margins of the ordained life in the civil war of politics at that time. I think this weakness was more akin to Jesus' wisdom of an upside-down kingdom in which the weak are strong. When all was said and done, this was a crucible moment for the intersection of spirituality and politics. It was in Tutu's weakness that he was used mightily to broker a future for South Africa.

Tutu was used tremendously during the fragile moments of South Africa's election, precisely because he was seen as nonpartisan. For example, Tutu and Stanley Mogoba, a former Robben Island prisoner who came to be the bishop of the Methodist Church in South Africa, went to see Chief Lucas Mangope, a member of the Freedom Alliance, to try to persuade him to return to the election process. This wouldn't have happened if Tutu was seen publicly as an outright card-carrying ANC member. Yet Tutu remained a radical figure. On one hand, Tutu lived in this beginning stage of Christian mysticism, modeling the image of God as a burning bush, one that burns and is purified but not consumed; on the other hand, Tutu's clergy were frustrated with his restrictions in South Africa's first democratic election. As we shall see now with Tutu's relationship with Allan Boesak, Tutu's own clergy were not the only ones frustrated with him.

TUTU AND ALLAN BOESAK

Allan Aubrey Boesak was born in Kakamas, Northern Cape, as one of eight children. His father, a school teacher, died when Boesak was six years old. He was raised in Somerset West and worked as a child laborer to help support his family. At fourteen, he became a sexton in the separate colored sector of the local Nederduitse Gereformeerde Sending-Kerk. After graduating from Bellville Theological Seminary, he worked as a pastor in Paarl between 1967 and 1970. In the early 1970s, he studied at theological institutions in Kampen, Holland, and New York, gaining a PhD in 1975. On his return to South Africa in 1976, his parish was in Cape Town's Bellville South.

He came into prominence when he was unanimously elected head of the World Alliance of Reformed Churches (WARC) in 1982. He became a world celebrity when he introduced the motion that apartheid was a heresy, at the 1982 WARC conference in Ottawa. Boesak said, "In South Africa apartheid is not just a political ideology. Its very existence as a political policy has depended and still depends on the theological justification of certain member churches of the WARC. For reformed churches, this situation should constitute a *status confessionis*. This means that churches should recognize that apartheid is a heresy, contrary to the Gospel and inconsistent with the reformed tradition, and consequently reject it as such."[28]

Boesak's statement here led to the suspension of the white South African Reformed churches from the world body. Tutu saw Boesak's position as profound leadership, and a thorn in the side of the Dutch Reformed Church. He and Tutu seemed to hit the world stage at similar times. For Tutu it was in 1978 heading up the SACC and winning the Nobel Peace Prize in 1984. For Boesak, it was when he presented his theological critique of apartheid in 1978 and was elected as head of WARC in 1982.

In January 1983, Boesak's call for a united front against apartheid resulted in the formation of the United Democratic Front (UDF), an umbrella organization that swiftly became an essential antiapartheid group in South Africa. Boesak provided the first signature to UDF's "million signature petition" against the South African constitution of 1983, which provided separate chambers of Parliament with limited powers for colored and Indian minorities but excluded the twenty-four million black majority altogether. Boesak described colored and Indians who went along with the new parliament as "the junior partners in apartheid."[29]

This was also the time when the Nobel Committee was about to announce that Tutu would receive the Nobel Peace Prize. The Nobel Peace Prize never stopped Tutu and Boesak from working together very closely in the decade that followed. The most distinct tension between him and Tutu was a theological difference: Tutu's Anglican theology did not approach the relation of public politics and theology the way Boesak's Reformed theology did. Boesak's Reformed faith tradition encourages challenge and reform. This Reformed tradition says that we are put on this world to change this world, and that is what reformation is all about. For example, Boesak was known for his activism and civil rights marches but, as bishop, Tutu had a different role to play.

In October 1986, in his position as moderator of the Nederduitse Gereformeerde Sendingkerk, a segregated black branch of the Dutch Reformed Church in South Africa, and president of the World Alliance of Reformed Churches, Boesak pleaded for unity. He argued that apartheid could not survive in any new political formulation. He said it was a matter of urgency that they listen to his appeal for unity based on the rejection of apartheid. In this way and others, some might see Boesak as a Reformed theologian fitting the role of national confessor better than Tutu. But perhaps Tutu's role as confessor can best be understood in the context of Anglican spirituality, in which confession indeed is performed individually and publicly.

On one hand, Tutu became the spiritual father of a nation, and on the other activists like Boesak contended that the TRC did not go far enough in providing the confessions of big business and the ongoing benefactors of apartheid. In this sense Tutu's Anglicanism provided him with international support but did not fully confess its own complicity in apartheid. On an international level, Tutu, as the highest-ranking black clergy figure in South Africa, was pressed to lead opposition to the National Party. And yet, as he arose in the Anglican church hierarchy, his constituency became more complex. And as the Nobel Peace Prize winner, he served as black South Africans' unofficial ambassador to the world at large. The form of protest he was able to engender on an international level was economic sanctions, always being persistent with the point that sanctions offered the last hope of avoiding a "holocaust" in South Africa. It must be noted here as we discuss Boesak's role that Tutu was not the only international Christian voice coming from South Africa in the fight against apartheid, and Tutu would be the first to acknowledge this.

Boesak and Tutu worked together to fight sham constitutions and to boycott fake elections. They both advocated that churches, civic associations, trade unions, student organizations, and sports bodies should unite to dismantle apartheid. Both used their differing Christian perspectives to excite communities to move beyond apartheid. Tutu, formed by Anglican monks, worked through a kind of Anglo-Catholic Christian mysticism in which God was moving people and creation through purgation and illumination into the ultimate ideal of union. Boesak preached with eloquence in English and Afrikaans through the tradition of the Dutch Reformed movement, freely invoking John Calvin to buttress his own political views. For example, Boesak said Afrikaners had distorted Calvin's theory of election by claiming that God had chosen the Afrikaner nation as a whole, rather than selected individuals.

Both Tutu and Boesak demonstrate God's purgation of so-called pure religion, especially those kinds of religiosity that inherently support the causes of affinity groups in politics. They both showed how purity of blood had become more important than spiritual calling. To undermine the legitimacy of National Party rule, Boesak turned his own theology of the Dutch Reformed Church on its head. In a 1979 open letter to the minister of justice, Boesak said the Bible teaches that "where there is no justice, authority of the government is no longer derived from God, but it is in conflict with God. Resistance to such a government is both demanded and justified." Boesak added that Calvin himself "echoed this sentiment when he wrote to King Francis in the letter published as the prologue to his *Institutes*: 'For where the glory of God is not made the end of the government, it is not a legitimate sovereignty, but a usurpation.'"[30] "Calvin also stated clearly that 'worldly princes' lose all their power when they rise up against God. Christians should resist such a power, not obey it."[31] And for those coloreds, Indians, and Africans not inclined to rebel against authority, Boesak laid the charge of subversion against the government. Those that resisted the government were being loyal to a higher authority.

It is quite interesting to note how Tutu responded to these tense times. "Nobody tries among my critics seriously to address the issues I am raising. My critics don't say, 'What you are claiming is wrong or invalid.' No, what they are saying is—'Tutu, you're a political predikant—that is the most important thing. And we want to establish that fact and when we have, we won't need to address the issues you are pointing to because you will have been thoroughly discredited!'" Tutu believed his critics were guilty of producing a monumental red herring and, sadly, were duping many who should not be duped. "They are not at present questioning the validity of my statement that apartheid is the most vicious system since Nazism—that forced population removal schemes which are the heart of apartheid are fundamentally and of themselves evil. No, they are not yet saying whether those statements are true or false or mischievous. It is as if I should say, 'Hey, that man is dying,' and instead of trying to establish whether my claim is true or not, they are saying, 'Hey, Tutu, are you speaking as a politician or a bishop?'"[32]

Tutu scandalized many when he declared that in God's last judgment God would reveal if we were fit for heaven by a set of criteria that could not be described as religious in the narrow sense, but by whether we had fed the hungry, clothed the naked, visited the sick and the imprisoned (Matt. 25:31–46). Tutu went so far as to say that entering heaven is not dependent on whether we pray or go regularly to church. Tutu's role as spiritual and political provocateur was often received as Tutu's ad nauseam activity. Tutu states, "It reminds me of what a Ghanaian woman judge said about the repeated efforts of the WCC to explain to people that the grants to liberation movements were for humanitarian purposes and yet many still did not seem to hear this word. I want to use her remarks about our own position. 'In Ghana,' she said, 'we have a saying, It is difficult to wake up someone who is pretending to be asleep.'"[33]

FREEDOM IS THE BEGINNING

Freedom is only the beginning. I don't know if Tutu was quoted as saying this, but I told Chris Matthews, an ABC journalist, about this concept when I accompanied Tutu to cast his first vote. That day was surreal, as folks got in long lines that wrapped around buildings and neighborhoods. This concept, that freedom is just the beginning, is major wisdom in learning how to move human communities out of poverty and violence. When in 1994 the first democratic elections were held in South Africa, Tutu's pivotal role as spiritual leader was vital in creating a stable atmosphere, especially his work of facilitating the political participation of Mangosuthu Buthelezi, a South African politician and Zulu chief who had founded the Inkatha Freedom Party in 1975 and was chief minister of the KwaZulu Bantustan until 1994. Buthelezi was also an Anglican whose participation in the elections saved countless lives, because there would have been civil war if he had not.

By now, more than twenty-five years later, most know the results of South Africa's first general elections, held between April 26 and 29, 1994. This was the first election in which South African citizens of all races were allowed to vote and run for office. Numerous voting agencies around the world came to observe, to ensure that these elections were indeed free and fair. All of this occurred under the direction of the Independent Electoral Commission (IEC). This marked the official end of apartheid.

As I accompanied Tutu to cast his first vote, I saw the long lines of people waiting peacefully to vote. In fact, altogether nearly twenty million people voted, without violence. As was expected, Nelson Mandela's ANC political party, whose slate also contained the labor confederation of the Congress of South African Trade Unions (COSATU) and the South African Communist Party (SACP), won with a sweeping victory of 62 percent of the vote, short of the two-thirds majority required to unilaterally amend the interim constitution. The ANC formed a government of national unity with the National Party and Buthelezi's Inkatha Freedom Party. This new National Assembly moved to elect Mandela as South Africa's first black president. (To this day, South Africa's Independence Day holiday is April 27.) I also had the privilege to attend Mandela's inauguration as president on May 10, 1994, in Pretoria.

In many ways, this first real election was not just about politics; it was about spiritual leadership. Tutu states, "How often did we not try to bolster morale of our people by declaring that our God saw, our God knew, our God heard and He would come down to deliver us from our oppression as He had done in former times. . . . And now it has happened."[34] Tutu's reasoning for practicing being impartial for these elections was profound. He believed that it was God's will for South Africa to be an example for the rest of the world, showing how a pluralist society with a diversity of cultures and ethnicities can thrive, and how the wealthy and the developing worlds can coexist.[35]

Nevertheless, in South Africa's first real elections, freedom was only the beginning in the mid-1990s. Apartheid had left a horrendous legacy, represented by a huge housing shortage, massive unemployment, and serious education and health care crises. The rural areas for black people were impoverished, without electricity, clean water, or proper sewage, so that cholera epidemics happened— in a country that pioneered sophisticated medical technology such as heart transplants. Once Mandela was elected, many perhaps had unrealistic expectations that could not be met by any government, certainly not overnight. Nevertheless, Mandela and others knew they would have to act quickly to improve the quality of life of the most disadvantaged, so that it would be clear there is a qualifiable difference between living under apartheid and living in a democracy. Resources had to be transferred from the defense budget and reallocated toward housing, education, and health care. But people would have to be patient and reduce their expectations to more realizable levels.

Speaking in Germany in those early days after the election, Tutu looked forward to international financial investments and, he hoped, aid, which would help "our infant democracy to succeed, because South Africa will be the locomotive to drive Africa's economic train," uplifting the entire continent. "We are going to succeed because God wants us to succeed. . . . We will be a paradigm for the rest of the world on how to solve similar problems."[36] Tutu concludes with joy: "We have come to say thank you to God for that incredible miracle that took place last week. . . . We made that profound scientific discovery: 'That we are all South Africans.' . . . We were transfigured. People walked into the polling station and when they emerged they were different people."[37]

Moving through the purgative changes of becoming a new South Africa takes us now to the second part of this book. I have tried to show how Tutu and his South African nation moved through a purgative stage. Tutu's life struggled within the ebb and flow of apartheid. In part 1 we have looked at the crescendo of apartheid to its highest tide in 1990, when Nelson Mandela was finally released from prison. Parallel to his nation's purgation, Tutu's spiritual life experienced his own purgation, as his ordained spiritual leadership emerged alongside his nation's struggles. In this chapter we saw some of the toll of those years on Tutu's significant relationships. The goal throughout part 1 has been to root out a deeper understanding of Tutu's spiritual life as he struggled to stay related both to his enemies and to his friends. Indeed, Tutu's relationships weathered significant storms, and some ran ashore during the onslaught of apartheid. Tutu's struggle to mend such relationships around him should help ground the reader for what now occurs as Tutu is chosen to be South Africa's chief confessor, in order to bring illumination for what happened under the evil of apartheid.

Such illumination is vitally important in Christian mysticism, to expose dysfunctional spirits that perpetually obstruct consciousness of the Holy Spirit. Purgation is the process of exorcising or washing out such demons. The next stage, illumination, is the process of finding clarity so as not to fall under the spell of such demons ever again. Tutu's spiritual leadership was such that he anticipated how South Africa could easily fall prey to such demons, if not careful. Tutu's stance as South Africa's confessor was determined not by whether the perpetrators of injustice were white, but rather by whether injustice was being perpetrated and human rights were being violated. Tutu's authority and basis for being concerned about injustice of any kind was always based in such spirituality. Tutu made his hope clear that after South Africa's first democratic elections, the momentum of freedom and justice would continue to be the case, whoever was in charge of the new government of South Africa.

PART 2
ILLUMINATION

"US-based South African comedian Trevor Noah has defended himself after being criticised by a French diplomat for saying 'Africa won the World Cup'. . . . a day after France beat Croatia. . . . More than half of the French squad can trace their heritage back to Africa."[1]

—*BBC News*

Tutu at a press conference about South Africa following the World Cup in 2010. Courtesy of African News Agency (ANA) Archives.

Chapter 6

Confessor as Tutu's Ordering Identity

Although we begin part 2 with political satire, there is a profound point that Trevor Noah makes when it comes to recognizing human identity. As a comedian who grew up in South Africa, and as an interracial child, Noah is deeply aware of how human identity has been used primarily as a means to an end, rather than an end unto itself. In other words, Noah's humor illumines the audiences who watched France win the 2018 World Cup, only to realize that France's team was predominantly black. The value of this humor is in its illuminative quality—showing how a once-oppressed identity was now being coveted on the world's stage. As Tutu has said, "Injustice, evil and oppression cannot last forever."[1] A miracle is unfolding right before our very eyes. In a postcolonial world we are beginning to witness an about-face of French society, now ferociously defending their inclusion of black identity. This is an excellent example of how to understand the second mystical stage of illumination.

In part 2 we explore Tutu's spiritual life as he engages the newfound freedom of the new South Africa. This is the stage of illumination, as he encounters the vulnerability of beginnings and the habits that often entice many to return to their old ways. The guiding idea in this stage is that the spiritual role of confessor orders Tutu's complex persona as he negotiates even more complex South African

131

societies that have been seduced to normalize the evil of apartheid. As Tutu has said, some of the churches in South Africa helped enable apartheid to exist and thrive by propounding theologies to justify it.[2] This guiding idea of Tutu as confessor leads to the conclusion that his life and work affect inquiry concerning not only South Africa's context of apartheid, but its future as well. The reader will see a most fascinating life and witness God's presence amid humanity.

In particular, this chapter explores Tutu's role as chief confessor, hearing the confessions of those who committed crimes during a particular period of apartheid. With this in mind, this chapter demonstrates how illumination occurred as he moved into his role as chair of the Truth and Reconciliation Commission. Getting a new South Africa to confess its sins illumined a difficult but positive path forward for South Africa, but also took its toll on Tutu's physical health, as we will see in subsequent chapters. In this illumination stage we begin to see the fruits of Tutu's struggle to mend relationships around him. It is important to begin this second part of the book with a little more explanation in Christian spirituality of the illuminative stage of Christian mysticism.

ILLUMINATION

The second stage of Christian mysticism is illumination. In this stage, as Dionysius describes it, in the light of God we can learn to burn with love and move "unswervingly upward in the direction of the ray which enlightens. . . . With a love matching the illuminations granted them, they take flight, reverently, wisely, in all holiness."[3] One of the key texts for Christian mystics in understanding this stage is the metaphor of burning love in the Song of Solomon. "Ah, you are beautiful, my love; ah, you are beautiful; your eyes are doves. Ah, you are beautiful, my beloved, truly lovely" (Song 1:15–16). As discussed above, the Christian pilgrim begins the mystical process to find God by purging self-knowledge, whereas here in the second stage God's Holy Spirit inflames human will with love to follow where the Holy Spirit leads, now no longer obsessed with self-love. In short, the pilgrim can see where to go and whom to truly love.

In illumination, the Holy Spirit facilitates the alignment of human and divine will. For Christian mystics, this is why Jesus constructs the Golden Rule, "'You shall love the Lord your God with all your heart, and with all your soul, and with all your mind.' This is the greatest and first commandment. And a second is like it: 'You shall love your neighbor as yourself.' On these two commandments hang all the law and the prophets" (Matt. 22:37–40). Purgation begins this process by gently cleaning humans of the desire to love only the self, and then burning into the will the warmth of God's love. Thus the human will is shaped to be compassionate, as God is compassionate. "Your anointing oils are fragrant, your name is perfume poured out" (Song 1:3). Just as human skin becomes vibrant with healing ointment on it, so the human will, when it receives the Holy Spirit, becomes alive with love, even toward former enemies. Indeed, this mystical and metaphorical language may be too esoteric for some, but for Tutu, who also preached sermons and studied biblical texts like the Song of Solomon, there was a practical aspect of this kind of Christian mysticism.

Given the myriad kinds of spiritualities and interpretations as to which way to find God, Tutu knew that he needed an astute theology that could challenge the state religion of apartheid, constructed initially by the Dutch Reformed Church. For the Dutch Reformed, the language of Christian mysticism carried little value, especially since their state religion could spread simply by the force of a gun.[4] Even more, the architects of apartheid were theologians who needed to justify the construct of a "white" race that could somehow supplant Israel as God's chosen people. For the Dutch Reformed, there was little patience for Christian mysticism, which provided the frame of reference in which religious practices were mere means to an end.

In other words, the beauty of Christian mysticism for Tutu was that it would never allow itself to become a state religion. It understood that although God chose Israel, God was doing a new thing by adopting Gentiles into God's kingdom as well. The concept of a "white race" was antithetical to this new thing God was doing, because a select group of Europeans tried to change the paradigm so that now they were the natural chosen race. The methodology of Christian mysticism is needed here in order to purge this narcissistic disorder. The corrective is the inoculation of becoming a Gentile in God's kingdom, which guards against the disease of dysfunctional identities. Christian mysticism would forever guard against such disease.

Christian mysticism contained the inoculation against the disease of identity disorders. Now Tutu's identity reflected a spirituality in which relationality emerges. This benign awareness of the other emerges in the linkup between the Spirit of God and human willpower. We move into illumination, when the human will and human reason grasp the humility to realize there are both God and idols of God. In such a realization a brand-new way of seeing the world emerges. Human will and reason are now informed by the frame of reference of God who sprinkles human will and reason "with the hyssop of humility." In this new frame of reference, human reason and will are inspired by the Spirit of truth and set alight by the fire of love.[5] This is illumination.

Bernard of Clairvaux, a French Christian mystic of the twelfth century, saw this kind of illumination as a way in which the soul of the mystic is set on fire with the love that the bride has for the bridegroom. The attitude that the bride expresses in saying, "Let him kiss me with the kisses of his mouth" (Song 1:2), is that of the soul thirsting for God. Human beings do not relate to God as machines or slaves. This light in the Song of Solomon is quite different from the attitude of the slave who fears the face of a master, or the servant who looks for wages from a lord's hand, and it surpasses that of the disciple who merely is attentive to the teacher.[6]

In this second stage of illumination, the mystic sees relationality more clearly—especially those relationships that lead toward the healing of the nations. In this stage of illumination, there is a deeper longing for the last stage, union of will and reason with God. In the last mystical stage of communion with God, an ethic of love emerges in which there is an ardent sense that the mystic approaches God with unreserved candor that overcomes all fear and develops the audacity to become one with God. In the words of Bernard, "It is an ardent love, blinded by its own excess to the majesty of the beloved. For what are the facts? He is the one at whose glance the earth trembles, and does she demand that he give her a kiss? Can she be possibly drunk? Absolutely drunk! . . . How great this power of love: what great confidence and freedom of spirit! What is more manifest than that fear is driven out by perfect love!"[7]

It is this audacity that distinguishes this second stage of Christian mysticism, in which the love of the bride disallows a relationship with God like the attitude of the slave. In this second stage the mystic overcomes all the reticence toward God, because of the paradigm shift in which there is an actual recognition of God beyond self. All things change then by this illumination, which is uncharacteristic for the first stage, in need of purgation.

While Bernard calls the first stage of purgation the kiss of the feet, he describes the second as that of being lifted up to kiss the hand of Christ. In the process of Christian mysticism, God first cleanses soul and then raises it up. How? By giving the consciousness to see where to be bold to love. Love requires both boldness and vulnerability, because in this second stage of illumination one cannot separate how self and community are dependent on God's love and grace. Bernard puts it this way: "I see it as the grace of the beauty of temperance and fruits that befit repentance, the works of the religious person. These are the instruments that will lift you from the dunghill and cause your hopes to soar. On receiving such a grace then, you must kiss his hand, that is, you must give glory to his name, not to yourself."[8]

So how does such Christian mysticism illumine Tutu's spiritual life? My thesis in this chapter is that Tutu's role as national confessor operates from a distinctively theological model of relationality, in which forgiveness informs human identity, and a Trinitarian image of God involves the flourishing relation of persons. In short, not to forgive assumes there is no such image of God among humanity.

For Tutu, more specifically, not to forgive assumes there is no future for South Africa.[9] Further still, Tutu believes in forgiveness and repentance, and practices both because his context of white justification of apartheid and black political liberation is shaped by competing claims on God's election. In the end, these claims are in fact reduced to epistemological privilege of race. Instead of adopting the conceptualization of God's privilege of race as determining identity, Tutu adheres theologically to a metanarrative of God's forgiveness, in which conflicting racial identities are expressed and defined in the reconciling concept of *imago Dei* revealed through Jesus Christ, who manifests the plentitude of relational personhood.

In my previous work on Tutu, I have shown that Tutu is a rather conventional theologian who believes what the church believes. At the heart of Tutu's thought, I have argued, are his Anglican ecclesiology and the African concept of Ubuntu, both of which inform how he appeals for South Africa to move beyond the theological constructions of apartheid. In light of an ecclesial Ubuntu, Tutu disallows recourse to radical, interpretative schemes of black political discourse, in order to save white people from the effects of black rage. In short, I argued in previous work that Tutu's gift to South Africa (and to the world) is in how Christian orthodoxy is narrated in a context of conflicting racial identities in a manner to make their lives intelligible to each other.[10]

For Tutu one of the primary means of enlightening his audiences was through storytelling, and he was a master storyteller. Just as we have seen Bernard's Christian mysticism of the Song of Solomon, the purpose of telling spiritual narratives is to help others reach the stage of illumination, in which deeper wisdom can be discovered. In hearing the stories, the disciple would be put in the place with the most potential for epiphany and insight. From such outcomes the disciple would move from purgation to illumination. One such story from the Desert tradition of Christian mysticism was perhaps first told by the founder of the Christian monastic tradition, Antony. Desert Fathers and Mothers helped to illumine their disciples with such desert sayings by helping them to ask the right questions, so they could have the chance of being illumined by the right answers. The story goes like this:

A disciple came to a monk in the desert and asked, "What kind of prayer is not acceptable before God?"

The monk said, "You already have your answer because you have learned how to ask the correct question."

The disciple persisted, however, and needed clarity from the monk.

The monk capitulated to the young disciple and said, "Okay, if you want examples for prayers that are not acceptable to God, then do not ask for revenge and do not pray for yourself."

"How can this be?" The disciple asked. "How can prayer not be for yourself?"

The monk answered, "If God bears with us, who are sinners and who often offend God, how much more is it right that we should bear each other's burdens and put up with each other. So, it is not good that we should ask for things for ourselves because such prayer is a sign that we do not believe in God—that God already knows what we need even before we ask."

The disciple then asked, "How should I then pray?"

The monk said, "Pray for repentance. Pray that the lost will be found. Pray for friendliness toward those who wish you harm and love toward those who persecute you. If you do these things, you cannot help but become that very prayer."[11]

In the Desert tradition, this story was meant to help people distinguish goodness from evil and God's actions from immoral ones. It is only fitting in this spiritual biography of Tutu that a contemporary moral story be told to understand illumination in the South African context. This is the fable of Rabbit and Lion that I learned from South African theologian Tinyiko Sam Maluleke.[12] Maluleke was brought up partly in rural South Africa, where his elders told him fables of "clever Rabbit" and "gullible Lion." These fables in particular occupied a special place in Maluleke's heart. The point of illumination in them appeared to be a simple one: "although Lion was big, strong and powerful he was much too idiotic [to] be a match for the small, weak, harmless but very clever animal called Rabbit." These stories were so illuminating that they always succeeded in drawing children completely into the web of the storyteller. The illuminating point of the Lion and Rabbit stories was to show that strength alone was not enough, and that even the weak could have creative resources for their own survival. The story goes like this:[13]

> Lion travels far and wide searching for Rabbit. In a series of clever ploys Rabbit continually makes Lion look like a fool. Lion's dignity begins to sink among the animal kingdom, who before had seen him as royalty. Now, Lion is only laughed at. Raging with anger, Lion now pursues the end of Rabbit once and for all. After searching long and hard, Lion finds Rabbit chomping on a delicious meal, unaware that Lion is at the entrance of the cave.
>
> "Hey! Checkmate! You are dead today, little friend," Lion growls as he moves stealthily toward Rabbit, who now has no way of escape. What Rabbit does have, though, is wit and cunning. Rabbit stands on his hind legs, like a herald proclaiming an announcement of life or death, and shouts: "King Lion, I'm afraid I feel seismic tremors in this cave! It will no doubt collapse and kill us both! You are the powerful one—do your duty and hold up the cave entrance while I seek help from our compatriots in the animal kingdom."
>
> Caught in the moment, Lion raises his powerful forearms and paws to hold up the cave roof, as Rabbit quickly darts out, laughing. Yet again, Lion looks foolish.

Maluleke's analysis of the fable is astute, because he focuses on the possible epiphanies in the fable. Although Lion may look foolish, the fable also displays how the weak can easily satirize the ignorance of the powerful. Maluleke states, "Rabbits may not have brawn but their intelligence is both admirable and entertaining. But this is not merely a matter of fun and laughter. Rabbit's life was in danger; what is a little lie if a life is saved? After all, Rabbit's clever lie led to no loss of life; Lion has only lost what he has always been losing, namely his dignity and his face." An epiphany occurs, however, when Maluleke turns to get another vantage point on the fable—that is, what if Rabbit is not that good of a character? "Is there nothing to be said for Lion's generosity in suspending a selfish desire for revenge in the light of what he believed to be a much more serious calamity?" The moral of the story must be drilled down to seeing that Lion may have the grace to imagine cooperation with one's mortal enemy in times of crisis—something Rabbit seems incapable of imagining. "What if the roof had indeed been collapsing? Would we not sing the praises of Lion, the unselfish one? Then Rabbit would have been exposed as selfish and small minded: Lion holds the roof when Rabbit flies giggling away, enjoying the good life in some other corner of the country. That is to say, the moral of the story is not without complexity; the 'stupidity' of Lion is not without its redeeming qualities, nor is the inventive intelligence of Rabbit without its flaws."[14]

Like Maluleke I agree that the Lion and Rabbit fable offers several vantage points to see the complexity of apartheid South Africa. On one hand, black South Africans were Lion—cheated and ridiculed. The whites could be seen to look like Rabbit, being small in number though controlling a disproportionate amount of power over black South Africa. When Lion resolved to end it once and for all with Rabbit, this could easily be analogous to the uprising of black South Africans resisting apartheid. When I arrived in South Africa in the early 1990s, this may indeed have been when Lion's final solution was being put into place, since this was the pinnacle of international pressure, with Mandela's release and the start of the first real democracy in South Africa. And here it must be added that the spiritual work of the World Council of Churches Program to Combat Racism should be counted into this final solution. "Rabbit was finding less and less forest in which to hide. Slowly but surely, Rabbit was exposed."[15]

The insight of the fable is that the character fault was just as pronounced with Rabbit as it was with Lion. If South Africans were not careful, Rabbit's cunning would raise its ugly head once again as, for example, when the ANC suspended its armed struggles while the police seemed to intensify their clandestine violence from 1990 up to election time in 1994.[16] Was it yet another ruse when de Klerk wanted a Reconciliation Commission, and not so much a Truth Commission, so as to gain key protections before giving in to Lion (a black majority government)? In light of these complexities of Lion and Rabbit in South Africa, Tutu has to defend the setting up both a Truth and Reconciliation Commission that would appear to benefit the white perpetrators of apartheid in being granted amnesty while black people could be tricked once again in their inability to do anything concrete to repair a history of apartheid.

Whenever I am asked to provide academic lectures on Tutu and South Africa, in my question and answer sessions at the end, audiences inevitably want to know about the continuing disparities in South Africa in particular and Africa in general. More than twenty-five years after the elections, both contexts still struggle with poverty and unequal opportunities. Like Native Americans, black South Africans still live in townships, while whites live in suburbs and an upper-class existence. There seems to be an increase in the crime rate in postapartheid South Africa, especially among poor black townships, although this is not the case in high-security residences of postapartheid white South Africa. What makes the news is in how crime is now creeping toward the high-security residences of white people. Maluleke concludes, "To all intents and purposes, therefore, the majority of black people remain in the same—if not worse—situations both socially and economically. They could be excused for feeling that, like Lion, they hold the roof of the cave while Rabbit enjoys the fruit of the land!"[17]

Tutu's genius was that he understood the complexity of reconciliation, that is, unless one is authentic in anger against injustice, there can be no true reconciliation. In telling one's own true account of reality out loud and in public, one participates in the illumination process of exposing the harm that is being done. Herein the power of one's own story is vital, as well as the space in which such a story can be heard. Maluleke states:

> Surely this situation has something to do with reconciliation in the country. How can there be reconciliation while the gap between rich and poor is not only widening, but also retaining its essentially racial nature? How can there be reconciliation amidst such violence? The South African media has never tired of reminding us that we are arguably the rape capital of the world! An even more ominous enemy has been the HIV-AIDS scourge. At present one out of every nine South Africans is living with the HIV virus: it is a staggering statistic. It seems as if one day we celebrated the end of apartheid and installed Nelson Mandela as president, then the very next we were re-colonized by both HIV-AIDS and the forces of globalization in which the local currency is being daily devalued.[18]

South Africa's complex context cannot be explained by static characters like dumb Lion and clever Rabbit, because we do not always know when Lion transforms into Rabbit and vice versa. Each could arguably represent the other, as white South Africans could claim to be Lion with their industrialization for South Africa that holds up the roof of the cave. And even black South Africans are identified with clever Rabbit, who gets by gaming politics and colluding with wily political partners. The problem is that often when arguments are made that blacks need whites and whites need blacks, there are usually suggestions that blacks lack the capacity to administer a nation-state. Tutu's spiritual insight here was that interdependence is different from codependence. The simple point is summed up in the proverb of Ubuntu: "A person is a person through other persons." In short, Lion and Rabbit are not just two characters. They are myriad characters. Today, Lion is not always Lion nor Rabbit always Rabbit. Maluleke concludes:

> Almost every political province has its own tribal Lion and Rabbit permutations. In the northern province, the Rabbit is sometimes represented by the Northern Sothos while Vendas and/or Tsongas become the Lion— depending of course on one's tribal affiliations and political leanings. Yet for many people in the northern province of South Africa, it is the Xhosas and the Zulus who are the Rabbit: aren't the Xhosas and the Zulus running the country today? Others would say the Lion is women, while men are the Rabbit. Yet still for others, the real Lion is the struggling and cheated rural poor while urbanites are the Rabbits, who escape the sweat of farming rural communities. The new black elite is another identifiable community of Rabbits thriving in the face of an impoverished and unemployed black majority of Lions.[19]

BIRTH OF THE TRUTH AND
RECONCILIATION COMMISSION

The Truth and Reconciliation Commission illumines the complexities between Lion and Rabbit. South Africa was not the first to set up commissions like the TRC. Between 1971 and 1995 there were around thirty countries with some such commission. In fact there were about twelve African countries experimenting with such commissions. Even Uganda under Idi Amin's government in 1974 had such a commission, although he oversaw the killing of more people than is ever realized today. In order not to repeat such mistakes of the past, scholars like Daan Bronkhorst believe is vital to be students of such history.[20] So Bangladesh was one of the first countries to initiate such a commission, which investigated war crimes in 1971, followed by Uganda's commission and other countries, including Bolivia, Israel, Argentina, Guinea, Uruguay, Zimbabwe, Philippines, Chile, Chad, and others. Since the TRC in South Africa, other countries have used a similar model, including Rwanda and Northern Ireland. Maluleke states, "TRCs are part of the search for a way to expose, and use positively, the fact of mutual dependency between the Lion and the Rabbit."[21] With seemingly recalcitrant situations like Israel and Palestine, David Shipler states:

> Whatever happens in war or diplomacy, whatever territory is won or lost, whatever accommodations or compromises are finally made, the future guarantees that Arabs and Jews will remain close neighbors in this weary land, entangled in each other's fears. They will not escape from one another. They will not find peace in treaties, or in victories. They will find it, if at all, by looking into each other's eyes. The time has passed when Jews and Arabs could face each other in simple conflict. They live together now in rich variety. There is no single Arab-Jewish relationship; there are many, and they require an elusive openness that must somehow run against the forces of war, nationalism, terrorism and religious certainty.[22]

In light of such recalcitrance, how would South Africans deal with the legacies of the apartheid era? This had been the question lingering over the South African nation for over a century. Upon the final victory of democratic election in 1994, the ANC wanted to set up a "Truth Commission," but their adversary, the National Party, advocated for a "Reconciliation Commission." The ANC, Nelson Mandela's party, was concerned about the victims of the apartheid period, while the NP, F. W. de Klerk's party, sought amnesty for the perpetrators. The result was the National Unity and Reconciliation Act of July 26, 1995, which established the Truth and Reconciliation Commission (TRC). At the end of the day, the TRC provided a compromise approach for apparently opposite interests. These disparate interests are stated clearly in chapter 2 of the Act, which describes the "objectives of the Commission" as follows:

§ 3 (1) the objectives of the Commission shall be to promote national unity and reconciliation in a spirit of understanding which transcends the conflicts and divisions of the past by

(a) establishing as complete a picture of the causes, nature and extent of the gross violations of human rights which were committed during the period from March 1, 1960 to the cut-off date,[23] including the antecedents, circumstances, factors and context of such violations, as well as the perspectives of the victims and the motives and perspectives of the persons responsible for the commission of the violations, by conducting investigations and holding hearings;

(b) facilitating the granting of amnesty to persons who make full disclosure of all the relevant facts relating to acts associated with a political objective and comply with the requirements of this Act;

(c) establishing and making known the fate or whereabouts of victims and by restoring the human and civil dignity of such victims by granting them an opportunity to relate their own accounts of the violations of which they are the victims, and by recommending reparation measures in respect of them;

(d) compiling a report providing as comprehensive an account as possible of the activities and findings of the Commission contemplated in paragraphs (a), (b) and (c), and which contains recommendations of measures to prevent the future violations of human rights.[24]

Given the above context of victim and perpetrator discovering compromise, the origin of the TRC is inextricably linked to the evolution of South Africa's negotiated settlement. The greatest goal, shared by both black and white South African leaders, was that the South African transition would happen not by force of arms, but through dialogue and an eventual negotiated settlement. Here, it must be understood that this transition is fundamentally different from that which, for example, Nazi Germany underwent after World War II, or the revolution that saw Mengistu Haile Mariam deposed from power in Ethiopia in 1974.

In each of these countries, the conflict produced a clear victor. After World War II, the Allies were able to take occupation of Germany and impose their version of justice on the Nazi regime at Nuremberg. In a like manner, the Ethiopian People's Revolutionary Democratic Front (EPRDF) overthrew the Mengistu regime after a period of civil war. One of the EPRDF's first acts after taking power was the establishment of a Special Prosecutor's Office to try members and supporters of the old regime responsible for widespread violations of human rights. In both cases the approach to those who had committed gross violations of human rights could therefore be imposed in terms dictated by the victorious party. Predictably, both parties chose prosecution as the primary mode of dealing with the past, not only because they believed this to be right, but also, crucially, because they were able to do so.[25]

These situations can be contrasted with the transition from military rule to democracy in Chile in 1988. When General Pinochet, the former head of the Chilean junta, agreed to restore power to an elected civilian government, he still commanded sufficient power to ensure that he remained in office as head of the armed forces. As a result of the continued influence and strength of the military, the new government was effectively unable to bring charges against those who had been responsible for assassinations, torture, and "disappearances" under Pinochet's rule. Although the new government in Chile did establish a Truth Commission in order officially to investigate, record, and acknowledge human rights abuse under military rule, those who were responsible for these abuses remained unidentified and unpunished. If Germany and Ethiopia represent one element in the justice policy choices that confront societies during a transition from authoritarian to democratic rule, that of prosecution, Chile represents the other end of the spectrum, blanket amnesties for those who committed gross violations of human rights.[26]

South Africa occupies a position somewhere between the two. South Africa's negotiated settlement produced a markedly different balance of power from that which prevailed at the time of the German, Ethiopian, and Chilean transitions. In South Africa, the struggle between the liberation movements and the former government had reached an impasse, a stalemate, in which neither side could claim a victory. Furthermore, the South African conflict led to a deeply divided society that produced, at the time of transition, a great deal of hostility, mistrust, and instability. A lasting and peaceful settlement could not have been achieved if one side was to embark on a series of prosecutions against the other. It was therefore important to develop a way of coming to terms with the past that neither concealed the occurrence of human rights abuse nor threatened to destroy South Africa's new democracy. The TRC was precisely such an initiative. By fully investigating human rights abuses and making the granting of amnesty conditional on full disclosure, it aimed to discover the truth about the past. In order to consolidate democracy and promote national unity, those who established the TRC chose truth above prosecution. Many critics would say that the TRC chose conciliation above justice. In fairness to the TRC, their work is admittedly still undone, as a reparations policy designed to assist those who suffered as a result of abuse remains unfinished. The TRC recommended that victims of apartheid should receive a monthly grant of up to 2,000 rand for a period of six years. In 2018, President Cyril Ramaphosa found himself under increasing pressure to follow up on such reparations for victims under apartheid.[27]

STORYTELLING

Tutu as chair of the TRC was charged with the task of establishing "as completely as possible the nature, causes and extent of gross violations of human rights committed" during a selected period (about March 1960 to December 1994). Furthermore, the Commission was empowered to grant amnesty in exchange for what it termed a "full disclosure" of truth about violations of human rights. Also, the Commission was to establish the fate of victims, enable them or their survivors to tell their stories, and make arrangements for possible measures for reparations. Structurally, the TRC was made up of seventeen commissioners divided into three committees: human-rights violations, amnesty, and reparations and rehabilitation. These committees were assisted in their tasks by an investigation unit as well as a research department, among others. The broader aim of the Commission was to steer the new nation out of hostility and division toward unity and reconciliation by coming to terms with South Africa's past.[28]

After conducting investigations and hearings of some 20,000 victims and 7,000 amnesty seekers for about two years, the TRC submitted its report and findings on October 29, 1998, to the then state president, Nelson Mandela. It is important to note that while the South African TRC has officially completed its task, the amnesty committee continues in one form or another. For example, the South African President's Fund currently holds 1.4 billion rand spent on exhumations and burials of antiapartheid activists and victims. There had been 14.5 million rand spent on basic education for TRC victims who made claims, and 6.5 million rand spent on higher education since 2014. In October 2018, twenty years after the TRC released its recommendations, there was a political movement for Ramaphosa to include 80,000 claimants for reparations. A response from Ramaphosa was expected sometime in 2019, which he indeed provided concerning expropriation of land in February 2020. Ramaphosa stated that the South African government will press ahead to distribute more land to the black majority. He also warned that a failure to do so would perpetuate the injustice of apartheid. All of this momentum, however, was shut down due to the COVID-19 pandemic.[29]

In *Truth Talk*, the official newsletter of the Truth and Reconciliation Commission,[30] Tutu saluted the remarkable magnanimity and generosity of spirit of South Africans who exposed their pain to the world. Tutu believed that the vast majority of South Africans should, by right, be consumed by bitterness, anger, resentment, and the desire for revenge. By displaying a willingness to forgive, however, South Africans, through the TRC, paid a high price for the freedom South Africa would come to enjoy. For Tutu, that price was multifaceted. First, the high price for freedom in South Africa related to the suffering they experienced as a result of gross apartheid violations. Secondly, to speak about these violations was no guarantee that the South African nation would embrace healing. Thirdly, there was the concern that the perpetrators of apartheid may get amnesty without even apologizing for what they did. Fourthly, the victims who testified in the TRC hearings relinquished their rights to institute civil proceedings for compensation.

Tutu defended the high cost of the TRC by saying that whatever reparation the victims of apartheid may get, such reparation would never be able to match the high cost of suffering during the apartheid era. This high price would show that South Africans hoped for the future more than they resented the past. This was often a struggle, however. Sometimes Tutu was resented for granting forgiveness so easily. Other times he was criticized for not granting it easily enough.

One who criticized Tutu was Professor Richard Vanderross, who talked about Jesus' free, unsolicited forgiveness on the cross. Given this, how could Tutu demand a show of repentance during the TRC? Tutu's theology said, in effect, If you confess I must forgive, but you can't appropriate my forgiveness unless you engage in restitution. Tutu, in his book *No Future without Forgiveness*, talked about being stuck in a dank, dark room. You can see the sunlight outside waiting for you, but you have to open the window to appropriate it.[31] It was a lovely way to describe forgiveness. He also told a story about the stolen bicycle. You just can't come back after stealing it without confessing that you took it and then giving it back.

Underlying much of Tutu's rationale for the TRC was his atonement theory, in which he understands the process of creating a future, a process in which communities practice forgiveness. Tutu states: "We regret that there are still both victims and perpetrators who are not coming forward. . . . There is something I would like to say to those perpetrators: . . . The truth will eventually win out. . . . When you come forward to confess you are guilty, you will lighten the burden for us all."[32]

Tutu's atonement theory for a future South Africa assumes that there is no such thing as a reprobate.[33] As a confessor, Tutu is trained to be sensitive to even a flickering ember of remorse, in the hope it could be nurtured into a flame of reconciliation. Tutu believes that "we all have the capacity to become saints."[34] It is not surprising that South Africa needed Tutu to head the Commission, which was headed actually by two churchmen.[35] The TRC was described as a mixture of the ecclesiastical and the judicial. Implicit to the theology of the TRC is that civic judges cannot discover "the truth"; instead, like Pontius Pilate, they merely satisfy themselves as to the discharge of an onus. Tutu's theological impetus of community, however, understands true confession occurring between sinners and the only sinless one, the triune God—the only one qualified to judge whether the truth has been told and forgiveness merited.

Critics of Tutu's theological impetus behind the TRC state that the idea of a person being "required" to confess "the truth" to a human commission in the name of the law, dressed up in the robes of the church, takes one back to the Inquisition. "If we were the Inquisition we would have had electric prods," Tutu chuckles, going on to say that the people who perpetrated the crimes must be persuaded that their confession is central to their own healing, not their prosecution. The National Unity and Reconciliation Act makes clear, says Tutu, "that the truth is sought . . . for the purpose of healing the land."[36]

It is vital to see Tutu's theological contributions, more particularly his articulation of forgiveness and repentance, in order to understand the impetus for his political involvement in the TRC. The security forces would not have contemplated a settlement without the prospect of amnesty given from the legitimate authority that Tutu offered. Even more practically, it would have been lengthy and expensive to convict even one person of crime during the allotted time of apartheid violations. Tutu continues, "It is a very heavy price. But what is the alternative?"[37] It was costly for those who confess publicly, but the community had to also look at what would happen if there were no public confessions. In many South African communities, however, the people asked: But where are the confessions? Where are the perpetrators who committed these ghastly deeds? If confession is crucial for the healing of the nation, why are they not coming forward voluntarily?

Despite his being accused of forgiving criminals, many South Africans believe that the TRC under Tutu's leadership was the best way to deal with affliction, so that the nation would not be held hostage to the past. During the TRC hearing, victims and survivors from all sides of the political spectrum told of their suffering during the apartheid era.[38] This led people in some communities to dub the TRC "the Kleenex Commission," because of the tissues used by witnesses to wipe away their tears.

The Amnesty Committee, which made the decisions on whether to grant amnesty to perpetrators, because they were dealing with prisoners whose crimes were already known, conducted hearings in which people had grave difficulty providing complete disclosures. New information was slow in coming in revealing what happened under apartheid. The hope of the Amnesty Committee was that by summoning people such as police generals, investigative inquiries would reveal new information that would subvert any future machinations of apartheid. This was one of Tutu's most potent political arguments in favor of the TRC. If members of the corrupt police could convince the Amnesty Committee that they had made full disclosure of their acts and that they were politically motivated, then they were entitled to amnesty. Such disclosure was not simply to grant amnesty for the guilty; even more important, such disclosure would ensure that those agitating for a return to apartheid would fail.

In the face of thousands of political deaths exposed by the TRC, Tutu's wisdom advocated for a legitimate police force created by a legitimate government. Tutu suspected clandestine activities of what was known as the Third Force, which sought to disrupt any peace negotiations and a date for elections. Tutu stated, "We are going to have to purge the security forces on both sides. . . . If people were forced to implement laws that said that 'black people are nothing,' it would be surprising if they were not themselves dehumanized. . . . The Christian . . . must say no to politicians who want to divide people."[39]

These perpetrators of affliction did not even have to say that they felt sorry for what they had done, as long as they gave complete disclosure that would implicate those who created the infrastructure of apartheid. White right-wing groups, however, knew that they would have too much to lose in the event of a civil war, but one could not rule out limited state terrorism. Also, if groups like Inkatha and the Afrikaners and the Tswanas become even more alienated from the constitutional process, then violence was likely to escalate, not decrease. This was why the principle of Ubuntu was so important: "We are going to be free, black and white together." Although the TRC may have been a compromise South Africa, it is important to recognize the disaster that it prevented. In apartheid South Africa, white people had immense power, although they eventually were unable to suppress the black mass population anymore. Tutu led a movement to intensify international outrage and economic sanctions to disqualify the apartheid regime. So, to return to our earlier parable, instead of Lion declaring checkmate, the situation was more like stalemate. In the early stages of moving from prisoner to president, Mandela stated: "If you want to go to war, I must be honest and admit that we cannot stand up to you in the battlefield. We do not have the resources. It will be a long and bitter struggle, many people will die, and the country may be reduced to ashes. But you must remember two things. You cannot win because of our numbers: you cannot kill us all. And you cannot win because of the international community. They will rally to our support and they will stand with us."[40]

Mandela knew that if South Africa exploded into an outright civil war, very little could be done. The fickleness of a white international community during those days could easily become dormant and define South Africa's problems as of little self-interest. Here Tutu's spirituality played a large part in further defining how self-interest is not as valuable as interdependence. As Maluleke helps us conclude, "In other words, TRCs are here to help the Lions and the Rabbits take shared responsibility not only for their survival but for their shifting identities. Whether they do—and can—succeed is, of course, another matter."[41]

RELATIONALITY AS SUBSTANCE FOR ILLUMINATION

Confession of sin as the practice of telling one's story in public is a practice in the church meant to remind the disciple that evil is not the ultimate reality of creation. Knowledge or illumination of sin provides the reference point; it does not normalize evil's existence. To understand confession in a more proactive way, confession is the practice of the presence of God amid humanity. Understanding the spiritual life and work of Tutu in South Africa requires an understanding of the relationship of confessor and confessed.

Illuminating who is the confessor and who is the confessed is central to how Tutu negotiated his public identities around spiritual convictions. Tutu's spiritual convictions did not occur in a vacuum, but through significant relationships. Even as Tutu recalls his first religious experience, he cannot do so without recalling who helped him interpret God in his life: "I was born into a Christian family and it was taken as real that God was there."[42]

There are many relationships that helped Tutu interpret God in the world. Tutu's more formal mentors were people like Francis Cull, Trevor Huddleston, Ambrose Reeves, Michael Scott, Joost de Blank, and others "who have given the gospel of Jesus Christ great credibility amongst the deprived and disadvantaged."[43] In addition to such relationships is the profound character of Nomalizo Leah Shenxane Tutu, Desmond's wife, who had a tremendous impact on Tutu's development.

LEAH TUTU

Nomalizo Leah Shenxane, also known affectionately as Mama Leah, was born on October 14, 1933, in Krugersdorp, two years and seven days after Desmond. As she grew up, she became a teacher, a nurse, and an assistant to the registrar at the University of Botswana, Lesotho, and Swaziland, between 1970 and 1972. She was the director of the Domestic Workers and Employers Project of the South African Institute of Race Relations from 1976 to 1984, and in 1988 she cofounded the Desmond Tutu Peace Center, which is now the Desmond and Leah Tutu Legacy Foundation.

She married Desmond Tutu on July 2, 1955, and they subsequently had four children. They renewed their marriage vows in 2015 in Soweto. During the marriage renewal, reporters learned about the humor in Desmond's initial wedding proposal to Leah. He told her, "My parents want me to get married." In a later letter, she responded with her own humor: "I will help you to be obedient to your parents."[44] This was how they began their marriage, enduring sixty-three years and counting as of the writing of this book. Mama Leah, which I called her when living with the Tutu family at Bishopscourt, is a powerful woman who has withstood the tests of time and apartheid. As of the writing of this book, Mama Leah relied upon her supporting cane to move from place to place, her limp no doubt the result of her longevity and struggles in apartheid South Africa. Many do not know her power of activism, being the cofounder of the South African Domestic Workers Association (SADWA), a South African organization bringing relief to many women working subserviently in white households. SADWA's legacy is still celebrated to this day.

At an occasion in honor of Leah, older women started a struggle song of domestic workers: "My mother was a kitchen girl, my father was a garden boy, that's why I'm a unionist." As they sang they also contagiously made others sing and dance. At this same occasion a well-known writer, Sindiwe Magona, honored Leah with this line of a poem in Afrikaans: "As dit goed gaan met die familie, sal dit goed gaan met die nasie" ("If the family does well, the nation will do well"), a reference to the legacy of the Tutu family. There were many times during the apartheid years that Leah provided the substance of hope that sustained Desmond. The power that exudes from Leah is in how those perilous times did not paralyze her. Desmond spoke often in public and private how the foundation of the family and infrastructure underneath his public ministry was his wife.

I recall Leah's acts of kindness from my days living with the Tutus, such as allowing me to use her car or sending over to the chaplain's quarters a nice dessert for me to eat. She turned the colonial church's compound at Bishopscourt into a home that welcomed strangers. Desmond's relationship with Leah was foundational, because each was easily interchangeable in the apartheid years. Tutu's enemies knew they could hurt Tutu by hurting Leah. But she stayed strong, even defiant, against apartheid. The story is told of when Leah was gardening and a large military truck passed by. "She stood up quickly and looked for a little stone to throw in the direction of the might of the apartheid army. We now know, of course, that the little stone won."[45] It must be mentioned that Leah raised with Tutu a family of highly educated children. Jonathan Jansen, the South African scholar, concludes that in contrast to a society often filled with corruption, family strife, and even activists who now look to their own selfish interests, the Tutus symbolize people's dreams for what their country ought to be.[46]

In one of my Tutu Travel Seminars, a participant noticed in our conversation with Desmond and Leah how she would often finish his sentences. After learning about Tutu's rigorous daily schedule, someone asked how they found time to be together. They made sure to spend time together in morning after Eucharist, at breakfast and lunch, and in the evening after evening prayer. They avoided most diplomatic parties and events, preferring to stay at home.

They also traveled together, and they traveled a lot. Leah Tutu's default position was that if she was available she would travel with him. When they went abroad, his travel expenses were quite pricey, because Tutu wanted equal accommodations for those traveling with him, which included Leah. Organizations resented the fact that they would have to pay for three first-class airfares to get Tutu to come and address them, but that was the rule. If you wanted Tutu you had to pay for him, and he required that his wife and staff be treated in the same way that he was.

Leah anchored the family in Tutu's hectic days of leadership. So when Tutu went to study in London, the first thing he made sure was that Leah would come to King's College London with him. There was a theological fund financed by American Protestant money, but finances were still tight. The CR monks sponsoring Tutu didn't want to include Leah at first but later accepted. Then she told them she was bringing the children. Keep in mind she'd given up teaching and went to study as a nurse, so Trevor and Thandi had been left with Tutu's parents for about two years. The monks eventually found a way to support sending two children, but could not afford a third, so Naomi stayed behind. But then a white woman, a close friend of the Tutus, raised the money to send Naomi with a priest to London.

Some monks grumbled about this expense. As a result, Tutu was seen by some as a spendthrift. There was some tension and criticism against Tutu, but I think much of it was based on hypocrisy and double standards. Most of these monks were from these British upper-class families. Huddleston went to Langsing College. Tutu's mentor Elrod Stubs went to Eton and Oxford. They came from families where the eldest son inherits land and title, and the next one goes into church, and next one to the military. They were stacked with aristocracy, which they tried to overcome. Although they lived modestly in Mirfield, nevertheless they were monks whose every need was taken care of. Their worship was absolutely beautiful, especially with plain chant and powerful liturgy, but the fact is that they didn't come from poor backgrounds, they were supported by the monastery, and they did not have families to support. It was difficult for an English monk to understand the financial struggles of Leah and Desmond in London in the 1960s, much less their struggle against racism.

England was very important in Desmond and Leah's life. Despite the racism they faced there, it was in London that they realized how badly black people were treated in their home country of South Africa. Living in a society in which ill treatment occurred regularly meant that they probably experienced racism on a daily basis. One cannot imagine how white societies of those times segregated and isolated a black person's self-esteem. When you went into town to shop, you felt it. When you did anything, you faced racism either consciously or unconsciously. This was one of the reasons that Leah really struggled returning to South Africa the second time, after four years abroad. One time she sobbed on the shoulder of Tutu's personal assistant, "If I go back home and walk on the sidewalk when a white person is coming, I have to step off or get pushed off."[47] Leah shared in these kinds of experience, but if that was the South African way the world was made, she was just as convicted as her husband to change it. She shared Tutu's vocation to raise the global consciousness about the evil of apartheid.

In retrospect, when Tutu went to town to get a newspaper as a small boy for his uncle during World War II, he realized even then the need for such consciousness raising. Tutu followed the war news because his father's brother was in the South African forces, which went through Kenya, Ethiopia, and Egypt during the war. He and his uncle would open the newspaper on the sidewalk in such eagerness to find out what was going on, but whites walked around nonchalantly, as if a fish does not know it is wet. Perhaps such nonchalant behavior was due to white South Africans being indifferent to black people in public. In South Africa during the war there was the shortage of available men, due to the expectation of arming only men of European descent. Also, the declaration of war on Germany had a narrow majority in the South African parliament and was far from universally popular; thus conscription was never an option. More than 330,000 men volunteered to serve in the South African army during the war.

Indeed, without their increasingly global reference point, Desmond and Leah too to some extent might have been fish not knowing the extent of wetness. Leah's relationship with Desmond is a profound lesson about illumination. The context here is in how we need to allow space and time to recognize the emergence of identity—especially spiritual identity. For example, it took space and time to recognize the resurrected Jesus in Luke 24. In this text, after his crucifixion, the resurrected Jesus joined Cleopas and a friend walking on the road to Emmaus. While they were talking and discussing, Jesus himself came near and went with them, but their eyes were kept from recognizing him. Perhaps they could not recognize Jesus because they lacked a frame of reference to recognize a living Jesus after witnessing the gore of his crucifixion.

Jesus asked these distraught disciples, "What are you talking about?"

They provided a sarcastic response to Jesus: "Are you the only one around who doesn't know what just happened?"

"What things?" Jesus asked. "Was it not necessary that the anointed one you believe in should first suffer and then be seen for who he is?"

It is interesting that the questions in this passage continue in their intense nature as Jesus, the stranger, finally took the bread and blessed and broke it and gave it to them. For they asked, even upon finally recognizing Jesus, "Did not our hearts burn within us while he talked to us on the road, while he opened to us the Scriptures?" But it wasn't through the Scriptures that they recognized Jesus; rather, it was through the breaking of the bread. If you extend this lesson of how Jesus' identity emerged, you see another onslaught of questions as Jesus stood among the rest of the frightened disciples. And Jesus asked, "Why are you frightened, and why do doubts arise in your hearts?" But again, Jesus did not answer their questions in the manner they expected. He simply showed his hands and feet. He said, "'Touch me and see; for a ghost does not have flesh and bones. . . .' And when he had said this, he showed them his hands and his feet. While in their joy they were disbelieving and still wondering, Jesus said to them, 'Have you anything here to eat?'" Interestingly enough, this was Jesus' last question in the Gospel of Luke, "Do you have anything to eat?" They offered a piece of broiled fish and he ate with them.

We can learn a lot about Tutu's spiritual life on the road to Emmaus. As in Tutu's ambivalent South African context of joy and disbelieving, Jesus' disciples experienced the same. In other words, in this human condition there were no static or pure spiritual experiences without the mixture of earthly or sinful experience. Jesus was standing next to the disciples, and yet they doubted. South Africa is now a free nation and still wrestles to be free. Likewise, in their joy the disciples were disbelieving and still wondering. This is the problem of emerging identity; it takes time to actually see what's there, or in this case *who* is there. In this narrative of Luke, the disciples must have felt beyond strange after first running for their lives because of Jesus of Nazareth, then knowing that he was crucified, and then seeing him before them asking, "Do you guys have any food around to eat?"

Jesus' question seems out of place, for such a one as he. Someone who was just killed is not supposed to worry about what's for dinner. Jesus' questions are awkward to us. They seep deep down and sit there, like an awkward dinner guest. In the end, it's really the question of God's presence that makes us so awkward, underneath our patented responses to the whereabouts of God is an ocean of questions. The genius of Tutu's spiritual life is in how he reminds us that we too are on the road to Emmaus, we too are frightened disciples, and in our joy we too disbelieve and still wonder. This is why there are all these questions in us, and perhaps such questions within us can be seen as the convictions of knowing how God emerges in the world.

Theologian James Loder has an interesting interpretation of this questioning process in the Emmaus event.[48] He calls it a process of scanning. Scanning for Loder is the internal dialogue that finds and grows the hope that is already there by establishing a context of rapport and tracing down the roots of that hope in the realities of personal, social, and cultural history. There one finds, in solutions of the past, prototypes for the "new" solution that will open the future.

This is also a beautiful description of Tutu's leadership in the Truth and Reconciliation Commission. I agree with Loder's reading of the Gospel of Luke that the risen Christ does in this Emmaus narrative what his Spirit does in the contemporary transformation of human beings. In other words, the questions in us are the signs of the Holy Spirit convicting us to see what's really there. But how can questions be convictions? Questions here are convictions in the sense that they pose between us and Jesus tangible signs that we are still alive and emerging in our capacity to recognize God and each other.

As we have learned through discussion of purgation, in Christian mysticism, there is the need for an honest void of God's presence to open up before the two disciples can recognize Jesus. His tragic death and their consequent disillusionment in the early part of the narrative are the face of a deeper void, the total annihilation of their lived "world" and the expectation that not only their hopes but also the hopes of their ancestors will come to nothing. They have nearly lost all faith. As stated before, it is important to recognize that their disillusion is comingled with joy. Loder has insight when he says these two men do not recognize that the conflict they feel is not fundamentally derived from their broken hopes for Israel, but from the fact that they had inadequate hopes for Israel to begin with. Jesus' death only begins to expose the conflict in which they were already unconsciously involved. In other words, their hopes for Israel had always been too small. Thus, the divine initiative that Jesus submits to in crucifixion is not a creation conflict; rather, it is an exposing, focusing, and intensifying of a preexisting conflict that these disciples unconsciously brought into their original relationship with Jesus.

So it is with Tutu's spiritual leadership in South Africa. Here we see the presence of Christ in contemporary experience. Much of Tutu's spiritual work was to get us to have a greater hope for South Africa—one in which even white South Africans could discover their emerging identity. Tutu, trained in Christian mysticism, understates the ambivalence of being Jesus' disciple, that Christ's crucifixion and resurrection cause both conflict and joy in us. The conflict is simply the struggle to allow our hope to be more than an individual hope. Because of the Holy Spirit, there can never really be an individual hope, because such Spirit resonates through the self into the lived "world" and back again. If hope is only for the individual, such a person stands on the threatening edge of ultimate void. If hope is communal and interdependent, however, it cannot help but be conflictual and joyful. The Holy Spirit stubbornly persists in the emerging of our identity, offering the hope of transformation in the midst of an otherwise hopeless situation.

The good news here is that Christ walked alongside the disciples to Emmaus.

By cultivating and directing the process in which they are already immersed, he fostered what had been revealed in the crucifixion and the resurrection. The dialogue between the presence of Christ and the self-in-conflict is the means by which he sought to reopen the self to the transcendent. The crucifixion and the resurrection are powerfully demonstrated by the broken bread, because Christ's brokenness is what unites us as we are invited to take such brokenness into ourselves. It is not merely a union of brokenness, because the bread is embraced by resurrected presence. The crucifixion and resurrection are drawn into the most powerful tension possible to produce a new reality in us.

We thus celebrate in the Eucharist a startling new way of looking at things. In effect, in the Eucharist, our eyes are opened just as Jesus the stranger vanishes. Now we see Jesus the broken and resurrected one standing in our midst, showing us the purpose of living in the tension of brokenness and resurrection. Brokenness and joy are ever within us, scanning us, questioning within us to lead us out of false hopes and into transfiguration. Thus, the broken body received from the risen Lord presents a whole new reality, a startling new way of looking at things. In effect, and in fact, "their eyes were opened." But he vanished! Loder asks the interesting question, "How is it that when their eyes were opened, they could see less? This was a marvelous thing because the new Israel was not to be external to them, bound to one place and time, one space and person. It was to be the new reality in which all persons could live, and they became able to compose the 'world' as his World; that is, as it promised to be composed for them, ahead of them, and from beyond them."[49] The holy is also transformed for them, from one who establishes his rulership preeminently in the lived "world" of the cultic and political order of Israel, to the holy who establishes his World in and through all the dimensions of human existence. In short, Jesus' disappearance as their eyes were opened means that his true nature was revealed; they now "saw" the universal range, depth, and power of his lordship, which also included their particular existence. Of course, they could no longer see him "out there" after he had become the lenses through which they viewed all beings and even being itself. Faith as "seeing" always implies that Jesus' perceived physical presence is vital in the lived "world." At the same time we must come to grips with the fact that our lived world also needs to be transcended by the recognition that God is much more than this lived world.

In all of this, Tutu's spiritual life is the stuff that propels our substance of faith toward God. Tutu's restlessness and questions are also within us, questions that we long to ask God face to face. So we need not be afraid of the paradox that, while we are in joy, we too disbelieve and wonder. The Emmaus event in many ways describes South Africa's newfound freedom as it seeks to interpret its existence and nature in light of a resurrected nation. In this sense, South Africa is a young nation. Jesus provides the wisdom that to access the kingdom of God one must become a child. Being a little child means that we have to ask a lot of questions like a little child. In the midst of our conflicts and fear we must remain full of wonder and amazement. Those of us who walk around with all of the answers are the scary people, for we have in many ways fixed a God in our mental closets, a God that we can put on and take off at will.

In the wake of a new constitution and black majority rule in South Africa, Tutu represents both the black community, whose dreams he embodies in its relentless fight against apartheid, and the white community, who find themselves more and more reliant on Tutu's role as confessor. Because of the South African context in which Tutu so effectively articulated the sin of apartheid, his life is exemplary of how a confessor helps the afflicted negotiate the harsh realities of human hatred, particularly in societies founded upon racial hierarchies. Tutu consciously accepted the role of public confessor, thereby conflating his dual roles given him from dual capacities of church and state.

In other words, Tutu is both a man of intense spirituality and a representative of the established, institutional church in South Africa. As a black African, both as the head of a white Anglican Church and as head of a powerful Truth and Reconciliation Commission, Tutu represents a complex set of attributes or descriptions—that is, as a leader of a black community that has come to represent oppression (confusedly in both universal and contextual expressions), and as an international Christian leader with powerful influence in ecumenical circles. Tutu represents the black community (as described above), whose dreams he embodies in his relentless fight against apartheid, and yet he also represents the white community, whose economic power is just as strong today as it was in the colonial era. How does Tutu negotiate this complex set of attributes within South Africa? Tutu gives us insight into his situation back in 1983, stating, "I mean that there are so many glaring inconsistencies in the socio-political dispensation that any self-respecting person has to deaden his critical faculties to survive in South Africa without going mad."[50]

SENSE OF HUMOR

Through a particular Christian spirituality, Tutu learned how to order this complex set of descriptions laid upon him through his charisma, his sense of humor, and his lifestyle, the obvious expressions of his spirituality. Tutu understood the necessity of the spiritual life to make sense of himself and others. He stated, "We should be careful too not to be poisoned by unnecessary jealousy, clergy can be notoriously jealous. . . . It is so important to have a robust spirituality and life of prayer and a good spiritual director/counsellor with whom to talk such things over."[51] Others also understood how necessary the spiritual life was for Tutu.

My own observation of Tutu's ability to draw adherents to himself is that he worked through the paradox of his sincerity and his sense of humor. For Tutu, hearing confessions while at the same time making people laugh is part of his character. His simplicity of lifestyle along with his formal roles allowed Tutu to be an effective healer. Tutu stated, "I know, for myself, that I could not survive at all, if I did not worship, if I did not meditate, if I did not try to have those moments of quiet to be with the Lord. I would not be able to survive. I would collapse."[52] What attracts me to write this biography is that Tutu's intense spirituality embodies his relentless fight against apartheid.

The intellectual and spiritual development of Tutu is important, in that Tutu's character and voice effect not only the South African context, but also an international context of colonial history. Most important is that his Christian spirituality orders competing identities in himself. From this spiritual character Tutu is able to offer healing responses to the perennial questions of racism and human hatred.[53] Similar to how a confessor facilitates in the confessed movement from evil, Tutu's life is key to understanding South Africa's movement from destruction. In this light, the guiding metaphor I present is that Tutu is confessor for a world obsessed with the categories of race.

I claim Tutu as confessor because this spiritual role lends itself more to theological or public warrants in which Tutu unapologetically never leaves Christian spirituality while rallying political and international defiance of apartheid in South Africa. Herein lies much of the controversy that surrounds Tutu's life in politics, particularly the charge that his spiritual commitments often produced the kind of political resentments in which Tutu was seen as partial to certain groups. For example, the question was asked during my visit to South Africa in December 1999: What difference would it have made to the Truth and Reconciliation Commission if Tutu had not worn his episcopal cassock during the Truth hearings?[54] Ironically, Tutu's theological commitments, by which he understands human cooperation, led to political opposition from both blacks and whites who think either Tutu is, at best, an idealist, influenced too much by a Western genre, or, at worst, wrong in his attempt to be both truly African and truly the head of a white European colonial church. In other words, Tutu's competitive identities grow from his ability to act in diverse environments.

As mentioned above, Tutu's paradoxical characteristics enable him to act in different contexts. For example, the following two contexts are opened up by Tutu's sense of humor.

> You clapped for me and my family very warmly. I want to return the compliment but it would be a little odd if I did it all by myself and so since I know that at least tonight you are unlikely to deny me most things, I ask, how about joining me in saying, what splendid people God has produced in all of you. I have to be careful about this kind of thing, because last year my wife and I were in Australia and I was really going great guns in saying to a crowd of young people, 2,000 of them, the trouble with many of us is that we never really celebrate who we are, giving thanks to God for creating us as we are. How about giving yourselves a standing ovation and how about giving God a standing ovation for being such a tremendous God, and they did. They really went to town, brought the roof down, and without thinking at the end of it, I said, "thank you!"[55]

Another humorous example is found in the human need of God's mercy, found in the following account of Tutu's rendition of a story "of a great lady who was having her portrait painted. When it was finished she complained to the artist that it did not do her justice. The artist retorted 'Lady, you do not want justice. You need mercy.'"[56]

Very little academic work has been done on the role of humor and political satire to disarm violent societies of their resentments and hatreds. This biography makes some attempts at showing how Tutu's gift of humor is a key attribute of peacemaking.

CONTROVERSIAL IDENTITY

As a theologian, what further attracts me to his biography is that Tutu is a man of intense spirituality, and yet he is also someone who is representative of the established, institutional church, which in South Africa has often been described as the handmaiden of the oppressive system of apartheid. Tutu represents the black community, whose dreams he embodies in his relentless fight against apartheid, and yet he also represents the white community, whose imperial power is seemingly just as strong today as it was in the colonial era.

How can one claim confessor as Tutu's central metaphor for Christian reflection? And does this metaphor lend itself more to theological or political warrants? Tutu's life provides the illumination that in many instances it is a false dichotomy to juxtapose theology and politics. For example, even though Tutu unapologetically never leaves his spiritual basis, he is somehow able to rally political defiance against apartheid. In the end, though, Tutu is not able to achieve any success in this endeavor without managing various constituent factions. In other words, Tutu knows our relationships contain both theology and politics.

According to Simon Maimela's article in *Hammering Swords into Ploughshares*, different people in South Africa have contradictory perceptions of Tutu's role against apartheid.[57] My objective is to assess the extent to which these perceptions are true reflections of Tutu and his spiritual impact on South Africa. One such perception is in Simon Maimela's question: Is Tutu a political priest or a man of peace? What seems to make Tutu so controversial and revolutionary in the eyes of many white South Africans, and yet complacent and compromising among many blacks? The answer is in Tutu's resolve to work through the church to declare apartheid "the most vicious and evil system since Nazism." In short, Tutu's strength is in making the political struggle a spiritual struggle. Thus Tutu inspires the church in South Africa to dismantle apartheid so as to bring about a new South Africa, visions of which are seen in part 3 of this book. Tutu's spirituality is a commitment that has put him at the center of the political storm. He is viewed by the white establishment as having failed to neatly separate religion and politics so as to confine his ministry to the proper business of the church, namely, the spiritual sphere; and he is viewed by black South African scholars, such as Itumeleng Mosala, as betraying the struggle of the oppressed with too close a tie with European theology. Tutu's competitive identities of spiritual and political are Tutu's greatest controversy.

My bias in this controversy is to construct a particular view of Tutu's spirituality that affords him the crucial role of being politically effective in South Africa. How, as an archbishop steeped in the political mire of liberating his people, does Tutu still function as an archbishop of the Anglican Church? Tutu is unique, not only for being the first black archbishop of the Church of the Province of Southern Africa, but also for completely shifting the "establishment" attitude that often infects Anglican beliefs and pronouncements of the church and, as Michael Worsnip states, "serves to make the Church less courageous in its opposition, less vigorous in its protest and less potent in its rejection of government ideology than it might perhaps have otherwise been."[58] In this light, Tutu's spiritual commitments become political commitments, as he is thrust into a role in which his character and commitments change the traditional Anglican attitude of establishment. A letter to the editor in a South African newspaper captured the sentiment of those hanging on to the establishment: "I want to know why Archbishop Desmond Tutu is so busy condemning the violence committed at St James Church of England when he preaches Liberation Theology (lives are expendable for the cause). . . . Tutu is simply using this massacre of innocent people to further his own cause."[59]

It is my hope that the reader may also infer in what ways Tutu's character illumines the social and political realities of South Africa.

The unique Christian character and witness that Tutu offers is that Tutu's apartheid context disallowed any political foundation by which to appeal for equality on the basis of an existing constitution. For example, figures analogous to Tutu, such as Martin Luther King Jr., could draw from American civil religion and the US constitution. Tutu, however, resisted Western, radical expressions of political theology, since he was aware of differences between his South African situation and that of black Americans. The wholesale importation of Black Power became inappropriate.

Black South Africans did not enjoy any of the civil rights formally protecting black Americans in the United States, which ensured some tolerance of the open expression of Black Power in the US. During apartheid, there was no such formal protection in South Africa, where assertions of Black Power implied a legitimate claim to govern over the white minority. However, there was a church, in fact many churches, in South Africa. This made Tutu's recourse to Christian spirituality all the more important as common ground to appropriately situate justice. The political system of apartheid was a de facto religious system predicated upon white people as God's chosen. Spiritual resistance to apartheid was at the same time ascetic resistance to the demonology of making white people superior to black people. Therefore, Tutu's spiritual character makes Tutu's political impact greater in South Africa as he articulates a society able to confess its sin without such sin destroying hope and a future.

As a result, Tutu's apartheid South Africa was more theologically explicit than the US. South Africa lacks the US's formal dualism between church and state. This allowed Tutu's spiritual appeal to be interpreted as moral appeal. Although Calvinism has influenced the moral ethos in both the United States and South Africa, South Africa in particular, as C. Dunbar Moodie describes it in *The Rise of Afrikanerdom*, is largely defined by an interpretation of Calvinism that makes the Afrikaner civil religion a doctrine for a New Israel.[60] To this day, many Afrikaners think of themselves as descendants of seventeenth-century Calvinist rebels who fled religious persecution in Europe. For the ruling Nationalist Party of apartheid, God created the Afrikaner people with a unique language, a unique philosophy of life, and their own history and traditions. This divine election was stated in the moral appeal of Afrikaner nationalists in 1944, from which four years later apartheid would develop.

Early Anglican history in South Africa proves to be just as contentious as Afrikaners' civil religion. There were inherent and traditional connections between the English-speaking community and the British crown. Such connection was naturally apparent in the Anglican Church, in which military flags and memorials hung in Anglican cathedrals throughout the country, testifying to an English civil religion that pervaded South Africa at the turn of the twentieth century. Members of the Church of the Province of Southern Africa (CPSA) apparently found nothing incongruous about the Union Jack coexisting with the cross and altar, even when blood-stained from encounters with Boers and "natives." Perhaps the extension of the natural link between Anglican Church and British government developed somewhat uneasily into a link between Anglican Church and government in general, which would explain many patently ambiguous attitudes of the CPSA towards the Nationalists' government and its policies in apartheid South Africa.

All this makes Tutu especially interesting in that his political persuasion is rooted in a Christian narrative. He must convince a racial hierarchy that *African* divine election is just as true as the Afrikaner and English visions of divine election. In this competition of Christian narratives, Tutu's role as confessor is most apparent. Tutu becomes the mystical figure able to absolve the sin spawned from Adam and Eve, who defined self over and against the other, whereas God defines self within the other. This makes me keenly interested in the mystical bent of Tutu and his attraction to modern Anglican mystics such as Maggie Ross, who advocates spirituality in which human tears become a sign of the presence of God. Although mysticism is problematic in analysis even in theological discourse, I am primarily concerned with how his interest in mysticism and Christian worship facilitated his role as South African confessor, which in turn facilitated the destruction of both apartheid and the established government that perpetuated it.

RECONCILIATION OR COMPROMISE

The ongoing debate regarding the TRC is whether it brought reconciliation or compromise that favored the white community.[61] Reconciliation provides the potential for peacemaking in South Africa and the world as a whole, while compromise may end up covering up crimes that occurred under apartheid. As stated in the beginning of part 2 of this book, thinking that we can live ideally in a pure state as human beings is not realistic. So caution is needed here as we consider whether the answer here is either reconciliation or compromise. The temptation is to make the South African TRC a scapegoat to blame for the existing ills in society or to use it as an excuse for complacency.

It is true that the TRC's success may be overstated, as when one commentator declared that "never before in modern history has a people told their story so fully and so movingly."[62] Others complained that the TRC "failed to get a proper grip, . . . let alone pin it to the floor."[63] It is important to note here that in its final report, the TRC claimed to "have provided enough truth about our past for there to be a consensus about it."[64] In his foreword to the TRC report, Tutu stated that through the TRC, South Africans had managed to "look the beast of the past in the eye, . . . [so] let us shut the door on the past." Others describe the final report as brilliant, creative, and inventive.[65]

It is important to recognize that the debate over reconciliation versus compromise is far from finished. In fact, these two approaches cannot help but have elements in common. It is difficult to prove that granting amnesty to offenders, as in the Pinochet saga, ever brought consensus in the international community. Maluleke is helpful here, however, in offering three broad types of criticisms leveled against the South African TRC process.[66] The first came from conservative voices who prefer social amnesia. They dismissed the TRC as a witch hunt to embarrass whites and their political parties. P. W. Botha was perhaps the most famous exponent of this view, although some argue that even F. W. de Klerk held this view.

The second type of criticism was that though the TRC was meant to be a judicial commission, it did not consistently pursue "factual truth."[67] Politicians like Van Zyl Frederick Slabbert, a former opposition politician of the apartheid state, appeared to hold this view.[68]

The third type of criticism states that TRC took on an impossible task, in that its conclusions were limited in ways that put victims at a disadvantage, and was not brave and creative enough. Here Maluleke locates his own position and the criticisms of those such as Mahmood Mamdani and Colin Bundy.[69]

Mamdani, a professor of government and anthropology at Columbia University in New York, believes the TRC scratched the surface by dealing only with individual violators of human rights and in turn ignored the issues that led to the violence of apartheid. Instead of defining victims in this narrow way, Mamdani believes the TRC missed out on the opportunity of educating the white population, that although most of them were not perpetrators of apartheid, they were its deep beneficiaries. Mamdani further argues that the TRC—by focusing on a small minority of South Africans, perpetrators and political activists—has effectively absolved whites of responsibility for the harm inflicted by apartheid.

Colin Bundy, a fellow of Kellogg College, Oxford, is a South African historian and former principal of Green Templeton College, Oxford. Bundy influenced a generation of historians to envision the larger South African history. In other words, the TRC serves to separate the apartheid era from the prior history of conquest and colonization. Bundy believes the evolution of the TRC is more responsibly placed in the larger context of South Africa's apartheid history. To some extent Bundy explores the role the TRC has had in (re)writing that history—especially in how the TRC's final report contains a fragmented history.

Maluleke's criticisms mingled with the examples of Mamdani and Bundy are important because they highlight the complexity of separating reconciliation from compromise. He thinks the key failure was in not calling leaders and thinkers (as opposed to just the foot soldiers) to account for repentance in their role in implementing apartheid. Maluleke also concludes that the first type of criticism, that of the witch hunt, is oblivious to the main point of the TRC. However, the second type of criticism, he believes, of the judicial nature of the TRC, is one well taken. This is especially true in light of how South African discourse about reconciliation is not evenly spread between black and white, male and female. Much of the discourse remains white and male—that is, except for Tutu.[70] Maluleke names an interesting fact: none of the black members of the TRC except Tutu have published their memoirs of the TRC process, while almost all the white members have done so. Maluleke has wisdom here in saying that the South African TRC process is instructive, not because it was an unqualified success story but, rather, "because it failed in so many crucial and spectacular ways. It is what we learn from, and do with, these failures—once we have acknowledged them—that matters."[71]

The wisdom here is in focusing not on success or failure but on the emerging identity of individuals and communities into a nation and world. Focus upon success or failure misses the depth of how identity emerges in a fuller reference point. This is why spirituality and God are important. Maluleke believes that what both the critics and the praise singers often miss is the human factor. What is so valuable is that Tutu unashamedly believed in the "God factor" in all this. By this I mean Tutu's optimism was not based in irrelevant idealism; rather, his faith was such that he knew that South Africa as a nation-state would need the transcendent perspective of God to provide a proper reference point beyond self-centered interests and politics. I agree with Maluleke that the human influence of having two influential global icons like Mandela and Tutu, who put all their weight behind the TRC process, mattered a great deal. Here he quotes Albie Sachs, a former ANC activist and now a judge:

I think the TRC report is a brilliant document. I loved it because it was so uneven, it was rough, it had seams, you could see the stitching, and it was authentic, it was real. . . . It contained the passion, the variety, and even the contradictions of the process itself. . . . The TRC's mode of operation was unique. I always mention something that was completely strange to me: that Archbishop Tutu cried. Judges do not cry. We do not have songs at the beginning of the process. We do not have a comforter sitting beside a witness, patting their shoulders, giving them support. Court processes are not human in the way that the TRC processes were.[72]

To illustrate the God factor in the TRC process, we need to recognize the epic and almost biblical proportions of Mandela, a prisoner leading a country as president, and Tutu, unashamedly leading his country without withdrawing from his calling as a spiritual leader. In other words, there is a confessional element to the TRC process that should feel free to claim that Tutu's role as head of the TRC was not accidental or capricious but well thought out: to incorporate the spirituality of reconciliation. A South African journalist concludes: "If the grave and plodding Nelson Mandela is our reliable father, then the hyperactive little figure in ermine at his side [Desmond Tutu] is our naughty uncle, the one who carries all the family's emotional baggage, weeping for us when we grieve, dancing when we celebrate."[73]

Without the human spirit of the likes of Tutu and Mandela being infused into these reconciliatory structures, the structures would probably have collapsed under the intense criticism inspired by long-held mutual suspicions and painful memories. These significant relationships were important to display, in order to see more of the context in which Tutu matured. Tutu is fond of saying how much he depends on others to be himself. For example, Tutu describes Festo Kivengere, bishop of Kigezi, Uganda, as a person who helped form his character as an Anglican archbishop. Kivengere stood up to Idi Amin and escaped with his life to Rwanda just hours ahead of Amin's death squads. Kivengere returned to Uganda after Amin's overthrow to play a major role in the reconstruction of Uganda. Tutu visited Kivengere near the end of his life and later stated, "When I stood beside his bed I realized that his most eloquent sermon had been his life—the manner of his living it and how he gave it up. God be praised for his faithful and dedicated servant Festo. He is now a wonderful part of the cloud of witnesses around us, urging us on in the race that is set before us."[74] In the same way, I offer this biography to say that Tutu's own most eloquent sermon is his life. Tutu's life illuminated, however, does not occur without adventure and controversy.

Perhaps most controversial to Tutu's illumination is the question, To what extent does Tutu represent the "establishment" ethos of Anglicanism? I rely on the third stage of Christian mysticism, union with God, in order to answer this question. In the last part of this biography, I explore how Tutu's life coheres with the seeming contradictions of establishment versus grassroots or spiritual versus secular. In the last part of this book, in which the mystical stage of union emerges, one may see how contradictions exist among Tutu's spirituality, institutional church, politics, and relationships—and how they exist in the interest of truth (i.e., paradox). One may see how such union may illumine a better understanding of Tutu's life. Tutu's multiple identities need not be seen as contradictory or pathological. In fact, I will argue, Tutu provides permission to forge a union of new identities not foreseen. It is not only the church that forms Tutu. Tutu's context of apartheid South Africa also forms him, but his spirituality allows Tutu to overcome many of the seductions of apartheid that sought to normalize oppression and accept the illegitimate power structures as legitimate. Interestingly enough, it is through Tutu's spirituality that one sees that he could never behave as if apartheid were normal.

The greatest religious challenge in the new South Africa is the maintenance of what has become an amalgam of spiritual and political leadership, especially as displayed in the life and thought of Tutu. Now that major spiritual leaders in South Africa are dead, retiring, or moving to more reflective stages in their life,[75] a division has begun between spiritual leadership per se and spiritual leadership that also addresses political life.[76] Now, as South African society looks for the Joshua figures who will succeed Moses, it seems crucial that such a discussion of spiritual leadership should take place in terms of addressing the religious challenges in a new South Africa.

As an African American who lives in the United States, I have a special interest in providing such a discussion, since North American cultures have an extremely difficult time appropriating spiritual leadership that is, at the same time, healthy political direction. It is also important to raise this issue since the United States also seems to have a crisis of leadership with the election of Donald Trump. Tutu could have predicted this tension when speaking in the United States:

> It is one of the ironies of the South African situation that I can here in this great and free country, the land of the brave and home of the free, address so august a body as this and yet in my own country, the land of my birth, I would not be able to speak to a comparable body because I and 23 million other black South Africans are victims of the politics of exclusion. . . . America is a great country with great traditions of freedom and equality and I hope this great country will be true to its moto and tradition and will unequivocally and clearly take its stand on the side of right and justice in South Africa, for what the USA decides and does has a crucial bearing on what happens in other lands.[77]

The South African nation has depended terribly on Tutu's voice to articulate why forgiveness is better than retributive justice. What will happen, however, when South Africans are faced with future political crises without major public spiritual leaders like Tutu?

Tutu's context of South African apartheid presented the dilemma in which he, as ecclesial head of a historically white church, negotiated how to act effectively in a society so defined by race that both Afrikaner and African could claim

God's election as the chosen race. Subsequently, as head of the TRC in South Africa, to say that Tutu's urgency was simply to restore black people to a place of flourishing ignores his profound contribution toward reconciliation of races and toward restorative justice. Because of Tutu's Trinitarian spirituality, in which diverse personhood flourishes in unity, Tutu was obligated to articulate a theology of community in which all South Africans have an opportunity to grow toward unity. Without such a vision of forgiveness and repentance, there likely would have been no future for a flourishing South Africa.

We now look at Tutu's spiritual life as he engaged the newfound freedom of the new South Africa. Illumination is a vulnerable stage of beginnings, and habits entice many to return to the way things once were. But Tutu the confessor represented the clarion call to resist such habits. This guiding idea of Tutu as confessor leads to the conclusion that his life and work in South Africa affect not only the context of apartheid, but the nation's future as well. Getting a new South Africa to confess its sins illumined a difficult but positive path forward for South Africa, but took its toll on Tutu's physical health. Now we turn to examine the toll of such suffering.

Tutu walking to the voting booth in Gugulethu township to cast his vote, April 27, 1994. Author photo.

Chapter 7

Mystical Illumination of Community and Suffering

In our previous chapter we explored the initial stages of illumination in which Tutu learned how to navigate a South Africa in newfound freedom. The illumination of such freedom was cause to celebrate, but it also brought together the gravitas of the past and the need to live in the present moment, while continuously moving toward the future of union with God and human flourishing. In this chapter we move more deeply into the gravitas of illumination, in which remaining conscious of the past in order to live more wisely in the present and future can indeed be a suffering experience. With this in mind, chapter 7 demonstrates how Tutu's spirituality deepened all the more as South Africa's new identity emerged and as his physical health encountered great challenges. South Africa's new identity showed that the road ahead would not be easy. The metaphor here of a baby being born should help ground the reader in the birthing process of a new nation and the growing pains to come.

Throughout much of Tutu's life, he suffered. In 2018, as this book was being written, Tutu was admitted to a hospital in Cape Town for a series of tests before his eighty-seventh birthday celebration, at which the current South African president, Cyril Ramaphosa, spoke.[1] Delivering the eighth Desmond Tutu International Peace Lecture, focusing on restorative justice in South Africa, twenty years after the TRC, Ramaphosa was charged with providing a message that could contribute to international discourse about peace, human rights, and justice in an increasingly globalized world. The most important guest missing from the lecture was Tutu himself. Tutu's health did not allow for him to be present in person. He instead watched proceedings via video link from his hospital bed, where he received treatment for a recurring infection.

Humorously honoring Tutu in his absence, Ramaphosa explained that Tutu had not given him much choice in accepting the invitation to deliver the lecture. If he refused, Ramaphosa said, Tutu had threatened to stop praying for him. It was not a chance he could take. This was a rare moment of levity from Ramaphosa, who came to office after the turbulent presidency of Jacob Zuma, and who often appeared solemn and foreboding as he tried to steer his country forward. Ramaphosa's audience appeared slightly taken aback when the president used his platform to deliver a robust speech to those who doubted the need for accelerated land reform and economic transformation in South Africa. He decried the notion of freedom "when 10% of the population has more wealth than the remaining 90% combined. . . . We will not be able to say we have achieved freedom for all our people until we have corrected the historical injustice of accumulation by a minority on the basis of dispossession of the majority."[2]

The central thesis of his address was that peace in South Africa is impossible as long as economic inequality, landlessness, crime, and discrimination continue to flourish. At the end of his address, Ramaphosa turned his focus to Tutu and his clerical robes, embedded in the national consciousness, and his creation of the term "'Rainbow Nation' . . . out of the expectation that our nation would become one and remain one in perpetuity." Ramaphosa urged his listeners to dedicate themselves to national unity, and to remember that peace is inextricably connected to equality, and reconciliation to justice. A journalist attending the event, Rebecca Davis, concluded, "It was a strong speech. . . . But the Arch's absence robbed the evening of a certain magic, . . . a reminder of how deeply Desmond Tutu will be missed when he leaves us for good."[3]

Ramaphosa's speech reminds us of the work of illumination in staying conscious of the sins of the past while moving forward. Staying so conscious is difficult, because the default mode for many people and nation-states is to try to forget the past. For example, Wilhelm Verwoerd, the grandson of Hendrik Verwoerd, a prime minister of South Africa during apartheid, provides a case in point in the context of such suffering. He writes:

> As pointed out before I am indeed very uncomfortable with the political convictions exhibited in . . . conversations with my parents. I am more and more convinced that a fundamental moral and spiritual critique of Apartheid is necessary to help transform historical pain and to prevent further wounding.
> But in the process it is important to remain as honest as possible with myself; to ensure that in my radical distancing from Separate Development

I am not also running away from my own shadow. Am I genuinely prepared to also face the evil within me? I struggle to accept the literal reality
of being a blood relative, a biological grandchild. However, it seems to be
a more complex challenge to fully become aware and accept how my mar-
row and bones were formed by family-cultural milk. To be really honest
about the large degree to which for more than 20 years of my life I basically
followed in the steps of my Ouparents, Pa and Ma, Ooms and Tannies,
brothers, nephews and nieces.[4]

Verwoerd then narrates his encounter with Tutu during a follow-up to the
Faith Communities hearing of the TRC, where he and Tutu briefly met during
a tea break. Wilhelm Verwoerd was surprised by Tutu's generosity to continue
their exchange about ancestors and reconciliation at a later stage. So he later sent
Tutu two pictures from his youth, one of him sitting on the lap of his grandfather Hendrik Verwoerd, who was feeding him with a milk bottle, and the other
a black Christ painting.

Despite Tutu's fragile health he made time again for a pastoral cup of tea
with Wilhelm. Tutu said a short prayer and asked in Afrikaans, "Hoe gaan dit?"
("How are you?"). Wilhelm was aware of how little time he had with Tutu, so he
jumped in at the deep end by explaining the spiritual turmoil reconciling with
a troublesome ancestor. All this was exemplified in the two photos. Wilhelm
stated, "But I see it as part of my commitment to reconciliation to face the
pain that is represented in that painting, without demonizing my grandfather.
To look for ways how I can help to transform that pain, from a spiritual depth,
not just at a political level, and that's why I thought your wisdom would be very
precious."

Tutu responded,

> I think already the very fact of you being concerned about the anguish and
> the pain that was caused by a policy . . . which he didn't start, remember!
> He came in a long line of premiers. But he was a very, very clever man. He
> could argue the hind leg off a horse. One obviously wishes that he had been
> on the right side. Having said *all* of that, he was a human being like all of
> us, subject to the same pressures. At that time his white compatriots clearly
> wanted a separation between the races, that they should have a superior,
> advantaged position. I suppose he would have been silly—having gotten
> into power by those people—to do a somersault.

Tutu went on, in his role as confessor, to say that it is right to neither demon-
ize nor exculpate. Tutu reminded Wilhelm of those times in which Afrikaners
had just come out of a bruising war with the British to find a home. Tutu laughed
and shook his head at how these people, "my people," dared to call themselves
"Christians." This despite the glaring gulf between vision and practice. Tutu
concluded: "In any case, there is not very much you can do about it! He is your
grandfather. He is your grandfather. He is your grandfather." In Afrikaans, "Jy
het hom nie gekies nie ("You did not choose him"). He is there in your family."

Wilhelm recalls how some black people were furious with Tutu during the TRC for his strong emphasis on the need to forgive. Wilhelm states, "I am concerned that requests for forgiveness by people like me might have more to do with wanting to be freed from a burden of guilt than being rooted in a sincere commitment to restorative justice." Regarding the two photos, Tutu concludes, "This symbolism is part of the pain that you have to bear, I think until . . . I don't know when it will be that we will say, 'Ja, we have to vergewe' ('yes, we have to forgive'), and say, 'he was a product of his time.'" Tutu continues, "Do be careful that you don't want to take on a burden that is unbearable. Yes, acknowledge things that should be acknowledged. And then do what *you* can to make this world a world where such things will be more and more rare." Wilhelm stood up with both hands reaching toward Tutu, "Thank-you very, very much, Father. Thank you for your radical spirituality of including everyone. I hope you will be with us for many years to come!" Tutu responds with a large smile and a warm handshake, "I don't know about that, the way things are with my health. . . . One carries you in one's heart. Ek gaan nie opstaan nie, boetie. Man, ek sukkel...ek is nou 'n ou man" ("I'm not getting up, young brother. It is difficult for me. . . . I am now an old man").[5]

Such an encounter with Tutu illustrates how apartheid took its toll on all sides in South Africa and how Tutu in many ways was the filter. Needless to say, such a filtering process has taken its toll also on Tutu. I think Tutu's contemplative practices have allowed him to enter his elder years and longevity, however. In other words, Tutu has lived a full life. Along the way though there has been much joy but also suffering. In Tutu's advice to Wilhelm I think Tutu provides a theological response that comes out of the illumination stage of his life. This theological response is called theodicy. Theodicy is the question of how God can exist alongside evil and suffering. Tutu's answer is that God creates personhood in such a way as to allow the intelligibility of theodicy. In other words, without the correct relationship of persons, there will be no understanding of good and evil. The blessing here is never allowing the normalcy of evil and oppression. The person's infusion of God's image is the needed light to see how to grow and what to grow toward. The miracle is this: God created us to be infinite, because God instilled God's image in us. Tutu helps us understand this when he states: "The tremendous thing about each one of us is that we have a value which is an infinite value. It resides in the very fact of being created and so we say to the perpetrators of racism and apartheid, your policies are immoral, are unchristian, are unbiblical. You are taking on God for you are saying, God has made a mistake, that God, when he created some black, has made a ghastly mistake so that they have to go around apologizing for their existence. We don't have to apologize for our existence. God created us in his own image."[6]

God's image makes us all infinite. God's image is Trinity. The nature of the Trinity is *homoousios*, which is a description of Jesus used in the Nicene Creed for describing how Jesus is the same essence as God. This term *homoousios* is important concerning who Jesus is, in order to understand how the humanity of Jesus is in common with human beings. The same term, *homoousios*, was later also applied to the Holy Spirit. God as Trinity is not abstract mathematics of binding three individuals, for example, as the classification of reptile is common to a lizard and two snakes. Instead, *hypostasis* is a term that leads us past the category of anything individual, such as snakes and lizards, which are part of the reptilian classification.

Hypostasis, meaning "person," was used at Nicaea as a synonym for *ousia* (literally "to stand under," i.e., "sub-stance"). Over the course of the early church *hypostasis* came to be distinguished from *ousia* and is instead taken to mean "entity." Thus, in the Trinity there is one *ousia* (essence/being/substance) and three *hypostases* (entities or "persons"). So while Christ is both fully human and fully divine, these two distinctions of nature need not compromise the unity of Jesus Christ as a single *hypostasis* (person). In short, theological effort here is to show that there is no fraction in God's nature. *Hypostases* are infinitely united and infinitely different because they are synchronically the divine nature as they uniquely share each other's company. It is by opening up completely to one another that the *hypostases* are able to be *homoousios* without restriction, without being divided. Vladimir Lossky, an Eastern Orthodox theologian, helps us understand when he states, "The more they are one the more they are diverse, since nothing of the communal nature escapes them; and the more they are diverse the more they are one, since their unity is not impersonal uniformity."[7]

Outside of praise and adoration, outside of the personal relationship of faith, and outside of prayer, any Trinitarian language is false. It is only in a poverty of intellect that God lights upon the person who discovers the initial mystery of the Christian faith, namely the Trinity.[8] Tutu states:

> I want us to contemplate the fact that God had no need, has no need of anything or of anyone outside of God in order to be God. So Hegel the philosopher was way off the mark when he said God without the world is no God, because we know by divine revelation that God is fulness of being, pulsating love from all eternity because God is a fellowship, a community, God is a society from all eternity in which God the Son, who is coequal, coeternal with the Father pours forth in return His entire love and being on the Father. The love that binds them together is so immense that this love flowing between Father and Son is God the Holy Spirit. And so, God created us wonderfully, not out of necessity. He did not need us; but gloriously, He wanted us. . . . We are privileged to be God's . . . eucharistic persons who hold everything in trust for God and who are forever saying thank you God for your generosity. We return to you what you have entrusted to us temporarily—our time, our money, our talents, our future lives. We are but responding to and seeking to reflect only your own lavish and magnificent generosity.[9]

As mentioned earlier, Tutu believes that human persons are especially born as potentiality, and without such an environment, personhood does not survive. In other words, people need not kill each other upon a contrived premise that we somehow fully know what it means to be human. Acting with violence, because someone is black or white, gay or straight, or simply different from current norms, does not take into account the dynamic nature of becoming human. Instead, through the tenets of Christian mysticism we should rejoice in how God has created persons different, so that new meanings and identities are always possible.

Unlike many Western forces that seek to "establish" who a person or community is, Tutu's Ubuntu excludes Western environmental tendencies of grasping for competitiveness.[10] The beauty of Ubuntu is that instead of warring factions, instead of being manipulation and self-seeking, when one lives in Ubuntu, that person is "more willing to make excuses for others"[11] and even discover new meaning in other persons. Therefore Ubuntu is an attribute that distinguishes humans from other creatures who, Tutu points out, do not defer to each other, especially when food is involved.[12] Perspective determines actions, and Ubuntu provides an invaluable perspective in which different people may see themselves as more than rivals. "When you look at someone with eyes of love," Tutu believes, "you see a reality differently from that of someone who looks at the same person without love, with hatred or even just indifference."[13] This is how apartheid formed persons not to see the other as a person in common. The legitimization of apartheid structures created the worldview of victimization in which white people no longer saw black people as the common good.

Instead of perpetuating the system of apartheid, Tutu believes that Ubuntu means that personhood ultimately forms through the church, as the church witnesses to the world that God is the one who loves human identities into being. In other words, God's love is prevenient, there before everything else, and calls all justifications for control into account. As a Christian, no one can claim control of life. To gain the vision to negotiate how to be in the world is to access the life of grace in God.

For Tutu, any claim of control or power is delusory and foolish. Jesus teaches his disciples not to trust power; rather, one should trust the vulnerability of love. For example, Jesus entrusted authority, as Tutu explains, to Peter by telling him, "Feed my sheep." Underneath this trust was the awareness that Peter still had a lot of growing to do, because to trust Peter at that stage in his development was like trusting "a thief to become your treasurer."[14] This trust and vulnerability takes us back to theodicy.

If God is omnipotent and good, then why is there evil? Since God is both omnipotent and good, why should people suffer based on how they were created? In light of these problems Tutu asks, "God, on whose side are you?"[15] For Tutu it almost seems as if God wanted to let those who doubt God's presence have a "field day and give sleepless nights to those of His worshippers desperate to provide meaningful theodicies to a skeptical world."[16] God intends to transfigure and transform the world, but currently the whole of creation groans in expectancy of a new creation.

Any doctrine of creation carries the burden of dealing with the problem of theodicy, namely, why does God's good creation remain de facto violent and capricious? Theodicy is the problem of the integrity of creation. Theodicy brings us full circle back to the need for a confessor. Theodicy forces human beings to confess when we behave as if we are not created by God. Any break of human identity from the image of God is sin. The confessor acts as a mirror to this phenomenon and calls human communities back to the worldview that no one should have the hubris to think she or he created herself or himself. We have such hubris the moment facile explanations of race or sexual orientation are used to satisfy those in power.

For Christians, however, a lamb is in power (Rev. 5:12).[17] Tutu states, "In the Bible this primordial mythical harmony and peace were shattered by the advent of sin, so that there was now a brokenness in the entire universe."[18] In light of the inevitability of the breakdown of human systems into culture wars, theodicy questions seek to relate God's providence with creation's tragedy and violence. Despite this tragedy and violence, particularly resulting in apartheid, Tutu thinks that the South African history of apartheid "impregnated the moral universe."[19]

AMNESTY OR AMNESIA?

Before I proceed to discuss Tutu's presupposition of personhood as informing his views of forgiveness, a further word must be said about the controversy of the TRC and the unsung affliction of many South Africans.[20] Such affliction could be seen on October 11, 1996, when the former defense minister, Magnus Malan, and nineteen coaccused persons left their Durban court acquitted from the indictment of murdering thirteen persons, among them many women and children. The Malan trial took place before the Supreme Court of Kwa-Zulu Natal and referred to a massacre committed in 1987 in Kwamakutha, a township close to Durban. Many black South Africans bitterly interpreted this decision as a sign that even after the end of apartheid, everything is meant to remain the same.[21]

Further, the affliction of black South Africans is seen in government offices and other institutions in which top civil servants are still white. The same holds true in the banks and businesses. The fact that much of the economic power still resides in the white community explains why the Reconstruction and Development Program (RDP) did not progress more quickly. Those who prepared the RDP saw themselves as building on the tradition of the Freedom Charter, when in 1955 black leaders articulated a way forward for their needs and aspirations. Mandela stated, "However, in 1994 we are about to assume the responsibilities of government and must go beyond the Charter to an actual program of government."[22] The RDP was a vital step in that process. From 1994 to more recent times this program has evolved; today it is known as the National Development Program (NDP), which seeks to represent a framework of economic progress through 2030.

As South Africa moved beyond its first real democratic election, of Mandela, it experienced the affliction of both poverty and racism, as the formal black political party of the ANC took control. White South Africans were naturally nervous about such a transition, especially in light of their complicity in creating or benefiting from apartheid. Apartheid was an affliction no one could escape. In light of this affliction, Tutu was seen as a controversial figure as head of the TRC. Tutu is very much aware that the National Unity and Reconciliation Act was a compromise, and that South Africans, for the sake of peace, had to live with compromises. Tutu is fond of saying what the alternative would have been without such compromise. South Africa was on the verge of the most comprehensive catastrophe. Tutu states, "Had the miracle of the negotiated settlement not occurred, we would have been overwhelmed by the bloodbath that virtually everyone predicted as the inevitable ending for South Africa."[23]

This edge of catastrophe is illustrated most clearly by *Ubu and the Truth Commission*, a play by Jane Taylor, first performed under the directorship of William Kentridge at The Laboratory in Johannesburg's Market Theatre on May 26, 1997. This play is based on the scandalous character of Ubu in Alfred Jarry's work of the nineteenth century. Taylor fuses the fury of the Ubu legend with original testimonies from witnesses at the TRC. This character from Jarry was introduced first to French audiences as Merde (shit), now as Ubu, who has come to personify human greed and ignorance. He has come to signify Hanna Arendt's description of the "banality of evil." In short, *Ubu and the Truth Commission* is a dramatization and adaptation of evil into a contemporary South African context. Jarry's original Ubu wanders within a conscienceless domain where acts are unjustified by cause and unpunished by effect.

Ubu is forced to confront the consequences of his actions through the testimony of his victims. Significantly, Ubu, the only "nonpuppet" or costumed character in this multimedia production, is difficult to pin down and is not an entirely reviled character. His humanity is most apparent through his relationship with his wife, demonstrating traits both of perpetrator and victim with her. Ubu remains attached to his victims, who through their poignant, idiosyncratic narratives provide horror with a human face. One reviewer wrote,

> But while overseas audiences were reportedly moved to tears by their testimonies, South African audiences—agonizingly familiar with these anguished chapters of a shameful past—are inevitably anesthetized. The fact that in *Ubu*, bad ultimately seems to triumph over good does not allow the audience to experience the catharsis that leads to self-forgiveness. After confessing his crimes Ubu sails off into the sunset—thereby revealing the impotence of the TRC to gain restitution for the victims. And although the

production makes the point that in every situation of evil there are degrees of culpability, all the guilty in *Ubu* use amnesty as the prime bargaining chip and ultimately get let off the hook. At the very least, *Ubu* should be commended for refusing to indulge the audience in a fairy tale ending.[24]

Despite Tutu's logic that compromise and peace are better than retributive justice and war, such a play as *Ubu and the Truth Commission* challenges the Commission's lack of retributive justice through its lack of criminal trials. As I have stated above, the reason for the privilege of amnesty is in the belief that restorative justice lies in the negotiations that brought about an interim South African constitution and, as a result, the first democratic elections in 1994. In those negotiations political representatives used amnesty as a way of getting to the truth and closing the book on an ugly past. Traditionally justice is about punishment, usually imposing fines or prison sentences. But the Commission is based on the idea of restorative justice; although people escape jail, much more attention is paid to the interests of victims. This brings us to the part of the puzzle that is probably most crucial for the victims and survivors, the work of the Reparations and Rehabilitation Committee (RRC).

Because the RRC's work did not make headlines or radio and TV news, it was not widely known. But its importance was brought to public notice by Judge Ismail Muhammad, the deputy president of the constitutional court. Muhammad said that amnesty and reparations are like both sides of a coin: there cannot be one without the other. If the state removes people's right to sue others for the harm they have caused, or to have others prosecuted, then it must find another way of helping. Muhammad gave the important point that under the normal legal system many South Africans who suffered under apartheid would not qualify for help. For example, for many people the law said it is too late to sue perpetrators. But the Commission could suggest to Parliament other ways of helping people instead.

The sheer number of 50,000 cases of those who testified at the TRC portrays the magnitude of the task. As the TRC spread the net of hearings over each South African city and town, the contours of destruction created by apartheid emerged with growing clarity. I had the privilege of attending a TRC hearing chaired by Tutu in Worcester, South Africa, in 1996. Each hearing produced new variations of the daily horror. Whether it be the cynicism of the "special branches" of the police force and their struggle against "communist terrorism," the employment of 16,000 black "special constables" to instigate the "black on black violence," the dreadful disappearances and heinous tortures, the bomb attacks, the "necklacing"—as these horrors were unearthed, waves of shock flooded through the land. There was hardly a day without some reference to the TRC in the media. Jan Munnik, the advocate responsible for investigating complaints against the police, said that "there are hundreds of torturers," still out there, but it was difficult to expose them due to rampant police corruption.[25]

CHEAP GRACE OR INVALUABLE PERSONHOOD

For Tutu, the TRC does not misunderstand justice as cheap grace. Instead, deeply laden within Tutu's theology is an understanding of personhood that sheds light on the image of God as triune. One can never understand Tutu's political contributions until one understands his theology. From Tutu's perspective of Ubuntu, godless systems of justice encourage a high degree of competitiveness and selfishness. Such systems are a rejection of a triune God's creation of interdependence.[26] Tutu shows this as he recounts the creation narrative in which Adam needs Eve as a sign of our interdependency.[27]

> Apartheid says people are created for separation, people are created for apartheid, people are created for alienation and division, disharmony and disunity; and we say, the Scripture says, people are made for togetherness, people are made for fellowship.
>   You know that lovely story in the Bible. Adam is placed in the garden of Eden and everything is honky-dory in the garden. Everything is very nice, they are all very friendly with each other. Did I say, everybody was happy? No, actually Adam was not entirely happy and God is solicitous for Adam and He looks on and says, "No, it is not good for man to be alone." So God says, "Adam, how about choosing a partner?" So God makes the animals pass one by one in front of Adam. And God says to Adam, "What about this one?" Adam says, "Not on your life." "What about this one?" "No." God says, "Ah, I got it." So God puts Adam to sleep and out of his rib he produces this delectable creature Eve and when Adam awakes, he says "wow," this is just what the doctor ordered. But that is to say, you and I are made for interdependency.[28]

Tutu's interpretation of the creation narrative illustrates the profound truth that instead of being made for disproportionate differences, God's creation continually informs persons that identity and relationship go hand in hand. The obsession with individualism and self-achievement is countered for Tutu in Jesus' claims of discipling individuals to move outside of competitive cosmologies. Tutu states:

> Now the radical point about Jesus' question [re: the Good Samaritan] is: Who proved a neighbor to the man in need? You, gathered here, are in fact not meant to discover who your neighbor is (whom you are supposed to love as yourself as the second great commandment). No, you are meant to be asking, "To whom am I going to be a neighbor? Who is in need and whose need I must meet as a neighbor with this privilege and this responsibility?" You and I are the ones who are to be judged for failing to be neighbor to those in need.[29]

It is with this evidence of proving to be a neighbor that African community is intelligible. According to much of current African scholarship, African epistemology begins with community and moves to individuality, whereas Western epistemology moves from individuality to community. For example, Western definitions of "community" connote a "mere collection of self-interested persons, each with private sets of preferences, but all of whom get together nonetheless because they realize that in association they can accomplish things which they are not able to accomplish otherwise."[30] This definition of community is really an aggregation, a sum of individuals. Not only does this go against the true meaning of community, but methodologically, this definition of community becomes an ineffective, circular argument. Ifeanyi A. Menkiti states that John Mbiti's aphorism "I am because we are" does not include an additive "we" but a "thoroughly fused collective 'we.'" However, Tutu's Ubuntu anticipates its own problematic, namely, the needs of the many outweighing the few.

Tutu stresses the Christian definition of relationship, as opposed to other social forms of communalism, to define Ubuntu. Influenced deeply by the spirituality of the Anglican Church, Tutu is able to overcome any tendency to go to the extreme of discounting personality for the sake of community. For Tutu, being properly related in a theological Ubuntu does not denigrate individuality.

> No real human being can be absolutely self-sufficient. Such a person would be subhuman. We belong therefore in a network of delicate relationships of interdependence. It is marvelous to know that one who has been nurtured in a living, affirming, accepting family tends to be loving, affirming and accepting of others in his or her turn. We do need other people and they help to form us in a profound way.
>
> You know just how you blossom in the presence of someone who believes in you and who helps you have faith in yourself, who urges you to great thoughts and yet accepts you as who you are and not for what you have or can achieve, who does not abandon you because you have failed. And you know just how you tend to wilt in the presence of someone who is forever complaining and finding fault with you. You didn't know you could be so clumsy being all thumbs until you got to this lady's house and trust you to break her favorite antique or to drop ashes on her beautiful Persian carpet.
>
> Jesus has had tremendous faith in people and got them having faith in themselves with a proper kind of self assurance, exorcising them from the horrible paralyzing sense of inadequacy that plagues so many of us. After the resurrection He met Peter and did not berate Him for denying Him because he helped him cancel it out through a three-fold positive assertion: "Yes, I love you." To this man who had denied Him, Jesus gave not less but increased responsibility—Feed my sheep. Become—(you vacillating old so and so)—my chief apostle and pastor.[31]

It is worthwhile to explore a bit more what I mean by an African extreme of community. There are three senses of human groupings: first, collectivities, second, constituted human groups, and the third, random collections of individuals. African social and philosophical understandings of human society usually adopt the first usage of human grouping, collectivities, whereas the Western understanding is more like the second category, human groups constituted of individuals. The difference between the two is comparable to what is "organic" and "inorganic." Human collectivities are more symbiotic and act in concert, whereas, a constitution of individuals do not have symbiotic attributes and do not behave together naturally. In an African understanding, human society is something constituted organically, whereas in Western, egalitarian societies, there is more of a nonorganic organization of individuals into a unit more akin to an association than to an African community. These distinctions also play out on the level of personhood.

Many Western views of personhood include primarily the perception of the lone individual, whose essential characteristic is self-determination, whereas the African view of a person depicts the meaning or intelligibility of a person only in the context of that person's surrounding environment. In the African concept of Ubuntu, human community is vital for the individual's acquisition of personhood. However, in Western thought, especially in existentialism, the individual alone defines self-existence. Jean-Paul Sartre's individual illustrates this Western attribute. The Western individual is "nothing [and] will not be anything until later, and then he will be what he makes himself."[32] This Sartrean view of person is as a "free unconditioned" being, a being not constrained by social or historical circumstances. Such Western individualism flies in the face of African beliefs. Not only does the location of meaning solely within the individual separate Western discourse from African understanding of individuals and community. There is also the problem of materialism.

CATHARSIS

Some observers have described the work of the TRC as a cathartic process. They argue that this self-cleansing of necessity had to lead to a turmoil of emotions. Anger, sadness, grief, and shock had to be allowed to surface. Many black South Africans cannot accept the slogans so widely shared among whites, such as "Let bygones be bygones!" When white business people, for example, say that they accept the new constitution of South Africa, how does one know that such people are not engaged in selective acts of amnesia? The emotions that rise in many black South Africans conflict deeply with a disposition that is typical for Western European culture, which regards the past as over and finished. Although Europeans tend to honor their dead, they do not often live with the awareness that the spirits of the dead are still with them, and that it is of vital importance to reconcile the unredeemed spirits of the past.

This, however, is a conviction deeply rooted in black African spirituality. For Africans there can be no peaceful presence as long as the spirits of the dead are not laid to rest. So many relatives of murdered or disappeared persons asked the TRC to help them get back from the police whatever remains of their loved ones exist, in order to bury them in a decent and dignified manner. The burial is the ritual by which a lost member of the family can finally be brought home. This is the way in which the harmony between the generations is restored and maintained. The bringing home of the one who is lost, even the one who is guilty, to the place of the ancestors is a vital aspect of the peace of the living.

This is a spirituality that should not be denounced as belief in "spirits" but should be seen as a worldview that knows something of the fundamental connectedness of all life. It is a spirituality that sees each individual human being as a member of the community, a community that includes both the past and the coming generations. In this context, coming to terms with the past is more than settling legal claims; it is an act of re-membering, of bringing together what belongs together. African re-membering has a lot to do with healing, redemption, and liberation.

Tutu is in the heritage of African peoples whose concepts and rituals provide the notion of reconciliation with profound meaning. Concepts like Ubuntu help African peoples to transcend the violent mechanisms of denial and retaliation that are so typical for Western cultures. It is a misunderstanding of Tutu to think his forgiveness rests in itself. Forgiveness assumes the sovereignty of God, who is enticing all to repentance. White people in South Africa are faced with the question, Will they see the TRC as an opportunity to get a deeper grasp on the spiritual power of their black fellow citizens? Will they learn from them to work for processes of re-membering, of bringing peace to the past for the sake of the present and future? Will they grasp the great readiness of the victims to forgive them as a chance to leave the prisons of shame and the dungeons of denial so that all the people at the Cape of Good Hope can finally be of good hope?

To face these profound emotions is the beginning of healing. As one observes the history of Tutu and the TRC, one encounters something profoundly uplifting. As women and men recall their memories, they are again faced with all their pain and anguish. Yet, as these persons face their suffering, and as they name it in public, they leave the witness stand with their heads held high. They have been recognized in their pain, and this is the beginning of a renewed dignity. There is deep satisfaction, of course. Were they not destined to be annihilated? Now they are poised as heroes. When they were tortured in the prisons, were they not told, "Yell as loud as you wish, nobody will ever hear you!"? Now the nation hears. And the accounts of their suffering are received into the memories of the nation. They were made voiceless; now their voices can be heard across radio and television. Now the names of the torturers that were beyond reproach only a few years ago can openly be mentioned. This correction of history is restoring for all who have been humiliated. The Magnificat of Mary comes to mind: "He has brought down the powerful from their thrones, and lifted up the lowly" (Luke 1:52).

This profound satisfaction is not a subliminal form of revenge; rather, it expresses itself in genuine readiness to forgive. Many victims repeat the phrase expressed by a witness during the first days of the TRC hearings: "I am ready to forgive, but I need to know whom and for what."[33] There is no need to repeat that the TRC process was unprecedented and merits close international attention by persons involved in peace research, legal questions, religious studies, theology, social psychology, and other disciplines. In light of projections of millennial violence associated with racism, it would be important to study possibilities for transferring this process to other conflict areas.[34] It is significant, for instance, that some members of the TRC were invited to visit Rwanda in order to relate their approach to a country reeling from the aftermath of the genocide between Hutus and Tutsis.

The future of the African continent is uncertain as African leadership changes. The vanguard of African leaders like Tutu is slowly bowing out of leadership, while other major figures in black liberation, such as James Cone, have passed away.[35] As leadership changes, it will be interesting to see how an African leader maintains spiritual leadership that is also political leadership. At the end of the day, the success of African community depends largely on leadership that can meet some of the most pressing problems of Africa and the world. For example, in South Africa, the townships are still time bombs that need immediate attention. This would also seem to be the case in many inner cities around the world. Unemployment is rampant, as are the flagrant disparities between the small number of elites and the vast masses of the poor. There is an urgent need to establish spiritual and political reform.

In the wake of prophecies for a new millennium, Tutu's life offers explicit direction as to where (or where not) to look for a new South Africa. Trained in contemplative spirituality, Tutu is aware of the difficulty of keeping human attention fixed both on the divine realm and on political transformation. In fact, without mystical attention to both heaven and social transformation, human beings will err to one extreme or the other, that is, delusion or anarchy. Tutu can be understood through mystical discourse because it reorients Western imagination to the memory that persons are made intentionally, more than just by chance. One may learn from an intentional creation that Christian views of heaven and justice need not preclude deeper ecumenical and interreligious discussions. Among many spiritual and mystical traditions, attention to heavenly reality among earthly reality guards against a capricious understanding of existence, a materialistic understanding of reality that has become the heresy of the Western world.

Despite my own Western identity as an African American, my intention in this biography is to say that one may learn from Tutu's life the desire to pass beyond solipsistic existence into eternal participation with God, who knows how to contain infinity in creation. Tutu's desire to pass beyond Western individualism leads to my method of presenting him in this biography as a Christian mystic and saint. Rather than Western individualistic interpretations of mysticism as a personal reward system for individuals, Tutu's mystical language is rooted in the communal apprehension of mutuality with God and creation. In fact, Tutu's views of heaven and justice commend themselves to ecumenical and interreligious dialogue. From Tutu we learn the following as a paradox and not a contradiction: No one is born to die.

Tutu's spiritual life offers the paradigm in which mysticism is more about communal transformation than Western obsessions of self-fulfillment. This is mystical because an aggregate of individuals can transform into community despite a suffering world. Much of Tutu's thought centers on how the imagination of a perfect environment of personhood provides the proper vision of how to live on earth.[36] The weakness of my approach to a mystical Tutu is in the Western demise of the ability to see spirituality and justice as mutual concepts. This demise of the imagination, I suppose, is caused by Western thinkers like Karl Marx and Sigmund Freud, who believe that mystical attention is delusional and therefore irrelevant. With Tutu, who embodies the struggle for both spirituality and justice, my hope is to recover how mystical imagination is healthy and provides integrity for earthly existence.

In particular, my assumption is that human imagination of what human communities could look like creates a connatural reality between earth's "realized eschatology" and heaven's supernatural intervention. In other words, imagination continually shows persons the telos of their createdness. God is both at the end of creation's journey and at its beginning, coaxing communities to realize their unique distinction in God's self. God interacts with human personality in such a way that God and humanity remain distinct and yet in common. Human imagination, therefore, is a divine gift that is shared in common with God. It is a gift that enables human vision to see through the finality of personal existence. This "seeing through" enables sacramental realities beyond the simple conclusion that life is inherently violent and finite.[37]

The practice of nonviolence demonstrates in my framework that attention to heaven is not delusional; instead, such heavenly imagination self-fulfills an attention span for justice and peace and allows better vision of how to live here, now, on earth. Weil's spiritual writings provide special insight here: "The key to a Christian conception of studies is the realization that prayer consists of attention. It is the orientation of all the attention of which the soul is capable toward God. The quality of the attention counts for much in the quality of the prayer. Warmth of heart cannot make up for it. The highest part of the attention only makes contact with God, when prayer is intense and pure enough for such a contact to be established; but the whole attention is turned toward God."[38]

Prayer as attention to heaven should train persons to seek ultimate goals beyond just individual survival. Instead of seeking only personal salvation in heaven, the goal now becomes mystical—that is, living ultimately as persons in community. Attention to such mystery may prove overwhelming at times. Whether a person can maintain the fixed attitude of "attention" on this paradox, as Weil remarked in her essay on "The Right Use of School Studies," depends not so much on the goal of penetrating God as an object of prayer but on being penetrated by God.

Weil's insights are useful in Tutu's spiritual formation framework because she (like Tutu) offered a vision of self beyond banal and self-serving ends. Weil gives us the insight that never has the individual been so completely delivered up to a blind collectivity, and never have individuals been less capable, not only of subordinating their actions to their thoughts, but even of thinking. Weil helps us see that the world (at least the Western world) socializes persons toward irresponsibility, stupidity, corruption, slackness, and, above all, dizziness.[39]

Weil teaches us that any effort stretched toward serving self-interests alone does not reach. It is only after long, fruitless efforts toward heaven, which often end in despair, when persons can no longer expect anything, that, from outside us, the gift of community comes as a marvelous surprise. In other words, by seeking community, one discovers self. God's gift is the perfection of personhood, which is realized through efforts to realize community. Such attention or realization destroys the false sense of fullness found in individualistic ways of living.

Weil's insight about the paradox of the individual and community is also helpful in understanding Tutu's impact as she further elaborates on the problem of suffering. Weil provocatively stated, "The false God changes suffering into violence: the true God changes violence into suffering."[40] The call of Christ to Christian persons is to believe *through* affliction. Belief must percolate the skepticism of affliction. Instead of the assumption of much modern religious thought, that by an onrush of emotion the skepticism can be permanently dissolved, there must be a true confrontation of evil; otherwise life is lived in a dangerous illusion. Tutu illustrates what a true confrontation of evil may look like in his response to seeing a "new level of poverty and squalor" in Calcutta:

> I was truly devastated by what I had experienced. I wondered about God, about the reality of His love and caring. Why should so much unmitigated and seemingly pointless suffering be happening, especially when one looked on potbellied urchins who looked so dissipated and exhausted so prematurely? Was there any point in human existence? Now these and similar questions I could have asked in almost identical settings at home in South Africa. . . . So much avoidable suffering could happen just because human beings appeared to be incorrigibly selfish, for in my home country one had the distressing spectacle of the squalor and poverty of a Crossroads, a black slum near Cape Town, existing almost obscenely cheek by jowl with the affluence of white suburbia. Where *was* God in all of this? Was it all just sound and fury signifying nothing? Did human beings really count? Why did justice, righteousness and all the worthwhile things seem to bite the dust so comprehensively and often so ignominiously when their opposites strutted about arrogantly?[41]

Percolation of faith within affliction involves *attente*, attention on God, an operation that cannot be hurried. For Weil, this is the subjective counterpart of the operation of Grace itself. "Humility is endless, and *attente* is humility in action."[42] Through her concept of attention, Weil desired to be passive and recipient, rather than seeker and pursuer of truth, which made her reject the "consolations of religion."[43] True attention or apprehension of God shows persons that creation is at the point where love is just possible—a "love," for Weil, which is "not a state but a direction."[44] In many ways, heaven is such a direction. It is a love in proportion to the distance created between God and persons.

Weil's understanding of human attention sheds light on Tutu's spirituality; namely, Tutu learned to depend upon a spirituality in which God is capable of suffering. Sometimes human suffering is so severe that Tutu cries with Teresa to God, "No wonder your friends are so few, considering how you treat them." But suffering, far from saying God has abandoned us, thinks Tutu, says we are called to suffer for the salvation of the world. So when a church suffers, God relies on them to be the salt of the earth, for if we fail, to that end God fails. Tutu recounts how, in a favorite book of cartoons by Mel Calman entitled *My God*, there is a humorous scene depicting God looking somewhat disconsolate and muttering, "I think I have lost my copy of the Divine Plan."[45] Looking at the state of the world, Tutu concludes, one could be forgiven for wondering if God had any plan at all.[46] Continuing in a humorous tone, Tutu states further:

> I do not know about you but I have often found the best literature in most homes in the loo. Once I was visiting some friends, and I came across a book of cartoons entitled *My God*—It had charming line drawings . . . and I came out an hour later. Some of them were quite delightful. One showed God with all of us directing all kinds of contradictory requests to Him and God says, "I wish I could say 'Don't call me, I'll call you.'" The one I would like to refer to shows God looking somewhat disconsolate as He reads a poster which declaims "God is dead" and he says, "That makes me feel insecure."[47]

In a suffering world seemingly void of community, Tutu believes that human persons are especially born as potentiality. If human beings, for example, would grow up individually among wolves, they would not know how to be human. There would not be human posture or human ways of eating, sitting, and walking. Therefore human beings become persons only by living in an environment conducive to the interaction of diverse personalities and cultures. If there is no such environment, personhood does not survive. Tutu proclaims infinite personhood from Christ's teachings that one must be born again, and that even the reality of death may not hold us to meaninglessness. As Tutu states, "Who says that death is the worst thing that could happen to a Christian?"[48] The Western mind, on the other hand, asks the question of Nicodemus, "How can these things be?" Tutu adheres to Christ's response, "If I have told you about earthly things and you do not believe, how can you believe if I tell you about heavenly things?"[49]

UBUNTU AND SUFFERING

Tutu's understanding of community is found in his concept of Ubuntu, which implies that persons discover personality through interrelationship. Tutu believes that God creates personhood in such a way as to allow the intelligibility of heaven and justice. In other words, without the correct relationship of persons, there would be no understanding of good and evil. The person's infusion of God's image is the needed light to see spiritual growth and to see the telos of such growth, namely, heaven. Ubuntu informs an image of heaven in that it displays a communal milieu in which God resides. In God's environment, persons are created infinite, and are continually infused with God's triune, communal image.[50] Tutu states: "In our African idiom we say 'a person is a person through other persons.' . . . We are different so that we may know our need of one another. . . . We forget again that our unity is meant to reflect the unity of the triune God, a unity in the diversity of persons."[51]

Tutu's Ubuntu seeks a paradigm in which the affliction of African people can be transfigured through forgiveness instead of vindictive vengeance.[52] Instead of retaliation and a further competition of black and white Christian narratives for God's privilege, Christians in South Africa are to fall toward heaven and see that their God also was afflicted. Even if African people seem hopelessly trapped in the closed system of apartheid and racial classifications, the image of God is planted in all human beings in such a way that its slow, vegetative movements, responding to light, will one day manifest the kingdom of God. Weil's concept of God's grace as light that percolates creation is harmonious with Tutu's restorative justice.

For Weil, grace percolates through the interstices of creation. Light can percolate all things; it can remain stored up, like solar energy, in the darkest and most opaque substances, like apartheid. Therefore grace is hidden in the world, as holiness is hidden in those invested with it. Tutu provides this example:

> On the same trip to Calcutta I had the privilege of visiting the Home for Derelicts, which the compassionate Mother Teresa had founded. On that occasion I did not meet the great lady herself. This home was one where the veritable dregs of society were brought in to live out their last few days with some of their long-lost dignity restored. Many had festering sores and the dying must have in a real sense been disgusting. But now they were being tended by young nuns who wore truly beatific smiles as they cradled feeble persons in their arms, feeding them as if they were so many doting mothers with their favorite children. There was an almost uncanny lightness about the room. I experienced then divine love incarnate in the ministrations of those nuns, who treated their charges with a deep reverence as if they were caring for Jesus Christ Himself.[53]

Persons must await God's covert arrival, for light is always silent in its operation.[54] Weil's vision of injustice is the "rootlessness" of modern culture as not merely a rootlessness in nature, but even more as a rootlessness in time. The destruction of the past in Weil's view is "perhaps the greatest of all crimes."[55] Weil's penetrating vision consists of demolition work in which the sacred hermeneutics of the Western individual are challenged, that is, the modern obsession with "rights," the idea of material progress, even the gospel of work.[56]

"The great mistake of the Marxists," Weil has written, "and of the whole of nineteenth century, was to think that by walking straight on one mounted upwards into the air."[57] As postmodern theologians such as John Milbank point out, modern social theories, however humanitarian in impulse, are one and all impregnated with the seed of violence.[58] The beauty of Weil's vision is in the ironical notion that it is better to wait upon the past than to wait upon the future, for "the past presents us with something which is at the same time real and better than ourselves, something which can draw us upwards, a thing the future never does."[59] Therefore, movement to heaven is not so much an endeavor for the future as it is a cultivation of what is already considered this life.

Consequently, the past is a "need of the spirit."[60] The future, Weil implies, is the artificial bait that an unscrupulous leader dangles before a dissatisfied people. The food promised is liberty, which can be promised only in the future, thereby depriving the afflicted of it in the present, except in name. Such trickery can be practiced only upon the collective, which cannot know that it is the victim of deception: for "a crowd cannot add things together."[61] If the same chicanery is practiced upon a formed person, the result will be to make that person conscious of servitude. That is because that person preserves at least the memory of past freedom through that person's community. The collective ironically has "memory" only of the future. In other words, a mob has no past. "That is why a rabble can assemble day after day to listen, bemused and even exultant, to the same catalogue of unfulfilled promises."[62]

In the end, Weil's vision collapses hierarchy that engenders the idea that the oppressed are in such a condition because of a lack of intelligence; darker-skinned peoples are naturally oppressed because of the evolutionary process in which white people are superior. The idea of equality must be guarded against, because it is a force of instability; "it spells the end of that measure of natural equality which every stable society necessarily contains."[63] Thus the opposite of hierarchy is not, as the revolutionists believe, equality, but anarchy; for when hierarchy is disrupted, there is a violent oscillation between one form of inequality and another, issuing in a confusion that may be mistaken for adjustment or "progress." Uprooting people and dumping them as rubbish puts an end to every vestige of natural equality; it is the condition of being rootless that was the impetus of the oppressor in implementing apartheid. Rootlessness is the most severe form of affliction.[64]

Despite the beauty of Weil's work, the mysticism in Weil, the language of paradox and contradiction, often ends up in a lack of constructive display, which in my view seems to be corrected by the relational concept of Ubuntu. Weil is helpful in her theological claims, which suggest that rationalism is often sustained at the price of pretending that evil is somehow unreal. In this regard, Tutu seems closely aligned to Weil's conclusions as he states: "The last mark of the operation of the Spirit seems to be that those who are chosen to be His special instruments are destined for suffering. . . . Those who are God's friends are distinguished by the fact that they suffer. . . . There is unbroken link in the mystery of service and suffering, witness and persecution, stretching from the Old Testament to the New Testament. . . . A church that does not suffer cannot be the Church of Jesus Christ, the suffering servant of the Lord."[65] However, Tutu's Ubuntu offers a model beyond individual claims of rationality by which to solve problems of theodicy. Tutu states:

> What we know is that God's intention, God's dream, is to establish a fellowship that includes us all, in which the physical, moral, and spiritual environment share, where there will be wholeness (shalom), where there will be physical and spiritual well-being, where all will care for each other, where laughter and joy, compassion and caring, peace and sharing, life without end, goodness and righteousness, justice and reconciliation, togetherness and fellowship will have prevailed over their baneful counterparts. This is sometimes called the Kingdom of God. God calls on us to be fellow-workers with Him, to be agents of transfiguration to help Him bring this to pass when the kingdoms of this world become the Kingdom of our God and His Christ and He shall reign forever and ever. Amen.[66]

To say with "analytical" philosophers that such a "metaphysical" world is impossible, or that Tutu's eschatology represents emotionalism, presents false dilemmas between rationality and Christian faith.[67]

Instead of typical Western dualisms of rationality and faith, freedom and will, Tutu follows an Eastern theological tradition that places revelatory emphasis upon our relation to what God has already revealed in the world. Most importantly, Christ reveals the salvation of the world, but such a revelation does not require control or domination on our part; neither does it claim a banal observation of a "new heaven and new earth" already complete on earth. Instead, aligned to the Eastern church, Tutu's theological construct refuses the Augustinian and Pelagian split of grace and free will. God created us to be responsible for others, in fact to know our identity through others, because God desired that our movement toward God's life be a movement of participation in the divine life, a life that implies freedom. As Gregory of Nyssa states: "As the grace of God cannot descend upon souls which flee from their salvation, so the power of human virtue is not of itself sufficient to raise to perfection souls which have no share in grace. . . . The righteousness of works and the grace of the Spirit, coming together to the same place, . . . fill the soul in which they are united with the life of the blessed."[68]

Instead of only a disparity in creation between the elements of grace and freedom, Ubuntu exists between God and human beings, who toil together in the salvation of creation. This toil in many ways is a description of ascetic theology mentioned above as the study of spiritual disciplines and practices. Earlier, I reflected a great deal on how such ascetic discipline influenced Tutu through Trevor Huddleston and the CR. But Tutu was influenced by Christian ascetics throughout his life. For one example, Tutu states:

> I recall on one occasion speaking to an Anchorite [monastic living in iso-
> lation] and she spoke to me of her life of prayer and I said, "Please just tell
> me a little about yourself" and she said, "Well, yes Bishop Tutu, I live in
> the woods in California. My day starts at 2:30 in the morning and I pray
> for you." I am prayed for in the woods in California at 2:30 in the morning
> and then you are able to say, what chance does the government of Mr.
> Botha stand?[69]

The anchorite Tutu speaks of is Maggie Ross, whose book, *The Fountain and the Furnace: The Way of Tears and Fire*, explores why disciplines in the Christian life remain vital to our freedom. The story of the fall reminds us that our control of the knowledge of good and evil is only partial. In attempting to control evil, we not only compound our futile grasping at knowledge that is beyond our creatureliness, but we create a hierarchy in which human identities according to superior races are assigned to material creation. Even more insidious is that such a hierarchy becomes implicitly defined as God's created order. Ross explains that what seeks to remain invisible, namely, evil, seeks to be anonymous in the mystery of God, and remains beyond our categories of definition.

Ross, a profound influence on Tutu's theology, declares that what (who) saves us from evil is known in the familial nature of God who is so kenotic (invested in the act of pouring out of God's love through Jesus) that mercy is willing to enter and pour through creation, not only when it is at its best, but most of all, when it is at its worst. Kenosis is when God willingly limits God's power in the self-emptying action of Christ, as described in the Philippian hymn (Phil. 2:5–9) in which God takes the form of a servant, being born in the likeness of human beings. Ross concludes, "And God incarnate in Jesus is willing to be made an object by the creation in order to overcome the abyss between subject and object, and thus destroy death and the fear of death."[70]

Ross's view of kenosis, in which God has been emptied into creation, provides the conceptualization for Tutu to proclaim that loving God is authenticated by loving neighbor.[71] Tutu's theology is in sync with Ross's as he states, "God is will-ing to limit God, to inhale—whatever image seems appropriate, God is willing to become empty. Or rather, in this image, to make an empty place by dispers-ing a bit of the density of glory. God in this way, as well as in the incarnation, becomes involved with creation."[72]

Tutu also illustrates God's kenosis through Adam and Eve, who were befriended by God in such a way that God made them like God so that they had space to be persons, free to love God or refuse to love God, free to obey, or not to obey God. To be made in any other way would have denied God's kenotic nature, i.e., "God's readiness to limit the power of God, so that creation and humanity could exist in freedom and integrity."[73] Similar to Ross's theology, Tutu's understanding of God from all eternity conjures the image of a blazing furnace of holy love in which the Father pours forth all of God's being to the Son who, coequal and coeternal with the Father, pours back in equal measure his entire being in an eternal self-emptying to be filled without ceasing—with the Holy Spirit binding the Father and the Son together forever. Tutu concludes:

> This kenosis, this self-emptying, this self-giving is an abiding characteristic of our God. This utterly self-sufficient God created all there is because God loved it. God loves it now. And God will love it forever and ever, world without end. Human words are inadequate to comprehend and describe this divine mystery. In the end we can only be silent . . . . God created this world because God loves, and when things went wrong, because of sin, God redeemed it. God in Christ emptied God's being of divine glory and God paid the price for our sin. It is all mystery, ultimately, and we cannot hope to encapsulate it in words. Words become an obstacle and a barrier. Instead, we need silence in the presence of this God we worship and adore, to be emptied of ourselves and to be filled with God, and so to become more truly ourselves as we are filled with the fullness of God.[74]

Ross, an Anglican anchorite mystic, influences Tutu toward a kenotic theology in which the sacrificial and relational means by which God is present to the world are crucial for how we may serve society as Christians. God is present to the world through suffering for others. This kenotic nature of God becomes crucial for how Tutu envisions the church serving his particular context of South Africa. Kenosis presents a different kind of reality of love. Ross's account of kenosis demonstrates that to sin in the face of unalterable Love is much more painful than to sin in the face of an implacable authority. A person's return to God, having sinned, and having returned God's gaze, restores a loving exchange in which oppressive racial classifications can be broken down. The effects of apartheid's heresy are transformed. Caught up in kenosis, human turning to God enables even fragmented identities to be made whole through creation and re-creation in the pure fire of self-emptying Love.

Although kenosis is often relegated to mystical discourse as problematic in its lack of a display of sustained theological claims, Tutu's affinity for kenotic theology encourages him to conceive how disparate identities of race, caused by apartheid, can be reconciled in God's relationship to the world. Kenotic spirituality as articulated by Ross enables Tutu to proclaim God's justice as the act of self-emptying in a corrupted order that already sees itself as just and true. A view of a kenotic God allows for harmonizing the Christian narratives of the African and Afrikaner instead of furthering their competition. Tutu insists, "we worship a God who is a weak God. We worship a God who is a dying God. And through that death life comes."[75]

A theology of kenosis challenges conventional theology in its cultural assumptions that justify both anthropomorphic models of humanness and practices of political and economic power. The subversive force of kenotic assertion extends not only to theological discourse but also to the derivative forms of social power that justify political structures. Western preoccupation with dominance and power is no doubt linked to and derived from our imperial "image of God." Clearly when the discernment of the imperial image of God is challenged, such an image, and its public forms, can be exposed and exorcized as demonic. Through kenosis, such images are not only exorcized, they can now be deemed heretical. Tutu states:

> God is ready to jeopardise the success of God's enterprise by engaging as God's partners those such as ourselves, wayward or impotent as we know ourselves to be. The divine human partnership is termed theandric. We see it in the very composition of the Bible where God speaks in the inadequate human words of God's human partners—God's eternal Word spoken through time-bound words; God is ready to be understood and misunderstood as God's human partner can understand and misunderstand God. God is ever willing to be immersed in the human condition, the Human mess, not standing aloof on some inaccessible Olympian height to shout down useful advice, but God coming down ultimately identifying so fully with our condition that God had to become a real human being, thrust through with the excrutiating agony of the sword of our alienation and fragmented life. God calls us to be co-workers, co-creaters and co-redeemers with God.[76]

Most important for Tutu's spirituality is that God does not remain inaccessible, like some Aristotelian unmoved mover. God empties God's self to become involved with suffering people, even when they were cast into the fiery furnace. Human oppressors then see a fourth and mysterious figure walking about with the three that were originally thrown there (Dan. 3:24–27). The Old Testament, having struggled with the problem of righteous suffering, reaches a zenith in the so-called Songs of the Suffering Servant of Yahweh, especially Isaiah 52:13–53:12, and how this text describes vicarious suffering, that is, suffering not for one's own sake but on behalf of others, even on behalf of others for their salvation. Herein Tutu takes solace that there is a redeeming value for how black people have suffered, that perhaps here, with the Suffering Servant, there is a clue about the inevitability of suffering in the economy of salvation. Therefore, Ubuntu addresses the theodicy of African suffering in that their severe suffering is not in vain and that suffering has salvific significance.

There is identity and solidarity with the Suffering Servant, an identification that happened when Jesus agreed to be baptized, causing for some a theological problem. We see this in the conversation that Matthew records as having taken place between John the Baptist and Jesus (Matt. 3:6; cf. 3:13–16). If John's baptism was an acknowledgment of sin, how could the sinless one have needed to be baptized? We are again in the realm of mystery, the mystery of what it cost God to redeem us. "Which one of us can know what it meant for the all holy, perfect man to be so close to sin that he had to utter that awful cry of dereliction, "My God, my God, why hast Thou forsaken me?" (Mark 15:33–36).[77]

Since Jesus did not enter glory without suffering, and his glory accomplished the salvation of the world, the followers of this Jesus have no other way to heaven except through justice: the gateway of passion and crucifixion, through Good Friday (Matt. 10:24–25).[78] Jesus makes it abundantly clear that heaven without suffering is impossible (Matt. 10:17–39). In short, for Tutu, a person who is a person through others cannot follow Jesus into heaven without suffering (John 16:1f; Matt. 10:38; 16:24–26). So a church that does not suffer cannot be the church of Jesus Christ. Christ calls forth a beatitude on behalf of those who suffer for the sake of the kingdom's righteousness (Matt. 5:10–12). Tutu states, "The authenticity of our witness and loyalty will be tested by whether the world loves or hates us (John 15:18–21), for we must be like Our Lord and Master in this if we are to be His disciples. What Shylock says in *Merchant of Venice* applies to Christians aptly—suffering is the badge of all our tribe."[79]

With the attention of the person to God's presence in heaven, we are enabled to discover how to become enough of a person to commune with God. This view, that is, becoming enough of a person, safeguards our anthropomorphic tendencies of making an abstracted polis into heaven. In other words, human imagination is the corrective humility that in the world the search of the human soul for heaven is really the effort of staying awake as a person in the presence of God, rather than existing merely as an animal.

Tutu's mystical understanding of community was explored in this chapter in light of his response to his own suffering and suffering in the world. The mystical stage of illumination sheds this light on the struggle to stay conscious of the pain of the past and the courage to live in the present and press toward a future. The deeper we get into illumination, the closer we move to union with God and human flourishing. With this in mind, chapter 7 has demonstrated how Tutu's spiritual life deepened all the more as South Africa's new identity emerged.

We now will look more closely at Tutu's struggle with racial identity as he moved into his elder years. Coming to grips with racial identity continues to be a perennial problem, not only for South Africa, but for the rest of the world.

Written on a street near Bishopscourt, Cape Town: "I was Anglican till I put Tu and Tu together." Author photo.

Chapter 8

Tutu's Racial Identity

This chapter on how the mystical stage of illumination informs Tutu's spiritual life will examine more closely the confrontation between the church and racism. In helping the church of South Africa to confront their own racism, Tutu helped to renegotiate racial identity in a postapartheid society. Inasmuch as he conducted such a negotiation, he demonstrated his life's pursuit for a rainbow nation called South Africa. As Tutu articulated how God created humanity in God's image to be both particular and universal, he also explored how we can move beyond the narrow constructs defining what it means to be human. Such narrow constructs include the institutions of denominational Christianity, partisan politics, and more. Tutu's search for ever-new identity nevertheless illumines Tutu's restless character of spirit represented by Augustine's axiom, "My heart is restless until it rests in you." This irresistible pursuit in Tutu to go beyond limited definitions of what it means to be human has allowed him finally to move from this illumination stage to the last mystical stage, union with God.

In order to further understand Tutu's identity as confessor, it is important to see Tutu's image of the rainbow people of God.[1] The rainbow image was used by Tutu to inspire people of all races in South Africa to move past the idolatry of the white race, which seemed to think it had a license to control other peoples in

189

the name of God. Tutu reminds us that God gave the rainbow in the Bible as a sign of peace, or *shalom*, in which all of creation could exist in all its diversity while at the same time being God's one creation. Different colors could represent different people made in the image of the rainbow people of God. For Tutu, racism is the symptom of a dominant people who not only want to wrongly divide humanity into a hierarchy based on race but also want to carry such discrimination further, into inequities based on sex, gender, nationality, socioeconomic status, religion, and more.

The image of the rainbow acted as an antidote to the far-reaching virus of racism, which could easily evolve into other kinds of "isms" and hegemonic policies. So it was important to use spiritual language to get at the root cause of racism; hence, apartheid is indeed sin—in need of confession. We see how Tutu's identity was formed by his courageous struggle against the violence of racial categorization. South African leaders like Tutu risked their lives in order to envision a whole South Africa in which not only black and white people coexisted, but so did all of the rainbow nation. This risk was inspired by Tutu's spirituality, a spirituality that would not let him be content as long as others were being treated as less than the children of God they were created to be.

Christian leaders like Tutu provide an example in which the two prominent African and Afrikaner identities have to decide on building a constructive future or continuing to face the ravages of civil war. Not only have Christian leaders greatly affected black political protest in South Africa; South Africa's racial context also affected theology, which evolved into a theology of the oppressed and exploited. In the end, this dynamic process proved constructive for the South African church, which then influenced the creative process of truth and reconciliation. Thus divergences and convergences among Christian leaders allow for creative theological and political reflection so as to avoid a paralysis of constructive change in South Africa. Let us at least hope and pray this is the case. Tutu seems to best exemplify how to avoid this paralysis, because he recognized that he must now lay down his leadership mantle in order to allow others to lead. No doubt Tutu's spiritual training provided him the wisdom to know the humility and practicality of when enough is enough.

FORMING A RACIAL IDENTITY

In some ways it is anachronistic to describe Tutu in racial terms. In Tutu's mind, the search for identity was more in keeping with whether he was Xhosa or Tswana. According to some South African scholars, the gestation of South African (i.e., African and Afrikaner) attitudes toward culture and race happened as a result of the country's industrial revolution, which scholar Gail Gerhart describes as "that period roughly from the discovery of minerals in the 1860s and 1870s until the first major boom of manufacturing in the early 1940s."[2]

But it seems more correct to begin with the arrival of European colonists in southern Africa in 1652, as they used severe force to conquer African societies and to possess the land. As a complex relationship between the British and the Afrikaners developed in the nineteenth and early twentieth centuries, the process of conquest of the indigenous peoples of southern Africa was a central part of the development of a modern, industrial South Africa. Once white hegemony of the Afrikaners and the British was secure over the Africans, the demand for black workers, at minimal cost, grew tremendously for industries such as mining. In order to ensure white control over all aspects of African movement, a welter of pass and permit laws was instated to "expel all 'surplus' urban residents."[3] In effect, as Gerhart's thesis implies, Africans were viewed as commodities that a white government should control.

At the turn of the twentieth century, one encounters what may be called the Segregation Era,[4] 1910–48, a time in which the process of white control was at work through legislative acts directed at pushing Africans farther off the land. Through taxation, rural Africans were forced into wage labor, a process that defined away any access to the power structure of this new nation of South Africa. Shortly to follow was the Native Land Act of 1913, which prohibited Africans from buying land outside the limited reserve areas. As a result of this systemic control of Africans, by a newly formed government of Afrikaners, at the turn of the twentieth century African political organizations emerged, in reaction to what was perceived as inhuman "native" policy that discriminated against Africans in an Afrikaner economic and political system.

Before Tutu was born, these early African political organizations included in particular the South African Native Convention,[5] which first met in Bloemfontein in March 1909, a seminal organizing event in the history of African political activity in South Africa. The trigger that precipitated this formal African political unity was the release of the 1909 draft constitution for a united South Africa, a draft that had been unanimously approved by the parliamentary representatives of the four colonies: the Cape, the Orange Free State, Transvaal, and Natal. Concomitant to the passing of the draft act was the hindering of the right of Cape Africans to sit in parliament, thereby continuing the exclusion of Africans from participating fully in the political institutions of the new state. In response, blacks from all four colonies cooperated for the first time and formed an umbrella organization. At this meeting the SANC clearly spelled out their opposition to the terms of segregation in the proposed union of a South African state and stipulated nonracial conditions that would have to be met in order to make the proposed South African union acceptable.[6]

Here, in the struggle between Afrikaner and British conceptions of race relations, was one of the clearest signs of the beginning of an African national identity. The British placed Afrikaners in de facto concentration camps at the turn of the twentieth century as both the British and Afrikaners conducted their scramble for Africa. Partly as a backlash resulting from this experience of oppression, Afrikaner racism became more explicit in apartheid laws while British racism receded more to the background as its colonialism began to wane. In order to exist in what would become the nation of South Africa, early African leaders fought dramatically to be recognized as full citizens and complete human beings. As the plot thickened, the nascent identity of African political organizations continued to grow around nonracial ideologies that provided public awareness of the human dignity of the African peoples per se (i.e., Tswana, Xhosa, Zulu, etc.). A more concerted effort was made after the black delegation to Britain failed in their attempt to appeal the draft South Africa act. In 1912, the South African Native National Congress (SANNC) became a permanent national organization, as the various African groups from all the provinces gradually coordinated their efforts toward the political reform of nonracial unity. As segregation laws became more restrictive in the 1920s, the SANNC continued to evolve in its character as the main African political organization, and in 1925 it finally changed its name to the African National Congress (ANC).

As African political consciousness grew in this early South African society, white hegemony used different means to oppose the idea of nonracial unity. As a result of the momentum among the ANC to unite Africans around the goal of a nonracial Africa, the Native Affairs Commission in 1921 declared "that the town is a European area in which there is no place for the redundant Native, who neither works nor serves his or her people but forms the class from which the professional agitators, the slum landlords, the liquor sellers, the prostitutes and other undesirable classes spring."[7] In response to this vast array of societal ills from which whites form a derogatory definition of blacks, a political consciousness of protest eventually formed a counter African identity capable of surviving against a white government seeking sovereignty in a predominantly black land. Indeed, the increasing governmental control of black settlement, movement, and labor created a hostile environment for blacks, in which they had to struggle to maintain any semblance of hope for nonracial reforms.

RELATIONAL THEOLOGY

In order to access Tutu's spiritual contribution to the world by his work against apartheid, one must understand his integrative approach of relational theology.[8] A major distinction of Tutu's leadership is that he places universal requirements on the church's work in the world, to unite all peoples to each other and to God. Yet paradoxically Tutu maintains that in order for the church to be the church in South Africa, it must be faithful to the particular nature and work of reconciliation in South Africa. In short, there must always be the proper relation between the universal and the particular. Tutu wrote in 1984:

> We must have examples immediately that the alternative society which is the Church alive is possible and viable. It is important in a grasping, selfish society, for us to demonstrate in small or large church groups that it is

possible for Black and White genuinely to share. We may have to run the risk of breaking the law—but I think they have told us that they would much rather obey God than man. And unfortunately too many have been brainwashed into thinking that legally right and morally right mean the same thing. It is illegal in this country for church groups to meet for more than a day without permission. It is eminently not immoral to do so. And this sharing of worship and insights and resources must not be only for special occasions. It must be our lifestyle.[9]

Tutu devises a relational approach to theology by refusing the common either-or hermeneutic of juxtaposing contextual theologies against each other. For instance, Tutu refuses to separate black, African, and liberation theology. He is able to do this because of his strong emphasis on the universal church that all Christians are called to work through, in order to one day experience a reconciled creation.

Much of Tutu's insight concerning this complementarity comes from his Anglican tradition of via media, in which one should always seek to comprehend the whole. Thus Tutu is an African and black theologian, and yet he is also a liberation theologian who struggles with the theodicy questions of why the poor are always with us and how we may live harmoniously in a violent world. Black and white are inescapably bound together; if they do not move together, then they both will vanish, which, as Tutu would say, is an "alternative too ghastly to contemplate."[10] In order to place Tutu in further context, one needs to assess the development of South African political protest against apartheid in light of this ghastly contemplation. In light of a South Africa that was conquered by force and ruled by force, my central concern is to show how Tutu's relational theology accentuated his identity as South Africa's confessor—a deeply spiritual and political identity. This inquiry naturally leads to the question, What difference does the church make in South Africa's politics?

I presume that the crucial difference in maintaining black political protest in South Africa is the character of the community called the church that subverts any government's reliance on coercion as a means of political domination of creation. Our means of answering the above question concerning the impact of the church in politics can be seen through how Tutu acted as both political and Christian leader, a combined identity that has proven to be common to Africans in the forefront of black political protest.[11] By examining Tutu's hybrid identity as spiritual and political, it is my conclusion that the Christian church has become a major catalyst in moving South Africa away from a violent alternative too ghastly to contemplate. Crucial to this argument is the powerful impact of Christian missions on African politics, which is reflected in the backgrounds of generations of African political leaders.

Through peaceful methods, respect for constitutional propriety, and the strong moral assertions embodied in political demands, Tutu is one of the few leaders in the world who provide a symbiotic relationship between the identities of spiritual and political leadership, while at the same time being perceived as primarily a spiritual leader. Needless to say, black South Africans became more and more frustrated with the political system of a white government that sought to repress any significant social progress of Africans. But black spiritual and political protest continued to catch fire as in 1986 nearly two thousand blacks were arrested per day for passbook offenses.[12] Tutu stated, "The moratorium and release of pass offenders can only be welcomed. However, I hope there is not a sting in the tail. One has to be very careful that they are not going to find another way of harassing blacks."[13] The number of arrests was a fire of African political consciousness that had developed into the Black Consciousness Movement and black theology. A black renaissance existed in which Africans led national protests for a new identity as black people, an identity other than as commodities of white people.

By examining black political and Christian leadership, one discovers that the most significant political change in South African history is that African leadership encountered the intensified repression from the legal and penal system of the government during the 1960s—to the point of a complete ban on black political activity. For instance, this evolution of attempting to control black protest finally led to things such as the Riotous Assemblies Act (1974), which gave complete power to ban all African gatherings of protest against apartheid, an increased penalty for attending gatherings, and even more power for the police to control the crowds.

During the 1960s and 1970s, there was a temporary lull as African resistance reorganized in order to deal with a loss of leadership due to the apartheid government's severe bans on black consciousness organizations. During this period the church played a crucial role in maintaining the resistance to apartheid. Historian André Odendaal writes, "When the churches (one of the few remaining avenues of expression) protested near Parliament, church leaders, including Archbishop Desmond Tutu, were arrested."[14] Here Odendaal depicts a benign impression of church leaders filling the vacuum created by government bans on African political organizations, but the church has not always been viewed in such a positive light, as Tutu's joke of bitter truth shows: "When the white man first came here, he had the Bible and we had the land. Then the white man said to us, 'Come, let us kneel and pray together.' So we knelt and closed our eyes and prayed, and when we opened our eyes again, lo!—we had the Bible and he had the land."[15]

Most characteristic of Tutu is that he is a Christian leader who leads in political spheres only when necessary; this we may see through Tutu's refusal to be described as a political leader per se. But in this refusal, Tutu does not wish to imply any lack of political involvement. As Father Buti Tlhagale suggests,

> [Tutu] is not a political leader, although he is intensely involved in political issues. His involvement, however, does not recognize the "heretical dichotomy" between religion and politics. He is not a politician in the sense that his involvement is expected to lead to practical political reform

only. His involvement aims at bringing about a changed moral order which transcends and yet upholds the anticipated radical political change. The apartheid system must be replaced, not just by a political order governed by a Black majority, but by a new order built on the foundations of justice.[16]

And yet Tutu is a man who speaks boldly: "You whites brought us the Bible; now we blacks are taking it seriously. We are involved with God to set us free from all that enslaves us and makes us less than what He intended us to be. I will demonstrate that apartheid, separate development, or whatever it is called, is evil, totally and without remainder, that it is unchristian and unbiblical. If anyone were to show me otherwise, I would burn my Bible and cease to be a Christian."[17]

SPIRITUAL METHOD OF SOCIAL CHANGE

Tutu's method of relational theology encompassed both the Black Consciousness Movement of empowerment of oppressed peoples and the need for reconciliation among all races in South Africa. Only when the black community gained complete control to determine policies in South Africa would the possibility exist for correct reconciliation with whites on an equal basis. Therefore, through black liberation in South Africa, Tutu sought the correct relational complement of black and white liberation, because no one is a person in South Africa until blacks attain the freedom to open their God-given personhood and humanity.

In 1976, before being consecrated bishop and becoming general secretary of the SACC, Tutu was dean of St. Mary's Anglican Cathedral in Johannesburg. From this position he began a more explicit political involvement in South Africa. He wrote Prime Minister John Vorster to appeal that the government take more care to help migrant workers, black families, and urban blacks. Vorster replied by accusing Tutu of propaganda. As the country was boiling, Tutu warned that his people were made desperate by despair and injustice. In order to improve this situation, Tutu called for the repeal of pass laws and a national convention made up of "genuine leaders" who could work for a nonracial South Africa.

Change was inevitable; what mattered most for Tutu was the courage to help bring about constructive change. Tutu is often fond of saying about South Africa, "In this country we have so many people who want change so long as things remain the same."[18] This leads to Tutu's emphasis on forgiveness. Tutu believes that liberation for both blacks and whites will come about through the severe demands of forgiveness. Though he would never sanction "cheap grace," nevertheless he believed blacks must pardon white oppression by demanding repentance of the existing social order in South Africa. Tutu's view of forgiveness comes through his conclusion about those who believe religion has no relation to politics:

These persons tend to have an attenuated doctrine of reconciliation and want to avoid confrontation at all costs—to speak about a neutral God in situations of conflict, of injustice and oppression. They say God does not take sides and so the Church should not take sides, but must be somewhere in the middle. In an attempt to exercise a ministry of reconciliation such people present reconciliation as an easy option for Christians, and they speak about the need to be forgiving, especially to the victims of injustice, without making a call for repentance by the perpetrators of the injustice and for a redress of the unjust system—they will do this to such an extent that profound Christian words such as "reconciliation and forgiveness" are rejected with contempt by the poor and exploited because they appear to want them to acquiesce in their condition of oppression and exploitation and powerlessness.[19]

Ultimately, Tutu believes in forgiveness so that the victim does not assume the hideous nature of the one who inflicted suffering on them. Tutu worked diligently to prevent the point of no return in South Africa, in which further repressive policies of the South African government would generate a momentum of their own. As Tutu stated, "From our side we have done all that it seems humanly possible to do." Tutu's method of reconciliation sought to prevent such a bloody dénouement in South Africa. Unless something drastic was done toward reconciliation, Tutu wrote back to Vorster, bloodshed and violence would be inevitable. Two weeks later the Soweto uprisings occurred.[20]

In the days after the violent uprising that killed so many students, he addressed a crowd in Regina Mundi Cathedral in Soweto, speaking of "the courageous children who died on 16 June 1976": "God was always on the side of the oppressed and exploited, not because they are morally better than their oppressors. No, He is on their side simply and solely because they are oppressed. He wants them to be fully human. And when He liberates the oppressed he also liberates the oppressor, because whites in South Africa will never be truly free until all of us are free."[21]

Later, in Tutu's acceptance speech for the Nobel Peace Prize, he urged change in government policy, including the release of political prisoners and the end of the ban on political organizations. All of this was accentuated in 1985 by the desperate attempts of the Umkhonto attacks.[22] Tutu went on to observe that those regarded by whites as terrorists were considered heroes and martyrs by many blacks.[23]

A BIASED CHURCH

This discussion of Tutu's spiritual fight against the entrenched racism during the apartheid years is complicated by the church to which Tutu belongs. The complication is in how many white Anglicans in South Africa benefited in the acquisition of wealth and stature from a legal system that deprived black and so-called colored Anglicans. Yet many white South Africans alongside Tutu championed the cause to dismantle apartheid. This is complicated further by how long it took to take an official stand against apartheid after its implementation in 1948. For example, the Anglican Church instituted its own statement declaring apartheid as a heresy only in 1982. In this statement, given by Tutu, he called the universal church to do the same all around the world. It took ecumenical organizations like the SACC to help the Anglican Church in South Africa take its official stand. In the DNA of Anglicanism, in which church and state were not separated, there was not much muscle memory for the church to become subversive of government.

Was the SACC, however, subversive of the government in condemning apartheid as heresy? Yes, Tutu believed, if it meant God is subversive of all situations of injustice. With such an ally as God, Tutu concluded that racist governments would "fail because they are ranging themselves on the side of evil and injustice against the Church of God. Like others who have done that in the past, the Neros, the Hitlers, the Amins of this world, they will end up as the flotsam and jetsam of history."[24] For Tutu, as well as for many other Christian political leaders, God takes the side of the poor, the widow, the orphan, and the alien. In the end, the church was a biased institution in Tutu's spiritual framework.

Tutu's spiritual leadership becomes all the more important here in articulating a formal position of the churches to be against apartheid, especially since there was a lack of political leadership during heightened governmental intimidation. Church leaders had to fill the political roles by carrying on nonviolent resistance. But unlike the other African leaders mentioned in this research, Tutu remained reluctant to be a member of a political organization of any sort. The only exception one may find here is that Tutu often spoke to the National Forum Committee, made up of a wide spectrum of perspectives.[25] Despite Tutu's reluctance to be characterized as a political leader, the government found itself having to deal with him as such.

As we have seen, the South African government often accused Christian leaders like Tutu of being agents of a destructive revolution in South Africa. Botha lashed out against the SACC, accusing Tutu of being in line with Marxist and atheistic ideology. Writing to Tutu, Botha states: "You love and praise the ANC/ SACP with its Marxist and atheistic ideology. . . . You embrace and participate in their call for violence, hatred, sanctions, insurrection and revolution. . . . The question must be posed . . . whether you are acting on behalf of the kingdom of God, or the kingdom promised by the ANC and the SACP? If it is the latter, say so, but do not then hide behind the structures of the cloth and the Christian Church, because Christianity and Marxism are irreconcilable opposites."[26]

Tutu defended himself by saying that his theological position is derived from the Bible and the church, which both predate Marxism and the ANC. The Bible teaches that each person is invested with infinite value, instead of being valued through arbitrary biological attributes. Apartheid, in line with these latter criteria of value, claims that what qualifies a person for privilege and political power is biological. Tutu concludes, "That is clearly at variance with the teaching of the

Bible and the teaching of our Lord and Savior Jesus Christ. Hence the Church's criticism that your apartheid policies are not only unjust and oppressive. They are positively unbiblical, unchristian, immoral and evil."[27]

Tutu offers a sound response of an active church involved in the activities of the world. It is from this church that he is able to critique the interpretations of theological justification for apartheid so often found in the stories of Genesis and the tower of Babel. From this biblical narrative one may be led to misconstrue the Calvinist tradition's "ordinances of creation," in which God is believed to separate the chosen from the outcasts. For example, both liberation theologians and Afrikaner theologians use the story of a chosen people in the book of Exodus and their exodus from bondage as a paradigm for the sacred saga of the liberation of an oppressed people. But Tutu wanted to show that these passages of Scripture intend no such duplicitous intention to justify apartheid.

The book of Genesis provides the narrative of God's intention for a universe of *shalom*, a primal flourishing that was disrupted by sin. Thus Genesis ends with the disruption of the tower of Babel: "This is the ultimate consequence according to the Bible of sin, separation, alienation, apartness. It is a perverse exegesis that would hold that the story of the Tower of Babel is a justification for racial separation, a divine sanction for the diversity of nations. It is to declare that the divine punishment for sin had become the divine intention for mankind."[28]

The biblical narrative is instead a demonstration to us of God's mission to restore a primal flourishing through the enigmatic suffering of an incarnation of God and humanity. Apartheid denies this event of God's incarnation in Jesus by adhering to separateness, disunity, enmity, alienation of the human community. Therefore apartheid perpetuates a sinful state and is indeed sin. In this light, the story of Exodus becomes the liberation of all who are oppressed from such sin. What happens, however, when the church itself represents that which one should exodus?

THE CHURCH AND COLONIALISM

Contrary to the common political history of Africa, which so often caricatures Christian missions as allies of colonialism, Tutu was indeed able to distinguish the true character of the Christian church from the ideals of colonialism; but this is not to suggest that the South African political context involves an easy distinction between the ideals of a civil religion and the ideals of the existing white government. Bonganjalo Goba, an early participant in black theology in South Africa, describes this difficulty: "There was a feeling amongst those of us who were involved [in early black theology] that somehow we had experienced . . . a theological schizophrenia. We were split. . . . Part of our formation was terribly white, influenced by the western theology. . . . And there was another side to that in that we had our own [black] agenda which had never been addressed. So that the issue had to do with the identity crisis which we confronted."[29]

Simultaneous to the growth of African political organizations, the church offered a source from which one could neither accept inhuman treatment nor allow anything other than justice for all. In this source of the church, Africans found themselves simultaneously having to reject European material culture in order to search for one's own African name. For the African identity in South Africa, this became a search for a transcendent realm by which to escape the deadlock of oppression. What they found was the need to emphasize the spiritual side of "Africanness or African personality."[30] Dwight N. Hopkins states:

> Furthermore, the black political theological proponents share an extreme sensitivity to the bastardization of the gospel by the South African government and its church. They understand an attack on the white power structure is both political and theological; political because the separation of the races undergirds the raison d'etre of apartheid; theological because a heretical gospel confession and interpretation undergird white supremacy and the denial of racial fellowship. Therefore to disengage its political policy of apartheid, they must wage war on the theological justification. In brief, we discover a theology based on non-racialism (black and white together) versus a theology of apartheid.[31]

In the early formation of South Africa's government, leading church figures, both white and black and from various Christian denominations, called for integrationists' models that would remove the color restrictions from the draft South Africa Act. Such a petition was signed, for example, by the Anglican archbishop of Cape Town, W. M. Carter, in his first public act since his enthronement. And other liberal whites followed suit through other Christian denominations.[32] Although this indeed became a spiritual struggle, it was imperative that Africans have the opportunity to provide the national leadership necessary to bring about change. And indeed such leadership arose out of Christian missions that established educational training for blacks and colored people.

Christian missionary education received government backing around 1854, and to recent history, believes Peter Walshe, is seen to be one the greatest factors of shaping political awareness of a new class of black Africans.[33] Members of this new "educated" class of Africans used their awareness of "Christian moral principles for individual righteousness"[34] to counter the overall discrepancy between Christian doctrine and Western political ideals, on one hand, and the realities of white conquest, on the other.[35]

The political ideals of these early politically conscious Africans were influenced largely by the egalitarian principles that were disseminated in certain churches and church-controlled educational institutions in the country. Despite opposition from local white church members, the Anglican Church, for example, challenged the policy of the state by largely ignoring racial divisions, especially with regard to funerals and the administration of sacraments.[36]

From Christian missions, Africans began to articulate the eventual goal of full integration. Instead of violence, Christians advocated for a "nonracial" future of South Africa that no longer needed competing national identities to define a

South African unit. Instead of a Manichean deadlock of diametrically opposed positions, Christians encouraged a paradoxical view in which the birth of the South African nation could include two nations that comprised whites and blacks, both sympathetic to the other's plight.

Certainly one cannot paint an idealistic picture of the methods used by European Christian missionaries who sought to teach and convert their African "subjects" into what they conceived as Christianity. There were indeed gross assumptions of colonialism inherent in many Christian missionaries, as within David Livingstone's scheme that the "three Cs" must always go together: commerce, civilization, and Christianity. But on the other hand, Christianity, as a religious system, demanded more than the power-related structure of colonialism.

Lamin Sanneh, a Nigerian scholar of Christian missiology who taught at Yale University, offers a revisionist history in which Christian missionaries did not so much destroy cultures as became bound to them in the work of vernacular translation of the Bible. Through the need to translate, these missionaries facilitated among Africans the stimuli toward nonviolent rebellions for equal treatment for their own indigenous cultures.[37] Thus Sanneh agrees with the admittedly unconventional assessment of the ideological motive force of Christian mission as other than Western political and cultural dominance. He states that Christian mission stimulated indigenous language to express Christian teaching by adopting local religious vocabulary, but also adds this caveat: "It is undeniable, of course, that missionary endeavors in this field were not completely bereft of self-serving motives. . . . But no one can deny the irrepressible repercussions in the wider culture of missionary action. A more adequate way to define this is to view mission within the pluralist milieu of local cultures . . . [as] an integral part of Africa's pluralist heritage."[38]

Like Livingstone, many Christian missionaries approached God's justice as that which transcends all human ideological constructions, thereby calling one's cultural presuppositions into question. In this sense of humility, Sanneh quotes an American missionary: "I was a response to Dr Livingstone's call to come to Africa to help free and civilize and Christianize the Africans. . . . And then we began that . . . process of trying to peel away from everything . . . that was Western and white and European and American, and we started to search for what we called the 'naked gospel.'"[39]

This "naked gospel" was to be distinguished from the dictates of colonialism, which advocated conquest and power. Instead of falling prey to the abuse of worldly power, missionaries were to look beyond superficial converts of colonialism to the principle that conversion truly meant the restoration of indigenous foundations. And somewhere along this way of restoration, these missionaries hoped to find the kingdom of God.

From the perspective of absolute justice, Christian missionaries sought to provide a competing norm to the dictates of colonialism. From these Christian missions, African leaders were strengthened to fight in an oppressive world for an alternative political construction of justice.[40] Christianity contained a cosmology in which corporal reality is contingent to the transcendent state of resurrection and heaven. Who you are now and what you do in this world are in direct proportion to your future state of being; therefore, one need not blithely accept one's "lot" in life, but should appeal to God's nature of justice, in which this creation groans for a proper relation between action and being. A Catholic missionary gives a powerful account of this relation:

> With great reverence to the Masai culture, we went back to the naked gospel, as close as we could get to it, and presented it to them as honestly as we could. We let them play it back to us. . . . There was this constant playing it back and forth, until something emerged that I thought they or we never heard before. At the end, we began to see that what was emerging was the God of the gospel—one that we did not recognize before, . . . the God who loves evil people. That's incredible. This is a God who not only loves evil people, but loves me when I'm evil. . . . It's not the God we normally worship—church officials and authorities can do nothing with a God like this.[41]

Among a groaning creation, the community that seeks to display the ways of Christ's justice is what I call the church, a chosen body of Christians who practice the transcendent presence of a God, even if this God seems so absent in a violent world. But this church is not perfect.

As both Africans and Afrikaners construed Christianity to look forward to the achievement of an ideal society, that is, each in their own image, they perpetuated the tendency to abide in competing churches. That is, both nationalisms ended up claiming themselves as a people chosen by God. This problem of incommensurate churches leads us to a central question of this work, namely, how five African leaders seek to show how anyone chosen by God must understand and relate to a new power structure, one in which the lion will lie down with the lamb.

Although differences of leadership styles seem to occur among these African leaders, the unavoidable principle that lies deeply ingrained in each of them is the rejection of violence as the correct technique of conflict resolution.[42] For these African leaders, involved in this alternative discourse of Christian morality, other specific terms and means of political protest were required. Gerhart states: "Africans were battling against race prejudice and discrimination: could they in good conscience, and given the Christian ideals many had been taught to cherish, think of turning the tables on whites and of creating an order in which a white skin would automatically single out an individual as a target of suspicion and abuse? Emotionally, there was a temptation to vent feelings of bitterness and hatred against whites; but intellect and upbringing dictated restraint."[43]

Crucial to the argument presented in this work, the powerful impact of the church against racism in South Africa was reflected in the Christian educational backgrounds of first-generation African political leaders, that is, their temperateness and respect for constitutional propriety, and the strong moral assertions embodied in their political demands. From the early black mission-school graduates like Tutu we find a powerful Christian legacy of political witness. So powerful is this legacy that it produces a theology of liberation in South Africa that spreads the good news around the world that God is on the side of the poor and oppressed. Tutu's liberation theology also carried the positive experience of living in England, the motherland of the colonies. Tutu states:

> We were enfolded in a loving, caring, compassionate community. We were loved, accepted and affirmed and we blossomed. . . . So let me say all of you, our brothers and sisters, loved us into growing into who we are becoming. God was preparing us for our ministry in South Africa and you have had and continue to have a very considerable part in it. I believe that particularly your love has helped to preserve us from race hatred. . . . We have known different kinds of white people than those who have treated our people as if they were less than those created in God's image. For that reason therefore of infinite value in His sight. You helped us experience what it meant to be human beings and so we were able to go back into that situation in South Africa and be insulated in a sense against the corrosiveness of racial oppression and injustice. You have surrounded us in a wall of fire through your love and prayers and concern and we thank God for you so we have come to believe that this tremendous vision in St John the Divine (i.e., Rev. 7:9ff) would one day find fulfillment.[44]

Crucial to the argument in this chapter is the position that Tutu's spirituality was on the correct side of history in addressing the problem of racism in South Africa. Tutu as South Africa's confessor successfully facilitated the confession of the sin of racism from the ambivalent position of the church. In so doing, he helped to renegotiate racial identity in a postapartheid society. I mention ambivalent here because in Tutu's Christian spirituality he is very much aware that the institutional church can also become an idol or a pawn in the hands of governments. Inasmuch as he conducts such a negotiation against racism in the midst of an ambivalent church, he demonstrates his life's pursuit for a rainbow nation called South Africa.

Tutu enthroned as archbishop of Cape Town in 1986. Courtesy of Guy Tillim. With thanks to University of Cape Town Libraries Digital Collections.

Chapter 9

Leaving Church

Despite Tutu's commitment to the Christian church, we will discover here in chapter 9 how Tutu maintained his Christian spiritual commitments while also reaching out beyond the institutional church. As mentioned at the end of the previous chapter, Tutu's spiritual leadership was vital in filling in the gap of so many black political leaders who were imprisoned, killed, or exiled; yet such spiritual leadership was not always supported in the institutional churches Tutu represented. The title of this chapter, "Leaving Church," comes from Barbara Brown Taylor's memoir, in which she offers helpful insights that I use to explain this stage of Tutu's spirituality. This chapter also shows how Tutu welcomed ecumenical and interreligious dialogue, which befits the transition from illumination to union with God.

Barbara Brown Taylor, an American voted one of the most effective preachers in the English language, describes how upon leaving parish ministry she was asked what she preaches about now that she is not attached to a church. She describes how this question comes from those deep in the Christian faith, usually clergy: "Church is more than a place or a people for them; it is a primary source of identity." So their question does not come from any antagonism but from compassion. Brown goes on to say that she has not left the church, even though she no longer serves one particular congregation. She still works for the church, but the difference is in how the word "church" has expanded its meaning for her. "It no longer means . . . a self-identified community of believers. Instead, it means a far-flung bunch of people who are engaged in holy work."[1]

That question "What do you preach about now that you have left the church?" is one that helps us understand a similar response from Tutu: the church's meaning is much more than an institution, building, or denomination. An antecedent to this question must first be looked at: Has the church ever left Tutu? Tutu believed that not only did a nation-state like South Africa need a TRC process; so did the church. In this closing chapter in part 2, Illumination, we will look at the complexity of this question, especially in light of the disunity of the church. It is my presupposition that Tutu's life demonstrates a successful theological response to the modern worry of how divergent cultures may affirm each other as God's creation. But I must be quick to add here that even in my primary research on Tutu himself (i.e., serving as his chaplain, interviews, and gaining access to primary documents), it still remains difficult to explain the wonder of how Tutu not only survived but flourished in the midst of disunity.

Steeped in the political mire of his South African context, how did Tutu facilitate robust dialogue and a healthy transition of power, not just in South Africa, but in the rest of the world? In what way do Tutu's institutional church leadership and his leadership as chair of the TRC provide theological reality by which Ubuntu may come into being?[2] The analysis of this last chapter in Illumination shows how Tutu has influenced people against apartheid through his roles as archbishop and chair of the TRC.

What I have claimed as Tutu's central metaphor for his Christian spirituality is that of confessor. Does this metaphor lend itself more to theological or political warrants? This question is a false dichotomy, because Tutu sees theology and politics as part of the same fabric of what Taylor describes as "holy work." In other words, both as archbishop and as chair of the TRC, Tutu unapologetically never leaves theological discourse; consequently, he is able to rally political defiance of apartheid in South Africa. In the end, though, Tutu is not able to achieve total success in this endeavor without various constituent factions remaining in conflict. To what extent does this invalidate his holy work if in his "own backyard" there remain opposition and strife?

CONTEXT OF THE CHURCH LEAVING

Before we move to the final part of this book—that is, union—it is helpful to review an abbreviated history we discussed earlier of how institutional churches in South Africa reluctantly joined the struggle to end apartheid. In fact, the churches were divided themselves; making unity to end apartheid in South Africa was seemingly impossible, because of an absent church. When the government banned most popular political organizations under apartheid, it did not think that spiritual communities like churches would do anything particularly significant in opposition to apartheid. It must have been shocked to discover otherwise—especially because the church itself was divided.

The "multiracial" or English-speaking churches were living the life of apartheid just as much as the Dutch Reformed churches with their state religion. These churches were essentially inactive, mere spectators of the unfolding drama of apartheid. Baptists, Congregationalists, Lutherans, Methodists, Presbyterians, Anglicans (Church of the Province of Southern Africa), and Roman Catholics were still controlled by predominantly white hierarchies. Having been absorbed into the country's racist, capitalist culture, these denominational churches often conformed to the segregated nature of South African society.

The case of the Roman Catholic Church was symptomatic. As late as the 1960s, its schools, parishes, and seminaries were segregated; only 5 percent of the clergy were black; and 75 percent of its white priests, brothers, and nuns who were qualified teachers were to be found in white schools.[3] While churches condemned apartheid in principle, they were unwilling to confront the state actively. This makes Tutu's spiritual formation within the Community of the Resurrection all the more important, as there he learned to relate Christian spirituality to political impact. Other clergy—with very few exceptions—lacked such prophetic vision, and some harbored sympathies for the apartheid order.

In South Africa, approximately 70 percent of the African population are Christian; of these, almost one-third are members of independent churches. These churches and sects, numbering more than two thousand, were a world apart from the mainline denominations. They did not belong to the SACC; they were scornful of white-controlled organizations and in the main were apolitical. Only a handful of their leaders had identified with African political organizations in their struggle against segregation and apartheid.

While the churches were essentially quiescent, it is important to recognize that there were a few other outspoken white Christians who actively opposed apartheid and identified with the black struggle, such as the Rev. Michael Scott and Archbishop Joost de Blank. In essence, they condemned apartheid for dividing the human community, legally segregating Christians, and thus dismembering the body of Christ. It is even more important to recall that many of the outstanding black leaders of the ANC were devout Christians, like the Rev. Zaccheus Mahabane, Canon James Calata, Albertina Nontsikelelo Sisulu, Winnie Mandela, and Albert Luthuli, who led the Defiance Campaign of the 1950s and was in 1960 the first South African to win the Nobel Peace Prize.

In comparison with such individual Christian witness, formal church leadership remained unimpressive. Dualistic theologies predominated, focusing on otherworldly goals—examples of what Marx recognized as the opium of the people. As Luthuli realized, this was a dangerous situation for Christianity. The churches, he wrote in 1960, have "simply submitted to the secular state for far too long and some had even supported apartheid." Yet he believed it was "not too late for white Christians to look at the Gospels and redefine their allegiance."

However, he continued, "I warn those who care for Christianity, who care to go to all the world and preach the gospel. In South Africa, the opportunity is 300 years old. It will not last forever. The time is running out."[4]

It was from this low point in Christian witness that an increasing number of individuals and groups within the churches gradually began to articulate a prophetic theology, especially in the aftermath of the Sharpeville massacre of 1960 and the subsequent banning of the ANC and Pan Africanist Congress. What was to become a radical transformation in the understanding of Christian mission in a repressive society—the story of the emergence of an indigenous liberation theology in South Africa—can also be seen in Johannesburg with the December 1960 Cottesloe Consultation of the World Council of Churches (WCC) and the SACC.

Called to examine apartheid in the light of the Bible, the Cottesloe Consultation produced a mildly worded, even paternalistic, statement that was essentially critical of apartheid but not unanimous in the extent of its condemnations. Whereas English-speaking churches found apartheid "unacceptable in principle," delegates of white Afrikaner churches such as the Nederduitsch Hervormde Kerk (NHK) and the Herformde Kerk found separate development the "only realistic" approach to race relations and refused to sign the statement. The Afrikaans word *Nederduits* refers to Dutch Reformed churches. Delegates representing the Nederduitse Gereformeerde Kerk (NGK), the largest denomination within South Africa's Dutch Reformed tradition, did sign the statement but argued for a limited, yet still major, adaptation of government policy that would recognize a minority of Africans as permanent residents in "white" areas, where they would be entitled to civil rights.[5] The Broederbond, an organization of Afrikaner Christians, dismissed Cottesloe as a threat to the Afrikaner nation, which would only result in a multiracial and ecumenical disaster orchestrated by the liberal, even communistic WCC. Prime Minister Hendrik Verwoerd even used his New Year radio message to blast the signatories, and when the NGK synods met together, they decided to resign from the SACC and called upon their Cottesloe delegates to recant their signatures. The preeminent NGK delegate who refused to back down was Beyers Naudé. He had played a pivotal, irenic role at Cottesloe, but he had also come to the conclusion that apartheid was a heresy, indefensible on biblical grounds

At the time of Cottesloe, Naudé could not have been closer to the heart of Afrikanerdom. In 1958 he had been appointed acting moderator of the NGK (Transvaal) when he was already a member of the inner circle of the Broederbond. Deeply disturbed in his own conscience about the nature and practice of apartheid, Naudé was also fearful that its injustices would destroy the Afrikaners. Reluctantly, but with determination, he took a prophetic stand, metaphorically speaking, shaking his fist at his own people in the manner of a prophet in Hebrew Scripture. First, he initiated a journal, *Pro Veritate*, committed to ecumenical dialogue and to dismantling apartheid. Then, in 1963, he launched the nonracial, ecumenical Christian Institute of Southern Africa (CI) with the intent of converting the Afrikaner establishment and witnessing, in the Institute's own microcosmic community, to a new postapartheid society. Rather than being converted, the reaction of the Broederbond, the NGK hierarchy, and the Afrikaner political establishment was to turn on Naudé with a special ferocity, to extrude and vilify him as a traitor to the Afrikaner volk. He lost his parish, was defrocked, and, with his wife Ilsa, was cruelly ostracized.

After several initial setbacks, including its incapacity to reach Afrikaner leaders, the CI slowly gathered confidence in its unfolding theological understanding of the South African situation and began to move in new directions. Over the next fourteen years, before it was banned in October 1977, the Institute was to become a seminal group of approximately two thousand members, informed and stimulated by a deepening interaction with a new generation of black political leaders and black theologians. As a result, Naudé and his colleagues played an important and, at times, central role in the emergence of an indigenous liberation theology.

One of the early signs of this process was *A Message to the People of South Africa*, a document issued jointly by the CI and SACC. It rejected apartheid on biblical grounds, recognized God's kingdom as incipient in history, and called on Christians to struggle for the "salvation of the world and of human existence in its entirety."[6] Charity was not enough; every person was created in the likeness of a loving God and deserved justice, a condition that had to be cultivated by public policy. In challenging the prevailing culture of a dualistic Christianity that saw a world as a veil of tears and spent its energies preparing for the next, *A Message* was directed to those in positions of privilege and power; they were to reform society. It is important to notice, however, that while espousing a social gospel, the document was still essentially paternalistic—a call to white South Africans to establish justice for the poor. This tentative step toward a theology of liberation was not a call for the empowerment of the oppressed; nor was it a call to the poor to liberate themselves.[7]

The year following *A Message*, the CI, again in cooperation with the SACC, sponsored the Study Project of Christianity in Apartheid Society (SPROCAS). This two-year endeavor involved one hundred and fifty individuals (predominantly white) sitting on six commissions. It was essentially an academic attempt to detail the social, economic, and political consequences of apartheid. As another well-intentioned yet paternalistic response, a research project that stopped far short of activism and confrontation with the state, SPROCAS did not engender much enthusiasm among black leaders. It was also quickly overtaken by events. In 1968, the WCC initiated its Program to Combat Racism, which made grants to the exiled liberation movement for humanitarian programs. These grants triggered controversy within South African church circles on the issues of violence and civil war. By the early 1970s, the black trade unions were beginning to gather a little strength and managed to sustain several effective strikes.

In 1974, Portugal was forced out of Mozambique and Angola after years of debilitating guerilla warfare, and by the mid-1970s the Black Consciousness

Movement (BCM) had gathered mass support in the townships. In spite of a decade of severe repression, South Africa once more was drifting into political turmoil. In this context a new generation of black leaders emerged—for example, the young medical student Steve Biko—who were unimpressed with statements, appeals, messages, and study projects. Indeed, the CI's policies had begun to look like the state of affairs Naudé set out to overcome.

As the BCM spread from the segregated tribal colleges to black high schools and even grade schools, the CI turned to support the movement. Black leaders—for example, Oshade Phakathi as a community organizer, the young Reformed theologian Allan Boesak, and the Lutheran theologian Manas Buthelezi—came to play influential roles in the Institute as Beyers Naudé learned from and encouraged the currents of black theology that were part of the BCM.[8] In addition, the CI raised funds for the Black Community Programs (BCP) that were controlled by black leaders of the caliber of Bennie Khoapa, Steve Biko, and Barney Pityana. The BCP in turn initiated literacy drives using the techniques of Paulo Freire, sparked study groups on black theology, and established prototype clinics on leadership in townships.

When the police and army opened fire in Soweto on June 16, 1976, killing 176 school children and wounding hundreds, and the disturbances spread to other cities and further massacres of young protesters occurred, the CI was confirmed in its supportive and radical stand against apartheid. Consequently, it was inevitable that the Institute and its leadership would be banned, along with the Black Consciousness organizations, as they were, in October 1977. Shortly before these events, on September 12, Biko was murdered. Because of these multiple events, Naudé and his lieutenants became aware of the writings of theologians like James Cone in the United States as well as political theologians in Europe and liberation theologians in Latin America. By 1976, the Institute had also appealed for economic sanctions against the apartheid regime. In addition, Naudé took particular care to build up contacts and friendships within the black Dutch Reformed churches, a policy that contributed to the emergence of a strongly prophetic strain of liberation theology within the Sendingkerk and Kerk van Africa. While the CI was formally silenced in 1977 on account of these commitments, the spin-off effects of its witness were to continue as a challenge to the leadership of all South Africa's churches, including the increasing number of black clergy coming into positions of responsibility within most denominations. Key white church leaders were also profoundly influenced by Naudé and the Institute, including Denis Hurley, Roman Catholic archbishop of Durban, who sat on the Institute's board.

Allan Boesak, then the moderator of the Sendingkerk and president of the World Alliance of Reformed Churches, helped to free psychological control of the NGK, partly inspired by Naudé. This was done through Boesak's prophetic work, which aimed at breaking the dysfunctional relationship among black, white, and colored members of the Dutch Reformed Churches in South Africa. He spoke against the old terminology of mother and daughter churches and encouraged all three Reformed black churches to join the SACC. Boesak's theological writings have strong themes of hope, exodus, repentance, and liberation.[9] At this time, Boesak, a leading figure in the UDF, campaigned vigorously for economic sanctions against the apartheid regime. The same Ottawa Conference of the World Alliance of Reformed churches that elected Boesak president in 1982 expelled the NGK for heresy, for supporting apartheid. Tutu's leadership as general secretary of the SACC, and that of his successors—the unbanned Beyers Naudé and the Rev. Frank Chikane (Apostolic Faith Mission Church)—continued the prophetic witness pioneered by the CI. When the UDF was formed in 1983 to oppose the new dispensation of apartheid, Tutu, Naudé, and Boesak played major roles as patrons, which helped to legitimize the new organization.

Another important group in terms of refining a unified stand against apartheid was the ecumenical Center for Contextual Theology in Johannesburg where Chikane, Buti Tlhagale, and Albert Nolan made major contributions in analyzing South Africa in terms of structural injustice, race, and class divisions. Nolan states,

> The temptation for a Christian is to think that the most loving thing to do is to convert one by one those who sit on the thrones of injustice and thus to destroy the system. But change does not happen that way, because as long as the throne remains it will always be filled by others and the oppression will remain. The only effective way of loving our enemies is to engage in action that will destroy the system that makes them our enemies. In other words, for the sake of love, and for the sake of true peace, we must side with the poor and oppressed and confront the rich and powerful.[10]

NEVER LEAVING

Like Moses, who got angry at the people he was called to lead, Tutu found himself often stressed within all of these church struggles, but he never left the church, even as he was later called to the creative task of leading the TRC. Tutu's spiritual life is important in dismantling apartheid through his mediation of disparate identities. He represents a distinctive narrative of theological discourse with a complex set of attributes or descriptions. He is an African community leader who facilitates the emergence of his peoples out from under the ravages of colonialism, a hierarchical leader of the institutional structures of the church, and a product of a vibrant spirituality of the Community of the Resurrection. Tutu succeeds in the above mediation in that he in fact becomes transformed into an international, ecumenical Christian leader who claims catholic authority against apartheid structures. But how does he succeed and fail in juxtaposing these identities, in light of his primary identities as archbishop of Cape Town and chair of the TRC?

We see such tension in Tutu's relationship with Mangosuthu Buthelezi, a South African politician and Zulu chief who founded the Inkatha Freedom

Party in 1975 and was chief minister of the KwaZulu Bantustan until 1994. In the new South Africa, Buthelezi became minister of home from 1994 to 2004. In the midst of these identities, Buthelezi was also an Anglican. In light of the complexity of the political situation between Mandela's ANC political party and Buthelezi's Inkatha party, Tutu bore a heavy burden of spiritual leadership. For example, Mandela, when he addressed the Anglican Consultative Council, January 29, 1993, in Cape Town, praised Tutu for being such a vital leader when the country's legitimate leaders were imprisoned. At the same meeting, Buthelezi was critical of church leadership and said to Tutu, Buthelezi's own archbishop, "Let us campaign for Christian statements about the nature of man and society and let there be a way of connecting Church, humanity, God and the politician so that there will be a new South Africa which is just, and which is democratic and which is prosperous."[11] Buthelezi goes on to address both Tutu and the archbishop of Canterbury in a manner of confession.

> The appeal I make . . . is for us to understand that the Church in South Africa failed with apartheid because if it had not, there would never have been apartheid. . . . the Church was too confused in its thinking to avert the centuries of suffering which mankind has known. I have said all of these things in great humility.[12]

Even though Buthelezi showed overt hostility at one point toward the delivery of a prayer by Tutu, he wanted people to know that not all the accusations flung at Inkatha by its political opponents by the churches, by civil rights lawyers, by the Black Sash, and by elements of the press have been justified. There was, however, ample evidence of Inkatha's resort to violence, or counterviolence, often led or encouraged at a high level of Buthelezi's Inkatha organization. Any fair assessment of the violence must conclude that the original sin is now hidden in the mists of the past, and that neither side has clean hands.[13]

As Buthelezi's archbishop and later as the chair of the TRC, Tutu's theology of Ubuntu acted as a conciliar catalyst by which theological reflection in the South African context assumed a different ethos, one in which the primary identity of Christian community is no longer subsumed in colonial conquest, racial identity, or cultural practices. For Tutu, the primary identity of the Christian community is in the characteristic of the faithful who gather for the sacramental sake of practicing the presence of God. Through such practice and presence, this church is further called to practice models of justice in the world. Lastly, Tutu's theological convictions provided the Anglican Church in South Africa the inspiration to practice Christian truthfulness differently than before in South Africa, thereby demonstrating Tutu's life as a theological model in South African society. In other words, Tutu shows how cultures may affirm each other as God's creation.

My emphasis upon tensions between Tutu's archbishopric and chairmanship of the TRC is instrumental in the following presentation and analysis because the political impact that Tutu made was in fact comprised of his hybrid identity as a Xhosa archbishop who chaired the TRC and who appealed for political change through the spirituality of the Anglican Church. He was not simply, as commonly assumed, a political actor in his South African context. He was first and foremost a church leader.

Tutu wanted to look at theology "from the standpoint of an African who has for far too long been made ashamed of his irreducible humanness because it was black, something for which he could not be held accountable. And this sense of shame has made me what I am, so that all reality for me must be distilled through this integral experience of being black and ultimately also human. Maybe it is a chip on my shoulder, but, pray, who could have placed it there I wonder."[14] Am I ambivalent, or is Tutu, about his theological identity? Is he "Xhosa archbishop," or "first and foremost a church leader," or somehow both, so that these representations do not represent conflict but congruence? If it is both, how is that so?

The challenge is to view Tutu amid the varying views of his impact on South Africa. Tutu's controversy is in how he is such a high-profile spiritual leader, often at the center of the political storm.[15] My aim is to construct a particular view of Tutu's spiritual impact in light of his unique expression of Anglicanism in South Africa. Tutu is unique, not only for being the first black archbishop of the CPSA and becoming chair of the TRC, but for also completely shifting the traditional "establishment" attitude, which he powerfully shows to be in obvious contradiction to beliefs and pronouncements of the church. And through a theology of nonviolence, Tutu is able to facilitate the destruction of apartheid and the established government that perpetuates it.

The best of what Tutu represents is his insistence that prayer, worship, and life itself are grounded upon dogmatic fact, that in everyday human experience head and heart are wedded. Herein lies the best of Anglican aptitude; namely, through a strong emphasis on habitual recollection, one is able, through the church, to discriminate what is good in the world. By balancing extravagance and poverty through a proper view of creation, by affirming individual and community, by maturing Christian character in the common office of prayer, and by adapting rather than copying customs from other nationalities, Tutu offers the world a new paradigm for the church being relevant in the world. Such relevance has not always been the case, especially in Africa.

As Barbara Brown Taylor instructed in the beginning of this chapter, there is a deep need for a deeper understanding of church, especially as this term was used in the racial and culture wars of South Africa. The recovery of one's own cultural roots is vital to the dignity of any peoples who have recently been oppressed, or still are oppressed, by people of other cultures. If the Christian church was used somehow to justify conquest, and the only Christ seen was a hegemonic Christ, then a deep wound was created that naturally harms the longevity of human communities.

Thus through the above context it is understandable how Christian missions have been both accused of facilitating oppression and praised as empowering those oppressed and considered the least of humanity. No substantial superiority need be claimed for Western culture, as such (its own relation to Christianity being problematical, as major Christian ethicists like Stanley Hauerwas so eloquently teach). What one must conclude is that in today's world, especially in light of the declining moral influence of the US under President Trump and the increased xenophobia around refugees and borders in Europe, the Christian must be more aware of how the church cooperated with colonialism, and how historically white churches had a lot to gain by separating human beings on the basis of race. Indeed, it is not easy to stay conscious of the church's complicity with colonialism when human habits naturally coincide with least resistance and the status quo. The problem here is that the status quo of who a Christian is has changed. For example, a thirty-six-year-old Nigerian woman is now the average mean of measuring Anglican demographics. For many "traditionalists" who advocate a return to the good old days, dystopian days lie ahead.

In such a bleak vision, what place is left for local churches? Tutu's spirituality suggests that there is no reason why particular local cultures should not continue to subsist within the universal framework as testimonies to the rich variety of God's work in human creation. The context in which African Christians are needing to work now includes the arduous task of relating Christianity, tribalism, nationalism, Pan-Africanism, and so forth. Over the years in South Africa, there has been resistance to the South African government by churches local and global. Mostly this resistance was manifest when the civil authorities interfered in the church's life of worship. South African theologians such as Charles Villa-Vicencio think of Anglican examples like Archbishop Geoffrey Clayton, who, in response to the Church Bill of 1957, encouraged such resistance by counseling his priests to disobey a law that prevented people from discharging their religious duty of participating in public worship. According to Villa-Vicencio, that was the point at which Anglicans could do nothing except resist. This was due to massive changes in Africa, such as Ghana gaining its independence in 1980. Encountering independence for many Anglican churches in Africa, however, meant tumbling back into the captivity of the colonial past.[16]

The dominant view in modern academic discourse seems to be that the church played a negative role in African societies throughout the colonial period. Christian missionaries are seen as actively promoting colonial advances made into African communities, while many condoned military aggression against the Xhosa and other tribal groups in Africa. This assault on African cultures created a milieu within which missionary attempts to lure Africans into their missions became that much easier. Initially rejected by the majority of Africans, missionary movements succeeded only when African structures of society crumbled in the frontier wars. To become a Christian was to be other than African. Weighing in on the matter, Tutu states:

It was Christian stalwarts such as William Wilberforce who were in the forefront of the movement to abolish slavery. It was the likes of the Earl of Shaftesbury who labored to soften the rigorous and evil consequences of the Industrial Revolution. It has been Christians who have been prominent in the Suffragette Movement, in the Civil Rights Movement in [the United States], and the struggle against apartheid. We are all proud of the courageous witness of the confessing church in Nazi Germany boasting stalwarts such as Martin Niemöller and Dietrich Bonhoeffer. . . . Church leaders have been involved prominently in the transitions from authoritarian rule to more democratic regimes in Africa and elsewhere. Very recently in a casual conversation, an African diplomat told me that the last hope for democracy and freedom in Africa was the Church. He held that the people were thoroughly disillusioned with politicians. . . . In Benin, the Roman Catholic Archbishop Monsignor de Souza was held in such high esteem that he was unanimously chosen to chair the National Conference on the Constitution of Benin. The churches there played a crucial role in that country's peaceful transition from a military dictatorship to multiparty democracy. The South African peace conference convened by the State President, Mr. de Klerk, was a flop because many major players refused to attend, whereas a peace accord came to be signed as a result of the churches and businesses forming a facilitating committee with enough credibility to be acceptable to most of the major players.[17]

So how does the church relate in a healthy way to cultural identity that is African? And what then is expected of the institutional church in the event of its deciding that the time to fight has come? Does an archbishop become an ecclesial general? Tutu rightly answers, "Hopefully not," and thinks "last resort" is important, but in terms of practical institutional church options, does not address the responsibility of the church. The church's theological response to a situation of oppression is one thing; its practical response to a situation of oppression is another. The future generations will be justified in asking what serious alternatives were engaged in by a timid church to bring the present regime to an end. Tutu reasons that the timidity of the church may be ascribed to the educational system: "It is designed to produce docile unquestioning creatures. . . . They are taught to survive by towing the line, not rocking the boat and keeping in the herd."[18]

Tutu's complex persona as archbishop and chair of the TRC opens doors for those who are disgruntled with organized religion. Tutu's spiritual life helps us to have our notion of God deepened and expanded to be open to otherness. He helped Afrikaner Christians see this light, and helped his comrades see the light of God in their enemies. In order to access the truth we need to stand aware that we do not to possess all truth or somehow have a corner on God.[19] Tutu tells the humorous story of a drunk person who crossed the street and approached a pedestrian, asking him, "I shay, which ish the other shide of the shtreet?" The pedestrian, somewhat nonplussed, replied, "That side, of course!" The drunk said, "Shtrange. When I wash on that shide, they shaid it wash thish shide."[20]

The moral of the story is that perspective determines the other side of the street. One's particular perspective depends on where we are and who we are.

As we think about leaving church, we must also think about how that perspective differs with our context, because many in Tutu's South African context never saw him as being in the true church in the first place. He was simply the politician. Of course, many who do not believe in the validity of a church would lack the reference point to care about anything called church in the first place. Tutu's complex persona helps us see how religion is one of the most potent perspectives that can determine the concept of taking sides.

The value of reading a biography is that the reader can learn from someone else's perspective. Indeed, Tutu's perspective is one that sheds light on how the accidents of birth and geography determine to a very large extent to what faith we belong. Tutu is quick to say that the chances are very great that if you were born in Pakistan you are a Muslim, or a Hindu if you happened to be born in India, or a Shintoist if it is Japan, and a Christian if you were born in Italy. The lesson learned in Brown's insight of leaving church is in how we should not succumb to exclusive points of view and dogmatic claims on a monopoly of the truth. It should be sobering to realize that you can easily have been an adherent of the faith that you now might denigrate, save for the fact that you are born here rather than there.

Tutu's holy work has been described in this biography as derived from the mystical roots of Christianity that fought hard against idolatry and sham Christianity. Tutu's formation in the prime of his years as archbishop and chair of the TRC allowed him to acknowledge the integrity of difference and resist the urge to co-opt such difference as a means to his own ends. Essential to his holy work was that we must welcome strangers and others and respect them as who they are, and walk reverently on what is their holy ground. The ultimate illuminative stage for Tutu's spiritual life was his ability to distinguish commonality without relativizing differences. In other words, Tutu could discern whether or not one person's side of the street led to destruction.

One such obvious example in this book is the perspective of adherents of apartheid. Yet, as we learned from Tutu's relationship with the grandson of Hendrik Verwoerd, we can still move toward compassion. Tutu teaches us how, where, and when to hold to particular and peculiar beliefs tenaciously, not pretending that all beliefs are the same, for they inevitably are not. As we will discover in the last stage of Christian mysticism, union, Tutu indeed holds onto his faith in the very act of reaching out to someone of a different faith in the Dalai Lama. Tutu's insight here is that we must be ready to learn from one another, not claiming that we alone possess all truth or somehow have a corner on God.

As Tutu and the Dalai Lama write in their *Book of Joy*, humanity should in humility and joyfulness acknowledge the reality that we need each other.[21] In such joy we are capable of living in the mystery of being particularly who we are, while also transcending our various categories to see how we relate to each other. Joy allows our particular categories of thought and imagining to be apprehended and conceived by others. As Christian mystics teach about the last spiritual stage of union, we shall never comprehend the Divine completely. So Tutu's illuminative stage comes to an end as we prepare to move to his stage, union with God. In this stage we shall see how Tutu seeks to share his life's wisdom as an Elder and sage. His identity as South Africa's confessor never really leaves him, however. He continues to elicit from others the need to share how the transcendent reality of God is present in their lives through compassion, joy, and forgiveness. Tutu's wisdom as sage helps people see that they are creatures of God, made in God's image. This supreme perspective helps us to know the other side of the street.

PART 3
UNION

Interviewer: Without becoming involved in politics, what is and should be the role of the Church in the peacemaking process?

Tutu: The Church has to be involved in politics. Politics is a crucial part of human existence and it is too important to be left to the politicians. If God's writ does not run in the political as well as in all other fields, whose does? The Church must be completely involved in employing all sorts of strategies to push the politicians in directions which will bring about peace, and that is inherently political activity. However, I believe that the Church as an institution should not be party-politically aligned, which is different from not being involved in politics. St. Paul made it clear that the Church of Jesus Christ is in the business of bringing about reconciliation, and in South Africa today that is very difficult to do if the Church is perceived as supporting one political party over another. Apart from trying to bring people together to make peace, we also need to preach constantly the need for political tolerance. We must continue to take the side of those who are marginalized, to publicize their plight and support their cause so their needs can be addressed through the ordinary political process. We also need to be as vigilant under a democratic dispensation as we have been during the years of apartheid. Democratically elected politicians are as vulnerable to abusing power as those created by apartheid. The Church should be active workers and lobbyists for peace at all levels of society, whether in the townships and suburbs in which its members live or at the highest levels of government.[1]

—Interview with Tutu in *RSA-Beleidsoorsig/Policy Review*

Security at Nelson Mandela's inauguration, May 10, 1994. Author photo.

Chapter 10

Tutu's Unifying Role

Almighty God, kindle, we pray, in every heart the true love of peace, and guide with your wisdom those who take counsel for the nations of the earth, that in tranquility your dominion may increase until the earth is filled with the knowledge of your love; through Jesus Christ our Lord, who lives and reigns with you, in the unity of the Holy Spirit, one God, now and for ever. Amen.[1]

—*Book of Common Prayer*

We now move into the third and last stage of Christian mysticism, union with God. In this stage, we begin with what such union entails and how it is demonstrated in the spiritual life. We will then explore the forces of nature that slowed down Tutu's accustomed ubiquity, in which he once traveled constantly and was often in the public eye. Then, through the remainder of the biography we will apply the tenets of this last mystical stage to Tutu's spiritual life as Elder and sage. As mentioned in the beginning of this book, I see such a stage in Tutu's life as representing a deeper understanding of holiness or saintliness. Tutu's saintliness is not for himself, but becomes a worldview in which we all can share a holy life.

This saintliness stands in direct contrast to apartheid's spirituality, in which only white people could make a claim to holiness. The true heroes and saints, apartheid spirituality claimed, were those of European descent and, even more particularly, Dutch. The argument here and in much of this biography is that the worldview of apartheid was really one of hagiography, in which separate development was de facto a different version of the spiritual life, in which white people saw themselves as saints. The spirituality of the Dutch Reformed tradition saw

221

itself in contradiction with Eastern and Western Christian spiritualities that celebrated the Christian saints. Nevertheless, this same Dutch Reformed tradition allowed itself to become part of a government policy that said white people were holier than black people. This policy, conceived and nurtured within the Afrikaans Reformed churches, also affected the so-called English-speaking churches. Whiteness transcended Christian denominationalism. In short, apartheid (separate development) was theologically justified as a Christian policy. The Bible was interpreted in this way, sermons were preached in this way, and Christian seminarians were groomed in this way, to eventually become heads of the South African apartheid state.

This is a heresy, because the Christian faith was falsely used to support a racist ideology. No one can effectively argue that apartheid was simply about politics, because it was inherently a spiritual enterprise to justify white power over darkness and black people. Tutu writes:

> [Apartheid] astonishingly denies the central act of reconciliation which the New Testament declares was achieved by God in His Son, Jesus Christ. Apartheid maintains that human beings, God's own creatures, are fundamentally irreconcilable, flatly contradicting the clear assertions of Scripture that God was in Christ reconciling the world to Himself. Reconciliation could be said to sum up aptly our Lord's ministry and achievement. To deny that He effected this is to deny not just a peripheral and fairly insignificant Christian truth, but the heart of the Christian message. Apartheid, is, therefore, a heresy.[2]

In this chapter, after reviewing the tenets of the last stage of mysticism called union, we will apply those tenets to how Tutu facilitated the union of spiritual leadership during the chaotic times of apartheid. Subsequent chapters will show how Tutu further consolidates his life work as clergy person and South Africa's confessor in his role as Elder or sage.

UNION

Whereas the second stage of mysticism, illumination, is defined by love's conscious desire for union with God, this last stage is characterized no longer by longing for union with God but by abiding in God's essential or pure love. Herein the mystic experiences the ecstatic joy of being united with God. Such union casts out fear and, strangely enough, desire as well, because in union with God there is no need for desire. Bernard of Clairvaux summarizes the threefold journey in which the pilgrim abides in union with God:

> In the first place, we fall at the feet of the Lord, and lament before him Who has made us the faults and sins which we ourselves have committed. In the second, we seek his helping hand to lift us up and to strengthen our feeble knees that we may stand upright. In the third, when we have, with many prayers and tears, obtained these two former graces, then at

length we perhaps venture to lift our eyes to that countenance full of glory and majesty, for the purpose not only to adore, but (I say it with fear and trembling) to kiss his lips, because the Spirit before us is Christ the Lord, to whom being united in a holy kiss, we are by his marvelous condescension made to be one spirit with him.[3]

This third stage differs in an important respect from the other two: the soul has no part to play in achieving it, whereas in the first two stages the soul is led up to humility by Christ and to love by the Holy Spirit. In other words, in the first two stages, purgation and illumination, the pilgrim moves freely to or away from God. Here in the third stage the pilgrim does something differently. She cooperates with the one who calls her. In her effort to exert herself to acquire humility and love under the guidance of Christ and the Spirit, the soul realizes something (or someone) more. The third stage becomes like the third heaven to which Paul refers in 2 Corinthians 12:2: "I know a person in Christ who fourteen years ago was caught up to the third heaven—whether in the body or out of the body I do not know; God knows." Here Paul alludes to the ambiguity of the third stage, namely, that since one cannot force unearned intimacy with God, something more is required in order to reach union with God.

Here the soul must be caught up by God. This last stage of union with God is therefore an experience that only God can provide. On one hand, if the human person provides the experience, then it is only situated from a subjective point of view. On the other, if God provides the experience of rapture, then mutuality between creator and creature becomes possible. From this description it is clear that the experience of mystic rapture is characterized by the involuntary state of trance, which no human being can manufacture on her own. This is analogous to sleep, which Evelyn Underhill refers to as "the suppression of the surface-consciousness called ecstasy."[4] On many levels sleep is an involuntary response. A person cannot just snap her fingers and fall asleep. An environment suitable to sleep must first present itself.

Once the soul becomes conscious of the presence of God, then an analogous involuntary rapture takes place, of being conscious both of God and self in common. Such union cannot help but become indescribable visions that enlighten the mind, body, and soul, and inspire the human will to abide in God's will. Etienne Gilson, a well-known French philosophical theologian, puts it this way: "First. The soul is freed from the use of the bodily senses; this constitutes ecstasy properly so called. In this sense it may be said that the first moment of this mystic slumber is *Extasis*. . . . Second. . . . The slumbering of the external senses is accompanied, in the mystic slumber, by an 'abduction' of the internal sense. By that must be understood that without falling asleep, but on the contrary remaining watchful, the internal sense is carried away by God, who illuminates it."[5]

In order to understand the spiritual life of Tutu, we must encounter this last stage of the mystical way, union with God, or communion. Here I think it is useful to mention the criticisms against Tutu in his idealism of Ubuntu and in the amnesty bestowed by South Africa's Truth and Reconciliation Commission.

Tutu's Ubuntu is similar to Martin Buber's concept of I and Thou. Buber states: "If I face a human being as my Thou, and say the primary word I-Thou to him, he is not a thing among things, and does not consist of things. . . . I do not experience the man to whom I say Thou. But I take my stand in relation to him, in the sanctity of the primary word. . . . Even if the man to whom I say Thou is not aware of it in the midst of his experience, yet relation may exist. For Thou is more than It realizes."[6]

As in the case of I-Thou, Tutu's language of relationality through Ubuntu may appear to be idealistic in the face of apartheid. As a longtime student of Tutu's life, I know about this criticism firsthand, either from watching him on television or writing about him in books. For example, when I was trying to get my first book on Tutu published in the 1990s, an academic peer review was emailed to me along with the rejection by the publisher. "Ubuntu is idealistic," it read, "and therefore of no analytical value." Indeed, the ardent love stage of love that provides the audacity for idealism can be critiqued and argued against, but in no rational way should it be easily dismissed as of no analytical value.

It was with the same type of comments that other publishers rejected my first book on Tutu, but I am thankful publishers like Pilgrim Press, the Church Publishing Inc., and Westminster John Knox Press published my books on Tutu. They trusted the analytical value of a world that believes in a multivalent way to God, rather than a world that dismisses such a notion outright. The lesson learned is that the baby should not be thrown out with the bathwater, but that some caution is called for when dealing with the idealistic or mystical way to God.

Bernard admits as much when he says that, in an absolute sense, this ecstatic union with God is possible only in the next life, when we are freed from the limitations of mortal reason, will, and body. Bernard concludes that when it comes to seeing God's face, "this vision is not for the present life; it is reserved for the next. . . . Neither sage nor saint nor prophet can or could ever see him as he is, while still in this mortal body; but whoever is found worthy will be able to do so when the body becomes immortal."[7] However, in this life some mystics may receive the grace of experiencing what might be called brief glimpses of eternity.

In the union stage of Tutu's life and witness we catch a Christian mystic's glimpses of communion and eternity. Perhaps this is why it is rare to find the amalgamation of spiritual and political leadership in one person. Leaders like Gandhi, Mother Teresa, and Martin Luther King Jr. are rare because moments of ecstasy are rare and of brief duration. Tutu's unusual leadership points to the importance of something so ephemeral as Christian mysticism, in that his formation and spirituality sustained him through the storms of apartheid into the new South Africa. Great Christian mystics teach us that the mystical way is therefore not one of continual ecstasy, but rather a life characterized by vicissitude. In other words, Tutu's life teaches us that even in union with God, we remain created by God. This may seem simple enough, but upon meditating on such union, it looks like segmented visits with the Divine followed by periods of returning to the beginning of purgation, moving again to illumination followed by union.

This reminds me of the critically acclaimed science fiction film in 2016, *Arrival*, based on the 1998 short story "Story of Your Life," by Ted Chiang. The film opens with a soliloquy in which the main character realizes that life is not lived in a straight line and that human language falters upon such a realization. Human language assumes a linear perspective. This is shown magnificently when the human characters try to communicate with twelve superior extraterrestrials called "heptapods," levitating above different countries around the world. The bulk of the movie pictures the main characters researching the heptapod's written language of complicated circular symbols. As Louise Banks, played by Amy Adams, studies the language, she begins to have visions of a child who seems to be her daughter. It is then that she realizes that true language is not linear.

Banks figures out how to ask why the aliens have come. They answer, "Offer weapon." However, China translates this as "use weapon," and the US and other countries follow suit in sensing these extraterrestrials beings may be superior and threatening, prompting them to break off communications altogether. Banks, a linguistics expert, argues that the symbol interpreted as "weapon" might mean "tool," and that China's translation likely results from the competitive nature of their interaction with the aliens. Not just China, however, fears the aliens. US soldiers plant a bomb in the Montana spacecraft. Unaware, Banks reenters the alien vessel, and the aliens eject her just in time to save her.

Banks realizes in the climax of the movie that heptapods have divided a message among the twelve spacecrafts because they want all the nations to share what they learn. They have come to help humanity, because in three thousand years they will need humanity's help in return. The word "weapon" really means "language." In order to learn the alien's language human beings would have to change their linear perception of time to allow "memories" of things that have yet to happen. It is revealed that Banks's visions of the young girl are premonitions of her yet-to-be-born daughter, Hannah.

As a Christian theologian I naturally interpret this film from my perspective. The plot of *Arrival* is similar to the story of the extraterrestrial Jesus, who came among humans and experienced the same reaction of human beings feeling threatened. Jesus too said he brought a weapon, a sword (Matt. 10:34). And the climax for the Gospel of John (1:14) is in how Jesus is the ultimate language, the Word, who causes human beings to learn to live and perceive reality in a different way. The movie helps to illustrate the importance of mysticism, in that we are all too easily enticed to attack what we do not know, instead of being open to that which transcends our point of view.

The threefold method of Christian mysticism therefore looks cyclical and not linear from a human perspective. The good news in all of this, as Bernard states, is that God's desire will be given completely to us "even while still a pilgrim on earth, though not in its fullness and only for a time, a short time. For when after vigils and prayers and a great shower of tears he who was sought presents himself, suddenly he is gone again, just when we think we hold him fast. But he will present himself anew to the soul that pursues him with tears, he will allow himself to be taken hold of but not detained, for suddenly a second time he flees from between our hands."[8]

So, on the one hand, my early critics were correct to reject my approach to Tutu's life and thought, because, in spite of the intensity of Christian mysticism, its transitory character makes union in this life incomplete. On the other hand, the vicissitude of the mystic's experience is not without purpose. Tutu's life is such an example. In the dark night of the soul of South Africa, one could still hear Tutu's voice crying in the wilderness that there still is God—crying that we all still belong together as black and white people. This last stage of union with God is aimed first at purifying the love of the soul by making it live by faith alone. "The lover flees from the arms of the bride and abides for some time far away to try her faithfulness; she, desperately unhappy about her isolation, mourns and sighs for the lost one, until finally he returns and the joys of love are renewed."[9]

This is where Tutu's idealism is of most analytical value. Tutu's life aims not only at loving God for God's own sake; due to the nature of God's reciprocity, Tutu's life aims also at filling the soul with love for others and creation. Loving God entails loving others not for their own sake but for the sake of God, and bringing them to love God as well. We are able to analyze such cyclical love as absent when gunshots are heard and human beings are perceived as inferior to others.

In part 1, through the Christian mystical concept of purgation, I tried to show how Tutu's spiritual formation was as rigorous as it was because it was tested by the fire of his political context. In part 2, it was from such formation that Tutu was illumined to navigate the troubled water of an apartheid South Africa. In this last part, I seek to show how his spirituality has facilitated unity, often in strange places, as Tutu's spirituality has matured in his senior years. Tutu will be the first to say such facilitation of unity in South Africa was not his alone; he was a catalyst amid myriad leaders trying to organize an exorcism of apartheid.

In this last part of the book, we look at Tutu's spirituality in his years as Elder, in which his leadership becomes more explicitly international and interreligious as he joins other important individuals and groups to refine a unified spirituality in the world. So much of Tutu's spiritual work has been about bringing his South African society along with him in his own mystical formation of purgation, illumination, and union.

In Tutu's later years, his spiritual stage is more about applying his theology and wisdom globally. Tutu's spiritual leadership assumes a church capable of unity with those who heretofore were considered heretics, outcasts, and sinners. John de Gruchy provides wisdom here: "To regard the unity of the church largely in spiritual and invisible terms is to misunderstand the teaching of the New Testament, and in the end, to compromise the witness of the church as it struggles against racism and other forces that divide and separate people on the grounds of culture and ethnicity."[10] Such wisdom helps Tutu guard against the so-called "age of miracles" in the late twentieth century, which witnessed the collapse of communism and the freeing of the East European and Baltic states. It was not so much an age of miracles as it was the pragmatism of South Africa to change.

In December 1991, de Klerk, realizing that his own country could be swept by revolution, decided that the system of apartheid was incompatible with the aim of a peaceful and prosperous South Africa. Shortly thereafter a Convention of a Democratic South Africa was called to set the basis for a future democratic constitution, in order to plan for a united South Africa and a common citizenship. The path to democracy was never going to be smooth; the National Party and the Transitional Executive Council, responsible for government in the run-up to the elections, limped from one crisis to the next. While the ANC and the National Party argued over the constitution, the violence continued.

When the deadline for registration for the elections passed, the notable absentees were the right-wing Afrikaner Volksfront and the Zulu nationalist Inkatha Freedom Party, led by Chief Buthelezi. Both feared the future dominance of the ANC. South Africa reverberated with the calls from Chief Buthelezi to his fellow Zulus to lay down their lives for their beliefs, and from white right-wing groups threatening civil war. De Klerk realized his own political leadership would be better served by being practical. He originally envisaged a federalist South Africa, before he saw that economic and demographic realities made the vision of a "little Europe" impossible. Tutu realized the Conservative Party had a diversity of views, and would need a skillful leader to represent it. In his wisdom, he agreed that it would be unfortunate if the ANC won an overwhelming victory, which would give them the right to draw up the constitution on their own, potentially marginalizing other groups.[11]

Tutu was prophetic in those days as to how unity works, at least on the human level. Tutu's spiritual wisdom was such that he knew that in order to reach union, one would need first to encounter purgation and illumination. South African politics would be sorely tested during the period of power sharing in those years of multiparty democracy. Wise leaders of the ANC like Mandela knew early on that it would take a great deal of work during the birth of a democratic South Africa, because a final constitution would need to be drawn up, an executive president elected by the national assembly, and constitutional court and a bill of rights established. Faced with civil war at worst and prolonged political violence at best, Tutu knew spiritual leadership was vital during this time. The virtue of patience and courage of action became the Zen balance in which Tutu waited to discover whether the struggle against apartheid created within South African ranks an artificial unity or a purer unity. Paradoxically, peace and democracy could well spell division. Tutu was well aware of the peril of church division in the face of the urgent issues of the new South Africa. He urged the churches to continue to work together, as they had done in deescalating tensions after Chris

Hani's assassination, and urging Freedom Alliance members to take part in the elections.[12]

TUTU'S UNIFYING ROLE

Tutu's spiritual formation prepared him toward the last stage of Christian mysticism, union, through his role as confessor. Tutu literally became South Africa's confessor to help his nation confess the reality of a wide spectrum of apartheid evil. Again, as mentioned earlier in this chapter, this was extremely difficult to do, given that the concept of apartheid itself was understood by white people to treat them as being holy and set apart. Tutu states that at the very moment the perpetrators of apartheid had intensified its repressive policies, "they must have been totally flabbergasted by the Defiance Campaign to disobey all apartheid laws."[13] Tutu's leadership was crucial, as he led the church to be relevant to society and, even more, to demand that society take seriously a corporate identity capable of diversity and unity, the merging of different peoples and contexts in which we are much more than the sum of all our parts. He had confidence that underneath it all were human beings trying to know what was truly holy and good.

Like any good confessor, Tutu made his nation conscious of the choices between good and evil, even when those in power fiercely tried to hide such consciousness from the South African and international public. One would indeed have to confess whose side one was on, as he wrote in 1980:

> I am sure most people would agree that we in South Africa really have only two options available to us. Anything else is a refinement or adjustment of one or other of these options. The first option is that things remain fundamentally as they are at present, i.e., with political power exclusively in the hands of the whites (or nearly so). They would be the ones who as now call the shots. This could happen through an acceleration of the present Bantustan policy when we would arrive at the logical conclusion of the apartheid policy as described by Dr. Mulder whilst he was minister of what was then called Plural relations. He said this so to be clear that there would be no black South Africa. Black South Africans would be assigned to some homeland to exercise their political and other rights, . . . but some blacks could be co-opted into the system to enjoy considerable benefits and privileges—as a middle class that would be a buffer between the have whites and the have not blacks and as such beneficiaries become some of the most dedicated supporters of the status quo which had blessed them so singularly. But for the rest, they would be consigned to the outer darkness where there would be weeping and gnashing of teeth.[14]

As in the quote above, Tutu had the gift of turning political speech into spiritual speech. Such priestly leadership is seen as churches resisted apartheid through the South African Council of Churches, which inspired the Standing for the Truth Campaign. The South African government realized that it would have to increase the level of repression to an intensity that would be quite unacceptable to the international community. Herein, Tutu's leadership rose to the level of spiritual confessor, not only for South Africa but for many other nation-states in turmoil. The nation-state that related well to South Africa was the United States. Tutu remembers:

> We should have come much earlier to the United States. We had to postpone our departure because of the upheaval in our land. . . . [For example] we went to a black township called Wattville and we went into the home of an old lady and we said, "Can you tell us what happened?" She said, "Yes, Bishop. My grandchildren were playing in the front of the house, in the yard. . . . The police went past here chasing school children. They didn't find them. There was no riot happening at the time, and the police came down the street and swept past my house and they stopped. Bishop, I was sitting in the kitchen which is at the back of my house when one of my children rushed into the kitchen and said, 'Mommy, please come.' I rushed out. My grandson of six was lying just inside the front door. Shot in the back. Dead. Only six years old." . . . What in the name of everything that is good could a six-year-old do to police armed to the teeth? How do you manage to shoot a six-year-old in the back?[15]

Those in the United States could relate to the racial tensions that remained since the time of slavery. African Americans were still experiencing racial profiling and narratives similar to that of the South African grandmother. As Tutu first began encouraging people in the US to help facilitate the demise of apartheid, leaders in the US maintained that they demonstrated their opposition to apartheid and support of peaceful change toward racial justice by imposing restraints on relations with South Africa. Arms sales to South Africa were embargoed beginning in 1963, and in 1977 the United States joined the United Nations in imposing a mandatory arms embargo on South Africa. In February 1978, the US government issued regulations in compliance with a UN Security Council resolution to prohibit exports destined for the South African military, police, or apartheid-enforcing agencies. The US also prohibited direct loans to finance US sales to South Africa. The US also opposed apartheid by refusing to recognize the independence of the four so-called independent homelands.[16]

Where Tutu's unifying role as a spiritual leader on the international stage ran into trouble was with the new Republican party under the leadership of Ronald Reagan. Reagan's administration refrained from acting directly against South Africa, simply advising that whatever formula devised must rest on the consent of all the governed.[17] The following segment of a news report illustrates what Tutu was up against.

> **Desmond Tutu:** Apartheid is as evil, as immoral, as unchristian in my view as Nazism. And in my view the Reagan administration's support and collaboration with it is equally immoral, evil, and totally unchristian.
> **Reporter:** Under mounting pressure from Congress Reagan finally agreed to meet with the Nobel laureate. President Reagan tried to explain his

policy of quiet diplomacy to Bishop Tutu, who has called that policy totally unchristian because he claims it encourages apartheid.

Desmond Tutu: I sought to do my spiel on South Africa and sanctions and so on. And he was not particularly impressed. Reagan said you know these people supported us in World War 2. I said, Mr. President, your history is bad. These guys you're talking about, the South African apartheid regime, most of them supported the Nazis.

Reporter: Afterwards Tutu said the meeting was friendly but—

Desmond Tutu: We did say that we believe that this policy had in fact worsened the situation of blacks in South Africa.

Ronald Reagan: I have to disagree with him on the fact the situation has worsened. It has not. We have made sizable progress.

Desmond Tutu: There has not been a let up on the forced population removals. There has not been a let up of the denationalizing of blacks, turning them into aliens. And we haven't seen as it were the quid pro quo of constructive engagement.[18]

In 1986 the US Congress (over President Reagan's veto) passed a stronger sanctions bill against South Africa, and in 1988 the Senate Foreign Relations Committee approved measures aimed at cutting off virtually all US trade with South Africa and forcing American firms to withdraw almost all investments from the country. This newer bill did not pass the full Senate, but after 1988 all US corporations with subsidiaries in South Africa would have to pay US taxes in addition to those owed to South Africa. Furthermore, a divestment campaign strengthened in the US, seeking to force US corporations to end their support for white minority rule by severing all ties with South Africa. Many states, cities, counties, colleges and universities, as well as a substantial number of churches and other organizations, adopted binding measures requiring the sale of stocks and bonds in US corporations involved in South Africa.[19]

SANCTIONS

Tutu's spiritual leadership also focused on using money as a tool to make South Africa give up apartheid. This is not as unusual in spiritual leadership as one might think. In fact, a majority of Jesus' teachings are focused on the human and divine encounter of giving away everything in order to find true wealth. It is the spiritual paradox of losing identity to find it or, in Jesus' narrative, the paradox of losing life to save it. In Christian mysticism this is called *kenosis*—the notion of giving of self and still remaining a self. Similar to the burning bush that is not consumed (Exod. 3), following Jesus entails a losing of self in order to find the real identity to which we are called. And there is no more complicated self than those labeled as rich or poor.

In many ways, Tutu becomes a spiritual director for the world, in this sense of finding a truer identity. A decade before Tutu became the chair of the Truth and Reconciliation Commission, he was seen as a national and international confessor to which others could tell their stories of suffering, in hope of some kind of absolution and restoration. Tutu, however, was not the kind of confessor that one easily dismisses as cloistered and irrelevant to real life. On the contrary, Tutu's fame grew as a confessor as he took on the collaboration of Western countries with the evil of apartheid:

> By law, a black father . . . being fortunate to get a job, must leave his family in the Bantustan homelands to eke out a miserable existence while he comes to the white man's town as a migrant laborer to live an unnatural existence in a single sex hotel for eleven months of the year. He is, then, prey to prostitution, drunkenness, and sodomy. The migratory labor system is the legal policy of the land, eating away at the vitality of black family life, again, not accidentally, but of set deliberate government intent. That is how you keep the costs of production low because the migrant is paid as if he were single. Now it is important for those who invest in South Africa to know that it is this kind of system, whether they like it or not, whether they intend it or not, it is this kind of system which they buttress by their involvement there.[20]

For Tutu, those who invest in South Africa invest in a system that is evil, and just as unchristian and immoral as Nazism ever was. Any country that invests in a system that depends on black misery and suffering is evil. Tutu explains how many in Western countries justified themselves: "If someone else says to those who invest in South Africa, 'Hey, why don't you pull out?' They will be the first to say, 'You know, the people who will suffer the most if we pull out are blacks.' Baloney! For all these many years they have depended on black misery and suffering. What makes them suddenly become these wonderful altruists who care about black suffering?"[21]

Tutu's celebrated leadership of sanctions against his own country presented a further question, how to move South Africa away from an impending civil war. Tutu responded to an interviewer who asked if there was a particular moment he felt was a turning point in the fight against apartheid: "I believe that when the South African Council of Churches and I were awarded the Nobel Peace Prize, . . . it said the world was watching. . . . And it gave a high profile to our cause and helped to persuade especially the United States to impose sanctions, which I think were quite critical."[22]

Tutu announced in 1985, when he was enthroned as bishop of Johannesburg, that, should apartheid not be dismantled or not be in the process of being dismantled within eighteen to twenty-four months, then whatever the legal consequences, he would quite specifically call on the international community to impose punitive economic sanctions on the government.[23] Up to that point Tutu had not yet campaigned for disinvestment. He had called for political, diplomatic, but above all economic pressure as a last chance to avert the bloodbath.

When Tutu began to advocate for sanctions, he began to be criticized by both whites and those blacks who worked within the system. Because the focus turned to money, this was not a strange coincidence. It must be noted again, however, that Tutu first said there ought to be investment, but on strict conditions, to be implemented within eighteen to twenty-four months. He also said that workers should be housed as family units near the workplace of the breadwinners and no migratory labor should exist. He advocated for black workers to be unionized with no influx control and pass system. And he called for investment in black education and training.

Tutu began to move toward sanctions against South Africa when the above conditions of investment were not put into place. Tutu knew that South Africa must suffer consequences of their failure to act. White South Africans could no longer dictate what methods of change could be implemented by blacks to try to change the system. After all, black South Africans did not even have the vote, so how could the South African government say they must not call for international intervention? What alternative would be left except violence? What would they have done if they had been in the place of black people?

As a spiritual discipline of integrity, Tutu never said anything abroad that he could not say in South Africa. He challenged anyone to quote one single thing he said abroad that he had not said many times before at home. This challenge was accentuated in his criticism of Reagan's "constructive engagement" with South Africa. Tutu called such constructive engagement evil, immoral, and unchristian. When white South Africans asked for prayer in the threat of external aggression in the cold war against the Soviet Union and communism, Tutu said blacks had no fear of such external enemies. Black people were already victims in the vicious system of apartheid, not communism. Their major concern was internal, not external.

Though he received criticism, Tutu did not regret his statement about the Russians. People chose to hear what they were already disposed to hear. Tutu explained, "I said that though blacks by and large rejected communism as being atheistic and materialistic, they would nevertheless welcome the Russians as their saviors from the pernicious evil of apartheid, that for them anything must surely be better than the hell they experience daily in the land of their birth." Tutu wanted to make clear that apartheid gave a bad name both to free enterprise and to democracy. "When you are in a dungeon and someone comes to rescue you, you do not ask about their credentials and pedigree."[24]

As apartheid began to crumble under the weight of sanctions, Tutu threw his hands in the air and shouted "Yippee!" when he heard that negotiators had agreed on an interim postapartheid constitution for South Africa. "I think we have got to rejoice that this awful, awful, ugly, evil system . . . is officially at an end," he said. But Tutu cautioned, "While we ought to be filled with a wonderful euphoria, we are not, because people are just stunned by the violence. . . . Let them be ready now to invest in our country."[25]

It is interesting for Tutu to look back on the difficult matters of calling for sanctions against his own country. Thinking back to the 1980s he says, "Every time I have spoken to the State President he always says, 'When are you going to tell them to lift sanctions?' Sanctions are effective! Sanctions got the government out of Angola, Namibia is now independent thanks to sanctions." Tutu goes on to reflect on the double standard of overseas governments who wanted to reward de Klerk's leadership in the 1990s right away by lifting sanctions. Tutu states, "These were the same people who said sanctions are not effective! Sanctions have worked—to say otherwise is to talk baloney. I have always known that, and the government's response has always shown that they have always known that also."[26]

As confessor, Tutu facilitated a united spiritual witness together with the resilience of the people to persuade President F. W. de Klerk to undertake his remarkable and very courageous initiatives, including the release of Nelson Mandela and others, and then the unbanning of political groups such as the ANC, PAC, and SACP. The subsequent developments in South Africa were in part due to the witness of spiritual communities all around the world advocating for sanctions against South Africa as a means of nonviolent protest. It took Tutu's spiritual witness of naming demons and duplicity to help South Africa see itself as a nation in the world and for the world, to see a legitimate South Africa. We are in Tutu's debt for such illumination and union. Spirituality mattered a great deal in these complicated realities of how to see human value, as Tutu has boldly pointed out the theological complicity of the many South African churches that shored up the apartheid system.[27]

NONVIOLENCE AND JUST WAR THEORY

The greatest challenge in the new South Africa was the maintenance of what has become the union of spiritual and political leadership. Tutu's context of South African apartheid presented the dilemma in which he, as ecclesial head of a historically white church, negotiated how to act effectively in a society so defined by race that both Afrikaner and African could claim God's election as the chosen race. Subsequently, as head of the TRC in South Africa, Tutu's urgency toward restorative justice was not simply to restore black people to a place of flourishing. Such an interpretation of Tutu forfeits his profound contribution toward the current substance of peace. After his success with the TRC in South Africa, Tutu was sought out the world over to lend his help. Here are some of these commissions or beginning stages to form such commissions in which Tutu either was consulted, was directly involved, or played an influencing role:[28]

- Algeria's Inquiry Commission in Charge of the Question of Disappearances, formed in 2003 to investigate human rights violations that occurred in the 1990s
- Brazil's nonpunitive National Truth Commission, approved in late 2011

- Canada's Indian Residential Schools Truth and Reconciliation Commission, which investigated from 2008 to 2015 the human rights abuses in the Canadian Indian residential school system
- A Truth and Reconciliation Commission, mandated in a peace agreement in the Democratic Republic of the Congo in 2004, issuing an administrative report in 2007
- Gambia's Truth, Reconciliation and Reparations Commission (TRRC) Act, enacted by the National Assembly in 2017 to investigate human rights violations during the period of Yahya Jammeh's rule
- Honduras's Truth and Reconciliation Commission to investigate events around the 2009 Honduras *coup d'etat*
- Mauritius's Truth and Justice Commission of the Mauritius, an independent truth commission established in 2009 that explored the impact of slavery and indentured servitude
- Northern Ireland, in which a documentary filmed Tutu facilitating discussions between families in conflict[29]
- Rwanda's National Unity and Reconciliation Commission, formed in 1999 to promote reconciliation after the genocide
- Sierra Leone's Truth and Reconciliation Commission, which investigated the end of the Sierra Leone civil war in 1999
- Solomon Islands' Truth and Reconciliation Commission, launched on April 29, 2009, to address the trauma during the five-year (1999–2004) ethnic conflict on Guadalcanal
- Two commissions in the United States: The Greensboro Truth and Reconciliation Commission, a nongovernmental body that ran from 2004 to 2006 to investigate deadly events in the city that took place around November 3, 1979, and came to be known as the Greensboro Massacre; and the Maine Wabanaki-State Truth and Reconciliation Commission, which investigated child welfare issues among the Wabanaki peoples

Because of Tutu's Trinitarian spirituality, in which diverse personhood flourishes in unity, Tutu is obligated to articulate a substance of peace in which all South Africans have an opportunity to grow toward unity. All of this makes sense in South Africa, but not in other truth commissions. In order to further understand Tutu's unique leadership, some understanding of his view of peacemaking is in order. Tutu is instructive for how one may understand strategies of nonviolence as leading to a substantial peace, not only for South Africa but for the rest of the world. Mahatma Gandhi is also instructive here as he states, "We must be the change we wish to see in the world."[30] Tutu's peace leadership, in comparison to Gandhi's characteristic visceral emphasis and Martin Luther King Jr.'s poetical prowess, is in how Tutu adroitly disarms enemies in order to bring warring parties together. He does this by telling stories. "Do you remember taking off on a flight during a storm with dark overcast skies? And then your plane breaks through the bank of clouds and there above the clouds the sun is shining gloriously golden. . . . Nature seems to teach us . . . peace and calm almost always happen after turbulence."[31]

Tutu goes on to comfort his South African audience, warning them that there will be turbulence and periods of transition. South Africa could have been in a much worse situation, facing an abyss of racial turmoil, but he reminds his readers that they together pulled away from that precipice. He encourages his audience that this is so because God is with us and we are made for interdependence. God creates through interdependence, as Psalm 23 indicates. God is also interdependent with us, as God walks with us through the valley of the shadow of death. We are not spared birth pangs or anxiety, but God is with us, and has created humanity to experience peace, justice, compassion, and reconciliation.

Not all spiritual strategies for living lifetimes of nonviolence look the same. For example, Christian thinkers today wonder how to do significant research and education on the possibilities and limits of just war theory for the sake of a nonviolent world. Such just war theory goes back to early Christian thinkers like Augustine of Hippo, who provided the basic worldview for conducting a just war. Because of the fifth-century context of Augustine's thought, theologians posit that the degree of lethality in most wars in the twenty-first century has risen so precipitously that the degree of proportionality—a necessary proposition in just war theory—can never be satisfied. Still, such theologians, like Tutu, may see the necessity for force or violence if used for "the common good." Later in this chapter I will engage Tutu's understanding and practice of nonviolence. First, let's explore the roots and thinking of just war theory.

The evolution of the just war concept has its roots in classical antiquity. Plato formulated a code of just war, although Aristotle was the one who phrased it as "just war." Plato, within the context of the wars between city-states, wrestled with the problematic thought that Greeks would wish to exterminate fellow Greeks. He helped to establish the parameters within which rational people would wage war as the ultimate way of settling disputes. The just war was meant to vindicate justice and restore peace. Beyond Plato and Aristotle, just war theory can be traced back to Cicero (d. 43 BCE), Ambrose of Milan (ca. 339–97), Augustine, Aquinas, who further developed just war theology as a part of the Christian ethos, and Luther and Calvin, who carried just war theology into the Protestant Reformation.

Pacifism, as a Christian doctrine, is articulated and enacted particularly through church groups emerging from Anabaptist traditions and, later, Quakers. But these groups gave different emphases to understandings of nonviolence. These marginalized groups are important variations in the historical tradition of the church, which has at times operated firmly in the service of the rulers and at other times struggled to distance itself from oppressive rulers by affirming an alternative liberative tradition.

In Christian history overall, however, three attitudes are to be found toward war: pacifism, just war, and holy war. The early church, persecuted by a pagan state, was pacifist until the time of Constantine in the fourth century. At that point, through the early church's close association with the state and the threat of the barbarian invasions, Christians took over the classical world's doctrine of just war, especially as Ambrose and Augustine added Christian elements to understanding just war.[32] As the church grew complicit with European coloni- zation, the interpretation of peace changed as well. The twentieth century gave way to two world wars in which the church's three positions of just war, pacifism, and holy war resurfaced. This was a confusing time for the church's convictions concerning peace and human flourishing. Tutu is helpful in describing his own confusion.

> There is much puzzlement in the black community. Not only did the west go to war with the approval of the church, it lauded to the skies the Under- ground Resistance movement during World War II and regarded Diet- rich Bonhoeffer as a modern day Christian martyr and saint (and I believe rightly) even though he was involved in a plot to assassinate Hitler, the head of his home country for which involvement he was executed. Most western countries have their history written in blood. The USA became independent after the thirteen colonies had fought the American War of Independence. But when it comes to the matter of black liberation the west and most of its church wake up and find themselves gone all pacifist.[33]

Often the question of just war is thought out during specific episodes of battle, as when a chaplain might advise a commander on the "just" engagement of a target. Because of the chaplain's counsel, there are instances where attacks are actually called off. The just war theory has several requirements, but they are often misappropriated in the twenty-first century. The 2003 invasion of Iraq is one glaring example. First, you need a just cause in order to attack. Was there a good cause to overthrow Saddam Hussein? Second, the "legitimate authority" must decide the use of force. That authority is not the US government but the United Nations, as President George W. Bush acknowledged in his speech in March 2003. Third, you need a reasonable chance of succeeding. Fourth, you must seek to avoid killing noncombatants, which means using the right amount of force, what theorists call proportionality. Jean Bethke Elshtain, a prominent American ethicist who is also a devout Christian, argued in an article published October 6, 2002, in the *Boston Globe* that a preventive strike on Iraq was mor- ally justifiable. She acknowledged that she was swimming against the tide but insisted that thinking on the question of just war theory in relation to the Iraqi situation misses the point: "There are times when justice demands the use of force as a response to violence, hatred, and injustice." Was this one of those times?

Elshtain wrote that a preemptive strike was moral because Saddam Hus- sein was an evil tyrant on the moral level of Stalin, and he has never wavered from his goal to possess atomic, bacteriological, and chemical weapons. He had already used chemical weapons on his own people. This is a just cause for war, she argued: the prevention of the use of these so-called ABC weapons of mass destruction. Then there was the actual goal of the war. Just war theory does not see regime change as an acceptable cause for attacking. Elshtain acknowledged this but argued that rogue regimes deserve their own destruction. Yet she didn't say who determines the just cause for taking down a rogue government.[34]

Elshtain shows us that in just war theory, the aim of the attack must be clear. In the twenty-first-century Western world, however, this can appear as a democratic government must be installed after the war; otherwise the cost in lives is unacceptable. A concrete example for why such clarity needs to be made may be seen through the correspondence of Episcopal bishop Pierre Whalon. As a bishop, Whalon expressed that he was very concerned that the church be able to speak cogently to the situation, for many of the people who could decide the use of force against Iraq were Episcopalians, not to mention Christians. Moreover, moral questions are never merely the province of Christians. All people, no matter what their religious stance, Whalon wrote, must choose the good and avoid evil. There can be no docile position in the face of evil.[35]

As illustrated in Tutu's dealing with the Iraq war, the substance of peace does not mean placid behavior. Tutu remained fearless in his confrontation with world leaders who seemingly took their nation-states mindlessly into war. This was not grandstanding by Tutu, because his challenge of such leaders grew out of his moving his South African church out of its own inertia into a movement against violence and oppression. The problem here, however, is that political forces may view the church's defiance as itself a threat. For example, on the verge of South Africa's democratic election, Tutu believed that feathers had been ruffled and hurts inflicted by what many had experienced as abrasive and turbulent.

For Tutu, such confrontation could not be avoided, and in any case the gospel is almost always disturbing to comfortable status quos. Tutu's hope was for a different emphasis, to invest in the "inner life" of the church, to heal and nurture people, and to help them to bring about transformation around them.[36] For example, being a spiritual leader meant handling the vehement criticism, even abuse, that Tutu had to handle from the white public concerning his nonviolent call to boycott the 1992 Summer Olympics in Barcelona, Spain. It appears to have brought home to many whites the consequences of the violence far more effectively than his impassioned appeals that did not affect the white public as directly.

Tutu made it clear that he embarked on this course reluctantly. He told his congregation at St. George's Cathedral that he had thought he was done taking up this sort of role. Reflecting more on it to a journalist later, Tutu added that his plan had been to take a less central role once his country's political process normalized, but that one has to act when one "sees our country moving so inexorably almost to disaster."[37]

Despite these qualifications on the clarity of his own political involvement as a spiritual leader, Tutu vigorously defended the continued right of spiritual communities to become involved in political action in as clear a way as possible while remaining spiritual; for example, he constantly stressed that the church must remain autonomous and, in particular, must have just as much right now and in the future to act independently of political parties. In February 1990, within weeks of de Klerk's milestone speech releasing Mandela, this was underlined by the decision of the Anglican Synod of Bishops banning priests from being members of political parties, as well as their call for the African National Congress to abandon the armed struggle. The call for a possible Olympic boycott was made as an independent church initiative without consultation with politicians. When it was put to Tutu the following day that some in the democratic movement were unhappy that he had not consulted them, he responded sharply: "I am speaking, as I always have spoken, on moral and theological grounds. . . . I am not a lacky of political organizations." Perhaps Tutu articulated best the reason why spiritual leaders are needed on the frontline of politics while remaining spiritual leaders when he told a journalist that people were sad, angry, and starting to lose hope that some new order would take shape: "We could easily see the situation degenerate into all-out civil war. And we want to avert that."[38]

Being consistent, some thirteen years later, in 2003 Tutu called for Tony Blair, the prime minister of Great Britain at the time of the invasion, and President George W. Bush to stand before the international criminal court in The Hague because of the physical and moral devastation caused by the Iraq War. Tutu thought that the former British and US leaders in 2003 lied about Saddam Hussein having weapons of mass destruction as part of their case for a just war. In 2012, Tutu refused to join a meeting in attendance with Blair, again because of Blair's complicity in the invasion of Iraq. Tutu went so far as to say that the invasion left the world more destabilized and divided "than any other conflict in history." Blair contested Tutu's views and said Iraq had become a more prosperous country than it was under Saddam Hussein. "I have a great respect for Archbishop Tutu's fight against apartheid . . . but to repeat the old canard that we lied about the intelligence is completely wrong, as every single independent analysis of the evidence has shown."[39]

Tutu never supported the invasion of Iraq on grounds of just war theory because there was never any clear evidence of weapons of mass destruction (WMD). So, as he wrote for the *Guardian*, he thought it immoral of the United States and Great Britain to invade Iraq in 2003 on the premise of the existence of such weapons. He argued these nations should have recognized the complicated world we live in, with advanced technologies and communications systems making interconnection ever more possible. With these resources at their disposal, he thought, these wealthy countries should have been able to see beforehand that Iraq lacked WMD. Tutu described the Western leadership in the US and UK as behaving like playground bullies who were pushing international relations further apart.[40]

Before the invasion of Iraq was ordered, Tutu called the national security advisor Condoleezza Rice to argue that United Nations weapons inspectors needed more time to determine whether WMDs existed in Iraq, and therefore potentially bring the rest of the world into agreement with the plan for invasion.

But his advice wasn't heeded. Tutu goes on to argue in the article that the Western world often hides behind duplicity to determine who exhibits good political leadership and who should be terminated or sent to the International Criminal Court, while Tony Blair is spared reprobation.[41]

Tutu believes we cannot look away from the cost of such duplicity. Ridding Iraq of its so-called despotic and murderous leader has cost a staggering sum, with an average in 2011 of 6.5 people dying there each day in suicide attacks and vehicle bombs, according to the Iraqi Body Count project. As of the spring of 2019, between 183,249 and 205,785 Iraqis have died in the conflict since 2003, and millions have been displaced.[42] The US casualty status of Operation Iraqi Freedom is nearly 4,500, as of April 2019. American soldiers had been killed and more than 32,000 wounded.[43] On these grounds alone, thinks Tutu, in a consistent world, those responsible for this suffering and loss of life should be just as accountable as African and Asian peers who have been made to answer for their actions in The Hague. Tutu concludes that the direst outcome of the death tolls in Iraq is that the leaders responsible betrayed their duty as "custodians of morality. . . . The point is that Mr. Bush and Mr. Blair should not have allowed themselves to stoop to [Saddam Hussein's] immoral level."[44]

For Tutu, it is unacceptable for leaders to take drastic action on the basis of a lie. Further, there is usually no acknowledgment or apology when they are found out. What does this teach our children? Tutu's appeal to Blair was not to talk about leadership, but to demonstrate it. Tutu states, "You are a member of our family, God's family. . . . So are our brothers and sisters in Iraq, in the US, in Syria, in Israel and Iran."[45] In 2012, Tutu was slated to attend a conference with Blair at the Discovery Invest Leadership Summit in Johannesburg. Before the event Tutu felt an increasingly profound sense of discomfort about attending a summit on "leadership" with him, and decided to withdraw.[46]

TUTU AND JUST WAR

Despite his opposition to the US-led invasion of Iraq, Tutu seems to be an adherent of just war theory. As I am both a disciple of Tutu and a pacifist, I have always found this to be a disturbing position. Upon more discussion of his position, however, the reader may come to see how Tutu's position makes sense in light of the tragedy of apartheid South Africa. Tutu constantly called for non-violent means to end apartheid, but often found himself feeling as though there was little alternative to changing those who controlled the system than through the use of violence. Tutu explains: "And yet how strident is the opposition overwhelmingly from whites to economic sanctions. We blacks cannot vote. Now we must not invoke the non-violent methods which are likely to be the most effective. Then what is left? If sanctions should not be allowed or being applied, fail, then there is no other way left but to fight for the right to be human and to be treated as such. Can someone show us a different conclusion?"[47] In this quote the reader finds the summation of Tutu's Christian realism.

Nonviolence is the Christian norm; however, how does one translate this norm into a hostile world? Other evidence of Tutu's acceptance of the legitimate use of force can be seen in such statements as, "Should the West fail to impose economic sanctions, it would then be justifiable in my view for blacks to try to overthrow an unjust system violently. But I myself am committed to the way of bringing an end to this tyranny by peaceful means. Should this option fail, the low-intensity civil war I referred to at the beginning of this essay will escalate into a full-scale war."[48]

Although I am a disciple of Tutu, I believe that in Christian spirituality, any conceptualization of just war is anachronistic; we need to unlearn the self-fulfilling prophecy of violence. This requires Christians to constantly practice peace. In other words, talk of just war originally meant something very different from the way we want to use it today. Indeed, no debate about just war has prevented a war; rather, it calls all involved to a conversation and the review of a moral checklist. Theologically, the early church expected God's kingdom to dawn imminently, as it faced a hostile government that sought to eradicate Christianity as a subversive influence in the Roman Empire.

For early Christians, the pertinent question was whether or not to take up arms, either in self-defense or in the service of the state. But in the post-Constantinian era Christians readily fought for the empire under the insignia of Christ. The theological question had changed to what constituted a just war. This theological question has never been answered, because how could any Christian formed in the Sermon on the Mount envision a constitution of just war? Christians are formed to make peace, and, as Tutu believes, "Peace is achieved through active cooperation."[49] A theological imperative was the establishment of criteria to draw distinctions between wars with a just cause and end, and wars of material greed, national pride, vindictiveness, power, and the like. Paraphrasing Aquinas, Tutu provides the criteria for just war:[50]

> We try to use the very strict set of criteria that we use to determine when it would be justifiable for Christians to go to war, the so called "just war" theory. . . . According [to just war theory] once the criteria have been satisfied, e.g., have all other nonviolent means been exhausted, is the cause just, are the prospects of success good, will the situation that results be better than that which it is intended to replace, are the methods just (in the case of war, will every effort be made to ensure that innocent civilians are not unnecessarily injured and the war is to be declared by a competent authority?).[51]

Soon a related question emerged concerning the responsibility of Christians regarding tyrannical rule. To what extent were they permitted or obligated as Christians to resort to arms to remove the tyrant? For example, young white males (usually English-speaking white males) asked whether it was theologically legitimate for them to fight in the South African Defense Force, since it was involved in the military occupation of Namibia, cross-border raids, and war in the townships. These young white males articulated their protest against being drafted into the South African military in terms of traditional just war theory. Regarding this matter, Tutu states: "People—and young people specifically—are less and less willing to be used as cannon fodder, fighting to uphold corporate interests or the rule of the elites. . . . And understanding of this gap [between north and south], and its economic and colonial origins, can only help us to formulate solidarity."[52]

In other words, the problem of defining a just use of violence depends on who is interpreted as oppressor and victim—as terrorist or freedom fighter. After all, Nelson Mandela was once described as a terrorist and even went to prison under what was known in South Africa as the Terrorist Act to protect the state.

A REBUTTAL TO JUST WAR

What is terrorism? According to the US Department of Defense, it is the unlawful use of force against individuals or property, with the intention of intimidating societies for ideological purposes. This definition assumes that wars can be fought by states only. But one person's terrorism is another's martyrdom. For example, what constitutes terrorism, guerilla warfare, or legitimate defense? Tutu explains further: "The USA supports quite vigorously those called Contras in Nicaragua, who seek to overthrow a valid government legally decked in what independent observers considered to be free and fair elections. The Reagan administration also supports Dr. Jonas Savimbi and his Unita forces which are bent on toppling the MPLA Luanda government."[53]

Tutu's insight into Western bias raises the interesting question, When Christians go to war, what are we defending? The answer usually leaves Christians embarrassed, especially if such Christians are committed to the spirituality of the church in which the formation of community is essential. In Christian spirituality, there can be no conditional obedience to the principle of violence. Just war assumes one can separate noncombatants from combatants on the basis of universal evils, but without universal criteria for good and evil, there is no way to respond to moral anarchy in war situations. In other words, a double-standard morality always exists in just war criteria. Even advocates of just war acknowledge this failing, relying instead in ambiguous situations on the necessity of taking a stand for the common good.

Christian ethicists such as Stanley Hauerwas disagree with a methodology by which to adjudicate universal evils. In other words, Christians should respond in war situations, not on the basis of universal principles of what is right or wrong, nor on the basis of assuming a liberal ideal of freeing a world of war, but on the basis of the Christian way of life determined in Jesus. In addition, in the twentieth and twenty-first centuries, the church and the world face nuclear, atmospheric, and biological war that threatens all of creation. How could such war ever be justified? The church determines a response of nonviolence because of the collect at the beginning of this chapter. The church does not respond on the basis of universal evils espoused in just war theory. As Christians we are a particular kind of people, with particular behaviors that should always increase community. Therefore, when one determines a spirituality of war or peace, what is determined is a particular spirituality in which faith commitments are made explicit.

Is there an explicit commitment to community as taught and practiced by Jesus? If so, we return to the original question, When Christians go to war, what are we defending? Are we defending the justice of the individual in the Western world? As Hauerwas teaches us, we do not go to war because of hatred but because of what we love. He states, "That is why Christian realism requires the disavowal of war. Christians do not disavow war because it is often so horrible, but because war, in spite of its horror—or perhaps because it is so horrible—can be so morally compelling. That is why the church does not have an alternative to war. The church is the alternative to war. When Christians lose that reality—that is, the reality of the church as an alternative to the world's reality—we abandon the world to the unreality of war."[54] Hauerwas's teaching is counterintuitive in the Western world, because we love our individual selves the most. For the church, however, to practice peace we must realize that our main love and obligation is to a person who would rather be crucified than take up arms. Herein is our difficulty to live peaceably in a world at war.

For Hauerwas, it is difficult to live peaceably, because our loves give slant to our vision as to how to behave in the world. Our loves create national interests and motivations for war. In addition, our loves perpetuate the double-standard methodology of believing in justice for all while all along another kind of justice is practiced by those in power. Tutu displays the double standard in the following way: "Many have called on the ANC to renounce violence and have not directed similar demands to the South African government which has destabilized the neighboring countries. Is it because the perpetrators are white and the victims of injustice black that this selective morality holds sway?"[55]

The problem with just war theory is that it creates a set of criteria for what Christian spirituality looks like that is different from what Jesus teaches us in the Sermon on the Mount. For Jesus, the spiritual person is indeed in the world, helping the world to practice peacemaking, meekness, purity, and the kingdom of God. For those who think Jesus' Sermon on the Mount is idealistic or irrelevant, the criterion for living in the world is usually about what is best for the survival of the individual. Therefore, heroism becomes the world's chief virtue. We learn from Hauerwas, however, that the problem with heroism is that it is unpredictable and successful wars cannot be fought this way. Heroism is an example of ordinary soldiers having the opportunity to shine through as heroes. You should never fight wars for ideals, because they become limitless. The problem with democracies is that you have citizen soldiers who do not know how to fight limited wars. In war there is an organic escalation in which you have moral adjudication lacking in a people incapable of fighting a realist war.

So far I have discussed the rationale for violence in the Western church, Tutu's responses, and a counterargument to the rationale of just war. The discussion so far has not been easy for me to objectify, since I am an advocate of unequivocal nonviolence and believe such a position is the essence of the practice of Christian spirituality. As I have tried to show, however, such a position of unequivocal nonviolence is not assumed by all Christians. And more difficult for me to consider, unequivocal nonviolence is not the position of some I consider saints, such as Tutu, who states: "Is violence justifiable to topple an unjust system? I am theologically conservative and traditional. I think the dominant position of my church regarding violence is this: We regard all violence as evil (the violence of an unjust system such as apartheid and the violence of those who seek to overthrow it). That is why we have condemned 'necklacing' and car bombs, as well as instances of violence perpetrated by the government and the security forces. This does not mean, however, that the mainstream tradition of the church does not reluctantly allow that violence may in certain situations be necessary. The just war theory . . . makes this point clearly."[56]

As I have mentioned, his position on the legitimate use of force challenges what is at the heart of my perception of Christian spirituality. Tutu's vital leadership in South Africa's history, when there could be no official black leadership, forced him into being the sole voice able to articulate pluralism and individual rights in the midst of the corrupt public discourse of South Africa at that time. In light of the oppressive and exclusivist discourse of apartheid, Tutu's ecclesiology readily accepts pluralist tendencies. Tutu states:

> One of the first things we should acknowledge is the cultural, religious, and racial pluralism of our day. Consequently, we must be as a Church, as Christians, [ready] to make our contribution to the establishment of democracy as part of a cooperative venture. The days are past when we operated as if we were the only pebbles on the beach. It was exhilarating for us in South Africa when we marched in Cape Town in September of 1989 to walk with arms linked with a Jewish rabbi on one side and a Muslim imam on the other. That united front forged between peoples of different faiths and ideologies made us more robust as we faced a formidable adversary in the brutal apartheid regime. We must build coalitions and forge alliances.[57]

In other words, in order to understand Tutu's position of just war, one must be fully located in the context of South African apartheid. One must then ask, To what extent could a spirituality of nonviolence become intelligible in an apartheid society? For example, in the South African context, Tutu states: "The elimination of violence is directly related to the elimination of state and institutional oppression. . . . Botha offered Mandela his freedom on condition that he reject violence. . . . Mandela replied, . . . 'It was only when all other forms of [political] resistance were no longer open to us that we turned to armed struggle.'"[58]

For Tutu, it is not so much a question of his own acknowledgment of a spirituality of nonviolence, which he in fact maintains. It was more a question of being a responsible hybrid leader of spirituality and politics in the tragic circumstances of apartheid South Africa, in which the only worldview at times was the need to defend the dignity of humanity. Tutu's genius was in showing that the primary violence in South Africa was the violence of apartheid, a context in which he was called upon to lead nonviolently, although realistically.[59] Tutu states: "The Government and its supporters provide the primary violence and terrorism in South Africa. . . . I myself condemn all violence as always evil, but I hold too that there may come a time when it would be justifiable to use violence to overthrow an unjust regime. That is the traditional and conservative position of the church. We must prepare people to be disciplined in nonviolent action, to disobey unjust laws."[60]

Having been a student of Tutu's for many years, I am only now beginning to make sense of his complex positions on just war. This is difficult, because I believe Tutu to be both de facto a nonviolent resister and yet a public Christian realist.

Tutu believes there are "remarkable" Christians who believe that no one is ever justified in using violence, even against the most horrendous evil. These are "pacifists" who believe that the gospel of the cross effectively rules out anyone taking up the sword, however just the cause. "I admire these persons," Tutu states, but "sadly, I must confess that I am made of far less noble stuff."[61] "I am not in Gandhi's league."[62] "I am a lover of peace and I try to work for justice because only thus do I believe we could ever hope to establish a durable peace."[63]

Tutu is fond of reminding people that God creates human beings in God's own image, and part of such an image is freedom. Freedom is an indispensable ingredient of the spiritual life, because freedom implies an uncoerced relationship. For Tutu, Jesus always challenges persons to opt to follow him or desert him, to obey him or reject him. Persons are not robots. In this light, Tutu refers to the parable of the Prodigal Son, whose conscience did develop, although slowly, and needed not to be violated in its development. So too Paul teaches us in the New Testament that one should allow the ongoing development of conscience concerning foods offered to idols. Paul teaches that those who are wise know there are no such things as idols (i.e., idolatry is that which mimics the truth of God) and can eat this food without spiritual defilement (1 Cor. 8). There are others, however, for whom to eat is to violate their conscience and so to sin. Spiritual decisions are based as far as possible on a sound understanding of all the factors that are relevant to the subject under review. This is why spiritual direction becomes a crucial practice of peacemaking.

It is from such biblical exegesis that Tutu challenges any imposition or forced compliance. One cannot impose spiritual growth on communities; instead, like the prodigal son, one must allow spiritual maturity to develop naturally and in due season. More specifically, this exegesis applies to his position on conscientious objection in the following way. Tutu believes, based on the above rationale of the freedom of development, that space and time must always be allowed for Christian maturity. For Tutu, this means that there is a legitimate Christian principle that persons are obliged to obey one's conscience. This legitimacy is modeled in most normal democratic countries, where conscription obtains provision and where space and time is made for conscientious objectors by the provision of an alternative form of national service.[64] So, for Tutu, just war is intelligible, as it hinges on the conscience of a person's development; such a conscience, however, must be intense enough to deal with the reality and inevitability of violence.

Before one concludes entirely that Tutu is a just warrior, one must fully understand Tutu's theological assumptions, as I have tried to do through Tutu's biblical exegesis of spiritual growth. More particularly, such an understanding of spiritual growth for Tutu depends upon the character of the community in which the Christian individual is to grow. Tutu explains:

> [We are] trying to make sense of the experience of a particular and definite community of believers in the light of God's revelation of who He is, the cardinal reference point being the man Jesus Christ. Engaged theology is one done with passion and sometimes not paying too much attention to the niceties and delicacies. . . . Why you see, what you apprehend, depend so much on who you are, on where you are. . . . When blacks— after many years during which their cautious protest was consistently ignored—opted in desperation for armed struggle, whites dubbed them "terrorists," which meant they could be ruthlessly imprisoned, hanged or shot. The will to be free is not, however, defeated by even the worst kind of violence. Such repressive violence has only succeeded in throwing South Africa into a low-intensity civil war which threatens to escalate into a high-intensity war.[65]

How then does one make sense of a saint like Desmond Tutu and his apparent avowal that just war is sometimes necessary? Despite the obvious answer that such sense has been commonly assumed, as Augustine and Ambrose also espouse just war, I think one makes such sense through our Christian practices of being the church.

Regarding the unique role of the church in a violent world, Tutu states, "The Church must face up to the possibility that it may die in this struggle, but what of that? Did our Lord and Master not tell of a seed that will remain alone unless it falls to the ground and dies (John 12:24)? We can never have an Easter without a Good Friday: there can be no Resurrection without a Crucifixion and death."[66] Tutu's understanding that Christians need space and time to grow is what gives him his vision for how postapartheid South Africa is to proceed. Christians are to proceed in the vision of God's image of peace. South Africans may be like the blind that Jesus healed, whose vision slowly increased with clarity and was not instantaneously fixed. South Africa, with the end of apartheid, is now on the brink of coming to its senses like the prodigal son who turned back in the direction of his father. We are to understand such direction toward God. Tutu concludes:

I believe in that great liberator God of the Exodus and of Calvary and so I have no doubt at all that we shall be free in South Africa, black and white, for it is God's intention which cannot be frustrated forever and a new South Africa will emerge, truly democratic, nonracial and just where all, black and white, will be seen as of infinite value because all, black and white, are created in God's image; all, black and white, will strive to dwell amicably together as brothers and sisters as members of one family, the human family, God's family. And for this cause I am ready to give even my life.[67]

How we can participate in God's mission of reconciliation and restoration in the face of violence and war? A simple answer to this question is that Christians need to physically travel to the economically developing world to develop friendships and relationships with other human beings, so as to move these discussions out of the realm of theory and into the practice of love. Simply going there makes the difference.

In conclusion, Tutu's unifying force is crucial for the five most critical years of struggle between 1985 and 1990. This struggle, symbolized for most people during those years by Nelson Mandela's call for release from life imprisonment, found its expression in the spiritual leadership of Tutu, Beyers Naudé, Frank Chikane, Allan Boesak, and others in the SACC. It found expression because the voice of spiritual communities like the Christian church could be heard across the world. Christian spirituality had so far not been silenced by banning orders, total restriction of movement and assembly, and the massive use of military force. It was this spiritual force that Tutu used that goes unsung in South Africa's movement toward union.

We now move into the next chapter with an eye toward understanding Tutu's unifying role as confessor. Tutu, again providing a unifying role in the midst of some of the most contentious issues, plays a major role here in challenging the theological worldview of apartheid as being holy and set apart. In so doing, Tutu facilitates union of spiritual leadership during the chaotic times of apartheid, without having to entertain violent resistance to South Africa's apartheid state. Increasingly Tutu was called upon to apply this theological worldview to many other issues beyond apartheid in South Africa to which we now turn. As we move to subsequent chapters in this union stage, the reader will notice how Tutu continues to offer nonlinear theological strategies to help both South Africa and international communities move closer to unity and peacemaking.

Tutu being interviewed before voting for the first time in Gugulethu township, April 27, 1994. Author photo.

Chapter 11

Unifying Role of Confessor

In a myriad of crises in Tutu's life mentioned above and the deadlock on negotiations to end apartheid, spiritual communities were forced into an urgent adjustment of their role in South African society. They could not afford the luxury of being just communities of worship. Tutu was increasingly called upon to articulate the relevance of spirituality among several contexts of political strife. He realizes this as he states, "We come out of this reflection with the conviction that we are faced with a situation which calls on us to return to the type of protest actions on which we were forced to embark before February 2, 1990 [when Mandela was released from prison]." And yet, as we saw concerning his own clergy, Tutu felt that discernment was needed concerning the relation between political practice and the spiritual life. This is especially true focusing on Tutu's role of confessor when it comes to the incessant problems of the twenty-first century: poverty, homophobia, racism, and sexism.

To be fair to Tutu's archbishopric and his leadership in the TRC, his focus was primarily on a spirituality of transformation for the church and world that would thereby change not only South Africa but other places in the world as well. In other words, apartheid's toxicity was endemic around the world in the forms of poverty, homophobia, racism, and sexism. But another of Tutu's aims was to address the tensions that arose in the church as a result of his leadership's position "in the frontline in the struggle." In many ways I assume in this book that Tutu did this by accepting his official position in history as South Africa's confessor.

Tutu understood the context of South Africa as derived from the imperatives of Jesus' actions and being, not from dysfunctional political dogma. So much of Jesus' ministry dealt with issues concerned with poverty, sexuality, and human identity. Because of Jesus, Christians cannot with integrity remain aloof from sociopolitical involvement. Jesus teaches us that our relationship with God demands and is authenticated by our relationship with our fellow human beings. God's reign on earth as exemplified in Christian spirituality is not a nebulous, Platonic ideal state in the hereafter. It is, as Jesus said, among us, and its signs are tangible, this-worldly effects: demons are exorcised; the hungry are fed and the naked clothed; stigmatizing diseases are cleansed, and the lame made to walk again, the deaf to hear, and the blind to see; sins are forgiven; and the dead are raised to life again. When all are exposed for who they are, when evil is overcome by good, when oppression and exploitation are resisted, even at the cost of freedom and life itself—then we have a real foretaste of heaven.

THE EXPANDING CONTENT OF CONFESSION

Tutu says boldly that he will not apologize for being "political," for the term means what the users want it to mean. If Tutu were to suggest that apartheid is just, very few whites in South Africa in the time of apartheid would have accused him of being political. But when spiritual leaders work on behalf of the marginalized, speak up for the voiceless, demand the empowerment of the powerless, "then we are accused of bringing politics into religion or vice versa. We shall go on resisting the evils of an utterly unjust and wholly immoral and unchristian apartheid, until these are removed by the dismantling of this diabolical system which has to be maintained by such evil means and at such great cost in human misery and suffering. We shall condemn and resist evil whether it is perpetrated by whites or by blacks, because our standards are not expediency but those of the Word of God, the Gospel of Jesus Christ."[1]

POVERTY

Spiritual leaders should be informed enough about their current contexts so as to be able to wade into the troubled waters of politics and economics. For example, the collapse of communism in the late twentieth century has in some quarters been equated with the triumph of Western capitalism. Good theology, however, should always question such assumptions and provide an even more subversive foundation, namely, that God is still relevant in providing human beings a reference point for where the truly good life is. It should question the shibboleths of this or that status quo. Perhaps in the twenty-first century what is most required by spiritual leaders is a prophetic stance against the ready assumption of Western capitalist triumphalism.[2]

Western history has already recorded the dangerous encounters of spiritual leaders wading in the turbulent waters of economic reform. As in the case of Martin Luther King's Poor People's Campaign and others, spiritual leadership is vehemently attacked when it turns its attention to why there is poverty and what steps can be taken to end it. Spiritual leadership is vital leadership when confronting poverty, because it exposes the root causes of why people are poor—greed, avarice, solipsism, and pride. For example, why is it that the affluent North manages to get richer while the poor South gets poorer, carrying an enormous burden because of neocolonialism and a hopelessly unjust international economic system that causes massive suffering for ordinary people.[3] Tutu believes that Christian spiritual leadership lags behind because Christians do not behave ecumenically as we should, and instead continue to splinter off into silos. Poverty cannot be addressed properly unless one's own house is in order. Here Tutu states:

> Our Lord prayed solemnly for the unity of His followers because the credibility of His own mission depended on it. . . . We have no option but to work and pray that we might all be one. And yet there seems to be a universal inertia in the ecumenical movement. There are conversations, discussions and plans galore, but hardly anywhere has anything of much significance actually happened. . . . They have somehow lacked something to propel them to take the logical next step—organic union, becoming one, in any sense that is of significance to their members or to the world looking on with desultory and waning interest.[4]

Tutu is bold enough to say that the church deserves to be marginalized if it is spending its energies on academic pursuits or in pleasing elites, as if the Scriptures had declared that "God so loved the church" rather than "God so loved the world." Herein Tutu expresses his particular concern for justice and for getting priorities correct. He believes there is an important corrective to the ecumenical movement to focus more on poverty than on picky theological issues such as whether or not a third-century saint belongs in a liturgical prayer. The movement of Christian spirituality needs to focus on tangible unity rather than a false set of pedantic alternatives.

For the liberal and progressive Christians, Tutu also has a prophetic word. It is just as wrong to argue over false dichotomies like unity *or* justice. It should never be a question of either unity *or* justice. It should always be a case of both unity *and* justice. Tutu believes that the South African experience is a good example; church engagement with unity and justice was a struggle, yet produced powerful outcomes, such as an end of apartheid. Even more starkly, Tutu believes that spiritual pursuits are made infinitely more hazardous and difficult when the church is divided. Tutu states sadly, "When our church held a consultation on mission, our overseas partners declared categorically, 'Apartheid is too strong for a divided church.'"[5]

Tutu believes the most critical reason why the church needs unity is so that the church can address the sin of why many people in the world are poor. The elephant in the room is the sin of an international economic system that depends on an indebted developing world. Tutu even goes on to say that a year's moratorium on debt repayments by these countries must be called, and then that debt should be restructured. Those countries that engage seriously in the process of democratizing, in upholding basic human rights, and in appropriate development benefiting the majority of their populations, should then have their debt canceled. Taking up this cause should be the focus of the ecumenical movement. Tutu believes that the unity of the church is important here to help prevent any unilateral processes that may further patronize and entrap global nations, as happened under European colonization. He states:

> Ubuntu . . . declares that my humanity is caught up and inextricably bound up in yours. . . . My humanity does not depend on extraneous things. It is intrinsic to who I am. I have value because I am a person and I am judged not so much on the basis of material possessions but on spiritual attributes. . . .
>
> [The West's] dominant achievement success ethic is taking its toll. People feel worthless, are often considered worthless, if they do not achieve. . . . Ubuntu might remind us of a biblical truth. . . . We don't have to do anything to earn God's love, we don't have to impress God. . . . Christianity is a religion of grace. Can we help as the Church to transform our societies so that they are more people friendly, more gentle, more caring, more compassionate, more sharing?[6]

Here I think Tutu provides a healthier understanding of how an ecumenical church can lead the movement to alleviate global poverty. An ecumenical church does not mean everyone should share a uniform understanding of how to practice spirituality.

HOMOPHOBIA

In Tutu's Christian spirituality, the stage of union with God requires interdependence and the understanding of how individual and communal destiny are bound together. God, while staying God, is mysteriously contingent and vulnerable to and with creation. God created us all in God's image. What is God's image? What does God look like? Most characteristic of God is that God is somehow three and one, diversity and unity, community in one. In the light of this image of God, church leaders like Tutu have fought valiantly to correct the delusions of God's image as French sociologist Emile Durkheim's composite of society.[7] Tutu's vital work against apartheid was his role in destroying the idols of a civil religion that existed to buttress the suffering of so many diverse peoples.

In Tutu's consistent spiritual role of confessor, Tutu did not separate any human oppression in which God's image in them was attacked. Tutu is on record as saying discrimination against sexual orientation is as evil as apartheid. In 2013 the office of the United Nations high commissioner for human rights launched a global public education campaign for lesbian, gay, bisexual, and transgender (LGBTQ) equality, using Tutu as a patron for the cause. The project kicked off in Cape Town and was supported by Tutu and others. The campaign, Free and Equal, focused on legal reform and public education to counter homophobia and transphobia. South Africa was chosen as the country to launch, because of former President Nelson Mandela's statements on unity and respect of dignity for all. Tutu stated at the launch, "I am as passionate about this as I ever was about apartheid. . . . We in our country will never really be truly free unless we all are. . . . We should become a society where people are free to be who God created them to be."[8]

For Tutu, this meant one could not separate attacks against black people from attacks against the LGBTQ community.[9] This is why freedom of sexual orientation is enshrined in the South African constitution, unlike any other constitution in the world. Of course their contexts are different. Of course power runs amok differently, in different ways against people of color and the LGBTQ community. For Tutu, however, there is consistency to human identity; namely, we are all made in the image of God. Of course there are contradictions within the variety of interpretations of what this means. It is not hard to hear the contradictions; just flip the channels on TV or Google "the Bible and homosexuality." Tutu's main point in Christian spirituality is in the need to find synthesis in the contradictions; even more, to find this synthesis in the form of spiritual practices that move human communities away from war and into restorative justice.[10]

In many social systems, homosexuality is considered "totally new and out of step with tradition and culture."[11] For example, in a statement issued by the Zimbabwe Council of Churches (ZCC), presiding Bishop Jonathan Siyachitema said that Zimbabweans should not be coerced into a practice of homosexuality that is totally alien to them.[12] Others argue strongly that Christian doctrine is based on the church's centuries-old understanding of marriage and sexual expression. The premise here is that the traditional teaching of the church on marriage, marital fidelity, and sexual chastity is the standard of sexual morality. Candidates for ordination are expected to conform to this standard. Therefore, many believe it is not appropriate for the church to ordain a practicing homosexual or any person who is engaged in heterosexual relations outside of marriage.

Given a seemingly divided church on the issue of sexual orientation, how does Tutu as confessor guide spiritual communities in the twenty-first century? This question is all the more important in light of the suffering of the LGBTQ community, as many are singled out to be killed or tortured. Same-sex relationships are illegal in more than a third of countries around the world and punishable by death in many of them. On the continent of Africa alone, homosexual acts are still a crime in thirty-eight countries, according to the rights group Amnesty International. To the African Christians who condone oppression of the LGBTQ community, Tutu states again, "I would refuse to go to a homophobic heaven. . . . I would not worship a God who is homophobic and that is how deeply I feel about this."[13] Tutu's conviction comes out of the torture of members of the LGBTQ community. Although South Africa since apartheid ended in 1994 has had some of the best legal safeguards, LGBTQ persons still have faced brutal attacks. For example, a lesbian was found dead, having been sexually assaulted with a toilet brush thrust through her vagina.[14]

If Stephen Biko had actually been a human person to Jimmy Kruger, there would have been no affliction. This is equally true for a lesbian person in the actuality of her humanity. The problem is that in our racism and homophobia, affliction is anonymous before all things. It deprives its victims of their personality and makes them into things, objects. This is what Weil referred to as affliction, the cold, metallic indifference that freezes all those it touches right to the depths of their souls. In such indifference, the other will never believe any more that they are anyone. Perhaps God calls on those who suffer to be as Simon of Cyrene, Tutu believes, so that they can resist affliction and move toward how affliction is healed. Simon moved in this direction by carrying Jesus' cross. Those who are God's friends cannot but be found near the cross, for they too seemed marked out for special suffering.[15]

If persons do not face this evil and challenge it as an evil, then the world will continue to operate as a blind mechanism instead of a vibrant creation. Weil concludes, "To wish that the world did not exist is to wish that I, just as I am, may be everything. . . . What makes wishes dangerous is the fact that they are granted."[16] In Christian spirituality there is the understanding that no one escapes God. Even in hell there is no escape (Ps. 139). The escape, the turning away, may assume the form of a search for "consolation," whether through a religion of wish fulfilment or schemes to justify one form of human identity over another. The way of defeating human limitations is the way of acceptance of reality as such. "From another angle, this necessity is nothing but a form of obedience."[17] As Tutu states, "Who says that death is the worst thing that could happen to a Christian?"[18]

Tutu offers a spirituality in which the LGBTQ community is inextricably linked to the black community, and from there to all communities in the midst of the struggle for humanity. Tutu states, "God gives us space to be human persons. He respects our autonomy and freedom. He expects us to be free to exercise our freedom, but He also expects us to accept the consequences of living in a universe made for free moral agents."[19] Here, Weil's concept of attention is helpful in showing the interdependence of free moral agents. The concept of attention for Weil is such that we cannot produce anything greater than ourselves. Any effort stretched toward goodness does not reach: "It is after long, fruitless effort which ends in despair, when we can no longer expect anything, that, from outside ourselves, the gift comes as a marvelous surprise."[20] These efforts, though, are needed, because they destroy the false sense of fullness. Here the call of Christ is to believe *through* affliction.

Belief must percolate the skepticism of affliction. Instead of the assumption of much modern religious thought, that by an onrush of emotion, the skepticism can be permanently dissolved, there must be a true confrontation of evil. Otherwise, life is lived in a dangerous illusion. Percolation of faith within affliction involves *attente*, attention to God, an operation that cannot be hurried. For Weil, this is the subjective counterpart of the operation of grace itself. "Humility is endless, and *attente* is humility in action."[21] Proper attention to God—namely, prayer—tests the intentions of the person praying. That is, true attention to God disallows the treatment of others as means for ends. In this respect, the concept of God's *kenōsis* also proves helpful, in that God never forces creation to be creation, although God allowed God's second person to be forced by it. Christian consciousness is formed by this narrative of God's interaction with creation, whether they acknowledge God's love revealed in Christ or not. Salvation comes in the turning toward God, so when a person acts in such ways as to know where God is acting, then that person displays God's presence in the world. Therefore, actions like justice and forgiveness are not so much what we choose to do, as what we become. Without justice and forgiveness there is never a rise above affliction. In both justice and forgiveness, the wound of creation is slowly transfigured toward a new heaven and earth.

Tutu's Ubuntu seeks a paradigm in which the affliction of people can be transfigured through a forgiveness that reflects justice. Instead of retaliation and a further competition of Christian narratives for God's privilege, we are to turn toward God and see that God also was afflicted. Even if humanity seems hopelessly trapped in the closed systems of different kinds of apartheid, the image of God is planted in human beings in such a way that its slow, vegetative movements, responding to light, will one day manifest the kingdom of God. Grace as light percolates creation.

In Christian spirituality, human value is not ultimately defined by this or that arbitrary chosen biological attribute. Value is in the fact that each individual person is created in the image of God, that each person is God's viceroy. Each person stands in the place of God. Paul goes on to say, "Your body is a temple of the Holy Spirit" (1 Cor. 6:19). You are a sanctuary, and to treat you as if you were less than this, is not just wrong (which it is), is not just painful (as it often is), but is positively blasphemous. It is a sacrilege to treat the temple of God, someone indwelt by the Spirit of God, by God the Holy Trinity, in such a way.[22]

In the end, Tutu's spirituality is such that God collapses the hierarchy that engenders the idea that the oppressed is in such a condition because of a lack of something (e.g., power or intelligence). Human systems of oppression, like the modern-day apartheid in which LGBTQ communities cannot function as human beings, uproot people and make unintelligible every vestige of natural equality that God's diverse creation invites humanity into. Apartheid is the condition of being rootless, which is the goal of the oppressor in implementing apartheid. Rootlessness is the most severe form of affliction.[23] In this regard, Tutu seems closely aligned to Weil's conclusions. Tutu's Ubuntu offers a model beyond individual claims of rationality by which to solve problems of theodicy.

Tutu's role as confessor exemplifies a different way of knowing God on the African continent and among those of African descent. I name this African epistemology through the mystical concept of unknowing or the apophatic way. The apophatic tradition becomes relevant through African practices in which individuality is unknowable apart from community. In other words, to truly know one's personality among many African cultures, one must first practice the giving up of self and individual rights. Such apophasis is strange to Western notions of self-contained spirituality.

Herein is the struggle, however, for African cultural worldviews; namely, how does the African individual ever recover any recognition of self outside of the dominant cultural pressures to stay a community? This became a major issue in Afro-Anglicanism when a gay priest, Gene Robinson, was consecrated a bishop in 2003. It is true that African epistemologies of knowing the self in community provide a corrective to individualistic spiritualities that see themselves as somehow self contained, but it is also true that individuality and uniqueness are also part of God's image.

The English word "spirituality" is Christian in origin. The very word derives from *spiritus*, the life-giving breath of God that enlivens creation and transforms the relationships persons are able to maintain as human beings. In other words, by the time members in African churches become conscious of their experience, God has already become an experience of an experience; therefore, the African church constructs an image of a reality that in itself is occurring before her normal, historical awareness can become operational to describe it. How African Christians know is not exclusively through the clarity of cognitive function, but through what is often seen as the obscure hermeneutics of particular communities calling themselves the church. African Christian spirituality begins not with cognitive function but with a communal sense of devotion and mystery; so the origin of the church is deeper than any individual mind can fathom.

African Christian spirituality originates in the unspeakable interchange between the Spirit of God and the human's spirit. For many African cultures, it is this experience of the Spirit pouring into identity and taking possession that elicits the distinctive features of what looks African, but more important to my argument, elicits a self-giving in return. Such response is not ecstasy in the sense of inspired inebriation or of divesting oneself of created reality, in order to live henceforth in God, beyond one's own self. Both of these elements can be part of the experience, but they are not its core. To know God is primarily worship: worship of the holiness of God, infinite and inexpressible, yet present in the soul. Much of African worship is about a discreet Yes, the consent to be possessed, to be at God's disposal, the ecstasy not of inebriation but of service to God.

Intimacy with the Holy Spirit cancels out the individual's objectivity, with its external, critical attitude, and replaces it with an attitude one can only describe as prayer. This prayer is total; it encompasses our beholding and our readiness to receive and give our contemplating and our self-communication, in a single, undivided whole. In fact, for the African, no other attitude but prayer is appropriate in knowing God. In an African worldview, a person can bear witness before others to the truth only provided that person has received the abiding, inner witness of the Holy Spirit. It is the "Spirit bearing witness with our spirit that we are children of God" (Rom. 8:16). The Spirit is the witness because the Spirit is the truth, the one who believes in the eternal life of the relatedness of God (1 John 5:6, 10, 11). Here the Spirit appears as the herald of the divine life, which makes its own presence felt. This life is the Son, given to us by the Father, and the truth of this life, the giving and receiving of this knowledge, the creativity, communication, and koinonia of the Spirit (2 Cor. 13:13).

Every genuine encounter with the Spirit presupposes an accepting and receptive consent on our part. One can see this in Mary, in her fundamental orientation to the Holy Spirit, or in Jesus, when he is being led into the wilderness. African Christian spirituality locates individuals in this way in order to know that God is the unearthing process of giving consent to a preexistent communal way of knowing. So Tutu was good at singling out Christian individuals in order to highlight the good of the whole community. It is on such an occasion that Tutu states:

> But we come to give thanks for the ministry of our brother and his family and to rejoice as the apostles did that they have been counted worthy to suffer for the name of Jesus. And so we do paradoxical things to rejoice and give thanks in pain for we must express our sadness that a country which claims to be Christian and can invoke the name of God in the preamble to its constitution even if it is an unjust and totally undemocratic constitution which excludes 73% of God's people, can expel a Christian worker, a steward of God's mysteries and think that working for God poses a threat to the security of the state.[24]

It is in Tutu's African Christian spirituality that he says this, in order that communal harmony leaves out no child of God. The Spirit in African culture for Tutu is the same as the Holy Spirit, who continuously calls the church and the world to live in the mystery of being one and diverse at the same time. This means that the diversity of our brothers and sisters who identify as LGBTQ is no exception.

SEXISM

Misogyny and the oppression of women are another such inordinate pattern that displays how particular individuals or groups are systematically oppressed. Tutu, as South African confessor, also played a major role in such public confession, as he would often point to the sinful consequences when women are oppressed. For example, Tutu discussed the problem of poverty, which still defines the continent of Africa, including the westernized South Africa. This problem is exemplified through squatter camps in Cape Town, such as Khayelitsha and Crossroads. Tutu explains that these squatter camps exist because of the South African desire for cheap labor. More specifically, the desire of the poor to travel great distances to live in such poverty is a theological one, as Tutu states: "What happens is that the women folk say, 'You know, when we went to church we were told by ministers, "What God has joined together let no man put asunder." And so, we want to fulfill our marriage vows. We want to be with our men.'" He explains further:

> Isn't it marvelous: "Family Day" in a country which deliberately, systemat-ically, by design of government policy, destroys black family life. But those women said, "We have had enough. We are going to be with our men folk, come hell or high water." Well, they have been getting hell. These women, because there is no housing available, so they build squatter camps, with homes constructed of flimsy plastic coverings. . . . I am glad, you know, that I am not Western; I'm glad that I am not white. I am glad that maybe I am also not civilized—because those who uphold these wonderful stan-dards every day . . . go out and they destroy those plastic shelters that the women have put up.[25]

Tutu's concept of Ubuntu once again comes into play in his beliefs about the vulnerable position of African women. Women have occupied an inferior posi-tion in African traditional society, but so too have they in the structures of the Christian church. Although the church has shared in the movement to educate and emancipate women in Africa, there still remain theological and sociological discrepancies for the development of women in the social and ecclesial structures themselves. Women are therefore increasingly prepared for a role that they are not allowed to play.

Sexist language is problematic in African tradition, but the translations of Bantu terms like *muntu*, "human being," from which the word "Ubuntu" is derived, have no sexist overtones. In English it is rendered as "man." Tutu states that the famous Tanzanian liberator Julius Nyerere confessed that it was Presi-dent Jimmy Carter who had taught him to say, "One person, one vote," instead of "One man, one vote." Tutu, therefore, had an impassioned plea to the church to cease treating women as second- or third-class citizens. African and Christian thinking about the human community still must take up this challenge. Tutu, however, is hopeful.

Tutu describes his hope this way. He was at the mass funeral for victims of the massacre at Uitenhage, when at least twenty people were shot and killed on March 21, 1969, the ninth anniversary of the Sharpeville massacre. At the funeral in Uitenhage there were more than a hundred thousand mourners. It was a volatile and tense situation. The police kept a very low profile, which helped to keep things reasonably calm. Tutu was sitting on the dais with church and community leaders, Allan Boesak next to him. In front of Tutu and Boesak, and behind the row of coffins, were two young women sitting on the grass. They had their arms clasped round each other's waist. One was black, the other white. They were out of earshot from Tutu as he whispered to Boesak, referring to the duo, "That is the kind of South Africa we are all striving for." As if the women could hear the whispering, they seemed to tighten their hold on each other.[26]

Sexism and homophobia impacted Tutu's family directly when his daughter, Mpho, relinquished her Anglican priesthood. Mpho said that part of her was "stripped away" when she had to relinquish her religious orders over her same-sex marriage.[27] Before such stripping away, she was known as the Reverend Canon Mpho Tutu van Furth, who followed her father into the spiritual leadership of the Anglican Church. She and Marceline van Furth, whom she loved, were married in a small private ceremony in the Netherlands at the end of 2015, but they went public in May of 2016 when they had a wedding celebration in Cape Town. Although other gay clergy functioned in the South African church, they did so by hiding their identity; in many cases male clergy never resigned from being clergy because they were gay. Indeed, they may never have been ordained if they had been public with their sexual identity; nevertheless, Tutu van Furth is one of the first female clergy members to have to resign. Sexism is at work here in that, although Tutu van Furth was ordained in the US, where the Episcopal Church allows same-sex marriage, she had returned to Cape Town, and was licensed to officiate as one of the first female "canons" (diocesan staff assigned by the bishop) in the South African diocese of Saldanha Bay.

Tutu van Furth describes how Raphael Hess, the Anglican bishop of Saldanha Bay near Cape Town, came to visit her: "He was incredibly caring and generous with me. I said to him: 'I know you're required to take back my license, but rather than have you do that, I'm going to offer to give it back to you.' To which his response was: 'For now.'"[28] Colleagues and other clergy in the diocese where Tutu van Furth served tried to be in solidarity, even were willing to submit their own clergy licenses in protest. She said, "I was incredibly moved. This wasn't an empty gesture—their livelihood was at stake. It was a real commitment." At the end of the day, Tutu van Furth refused her colleagues' solidarity, but said: "In South Africa I've had an incredible outpouring of support—and an incredible amount of sadness. People have said: 'Is this still the conversation? Are we still in this place?'"[29]

"My marriage sounds like a coming out party," Mpho explains, telling a BBC reporter that she was surprised to find herself in love with her wife Marceline. When she fell in love, Mpho was forced into a difficult choice between being a priest, being a woman, and being with the person she loved. It was, she says, one of the hardest choices of her life. "I shouldn't have to choose but in the end you always choose love. Everything else will fall into place somehow. When in doubt do the most loving thing."[30]

Marceline van Furth is a specialist in pediatric infectious disease and is based in Holland. She is also an atheist. Prior to the announcement of their marriage, Mpho's sexuality was never made public, and she had previously been married to a man with whom she had two children. Mpho and Marceline now have four children between them, ranging from ten years old to nineteen years old, from their first marriages.

Although same-sex marriage was legalized in South Africa in 2006, the Anglican Church's constitution and canons on marriage state: "Holy matrimony is the lifelong and exclusive union between one man and one woman." Hence, even with the progressive stance of the church against apartheid, same-sex marriages are not recognized in the Anglican Church of Southern Africa (ACSA). ACSA introduced pastoral guidelines for members who enter same-sex unions, but full acceptance remains unclear in the continued church storms regarding same-sex marriages.

So the practice when it comes to LGBTQ clerics in the church is that they must remain celibate. Mpho weathered the storms that arose because of her marriage—even the sacrifice of having her ministerial license as an Anglican priest revoked after her wedding. With such results forecast, during that time she handed her license back, she thought this was a more dignified option with the same effect. "It was incredibly sad for me," Mpho said, especially that she could no longer stand beside her father at the altar and celebrate the Eucharist.[31]

Leah and Tutu, at that time eighty-four years old, were very supportive of Mpho's marriage to Marceline. Mpho also realizes that her father had to be careful to allow the controversial conversation around same-sex marriage to unfold, instead of trying to pick a fight. Despite this, as we have already seen, Tutu's public views on homophobia have been known for quite a while. Mpho hopes that her marriage, however, will help such a conversation deepen toward the church's fuller acceptance of all people.

In the BBC article conveying her choice, Mpho declared that the pews of churches are full of LGBTQ people, and so are the pulpits. Both are afraid to reveal who they are. Mpho wants young people to see people who look like her serving at the altar, to realize that a priest can look like a "lipstick-wearing black woman in robes." Mpho's role in Tutu's life accentuates what he has preached and stood for in terms of the full inclusion of women.[32]

Two and a half decades earlier, in 1989, the Anglican Church in Southern Africa met to discuss whether bishops of individual dioceses, supported by their diocesan synods, could be permitted to ordain women to the priesthood. The final vote was 121 for and 79 against the motion. But this did not reach the two-thirds majority required for a motion of a "controversial nature," and that motion failed.[33] The arguments against full feminism or the full inclusion of women were described in a variety of ways. First, feminism was just another form of Western imperialism. It sought to divide black women from black men and thereby dilute the struggle. That is, since feminist theology is developed in the West, blacks in South Africa are always at the receiving end of cultural imperialism and must protect African tradition from further denigration. Louise Kretzschmar countered that though feminist theology developed from Western Europe and America, that did not mean it had no application elsewhere. The main reason for this early development in Western women, she said, was due to educational advantages over many women in the non-Western world. And she criticized those against Western influence as hypocritical, since many black male South African leaders readily accepted Western thinkers like Karl Marx. The origin of an idea should not determine its value nor restrict its subsequent development.[34]

Tutu, a supporter of women's ordination, felt that he had to work within the structures of the church for such change. For example, Wilma Jacobsen, in her autobiographical account, describes her struggles toward ordination when Tutu was archbishop. She spent three months in Cape Town with the main aim of spending time with the new archbishop, Desmond Tutu, who also was her diocesan bishop. She met with Tutu, who was encouraging and assured her of his own personal support for the ordination of women to the priesthood. He gave no guarantee, however, that the church would ordain her as a priest. He emphasized that the church could do no less than assist her in testing her vocation. He also assured her that he would speak to the diocesan chapter about the possibility of her ordination to the diaconate at some future stage. Tutu ordained her, the first woman deacon in the diocese of Cape Town, on Sunday, June 5, 1988, at St. George's Cathedral.[35]

Tutu's leadership in ordaining women was monumental, but he was not able to lead the church to unity over same-sex blessings. After his last Synod of Bishops in 1995, he said to John Allen that he wanted to raise this issue of same-sex blessings with the bishops. "I tried to raise the issue with them, but they said, 'No man, we just went through apartheid!'"[36] There had also been a huge fight over economic sanctions among Tutu's bishops, who took three years to support sanctions. So when it came to ordaining women, it was a major controversy in the church. Though Tutu lost the vote in 1989 by thirteen votes, he kept working the system, and in 1992 the measure was passed.

On the issue of sexuality that divided the communion, Tutu said that it was only natural this had become a dominating issue, that in times of turmoil, when the world faces issues like violence and HIV/AIDS, people long for clear stances, and to be with others who agree with them. "But this is not the answer," he emphasized. "It is to admit vulnerability and to embrace your brother and sister with whom you disagree."[37] Any issue that sought to exclude people from church was wrong, Tutu concluded.

Tutu reflected further on justice in postapartheid South Africa. Even though people had violently disagreed on who could be a South African, now they could come together as brothers and sisters in a unified identity, although some differences remained. He cited examples of how families had befriended the murderers of their loved ones, and commented that retributive justice "seems to prolong people's suffering." Through restorative justice, he continued, people began to understand each other's vulnerability and acknowledge their humanity. In the same way, anger can hurt one's health, but dealing with anger can be healing. "An enemy is a friend waiting to be made; that's the only hope for this conflict-ridden world."[38]

South African women's theological work, he believed, was vital here to bring hope to a conflict-ridden world.[39] More and more South African women were expanding the meaning of interdependent humanity, as they exposed patriarchy in legal, economic, and social systems that reinforce male sovereignty. Misinterpretations of God in "his" heaven seem to connote the norm of a divine plan and order by which males are to be dominant.[40] Such a theological norm allows for the "exclusion of woman from positions of authority in the institutionalized church, regardless of whether or not she is ordained, [and] the stereotyping of woman's role in these institutions, regardless of what her gifts may be, [which] are exercises in patriarchal views of humanity."[41] Tutu is an advocate of feminist liberation theology that provides a transformative view of humanity, in which persons of all genders discover newly integrated personhood. Transformation is the operative concept here, rather than equality, which denotes merely gaining access to structures and ideas that have been formed by male norms. The goal of the threefold mystical process of purgation, illumination, and union is one in which the social order itself needs to change.

South African women theologians are vital here, as they display what it means to be human from a woman's perspective. This relationality emerges from Jesus' Golden Rule that "You shall love your neighbor as yourself" (Mark 12:31). Such theological work should not be seen as a threat to male identity, but should encourage men to understand themselves more clearly. This is the premise also of Ubuntu, that in healthy relationality one must actively love self and neighbor. Such relationality is the essence of God's restorative justice meted out in purgation, illumination, and union. "The recognition of the full humanity of women does not merely demand theological assent. The injunction 'to love your neighbor as yourself' is understood as the practice of valuing women's humanity. This practice is based on love and justice. As such it is relational."[42] Relationality is the opposite of the alienation that homophobia, sexism, racism, and classism produce. Rather than alienation, correct relationality links us to Creator and creation, as we are intended to be. Therefore, relationality demands a change in societal structures in which male-dominated hierarchies and divisions form false gods.

RACISM

Much of the background of this book displays the sin of racism, but it is important to discuss more explicitly how racism is a sin that needs to be confessed. In Christian spirituality, persons and communities concede the need to be transformed to a new identity, a new perspective that fully encompasses the truth which Tutu states: "God does not love us because we are lovable, but we are lovable precisely because God loves us."[43] In racism the reverse is true. Human identity is not derived from love; rather, it is defined primarily in favor of whoever happens to have enough power to belittle other human identities. In racism,

God becomes a deformed image (nightmare) of human beings pretending to be gods. These human gods believe in their own images and structure a world only for themselves. They become a plurality of gods vying for power and control of what it means to be human. In Christian spirituality, persons and communities are liberated from the desire to separate human differences into a hierarchy of control, because such a hierarchy could not exist in the God who is love.

So in much of Tutu's spirituality, the common refrain emerges: "We are the children of the divine love and nothing can change that fundamental fact about us."[44] As Tutu's Ubuntu theology unfolds access to a new identity for South Africans, it also unfolds access to the culture wars around the poor, human sexuality and gender identity, and racism. For Tutu, all of these culture wars are sins, because they operate in a logic that is the opposite of God's love. Racism, classism, sexism, and homophobia are sins that operate in a worldview in which there are numerous gods vying for control to dominate human purpose. More specifically in these culture wars, the problem of race emerges as biological classifications based upon physiognomic differences determine who is superior and who is not truly human.

Racism is the same sin that cast Lucifer from heaven, namely, the hubris of trying to usurp God's image. In John Milton's *Paradise Lost*, Satan, also known as Lucifer, was once the most beautiful of all angels, and knew this, as he famously declared that it was better to reign in hell than serve in heaven. Because of his vanity, Lucifer rebelled against God and failed miserably as he was cast out of heaven. Satan's rebellion grew from his unwillingness to be interdependent with the community of saints. For Satan, such interdependence was codependence and weakness, as he claimed that angels are "self-begot, self-raised."[45] Somewhere down the line Satan forgot that he too was created; thereby the worldview of a creator became unintelligible. Satan's narcissistic world was all there was, and no one else really mattered in such a world. If they did matter, it would only be to serve it.

The severity of the sin of racism and resulting practices, like the North Atlantic slave trade, were no less evil than the machinations of Satan. In racism, a person's pigmentation and physiognomic appearance determine whether her or his spiritual status is high or low in the social pyramid. Those proclaiming a god of white supremacy think (consciously and unconsciously) that there should be both God's judgment and grace deciding "with a rigidity unknown even in the strictest Calvinist predestinationism where you are born and where you can live."[46]

Racism is a sin because it is based on a metanarrative in which whoever happens to be in power invokes a theology to justify their power. Thus a false God replaces the living God who loves creation, who *loves* humanity. Even more, in Christian spirituality, God becomes fully human and fully divine at the same time to direct humanity in the direction of becoming more like God. In other words, God provides a frame of reference that we are loved so much that God wants to show the extent to which God will go to make such love as intelligible as possible to human beings. God is willing to die to capture our attention, intelligence, and love. So racism is sinful in its attempt to occlude God's frame of reference that human identity is discovered in the concept and actions of love. In the worldview that is racism, there is no love, not even for one's own self. This is because love is no longer intelligible. What remains is only instinct, self-interest, and survival.

Racism helps us see the slow creep of a sinful worldview when we look around the world and ask the following awkward question: Why is it true—not just in South Africa, but also on a global scale—that the darker a person is in skin pigment, the more likely it is that this person is poor or oppressed? When Tutu was trying to control the panic of mass exodus out of South Africa during apartheid, he made the following interesting remark: "I would say to [South African expatriates], they are not going to escape the turmoil, wherever they go. Really. If they go to western Europe, racism is rearing its ugly head there. And why go through the hoop twice, when having done it once, you can now relax?"[47] Also, Tutu seems to reflect on the theodicy question of racism as he reflects on his international travel. Tutu has the privilege of having seen the resilience of black people around the globe, as he states, "among Black people in Brazil, among those in African countries who suffer from starvation, civil war, and repressive government, among the Nicaraguans and the Palestinians. Traveling to these places, I have often wondered how I can minister effectively to people who are suffering so much. When I have arrived there, I have always found that they have ministered to me."[48]

In light of the vulnerability of God's love, racism boils down to the potential problem of blasphemy, that is, desacralizing the image of God. If this is true for how white European worldviews may see black people, how might black people also participate in the sin of racism? The difficulty of this question is in how racism is defined primarily in how the dominant race uses power to control the structures in society, so that black people lack power and a full place in human societies. So, in effect, to ask if a black person can be racist is equivalent to asking a poor person to be an ascetic. In other words, the question carries a premise that easily slips in favor of the true racist. It is true, however, that black people in the Western world have privileged lighter-skinned black people, but such actions are usually countered by movements such as Black Power and Black Lives Matter to expose any such dysfunctions in society. And in more societies on the African continent and in the African diaspora, the concept of "internal racism" is exposed more and more as a vestige of postcolonial societies.

The better question for black people around racism is whether or not African communities make enough space for individuality and natural political dissent. In more communal societies, people may go to an extreme of making little space for individuality. The logical conclusion to Ubuntu and African conceptualizations of community seems to be that persons have no existence apart from their relations with other persons. In other words, the question must be asked on an ontological level: if the individual self is constituted by its relations with others, what are the proper relations between them? By what criteria are persons their very relations?

Tutu's genius of Ubuntu is to describe it in such a way as to avoid a dull uniformity. Homogeneity should not be the enemy of heterogeneity. We must help cultivate tolerance, which is the hallmark of the mature, of the secure or the self-confident who are not threatened by the autonomy of others and who don't have to assert themselves by an aggressive abrasiveness. As Tutu learned from his dealings with the Eloff Commission, there is often a conspiracy among government and powerful media to make people turn in on ourselves, to be concerned about belonging to like-minded affinity groups. We forget we belong to the world, and that we have sisters and brothers out there who share a common humanity.[49] By drawing attention to an important cultural concept such as Ubuntu, it is necessary to distinguish its benign meaning from its possibly abusive purposes. I have tried to show that Ubuntu, as a concept, is integral to an African perception of life and community.

Ubuntu is also an integral strategy for how Tutu negotiates how his South African society may proceed together beyond apartheid. Therefore, in light of South Africa's dealing with the growing pains of an emerging nation-state, these criticisms raised above regarding the possible dangers of Ubuntu must be taken into account. Now that Tutu has withdrawn from the world stage, I think that Tutu has taken it upon himself to make the dangerous extremes of African communalism more explicit. Tutu explains:

> I have to confess that to our shame in Africa, on the whole, we have not been able to accommodate differences of opinion. When you differ from someone, often that is taken to mean that you are an enemy. But that is actually not traditionally African, because in the traditional African community, the Chief was a good chief if he could work out a consensus, and a consensus occurs because people have different points of view. . . . In many parts of Africa we must acknowledge with a deep chagrin that the only change experienced by many ordinary people is in the complexion of their oppressors.[50]

Here Tutu provides a reference that few theological issues in recent South African history have been more controversial and divisive than racism.

There have been some spiritual efforts to address racism. The Program to Combat to Racism (PCR) in the World Council of Churches was one. The PCR gave public witness theologically that the apartheid state was racist, violent, and illegitimate. The key theological strategy was to show how racism is a pernicious and entrenched ideology supporting apartheid. Despite the popularity of "nonracialism" as a political vision and strategy for South African black leaders in the 1950s, the white apartheid government was unwilling to negotiate shared governance. In fact, South African leader Albert Luthuli got the Nobel Peace Prize in 1960 due to his work in South Africa advocating for a "nonracial" society in

South Africa. Luthuli was the first African, and the first person outside Europe and the Americas, to be awarded the Nobel Peace Prize.

Even Mahatma Gandhi's spiritual practice of satyagraha was formed in his battle against racism in South Africa. Racism is in fact a deeply spiritual issue, not only because of the way the Bible was used to justify apartheid, but primarily because racism flies in the face of the Christian understanding that all human beings are image-bearers of God. In terms of theological documents, the Kairos Document of 1985 may be the most explicit theological statement against racism in South Africa. *Kairos* in Greek means moment of truth; and indeed it was a moment of truth in the 1980s when there were constant states of emergency. This moment of truth was for apartheid South Africa, but also for the Christian church and all other faiths and religions.[51]

When the Dutch in the sixteenth and seventeenth centuries transplanted their Dutch Reformed theology into South Africa, the history of South African churches was very much bound up with the amalgamation of religion and politics. As we saw earlier, in the early 1980s the World Alliance of Reformed Churches declared apartheid to be a heresy and expelled the Dutch Reformed Church from its organization altogether. For the most part, it took the decade of the 1980s for the Dutch Reformed Church of South Africa to formally move away from supporting apartheid. In 1986 there was a call for all Dutch Reformed congregations to desegregate. Now the Dutch Reformed Church has expressed repentance for the sin of supporting apartheid. The hope here is that by confessing the sin of apartheid they will mature into a corporate spirituality that represents the God of love.[52]

The central conviction of the Kairos theologians was that Dutch Reformed theology, like apartheid, presented more than just a political crisis; it presented a spiritual crisis. In short, apartheid was sin—even more, a heresy. The Kairos Document sought to locate this crisis firmly in spirituality. The indictment here was that apartheid was being used as spiritual justification for racism, and thereby nurtured by Christian churches. The Kairos Document stated that apartheid leaders blasphemed God by creating a "state theology" that misused theological concepts and biblical texts such as Romans 13 to justify apartheid. The Bible is arguably the only book (in vernacular) that both black and white South Africans read and possess. The Kairos movement intentionally used the spirituality of the Bible to tap into a live wire that could disrupt dysfunctional white Christianity. Much was at stake here: Is the Bible really the "Word of God" when used to justify apartheid? The answer of the Kairos movement and Rustenburg Conference was a firm No! The challenge was to articulate an authentic Christian spirituality in which there could be a joint confession by those who benefited from apartheid to call it sin. Such a confession needed also to be received by those victimized by apartheid. South Africa as a nation was admonished to repent from economic, social, and political sin.

The concept of sin recognizes the incompleteness of confession and forgiveness if unaccompanied by repentance. For example, can land be returned in the present economic system? So much of the push-back to the TRC was based upon this question, thereby tempting South Africa to mimic the instability of Zimbabwe and other nation-states teetering on anarchy. How South Africa will move forward, displaying how this nation repents, will continue to depend on the willingness to embrace Ubuntu and the worldview of interdependence. For example, both white and black farmers are necessary in South Africa's economic recovery. Simply grabbing land back from whites creates an instability of infrastructure and anxiety in world markets, largely still controlled by many white Europeans. The wiser course by current political leaders like Ramaphosa is to continue nation building and black and white interdependence. Not to do this will tempt South Africa out of its miracle of truth and reconciliation.

The entire phenomenon of corporate sin—its logic, its impact, and the suffering it has caused—is extremely difficult to fathom. In Tutu's spirituality he often encouraged not only Christian communities, but all communities in South Africa, to confess the evil of apartheid. This bore fruit as the Dutch Reformed Church in South Africa in 1989 confessed their sin of apartheid in a public statement that read in part: "We confess with humility and sorrow the participation of our church in the introduction and legitimation of the ideology of apartheid and the subsequent suffering of people."[53] The Dutch Reformed Church even went so far as to say that any attempt to defend it was heretical. This public denunciation of apartheid was also motivated to avoid a split in the Dutch Reformed family of churches that were divided by race, that is, black, white, and colored. Leaders of the black and colored churches did not believe the condemnation had gone far enough, but went significantly beyond previous attempts by the church to distance itself from the policy of apartheid. Naturally, many of the white church expressed reservations about the final document, known as the Testimony of Vereeniging, which stated that it "unequivocally regards apartheid in all its forms a sin and irreconcilable with the Gospel."[54]

Johan A. Heyns, the leader of the white Dutch Reformed Church, confessed that apartheid had wrongfully divided the races in South Africa. Boesak and other leaders responded, "We have heard from the representatives of the Dutch Reformed Church confessions of guilt with regard to the establishment, maintenance and justification of apartheid. . . . We have heard their plea for forgiveness."[55] But Boesak and others were disappointed that the white church did not support another resolution, to support civil disobedience as a means of protesting apartheid laws. During this time, Boesak led the largest "daughter" churches associated with the mixed-race Dutch Reformed Mission Church; and the black Dutch Reformed Church in Africa was led by the Rev. Sam Buti. This confession of sin was the predominantly white Dutch Reformed Church's attempt to reconcile all of its churches divided by race. But apartheid laws in effect at this time in 1989 still enforced residential segregation, making such confession no more than a token gesture. This was a token gesture, like the Dutch Reformed Church's admission in 1986 that apartheid was a "scriptural error" and that race discrimination was a sin.

Christian spirituality encountered a "legitimacy crisis," exemplified by the case of the Dutch Reformed Church, whose members constructed a theology of apartheid. Such a theology was diametrically opposite to Jesus' command to love our neighbors as ourselves. Co-option of the churches in an apartheid state also makes one wonder how in other ways Christian spirituality may easily be misinterpreted and misused. All of this presents a serious challenge, not only to the Dutch Reformed churches, but to all who claim to practice a Christian spirituality.

The sin of racism requires special vigilance, since many use Scripture to justify how sin revisits multiple generations of human history. Many have conceived sin to hold groups of people hostage from the past to the present. It is as if, through Noah's curse of Ham or other misinterpretations, the sin of racism is especially difficult to forgive, since many believe the sins of the father shall be visited upon subsequent generations—except perhaps upon those whose skin has white pigmentation. This perspective of sin through generations is especially worrisome as the racist point of view sees South Africa as desperate with crime and violence, poverty and squalor, fraud and corruption, women and child abuse, disintegration of families, the high rate of HIV/AIDS infection, and climate change.

In conclusion, the major issues in South Africa easily reflect the major issues in the world. In a myriad of crises Tutu's spirituality was called upon to help unlock constant tensions that occur among human cultures and societies. Despite the fact that spiritual leaders are usually seen as impediments in such tensions, Tutu was often called upon to help solve such issues. Tutu realized the need for him to be a benign agent of change. And as we shall soon see, he also realized that it would be difficult to move completely off the public stage and into retirement. What becomes profound for Tutu in the next chapter is his ongoing insight that a good confessor also has to be a good confessee. In other words, he too has to be deeply aware of his own sin and weaknesses.

Michael Battle's ordination to the Anglican/Episcopal priesthood at St. George's Cathedral, Cape Town, on Battle's birthday, December 12, 1993. Archbishop Tutu kneels before Battle (the ordinand) for prayer and blessing. Author photo.

Chapter 12

Confessor and Absolution

In chapter 12 we discover how union occurs as Tutu becomes both confessor and confessee. There is long-standing understanding that whatever a spiritual leader undertakes to give, such as spiritual direction or serving as a confessor to the penitent, such a leader must also receive. A spiritual director must be in spiritual direction, and a confessor must give confession. Such is the principle of integrity when serving as a spiritual leader. Without such integrity, the authority granted to the spiritual leader quickly dissolves, and the power that flows from such authority is often dysfunctional and abusive. As Tutu grows into his identity as Elder and sage, such authenticity becomes his currency, by which he continues his spiritual leadership on a global stage. In other words, Tutu's character is trustworthy and reliable.

Through the authority given to Tutu as archbishop and as chair of the TRC, Tutu navigated a seemingly impossible task of truth-telling and reconciliation, given the hundreds of years of tragic and legal racism in South Africa's past and present. In this chapter we look underneath the authority given to Tutu, to gain a better understanding of the character produced by such authority. Tutu's identity developed in such a way that he was perceived as South Africa's confessor, but this occurred through how Tutu was often brutally honest and forthcoming.

271

In this chapter, my aim is to show how Tutu pursues an authentic Christian spirituality, which can give us a deeper understanding of Tutu's life. I argue here that an understanding of Christian spirituality based in either individualism or competitive identity shapes static understandings of spirituality. Unfortunately, many forms of Western Christian spirituality adhere only to European Enlightenment frameworks in which the individual is the sole adjudicator of discerning what is of the Spirit. As some individuals rise in material power, their worldview shapes the reality of what is spiritual. In response, non-Western liberation ideologies, dependent on violent authorizing criteria by which to adjudicate freedom, lash out against such oppressive worldviews of the powerful few. This has been the ongoing struggle within colonialization, in which Christianity was often used to bless Western worldviews.

Tutu's spirituality is all the more vital here, in that his life displays the interdependence between African (non-Western worldview) and Western spiritualities. South Africa grew to depend upon Tutu's bridge in order to move beyond the normalcy of apartheid, in which those of European descent tried to subjugate African people and make them think this is how reality should be and is even ordained by God to be. Tutu's integrity helped others resist the temptation to think apartheid was a normal way to live. Tutu helped a nation-state confess that the normality of apartheid was evil and, in fact, sinful.

The sin confessed was the heresy of apartheid. Of course, there are objections to the charge that apartheid is a heresy, such as that the term "heresy" seems farfetched to a twenty-first-century world or that apartheid is a political system not a theological one, or that apartheid is not relevantly analyzed if it stays in theological discourse (one can easily get distracted in such an academic discussion). John de Gruchy is helpful here when he states, "While we must beware of witch-hunts, self-righteousness, and anything which is destructive of persons and genuine human relations, . . . it must be said that if the Church is no longer concerned about heresy it has lost its passion for the truth revealed in Jesus Christ."[1] The insight here is not to be intolerant to other religions, but to be committed to the struggle for truth within the church, especially in light of a skeptical world that thinks religious sensibilities tend toward oppression of others. Tutu's individual spiritual life matters for the whole of his country, in that he shows why the life of the whole church matters to the life of politics, and how the political life cannot help but affect the church. In other words, the existence of both an apartheid church and an antiapartheid church makes God seem schizophrenic. Apartheid is a sin for this very reason.

Tutu's work as confessor was to wash away the false distinctions between a white God and a black God, which revealed more of a dysfunctional anthropology than a sacred spirituality. A dysfunctional anthropology focuses upon itself, instead of the intent of Christianity to reveal Jesus' pedagogy of truth and reconciliation. In the roots of Christian spirituality was the emphasis on authenticity in becoming a disciple of Jesus. No one was perfect except Jesus; therefore, any transference of sin on another was equivalent to Jesus' proverb of not looking for the speck in someone's else's eye when you have a log in your own eye (Matt. 7:3). Apartheid Christianity introduced the novelty of the white race as pure and holy, thereby disregarding Jesus' work to create a new humanity. The New Testament bears witness to this new humanity when it says that Jesus "has abolished the law with its commandments and ordinances, that he might create in himself one new humanity in place of the two, thus making peace, and might reconcile both groups to God in one body through the cross, thus putting to death that hostility through it" (Eph. 2:15–16).

Instead of adhering to this Christian teaching, apartheid Christianity introduced yet another division: the novelty of race and racism. The early Christian mystics would have seen this fundamentally as a heresy.[2] Apartheid, as a Christian worldview, made a person's ethnicity and physiognomy the crucial factor in determining the image of God among humanity. This factor would determine proper marriage, where to live and work, and whom to educate. It even determined which church you could attend. Such a novel Christian worldview, espoused by the entrenched Dutch Reformed churches in South Africa, such as the NGK and NHK, met resistance even from the other predominantly white Reformed churches around the world. It must be said here, however, that the other so-called English-speaking white churches in South Africa could not gloat in self-righteousness, as they too basked in the benefits of a white apartheid society.

In many Christian liturgies of worship, the confessor pronounces God's absolution or cleansing of sin to the people in order for them to embrace one another in peace. The liturgical practice is not meant for a congregation to run out and wash their sins away; rather, they are to realize that God's love has already made them clean. What is meant here by confessor and absolution in terms of the last stage of Christian mysticism is that union with God always requires the authenticity of confession and absolution. Again, it is a misconception to think that purgation, illumination, and union are somehow linear in movement. They are more a circular motion. What is interesting here is that Christian mystics catch such glimpses of union with God when they are most aware of their sin and absolution. Christians like Julian of Norwich, of whose monastic community Tutu was an associate, thought that the holier she became, the more aware she was of her sin. This is important to the claims of Christian mysticism, because in the later developmental stages for Tutu, he was acutely aware as an Elder that an authentic life is most valuable.

Christian mysticism offers a lens through which to see Tutu beyond the binaries that often exist between the global North and South. Instead of leaving the shape of the spiritual life in the hands of individuals, Christian spirituality must always be understood in the reality of community, in order for the spiritual life to become intelligible. My lens for seeing such community is the mystery of Jesus' understanding of the communal character of human nature that must constantly confess itself in order for absolution to make sense. It is not that I want to cause yet another binary of grace vs. work as entry into the divine life; rather, the need for absolution provides a humility that invites authenticity, rather than pretense and power struggle.

Jesus taught and embodied spiritual practices that ultimately led to community, with the greatest community encompassed in the relationality of the triune God. Such key practices associated with Jesus are aligned with the threefold method of Christian mysticism; namely, Jesus may be most famous for his rite of reconciliation: contrition, confession, forgiveness, and reunion. This rite of reconciliation has the same flow as the mystical way of purgation, illumination, and union. Contrition naturally has the same connotation of purgation in the sense of the burn and suffering when made conscious of one's own sin. The ability to then confess such sin is akin to the stage of illumination, in which one is aware enough to see what needs to be confessed. And the last stage in the rite of reconciliation associated with Jesus is union, which obviously weds the concluding stages of Christian mysticism and the rite of reconciliation. For the rite of reconciliation, the union stage is often overlooked or grasped in a sense as representing forgiveness. For example, many people think the essence of forgiveness is when the victim and the perpetrator embrace in the sign of reunion. What is important to learn here is that such a semblance of union does not represent the intent behind the concept of union in Christian mysticism.

First, Christian mystics teach that one should not ostensibly seek union with God, because by doing so one inevitably creates one's own self-fulfilling prophecy of what such union looks like and actually is. For example, the director in the book *The Cloud of Unknowing* counseled the disciple, "It is quite certain one cannot taste or experience God spiritually except by grace, whatever the extent of knowledge, acquired or natural. Therefore, I beg you to seek experience rather than knowledge: knowledge can often lead one astray through pride, whereas humble, loving experience does not lie. *Scientia inflat, caritas edificat* (Knowledge puffs up, but love edifies—1 Corinthians 8:1)."[3] Dionysius uses the following allegory to describe how one should carefully navigate the problem self-fulling prophecies of creating our own union with God. There is a man who has a huge block of wood lying in front of him, outside him. Inside him, however, is the intention to fashion a smaller statue of wood, and correctly measure and align it in the dead center of the wood. In order to show this wooden statue, he has to admit (confess) that the large piece of wood still exists outside of him. He must realistically gain skill and train his imagination to remove the outer wood case that hides the statue from sight.[4]

The analogy above speaks to the need for realism and trained imaginations in a complicated and violent world. Those who followed Jesus, especially in the tradition of Christian mysticism, sought union with God by defeating those forces endemic in the breakdown of human relationships. It may come as a surprise to those who think of Tutu only as a political actor, but it is especially appropriate to reflect upon Tutu as coming out of this mystical tradition. Trained by monks and nuns, Tutu learned to see spirituality in the light of community, especially healthy communities capable of the inclusion of diversity.

This search for diversity in community was one of the goals of the Desert Fathers and Mothers, who went into the African deserts to find complete relationality with the God of Jesus, who was creating for them a different reality in the midst of the powers of the world. Their goal was the mystery of community (communion), maintaining the particularity of one's created being, while at the same time becoming a catalyst for community. Religious communities today practice this mystery of community through their vows and disciplines, in which an offering is made to the world in the form of a vowed life dedicated solely to the love of God and neighbor.

Ironically, it could only be in the harsh expanse of the desert (spiritual and physical) that Christian communities and individuals could practice *ascesis* (disciplined spirituality), which carried the hermit beyond societal control into the union with God. Spiritual disciplines were undertaken in order to become a living martyr, constantly dying to self in the competitive world of demons and aridity. Jesus discipled those around him to move toward the demonic forces in order to cast them out from the world. Exorcising the evil forces allowed for persons to move into a deeper liberation, operating from a relational spirituality with God.

In other words, Jesus called those around him to be like the artist in Dionysius's allegory of the person shaping wood into a piece of art, and to cocreate a reality different from the prevalent forms of violence and oppression. Symbolically, this would be like shaping the wooden cross into a sign of resurrection. In so doing, Jesus' disciples were commissioned to empower community in the midst of anarchy. Christian spirituality, even in anchoritic (solitary) forms, displays the shape of empowerment, as well as conversion that leads to deeper forms of community. The ultimate beauty of Christian spirituality is that it can liberate human societies from the destructive dialectic of oppressed and oppressor, caught in perpetual deadlock as if this were all we were meant to be. Union with God is possible, but we must not seek such through dysfunctional human knowledge.

So union with God does not necessarily mean the absence of pain and struggle. This is especially so when we know that some of our brothers and sisters are not fully included in the human family. What does a Christian spirituality of union look like today, in light of seemingly conflicting identities (e.g., black, white, gay, lesbian, straight, rich, poor, women, and men)? I argue that union with God helps us figure that out, in the same way that Jesus taught his disciples to use their lateral brains and understand that when one loves God wholeheartedly, you cannot help but love your neighbor as yourself. This worldview of Christian mysticism offers movement beyond the limiting definitions of human beings as objects and victims. Through the spirituality of Jesus, human societies are taught to see diversity not as the enemy but as the genius of God's creation of community. What does it mean to live into Jesus' spirituality?

Jesus, having stayed quiet, responds not to Pilate's power but to his weakness, his fear, as he reassures him, "You would have no power over me unless it had been given you from above; therefore, the one who handed me over to you is guilty of a greater sin" (John 19:11). To be detached for Christ provides the insight that power is not just negative but also involves creativity, healing, and resolution. The exercise of Jesus' kind of power inevitably makes more of the other. This making more of the other is the key insight of Christian spirituality that forms Tutu's life and witness. This spirituality that makes more of the other looks like Tutu's visit to Taizé. He writes, "I was deeply impressed by the polyglot liturgy and the deep silence that interspersed the Scripture readings in several languages and the singing." Then, he said, he felt he received a vision, of "young South Africans of all races coming on pilgrimage to Taizé . . . to play and pray together in earnest for a non-racial future for our tortured land."[5]

A Christian spirituality of union with God worries about the difficult issue of pluralism and how it relates to particularity, especially that of the particular claims of diverse people. A Christian spirituality of union does not avoid the problem of pluralism and particularity; rather, such union seeks to be consistent by showing that pluralism and particularity are necessarily each dependent on the other for their definition. The very history of the spirituality of the Christian church becomes based upon this mystery of trusting the plurality and particularity of God in Jesus to show us more, not less, of the other. This is why I think confession and absolution are part and parcel of the last mystical stage of union. We live in union with God as we train our imagination and sharpen our skills to know others actually exist outside of self. And they actually matter to me and God.

RENEWED SPIRITUALITY

In union with God, Jesus teaches the world that the other, especially the poor and oppressed other, is to be embraced and healed. The challenges to this perceived spirituality of unity are currently articulated most by liberation and contextual theology. Tutu's spirituality is representative also of this theme of a renewal of spirituality to embrace the poor and otherness. In light of the miraculous spiritual practices of reconciliation in South Africa, it seems natural to view Tutu's theology and work as a way forward beyond both the individualism of Western spirituality and the liberation hermeneutic of violence and identity politics. It is also natural for me to be an advocate for Tutu's spirituality, since I was deeply influenced by my experiences of living with him.

Tutu becomes a contemporary exemplar through his work of explaining the complexity of human identity, in which particular persons may view liberation differently but always need to aim toward the goal of relational spirituality. This goal, however, has not always existed, even among prominent theologians. For example, one of the architects of black theology, James Cone, struggled against the dehumanizing forces of theologies derived from European rationalism, and refused to accept white identity. As I finished writing this book, Cone passed away on April 28, 2018, the anniversary of South Africa's first democratic election. Cone, a central figure in the development of black liberation theology in the 1960s and 1970s, argued for racial justice and an interpretation of the Christian gospel that elevated the voices of the oppressed. Cone described black liberation theology as "an interpretation of the Christian Gospel from the experience and perspectives . . . of people who are at the bottom in society." Cone concluded that the "Christian Gospel is . . . a religion that says God created all people to be free. But . . . for black people to be free, they must first love their blackness."[6]

Cone spoke forcefully about racial inequalities. which persisted in the form of economic injustice, mass incarceration, and police shootings. Tutu understood Cone's articulate voice, but always maintained the goal of reunion with God. Tutu states, "I myself believe I am an exponent of Black Theology, coming as I do from South Africa. I also believe I am an exponent of African theology, coming as I do from Africa. I contend that Black Theology is like the inner and smaller circle in a series of concentric circles."[7] While Tutu recognized himself in Cone's account of white dehumanizing forces, Tutu's emphasis on Christian spirituality made him emphasize more of a third way than Cone's black/white dialectic.[8] Cone's prophetic voice had to be hyperbolic in the midst of white, European theology, whereas Tutu's Ubuntu theology favored a more complementary solution of human identities in the South African context. Although Tutu deeply respected Cone's heroic theology, the problem he faced in South Africa was that there were many black identities (e.g., Zulu, Xhosa) and even multiple white identities (e.g., Afrikaner and British). Tutu offers these observations concerning the problem of racial identity within Christianity:

> Until fairly recently, the African Christian has suffered from a form of religious schizophrenia. With part of himself he has been compelled to pay lip service to Christianity as understood, expressed and preached by the white man. But with an ever greater part of himself, a part he has been often ashamed to acknowledge openly and which he has struggled to repress, he has felt that his Africanness was being violated. The white man's largely cerebral religion was hardly touching the depths of his African soul; he was being redeemed from sins he did not believe he had committed; he was being given answers, and often splendid answers, to questions he had not asked.[9]

Countering this "religious schizophrenia," a Christian spirituality becomes a crucial means by which to overcome this incessant ambivalence of being in one of the oppressed groups in need of liberation. For example, in the historically colonial church of Anglicanism, Africans found themselves more and more ambivalent in their encounter with European material culture, alongside their search for the spiritual side of African personality. Herein, Christian spirituality emphasizes the discipline of Christian personality to discern the deeper realities of liberation. Christian spirituality, as no doubt Cone would point out, should not naively assume that its goal of community has been achieved. For example, only when all African communities achieve their full share in determining policies in South Africa, thinks Tutu, will the possibility exist for true liberation among all races and cultures. This is the basis for Tutu's mantra, "Until all blacks are free, no one is free." Therefore, through a Christian spirituality of liberation enacted in the South African context, Tutu seeks the correct relational complement of black and white liberation, because no one is a person in South Africa until blacks attain the freedom to open their God-given personhood and humanity. In a real sense, this move by Tutu offers renewed spirituality away from the individualistic notions with which Christian spirituality is usually associated.

In Tutu's spirituality, it is important to attend to his own self-understanding on what spirituality actually means and looks like. Tutu would often say, "If I am so important, if I am so valuable, then it must mean then that every other human being is of equal worth, of equal value." How wonderful! This is why an authentic Christian spirituality is utterly subversive of any system that would treat a child of God as if he or she were less than this. Tutu would go on to say that all of this is the consequence of his prayers, faith, and spirituality. He would also say that those who label the content of his theology as idealistic have it all wrong. Every praying Christian, every person who has an encounter with God, must have a passionate concern for who is neighbor, because to treat anyone as if they were less than children of God is to deny the validity of one's own spiritual experience.

It is not merely wrong to treat anyone less than a child of God; it is not merely painful to the victim of our injustice, our oppression, our exploitation. It is fundamentally blasphemous, because all of God's children are destined for union with God. This person we demean is created in God's image. This other is a God carrier, a tabernacle of the Holy Spirit. To treat this person unjustly is to desecrate the dwelling of God. In Tutu's spirituality of union with God, division, disharmony, hostility, alienation, and separation are the pernicious results of sin. Any policies that make it a matter of principle to separate God's children into mutually opposing groups is evil, immoral, and unchristian. To oppose such a policy is an obligation placed on us by our faith, by our encounter with God. It is dangerous to pray, because an authentic spirituality is subversive of injustice. Oppression and unjust governments try to stop people praying to a Christian God.

Tutu rejects radical theologies incapable of reconciliation, because they do not fit his understanding of subversive spirituality, which I think offers a creative model in discerning human personality as interpersonality. In *Hope in Crisis: SACC National Conference Report 1986*, Tutu devises a relational approach to theology by refusing the common either-or hermeneutic of juxtaposing contextual theologies against each other. For instance, Tutu refuses to separate black, African, and liberation theology. Again, Tutu offers a renewed spirituality that rejects the usual Western binaries. Tutu's understanding of union with God is based on his strong emphasis on the narrative of unity, in which diverse people are called to work together, in order to one day experience a reconciled creation.

We are all called to live into the reality of a reconciled creation through the inter-personality of persons; therefore, the church is never allowed to lose conscious-ness of the reconciling work already accomplished in Christ (2 Cor. 5:11–21). The church's work is to stay awake to Jesus' spirituality of liberation, in which we are no longer slaves to violence and oppression. In a renewal of spirituality for Tutu, there is space for an African and black theologian, and yet, based on possessing both of these characteristics, he is a liberation theologian who strug-gles with theodicy questions of how persons at war may live harmoniously in a violent world.

COMMUNION

Christian spirituality is often criticized as being atomistic and "navel gazing," providing little recourse to social action, due to Western individualism. How-ever, as many Christians from the Latin American and African contexts have demonstrated, Christian spirituality need not be obsessed with self-fulfillment or the domination of the self over the other. In Tutu's spirituality, the emphasis of the spiritual life should be not so much on self-fulfillment as on the relational fulfillment between God and the world. Liberation spiritualities have always sought to hold on to relational fulfillment as the goal of the Christian life.

Such relational fulfillment is not unique to contemporary expressions of the Christian faith. For example, in the early church, the Desert tradition was about the communal formation of a radical Christian witness in relation to the cor-rupted forms of power relations in the world. Ascetic figures like Antony fought against those forces seeking to destroy God's community, whether such forces were found within the church or in the secular order. The goal of the Desert Fathers and Mothers was not to create anything new, but to return to the rela-tionality set forth by God's paradise given in the beginning of creation. The identity of the monastic did not preclude the larger goal of the radical redefining of society through the convictions of Christian identity. For example, Antony provided his contemporary society an opportunity to join an "elite" group of individuals; and yet, unlike the late Greco-Roman society of which Antony was a part, the Desert tradition barred no one on the basis of social pedigree. For an ascetic, one's social identity was gained both through contemplation of God's flourishing creation and through action against demonic principalities and powers that were ransacking human institutions. The thrust of the ascetic movement was to access supernatural power through the rigorous training of Christian character, in which the ascetic discovered and practiced a disciplined self in order to move beyond the ambiguities of self-definition in this earthly realm. Antony exhorts:

> Let us all the more exert ourselves in the discipline that opposes [the demons], for a great weapon against them is a just life and trust in God. They are afraid of the ascetics on several counts—for their fasting, the

vigils, the prayers, the meekness and gentleness, the contempt for money, the lack of vanity, the humility, the love of the poor, the almsgiving, the freedom from wrath, and most of all for their devotion to Christ. It is for this reason that they do all they do—in order not to have those monks trampling them underfoot.[10]

In the Christian mysticism in which the monastic movement flourished, the line was not clearly drawn between contemplation and action. In light of this ambiguous line, prayer and social witness often became indistinguishable for early Christians like Antony. This is vital in understanding the Christian spiritual tradition, because in order to avoid anachronistic church-against-world typologies we need to read ancients like Antony. These people followed a Jesus who gave up security, status, dominance, and reputation for the sake of building community.

Due to this emphasis on stripping false identities, the Desert tradition offered Tutu a profound resource by which to show his South African context that human beings are more than racial classifications defined by an oppressive government. The Anglican anchorite Maggie Ross became Tutu's spiritual director at one time. Her description of those in the early church deeply inspired Tutu's contemporary witness to articulate a spirituality of liberation. Ross is especially helpful in explaining the need to redefine human personhood in light of God. Ross states:

We need to read the ancients again and again. We need their wisdom. We need their signposts and road maps. We need the light they left behind as we follow them in this divine spelunking.

But we need most of all to recover what they most wanted to teach: that the whole point of the journey into the fiery love of God is self-forgetfulness, a self-forgetfulness evolving from a self-awareness that gradually drops away as we become ever more found in the adoration of God in whom we find our true selves. This movement toward completion no longer needs self-reflection, but needs to be aware only of God.[11]

The discovery of human identity in relation to God was the primary focus of the Desert tradition. The Desert tradition, from which Christian mysticism and the monastic movement originated, focused primarily on the achievement of a Christian character that serves as a *martyr* (i.e., witness) to communion with God. But how is this done? The answer is prayer. In the Desert tradition, prayer involves *anachoresis*, the art of disengagement. This ascetic concept is applied both individually and socially. On an individual level, *anachoresis* is the art of solitude.

Tutu explains that prayer is the physical necessity to shut up. Being in the presence of God allows us to know God; and to know God is to love God. We often think of silence as a negative thing or the absence of noise. But for Tutu, someone who is thought of as an extroverted public persona, silence is a positive dynamic of being in communion with God. For example, one cannot do creative thinking surrounded by distracting noise. Recollected calm in persons does not happen by accident; rather, it is fermented in them. Jesus shows his disciples this fermentation process when he calls his disciples to come away by themselves for a while. Tutu even leads a guided meditation to help his listeners better understand. Tutu leads this way: "Relax, think of yourself in a scene with Jesus in the synagogue when He heals the man with a withered arm. You are there. You smell the dusty, sweaty crowd. Is the synagogue full? Look at the Pharisees, some with shifty eyes watching to catch Jesus out. Can you hear Jesus calling out in anger/compassion for the man with the withered arm? You are there. What does Jesus say to the man? to the congregation of religious leaders? to you? What then does Jesus ask you to do?"[12]

On one level, Tutu's guided retreat seems otherworldly and typical of meditative practices that seem to relate to the here and now. Yet on a social level, it becomes a way to train the imagination to move beyond the oppressive ways of the world. Many do not know, for example, that the same is true of the monastic movement; it got its start by challenge the oppressive ways of the world. While in church, Antony, the founder of the Christian monastic movement, heard the Gospel passage in which the Lord tells the rich man that in order to be perfect, he must sell what he possesses and give it to the poor, so that he will have treasure in heaven (Matt. 19:21). Upon hearing this language of disengagement, Antony gained the courage to engage an oppressive society of late-Roman Egypt by undergoing a period of dark and isolated endurance in the desert.[13] This was no doubt caused by a society of economic insecurity, in which there were severe tax burdens and competition among village landowners. Therefore, on a social level, communion with God involves the political withdrawal (*anachoresis*) from the increased weight of taxation on folks living under the colonial rule of the Roman Empire.

The act of *anachoresis* itself, rather than any exceptional supernatural powers, was what the early church appreciated about the Desert tradition. Christians living in severe states of oppression saw through ascetic figures that power and prestige was redefined through acting out, heroically, in order to see how one might truly live in freedom. Monastic spiritual practices were not irrelevant to a social witness against corrupted forms of government. A more positive way of stating this is that the spiritual practices of the Desert tradition helped to train persons in community to see a truer form of the *imago Dei*. Tutu affirms this as an African and as a Christian. He feels that he needed to contribute to the emergence of a relevant spirituality. The spiritual is central to all that we do. Communion with God is to dwell in light unapproachable. In other words, learning to practice the presence of God helps us understand why we exist. In such communion, angels and archangels and the whole host of heaven do not cease to worship and adore God. God is the transcendent one who fills us with awe—the *mysterium tremendum et fascinans*. But God does not allow those in communion to remain in an exclusive spiritual ghetto. Our encounter with God launches us into the world, to work together in the residual effects of communion to establish God's reign on earth. Tutu believes that God's reign on earth is full of peace, justice, and caring. In this fullness human beings become agents who can bring about radical transformation.

Another resource offered by the Desert tradition is its excellent assessment of *anachoresis* as an explanation of social "death," which implies that the ascetic attempts to construct a new identity despite the lack of any normal social support. In this regard, the ascetic tradition offers Tutu an invaluable resource to resolve the incoherencies of the human identity in relation to a corrupted society. And such a resource will continue to offer support in postapartheid South Africa. Tutu explains the need for such deep reflection of the spiritual life for the future of South Africa. Tutu states,

> There is going to be increasing leisure time as technology and machines take over from humans. We are going to have to learn how to spend that leisure time creatively. We are going to have to be taught how to enjoy our own company; we are going to have to grow more contemplative, to be still at the core of our being, to be in touch with our real selves and with God. We have a God-hunger, and only God can ultimately satisfy that hunger. We must make space for transcendence, for prayer, for meditation, and so our democratic state will be determined in ensuring freedom of worship and belief and even the lack of it.[14]

In Tutu's explanation for why we need the deep reflection of the spiritual life, he addresses his own need to confess sin. The only good confessor is the one who also confesses sin. Tutu is the first to admit his weaknesses and struggles. For example, he realizes that Christian spirituality often exists in caricature, lacking answers to many questions of liberation theology, especially the charge that spirituality is often too weak to help oppressed peoples in the face of oppressors. Tutu also found himself sometimes in the precarious place of being both an exemplar of liberation spirituality and a critic of it.

By focusing on the relational and communal aspects of Tutu's spirituality, I risk incurring the wrath of contextual theologians, who surmise that my interpretation of Tutu's spirituality as confessor is too weak a concept to say anything meaningful about human struggles today, especially the concrete situations in which people suffer. In an interview with a Muslim woman, Amina Chaudary, at Boston University, Tutu confessed to her the sins of the Christian community. The context of this conversation occurred when Tutu was serving as Elder at a meeting in Johannesburg. Chaudary observed that she had the rare and distinct privilege to attend this meeting of Elders where she silently observed some of the most charismatic and influential world leaders working toward promoting world peace. She writes, "These leaders were motivated to establish a sense of reconciliation and cooperation between 'cultures' and 'religions.' As a Muslim woman who often feels her faith to be misaligned and misconstrued by a small band of corrupt polemicists, I wanted nothing more than to understand how it is that religion could be used as a tool to bring about peace when it has so often been utilized as a tool to bring about evil."[15]

Chaudary and Tutu's conversation turned to discussing how religion, a powerful source of peace and understanding, can also be used as a powerfully destructive tool. "When can religion become evil?" she asked. Tutu responded with a confession:

> It isn't religion as such that is violent or incorrect. Actually I don't know any religion that promotes violence. It is the adherents of whatever religion. Christians have to be some of the most humble and very modest in this regard. It is not any particular religion that is to blame. There is no religion in fact that I know that encourages or propagates violence in that its adherents should carry out. Christians are the last to be hoity-toity. Now that they talk about Islam as being a violent faith, when you look at the history of Christendom, the Crusades and the many wars of religion that were fought, the cruelty of Christians in burning what they believed to be witches and burning heretics, and then very recently they were responsible for the Holocaust it was Christians.[16]

A good confessor also has to be good in confessing sin. Liberation spirituality is profound in this focus on the poor and oppressed, who often remain victims in the midst of the pomp and circumstance of something called Christianity. Often, strangely enough, God's image of the suffering Christ is lost. I have already discussed that liberation spirituality seeks to articulate the need for the poor and the oppressed to rediscover their humanity in light of the image of God. Such a rediscovery is seen only in liberation of the poor and oppressed and their refusal to repeat the sins of the oppressor. Especially, liberation theologies derived from Latin America and Black Theology insist upon the rescue of those oppressed and oppressors to see themselves again as God's children. Tutu concludes that this recognition is the insight in being children of God: "For the oppressed the most vital part of the Christian gospel is its message of liberation from all that would make us less than the children of God—sin, political and economic deprivation, exploitation and injustice. It is also liberation to be people who enjoy the glorious liberty of the children of God, which must include political empowerment to determine the shape of one's destiny."[17]

The problem is not in any weak response of liberation spirituality per se, but in the extent to which those who champion the liberation spiritualities will go to rescue the oppressed. Could violence ever be condoned in such a pursuit? Until a clear Christian spirituality of nonviolence accompanies the spirituality of liberation, Christian spirituality will remain ambiguous and relative only to the one defining its meaning. In some sense, my conclusion here leads to the last chapter on the substance of peace in God. I hold up Tutu as a model of a Christian spirituality of liberation, because he shows us how to refuse violence as the normative means by which to rescue the oppressed. Although this may appear to some as weakness, he provides profound strength to look for long-term solutions that refuse violent short-term answers. Yet Tutu is not a pacifist and could be convinced in certain circumstances to condone so-called "just war." Tutu's theology can be categorized as radical in the rhetorical sense of seeking the root of the Christian faith through the church's practices, but not radical in the sense of juxtaposing political identities of oppression as the hermeneutical key to theology. In other words, he refuses the argument that the essence of human identity is political, and therefore in need of force and coercion.

In the end, Christian liberation spirituality is the work of making spirituality communal. At the heart of this vision for human identity is the life, death, resurrection, and ascension of Jesus, who returns warring identities back to Communal Being, the Triune God. In this vision, violence becomes blasphemous to the image of God. Christian spirituality becomes communal spirituality, in which interdependence of being always refuses violent practice and never turns away from constructive engagement with the poor and rich. Tutu helps us see how Western individualism can no longer shape how Christians engage the needs of the world, because just war criteria can no longer be met in light of weapons of mass destruction.

We must learn from liberation spirituality that there is a plurality of theologies, jostling and competing with each other, but they can complement and challenge one another at the same time. The *imago Dei* becomes the mystery that informs our spirituality; the divine life of God demands the concert of being. The danger of Western individualism is that it has little incentive to work for interdependent structures. In such a case the catholic (universal) church becomes unintelligible if there is no consensus of particular identities. The task of Christians then becomes to address specific issues that arise from the contexts of particular communities. These particular communities do not become obsolete or irrelevant when their usefulness has burned out, because Christian identity has learned to see human identity as eternal, made in the image of God. Christian identity becomes the catalyst in the world to refuse to negate the mystery and gospel that our image of God has been restored in Christ.

Communion with God takes seriously the image of God in the other, so much so that in order for theology to be authentic, it needs to be relevant to its particular contexts. Because Tutu's form of Christian spirituality focuses upon the context of spirituality, the need to dialogue across contexts is essential. Precisely because Christian spirituality constantly answers a different set of questions by different kinds of people, there is the requirement for diverse spiritualities. "So that we now find ourselves," Tutu concludes, "perhaps in a bewildering position of dealing with strange juxtapositions of different theologies, cheek by jowl with one another, complementing or contradicting one another."[18] Consequently, ecumenical and interreligious spiritualties of liberation have developed in varying contexts around the world in response to injustice and violence, as we saw with Christians, Muslims, Hindus, Jains, Jews, and many other religious groups in the case of the TRC.[19]

Expanding the worldview of Western Christianity becomes the great gift of Tutu's liberation spirituality. Liberation spirituality is vital in that it makes clear that any theology from the position of dispossessed non-Western people must alert Western people that there is no unilateral cultural way of knowing God and neighbor. In the end, Christian spirituality comes from an Eastern religion called Christianity and should not readily fit into defined Western interpretations of religion. Much of Western discourse operates within the European Enlightenment framework of the rationality of an individual who claims the primacy of identity (race, economic class, gender, or culture) as proper access to expose oppressive structures of thought. In the non-Western world, however, human identity is known more through the socialization processes of communities, which teach individuals to discern who they are in light of the community.

Much of the non-Western world would distinguish race as different from culture. The latter is a system of inherited concepts rooted in a way of thinking and acting in light of a community grammar demonstrated through stories and histories that shape peoples in a particular location. What is fundamental to non-Western cultures is the communal way of knowing. The rationale for a liberation spirituality is that only in the particularity of being Latino, Xhosa, French, Zulu, Portuguese, Yoruba, and so on may clarity be given to what is true or what is of God. And even in such particularity, many non-Western spiritualities such as African spiritualities have opened themselves, for good and ill, to Western ways of knowing. An African example of being open to other cultures and particularities can be found through the concept of Ubuntu.[20] As a result, liberation spirituality assumes a communal nature of the church that becomes instrumental in the transformation of demonic forces in the world (e.g., apartheid in South Africa) into authentic communal existence.

As a result of conflicting displays of who is most human throughout history, Christian spirituality has a vital role to play now and in the future, to show how interdependence is possible among incommensurate identities. Now more than ever, Christian spirituality will have to offer discourse in which warring identities may discover conclusions other than violence and war. We learn from liberation spirituality, however, to live into the continual need for deconstruction of any claim toward unilateral identity in the effort to expose structures of power, injustice, or surreptitious hegemonic orders. In contrast with an exclusivist, Western hermeneutical methodology, liberation spirituality is based upon theological criteria that seek to reconcile conflicts that naturally arise among all persons in their varying contexts and locations.

So I end this chapter the way I began. To define Tutu's authentic sense of Christian spirituality requires the thought and practice of liberation. Without attempting to impose a single definition of Christian spirituality upon the reader, I have invited an understanding of the field of Christian spirituality as the work of relationality and interdependence. The benefits of exemplars like Tutu—a deepened understanding of humanity, attention to the poor among us, communal ways of knowing, ecumenism, expanded worldviews—all are benefits that set forth a possible future direction for scholarly research in the field of Christian spirituality.

In summary, a Christian spirituality of liberation thinks through and practices human interpersonality that flourishes throughout this earth. In the end, attention to how all persons flourish will inform a deeper and more systemic form of human liberation beyond humanistic discourse based on violent revolution. A Christian spirituality of liberation seeks the comprehension of including hermeneutical privilege of oppressed groups, while at the same time holding such claims accountable to the goal of the image of God in the oppressors. The goal, therefore, is for all to discover healthy humanity in communion with God, who is revealed in the ultimate death of Jesus, who leads us to be on the side of the sinner, the despised, the outcast, and the downtrodden. But this God is not controlled by any particular group. God remains God. This is important in any context in which many human communities claim the control of God's liberating powers. The story of the tower of Babel illustrates this in Genesis 11. It demonstrates a false unity based on disobedience, a self-securing homogeneity. In such a context unity is oppressive and gathers people together for the wrong reasons.

Perhaps new to many readers is the understanding that liberation requires ascetic training toward God, who calls us to both prayer and action amid human conflict and war. Such training offers a direction away from the oppressive realities of the normal cycles of violence, in which today's oppressed end up being tomorrow's oppressor. Jesus' spirituality makes it possible to develop a different kind of history, in which a person must leave biological kindred to favor those recreated into kindred by God (Gen. 12:1 and Matt. 12:46–50). Liberation spirituality is the living testimony of breaking with false forms of relatedness gained through oppressive histories. Instead of promoting warring human identities, Christian spirituality, discipled by Jesus, moves us toward God's promise of a new creation and away from a future of violence and destruction. The end of Christian spirituality then becomes full participation in the mystery of being related in infinite and eternal ways.

In this chapter we have discovered how Tutu becomes both confessor and confessee. Without such integrity, the authority granted to the spiritual leader quickly dissolves and the power that flows from such authority can become dysfunctional and abusive. As we shall see more explicitly in the next chapter, Tutu grew into his identity as Elder and sage, identities in which such authenticity is vital. Tutu pursues an authentic Christian spirituality that can inform a deeper understanding of how and why Tutu was chosen as global sage. Tutu's authenticity is important here, as he becomes an alternative to non-Western liberation ideologies, dependent on violent authorizing criteria by which to adjudicate freedom. This has been the ongoing struggle within colonialization, where Christianity was often used to bless Western worldviews.

We now move toward Tutu as an Elder on the global stage, not just in South Africa, again providing a unifying role in the midst of some of the most contentious issues of the time.

Tutu Travel Seminar, a program of the Desmond Tutu Center at General Theological Seminary, meeting at Volmoed Retreat Center in Hermanus, Western Cape, South Africa, August 10, 2017: (front, left to right) Leah Tutu, Desmond Tutu; (back, left to right) Edwin Arrison (Anglican priest ordained by Tutu), Michael Battle, Maureen Hagen (deacon in Episcopal Church), John de Gruchy (South African theologian), Robert Nelson Smith (Episcopal priest and former CEO of St. Francis Ministries), Graham John Ward (Anglican priest and Regius Professor of Divinity, University of Oxford). Author photo.

Chapter 13

Sage Years

In this chapter I will discuss how Tutu has reconciled the idealism of peace with the difficult stages of his struggle against apartheid in his elder years as sage. We discover here who his coelders are and explore their charge to go into all the world as sages and advisors in their global roles. Tutu's unifying role in South Africa was never really separated from impact in the rest of the world. This was true especially when he as archbishop rallied international support to nonviolently fight the apartheid regime through economic sanctions. It was also true when Tutu as chair of the TRC was often consulted on the global stage on how a truth and reconciliation process could occur in other countries. With this in mind, chapter 13 looks at how union occurred as Tutu realized his profound work beyond South Africa. Much of this work, though done with little fanfare or recognition, is work he feels necessary in his role as a global Elder.

Tutu, at a press conference in 2010 in Cape Town, announced the time had come to slow down and watch cricket, after decades of struggling against injustice. The biggest beneficiary of his new lifestyle would be his wife, Leah, because a real retirement would allow him to serve her hot chocolate in bed in the mornings, as an attentive husband. His intentions were to serve as an elder to initiate and found this global program only for a short stint and then withdraw from public life to spend more time with his family. Tutu said that he would cut his workload to one day a week when he turned seventy-nine on October 7, 2010, before retiring completely in February 2011. He said further, "I have done as much as I can and need time to do things I have really wanted to do."[1]

Although Tutu retired formally as Anglican archbishop of Cape Town in 1996, and served as chair of the TRC until 2002 (although the TRC report was given to Mandela in 1998), Tutu continued to travel the world as one of the Elders. His sense of humor also never diminished as he approached moving off the world stage. For example, at the opening ceremony of the South African World Cup in 2010, Tutu described it as one of the most significant events in the country since the end of white rule, as he swapped his clerical robes for a football shirt and beanie and danced in his VIP seat. Tutu states, "The time has now come to slow down, to sip rooibos tea with my beloved wife, . . . to watch cricket, to travel to visit my children and grandchildren."[2] Once Tutu was to step down, he would no longer be available for media interviews, and no new appointments would be added to his schedule.

Just as we saw Tutu wrestle to unify the juxtaposition between politics and spirituality in South Africa during apartheid, so too we can discover a synthesis of the two in Tutu's later life, beyond South Africa. He said frequently, displaying an infectious smile, that there were many in South Africa who claimed that he was really a politician trying very hard to be an archbishop. Tutu often acknowledged the concerted campaign to vilify and discredit him, to simplify Tutu as an irrelevant religious person or an overstepping political voice. But true to one of Tutu's gifts—his sense of humor—he seemed always able to calm down the crowds or critics enough to listen to his perspective. He did this by telling some delightful stories. "You know the one of how when I died I went to heaven, but St. Peter consigned me to the warmer place. A fortnight later there was frenzied knocking on the pearly gates and when St. Peter opened them there was the old devil himself standing there. And St. Peter confronted him: 'En nou toe'—'what are you doing here?' And the devil replied: 'Well you sent Bishop Tutu down there to me and he is causing so much trouble, I've come to ask for political asylum!'"[3]

Tutu's self-deprecating humor was an important sign of his immunity to power politics. I found agreement about this with Graham Ward, an English theologian, Anglican priest, and Regius Professor of Divinity at the University of Oxford. He was staying at Volmoed, an intentional Christian community and retreat center in Hermanus, South Africa, where my Tutu Travel Seminar group often met with Tutu. I was asking the group to go around to say how Tutu formed their vocations as clergy and theological students. They were all complimentary in praising Tutu, as you might expect. When we got to Ward, his answer was more caustic; Tutu didn't affect him, he said, in the same way as many of the other members of our group. Ward's wisdom was that by putting Tutu on a pedestal, you do a disservice to Tutu. In this spiritual biography we have heard other anecdotes about Tutu struggling with ego, fame, and celebrity.

His use of humor and laughter was a purgative tool for Tutu; after all, when you traveled the world like Tutu, constantly in the audience of kings and queens, heads of state, and the seemingly most "important" people, you would need ways to keep yourself grounded and down to earth. That seemed to be the point Ward was making.

Chris Ahrends, Tutu's chaplain and assistant in the 1980s, said that Tutu experienced frequent verbal abuse when he was traveling back then, but didn't express any hurt or anger because of it. In the early years of Tutu's ministry at Bishopscourt, when he had just become archbishop, real tensions were also building up as Tutu's staff competed for attention. Both of these stressful situations occurred regularly for Tutu—tensions on his staff and tension in society. Allen remembers that in those early years, when Tutu would go away, in his absence tensions would build up and get quite rough. When Tutu got back, after morning prayer he would report back to the staff about his trips. In this reporting would inevitably burst forth his unique laughter, ebullience, and joy, which would dissipate the tensions of his staff. He had this extraordinary capacity, in the way Chris Ahrends put it, to function like a sponge for the hatred to which he was constantly subjected.

Later, when reflecting on the TRC, Tutu mentioned this sponge analogy and how a sponge is purifying. Sister Margeret Magdalen of the Community of St. Mary the Virgin gave him this imagery, he said, by telling him how Jesus coped with pain in ministry. She described how a vacuum cleaner keeps in the filth while a dishwasher spews it out down the drain. Jesus, somehow, absorbed all that came to him and then passed it on further into the cleansing life of God.[4]

Tutu's power was not his own; he relied on Jesus. Tutu practiced such reliance on a daily basis through his spirituality and disciplines, which could keep him calm in the midst of crisis. This sponge-like capacity completely overwhelmed any negative sense of ego or celebrity. Tutu would admit it himself, "I love to be loved." He used to say under apartheid that he developed a hide of a rhinoceros, but it wasn't actually true. He said he had developed this hide, but he hurt deeply when he was attacked and abused as a leader against apartheid. He did love to be loved, but he constantly did spiritual work on how this could be identified within himself as a weakness. To love to be loved can sometimes lead to a temptation to also be the center of attention. You have to consider the effect on someone like Tutu, who since 1984 has been put on a pedestal. Shirley du Boulay, an English woman who wrote a biography of him, quoted someone in Tutu's social circles in Johannesburg who went to visit a hospital with him. The person said Tutu was upset at not being recognized. John Allen also told me this story and said that although he had not quite worked this all out, the person registering this complaint against Tutu was probably a white priest. To be fair to Tutu, one must distinguish between Tutu's ego and the feeling that he was being belittled as a black person, and not treated as a white person would be in the same circumstances. All of that said, if you are put on a pedestal and treated a certain way, you develop certain expectations, which can come out as arrogant.[5]

TUTU AS ELDER AND SAGE

Tutu and the Dalai Lama developed a deep friendship in their later years, and Tutu invited him to deliver the Desmond Tutu Peace Lecture, an annual public event. The purpose of this lecture was twofold: to keep a continuing focus on the work and witness of Tutu's legacy, and to emphasize that justice and peace in South Africa are of vital importance on the agenda of all religious people and groups.[6] In 2011 the South African government denied the Dalai Lama's entrance, both to give the lecture and to celebrate Tutu's eightieth birthday. We will discuss this in more detail below. In many ways this controversy addressed how the substance of peace was vital not only among nation-states and ideologies. It was also necessary to address the violence spawned among religions. For example, the South African chapter of the World Conference on Religion and Peace asserts: "We are convinced that each of our different faiths expresses itself clearly in favor of justice and peace. . . . We regret the fact that religion has been instrumental in the past to separate us from one another. . . . We want to promote fellowship and mutual understanding across religious lines."[7]

In Tutu's latter years he began to focus more on this understanding of substantial peace among religions and in other ways as well, especially as he became an official Elder, which was an independent group of international leaders working together for peace and human rights.

The concept for being an Elder derived from the entrepreneur Richard Branson and the musician Peter Gabriel. Branson and Gabriel simply acknowledged the tradition in many communities that elders are looked to for guidance, especially in helping to resolve disputes. "In an increasingly interdependent world—a 'global village'—could a small, dedicated group of individuals use their collective experience and influence to help tackle some of the most pressing problems facing the world today?"[8] They took this idea to Nelson Mandela, and with his support, along with the help of Graça Machel and Tutu, the Elders were formally launched in Johannesburg in July 2007 and still exist.[9] The original class of Elders included Nelson Mandela (founder), Martti Ahtisaari, Kofi Annan, Ban Ki-moon, Ela Bhatt, Lakhdar Brahimi, Gro Harlem Brundtland, Fernando H. Cardoso, Jimmy Carter, Hina Jilani, Ricardo Lagos, Graça Machel, Mary Robinson, Desmond Tutu, and Ernesto Zedillo.

They were founded to be an independent voice, not bound by the interests of any nation, government, or institution. The premise for their existence is founded upon their commitment to promote the shared interests of humanity, and the universal human rights that all people should share. They believe that in any conflict, listening to everyone is paramount, "no matter how unpalatable or unpopular this may be." True to Tutu's own spirituality, the Elders aim to act boldly, speaking difficult truths and tackling taboos. Lastly, in humility they claim not to have all the answers, as they stress how all human beings can make a difference and create positive change in their societies.[10]

To be an Elder means no longer holding public office. This is important in forming an independence from any national government or other vested interest. Elders should be leaders who have earned global trust by demonstrating integrity and inclusion in their leadership. Their common commitment is to peace and the premise of universal human rights. In such a commitment, it is their hope that they bring diverse expertise and experience to the situations they encounter. In short, they hope to be peacemakers who bring wisdom in resolving conflicts around the world. These Elders should already have the integrity of making peace in their own societies, demonstrating how they were social revolutionaries who helped to transform their own countries by reducing poverty, improving the status of women, or championing nonviolent struggle. The criteria for becoming an Elder very much describe Tutu's life as someone who leads by example, "creating positive social change and inspiring others to do the same."

Tutu also met the criteria for becoming an Elder in that he brought a profound worldview to the table. In African spirituality there is a search for balanced destiny between the individual and the community that continues beyond death. This balanced destiny is practiced in African cultures around the world through understandings of God, prayer, justice, human beings, and the created universe. Through Tutu's life, we discover an additional encounter with African spirituality in how Christian spirituality is already embedded in the political through the binding together of individual and communal destinies. How African Christians understand themselves to be the church is not any different from how they understand the *polis* or the community that behaves in the world. Similar to definitions of the political, African churches offer a dynamic construction of individual and community in which the identities create each other. This notion of mutual construction can be seen in how African ecclesiology is defined through a wide range of relatives, neighbors, villagers, and ancestors, who share responsibility for the formation and discipline of individuals baptized in Christ's community.

In essence, African ecclesiology looks more like hospitality than a place or time, whereas Western notions of the church inevitably lead to the church as a building or a setting for Sunday morning. African ecclesiology begins not with cognitive function but with communal sensibilities of devotion and mystery, which an individual mind could never fathom alone. Tutu is proud of this perspective of the church in South Africa. Tutu observed that a large group of church leaders banded together, standing overnight in the rain at Mogopa, to protest the removal of a remnant of indigenous people, most of whom had already been forcibly removed from their land. "Our action must have contributed to some extent in restraining the authorities."[11] It is from this thesis surrounding a communal ecclesiology of African Christianity that I posit Tutu's unifying contributions to bring together seemingly irreconcilable differences. Tutu as South African confessor is especially important here in making the penitent aware of what needs to be confessed in the Western world today.

INDIVIDUALISM

As we have seen before, Tutu offers to theological discourse a much needed corrective to the individualistic, myopic work that often goes on in the Western world. Tutu is uniquely situated to make such a contribution, because of his unique blend of an African and Western ecclesiology. In the West, especially from the time of the Enlightenment, the self has been understood as a distinct individual, with unique value and distinct rights. Persons have the right to make something of their lives, to take responsibility for their life direction, to use their talents and gifts to the full. Such emphasis puts supreme value on the right of self-determination, self-achievement, self-satisfaction. It is often justified that such personal responsibility for the shaping of one's life is a good, and that it flows from the Judeo-Christian understanding of the dignity and worth of each human being.

What is weak in this personal dimensional worldview is the bonding of the person with the community. Especially in this century and particularly in North American culture, individual self-determination has become the norm for understanding spirituality. This Western practice of spirituality has profoundly influenced all facets of life, including politics, economics, and religion. This is important for Tutu's life, as he argues for the interdependence between faithful Christian witness and faithful political practice. For example, Tutu states:

> So the [Eloff] Commission declares the [SACC] has abandoned its proper work that of proclaiming the Gospel and of evangelizing the many who are untouched and not yet reached by the Christian message. The point is that the South African Government is extremely annoyed with the SACC for doing dastardly things such as providing scholarships for black children in rural areas, for looking after families of political prisoners, for providing legal defense for those appearing in political cases, for providing health education and agricultural instruction to enable poor people to grow enough food to educate themselves providing a clear water supply in rural areas etc.[12]

For Tutu, there is a false dichotomy in any human spirituality that somehow disconnects from the needs of the world—and this goes for political needs. Tutu concludes, "We belong to the worldwide church of God and to touch the SACC is to touch the Church of our Lord Jesus Christ."[13]

In the African cosmology, the uniqueness of each person is affirmed and acknowledged, but African individuality and freedom are always balanced by the destiny of the community. From Tutu's perspective, the Western world engenders affinity groups and individualistic agendas. For example, Western newspapers for a long time now have given very little coverage to the killings of black people, but make it headline news when the victims are whites. Every violent death should be one too many. Also, there is hardly any positive reporting in Western media on what goes on in the global South. When Africa gets in the news, as if to comply with a stereotype, only the bad news hits the media. The use of military force is another example of this. In the Western world, what dictates military action? This question is important, because there seem to be so many double standards as to what is in the best interest of countries in the global North. How is US interest in apprehending a warlord in Somalia different from taking a backseat in the Bosnian war? Is it because in the former case it is blacks involved, while in the latter it is whites? Why is it so easy for the US to attack Iraq for an alleged attempted crime, and yet Palestinians can be treated so harshly elsewhere?

For Tutu, the answers cannot be solely political in nature. There have to be spiritual answers as well. The unity of the church in its koinonia may have something to offer to a world that in some places is rapidly disintegrating.[14] Instead of Christian and other religious communities mimicking society, spiritual leaders should be able to transcend all sorts of barriers and distinctions and give hope to those who are floundering in this time of flux, wondering who they are. When Tutu was archbishop, he reminded his church, "We are to elect a new bishop for the diocese to succeed your much loved Kenneth. Let us place ourselves in God's hands and refrain from the manipulation and politicking that is appropriate in the secular world."[15]

Indeed, as we have learned from the contrasting viewpoints between African and Western, Tutu teaches us that Western and African understandings and practices of spirituality are distinctly different. When we disregard these differences, there can never be an intelligible discussion of how the one's practice of spirituality can inform the other's understanding of spirituality. For example, much has been written recently about Western abuse of the environment as stemming from a perversion of the biblical mandate to "fill the earth and subdue it"[16] and the need for a spirituality that will form persons and communities in care and concern for our earth. This problem, however, is uniquely a Western hermeneutic.

A divorce occurs between African and Western spirituality because Western Christian spirituality has rationalized an eschatology in which union with God and the restoration of the image of God (2 Pet. 1:4) are achievable only in the life to come. If we are to wait for the next life to be unified with God, then it becomes permissible to use force and to justify violence in this life. This has been the rationale of much of Western Christendom. Tutu advocates, however, that in African Christian spirituality there is not this Western false dichotomy between this life and the next.

The African Christian life does not allow any separation between how we live now and how we will live in the next life. In order for our relationship with Christ to be authentic, we must show concurrent characteristics of our mutuality with Christ. Christian spirituality is our cooperation with God in space and time; such cooperation seeds our ability to live outside of space and time with God. Paul states, "Work out your own salvation with fear and trembling; for it is God who is at work in you, enabling you both to will and to work for his good pleasure" (Phil. 2:12–13). The Western person, however, learns from an early age to interpret salvation personally and to see the world as that which is to be individually controlled. A person, in Western interpretations of creation, is a being who stands over and against creation in all its dimensions, using and abusing it for his or her own ends. Key to this Western worldview is the separation of the person from creation and from the world of nature. Therefore, domination best describes this Western epistemology, in which nature is made the servant of human needs, wants, and desires.

In contrast to the Western perspective, the African perspective is such that the uniqueness and goodness of humanity are seen in continuity with the goodness and value of all the other facets of creation. The various facets of creation—the sky, the sun and moon, mountains, forests and trees, rivers and water, plants and animals—all have at least implicit spiritual meaning and often explicit significance. In other words, human personhood is interdependent with creation. Instead of the Western perspective, in which humanity relates to the rest of creation as ruler to servant, African epistemology portrays relationality and interdependence, which acknowledge that the earth provides humanity its basic sustenance—air, water, food, and so forth—and thus the human community is called to steward it faithfully and carefully. From this African sensibility of interdependence and relationality Tutu understands Christian spirituality, and he displays this throughout his ministry in the world. Tutu's genius in Christian spirituality is to show in more detail what interdependence and relationality look like in the African context.

An African person practices the destiny of the community through what I describe as the sacraments of various initiation rites that have been, and to a certain extent remain, vital to the interpretation of what is African. The rites of passage practiced among African communities integrate the person into the society so that she or he may find identity within community. This rite of passage continues beyond death, since ancestors are regarded as intrinsically part of the community, able to influence events and guide the community. This emphasis upon maturity and passage into deeper stages flows from an African communal sense of personhood, in which the individual becomes conscious of herself through social interaction. A person discovers self through what is expected of personhood in terms of relationship to a clan, in which cultural norms and responsibilities become intelligible.

Through these initiation rites, all of life is seen as sacramental, full of visible signs of invisible grace. For the African person, all of life is one continuous movement of community, from birth to death and beyond. An African person acts therefore in concert with the community, not apart from it. Crucial to an African spirituality of community is the fact that the destinies of the individual and the community are bound together. When good is done, it is good for the entire community, and when evil is committed, the shame or the victimization affects the whole community.

In addition to his work of Elder, Tutu was instrumental in setting up a company of himself and six other Nobel Peace Prize laureates, including His

Holiness the Dalai Lama of Tibet, to visit Thailand in 1993. Their mission was twofold. First, they wished to draw attention to the continued detention of fellow Nobel Peace Prize–winner Aung San Suu Kyi.[17] Second, they hoped to learn for themselves the reality of the situation in Burma. Unfortunately, the ruling regime refused them permission to enter the country. Instead, they traveled to the Burmese frontier, where they spoke with some of the thousands of Burmese who had fled military rule in their homeland. There he heard of how Burmese troops forced women and children to become military porters and how they used civilians as human landmine sweepers. Five years of "constructive engagement" had given the regime the confidence to maintain its repressive rule.

Tutu said that it was time to admit that the policy of constructive engagement was a failure, just as similar actions had failed to persuade the apartheid regime in South Africa to make more than cosmetic changes. This meant for Tutu that an international arms embargo was a first step. Trade and investment restrictions should follow. International pressure could change the situation in Burma, he believed. Tough sanctions, not constructive engagement, finally brought the release of Nelson Mandela and the dawn of a new era in Tutu's country. Tutu states, "This is the language that must be spoken with tyrants—for, sadly, it is the only language they understand."[18]

In Tutu's later years he has had to deal with controversy surrounding his fellow Nobel laureate. Aung San Suu Kyi was eventually released from detention, but shockingly went on to become a major leader of a repressive regime in Burma, by then known as Myanmar. Tutu condemned the actions (or inactions) of Aung San Suu Kyi in her role as state counsellor (essentially, prime minister), effectively telling her that "Silence is too high a price."[19] Tutu called on her to speak up for the Rohingya people, a persecuted Muslim minority in Myanmar, and end military-led operations against them. In 2017, Tutu wrote Aung San Suu Kyi an impassioned letter. At this point, the United Nations estimated that 270,000 refugees had been driven out of Myanmar and crossed into Bangladesh. In his open letter, Tutu urged Aung San Suu Kyi to intervene and speak out. The situation was so serious that Tutu confessed his need to break his vow on public matters; yet Tutu remained consistent in his role as Elder to bring guidance to global conflict and interreligious conflict. Whereas once Aung San Suu Kyi was compared to Mandela as a symbol of wise and enduring leadership, in rule she has repeatedly refused to speak out against the military's campaign of violence against the Rohingya population. The assault has seen horrible destruction and thousands killed in what the United Nations has said amounts to ethnic cleansing. As of the publication of this book, Suu Kyi had not responded to Tutu's letter, other than to say to the Delhi-based network Asian News International media, "It is a little unreasonable to expect us to solve the issue in 18 months. The situation in Rakhine has been such since many decades. It goes back to pre-colonial times."[20]

Tutu wrote in the letter posted on social media, "I am now elderly, decrepit and formally retired, but breaking my vow to remain silent on public affairs out of profound sadness." Tutu continues, "For years I had a photograph of you on my desk to remind me of the injustice and sacrifice you endured out of your love and commitment for Myanmar's people. You symbolized righteousness." Suu Kyi's emergence into public life had allayed his concerns about violence being perpetrated against members of the Rohingya. He naturally thought she would be a champion of the oppressed. But Tutu observed that "what some have called 'ethnic cleansing' and others 'a slow genocide' has persisted—and recently accelerated. . . . It is incongruous for a symbol of righteousness to lead such a country. . . . If the political price of your ascension to the highest office in Myanmar is your silence, the price is surely too steep."[21]

In addition to this breach of his vow and yet consistency in his role as Elder, Tutu collaborated with the Dalai Lama on writing the *Book of Joy*. This book, published in 2016, is a series of dialogues on finding "real inner joyfulness." Tutu and the Dalai Lama spent five days together in Dharamsala, India, in April 2015, where they talked about joy as well as celebrated the Dalai Lama's eightieth birthday. Their time was spent "in deep dialogue and playful laughter as they share their experience of how to find joy in the face of life's challenges." This discussion became the text of the book, with Tutu and the Dalai Lama calling each other "spiritual brother." "The ultimate source of happiness is within us," wrote the Dalai Lama. "Not money, not power, not status, which fail to bring inner peace. Outward attainment will not bring real inner joyfulness. We must look inside."

Tutu responded, "Sometimes life can be challenging and we can feel lost. But the seeds of joy are born inside each of us. I invite you to join His Holiness and me in creating more joy in our world." Indeed, for both Tutu and the Dalai Lama this was a highly creative venture to articulate each other's spiritualities in a way that was intelligibly congruent for the rest of the world. Their premise in spirituality is that while happiness is often dependent on external circumstances, joy comes from a deeper spirituality. Joy animates life and lends meaning and purpose for why we are on earth.[22]

There was irony in such joy when Tutu was trying to celebrate his own eightieth birthday. Even though Tutu invited the Dalai Lama to deliver the lectures, Tutu's own South African government denied the Dalai Lama's visa entrance. Tutu used witty understatement from the pulpit to remind that government controversy is far from over, but he was determined not to let it dominate the celebrations on his eightieth birthday. Tutu denounced the governing African National Congress (ANC) as worse than the apartheid regime, and warned that he would pray for its defeat. But during a service to honor his birthday Tutu relied on humorous understatement to remind Kgalema Motlanthe, the deputy president, that he had not forgotten the controversy. "Thank you for coming, despite some of the hiccups we have had," Tutu said to laughter and applause at St. George's Cathedral, Cape Town. Tutu practiced his own restorative justice as he stepped down from the pulpit to embrace Motlanthe, who smiled and bowed his head. The controversy was in how, the week before, Motlanthe had shared toasts in Beijing with Chinese leaders who have called the Dalai Lama a dangerous separatist, and won pledges for $2.5 billion in Chinese investment in South Africa. The ANC denied Chinese pressure over the Dalai Lama's visa by simply blaming it on a slow process and calling on Tutu to "calm down." When asked if the Dalai Lama would be granted a visa, Motlanthe reportedly said: "I don't see why it should be an issue at all."[23]

I was present at St. George's Cathedral for the celebration of Tutu's eightieth birthday. The guest list included Graça Machel, U2 singer Bono, and the mayor of Cape Town, Patricia De Lille. Choirs and African drums filled the cathedral with music. Tutu, Bono, and other dignitaries embraced people along the aisles of the cathedral. Anglican Archbishop Thabo Makgoba led the church in singing happy birthday to Tutu, who received loud applause when he paid tribute to Leah, his wife of fifty-six years at that time. In a statement seemingly spiteful, President Jacob Zuma said in a videotaped birthday greeting that Tutu was admired by "thousands," despite the country having a population of nearly 50 million people. The Dalai Lama did deliver the peace lecture via video link, as his physical absence was symbolized by an empty chair.

In conclusion, we see that not only did Tutu become a global Elder; he also joined a family of global Elders to learn how to work collaboratively, even joyfully. Tutu brought a great deal to the table with his African worldview blended with his Christian spirituality. We even see Tutu's consistency of speaking truth to power with his sister sage, Aung San Suu Kyi. In our final chapter, we will look at how union occurred as Tutu moved toward his retirement.

> Everyday God will make the Sun
> to shine
> And every day
>   Our Actions will be
>   Reflected in God's light.
> And everyday
> At the End of Each day
> God will come
> And dip into the sun
> To gather each and every reflection.[24]

Michael Battle's ordination to the Anglican/Episcopal priesthood at St. George's Cathedral, Cape Town, December 12, 1993. Author photo.

Conclusion

How Can Tutu Retire from God?

Around the age of eighty-five, Tutu realized he would not be able to travel, due to his age and required medical treatments. He and Leah moved from their house in Milnerton, a suburb outside of Cape Town, to Hermanus, a seaside municipality known for excellent medical treatment and care for retirees. In fact, Tutu's friend and well-known South African theologian John de Gruchy gave Tutu his spot in line for the best retirement home in Hermanus. Tutu and Leah's spiritual community became an intentional community called Volmoed (meaning full of courage and hope), tucked away within the Hemel-en-Aarde (Heaven on Earth) Valley adjacent to Hermanus. This valley first came to prominence as a place of healing during the eighteenth century, when a leper colony was established there, and more recently when Camphill (next door) opened its doors to persons with Down syndrome. Volmoed, therefore, is more than a traditional retreat center, because full-time residents agree to pray and work together in light of God's life with them, to provide a place of healing and wholeness.

For about two years, Tutu lived in this healing and wholeness at Volmoed where I, as professor of church and society and director of the Desmond Tutu Center at General Theological Seminary in New York, would bring my Tutu

Travel Seminars to visit him twice a year. Participants in these seminars would be a mix of students, teachers, and clergy. As of the time of finishing this book, Tutu and Leah have had to move back to their home in Milnerton, due to the need for proximity to specialized medical care. With these transitions in Tutu's life, I realized more and more how Tutu's life is a guide to the deeper mysteries of living a good life.

In Tutu's later years he has become increasingly aware that religion is very much an accident of birth, geography, and history. Many Christians were scandalized by this view, that they are Christians largely because of where they were born. Had they been born in India, then the chances are very great that they would have been Hindus, or if born in Pakistan, they would have ended up (or, rather, begun their lives) as Muslims. For Tutu, this sociology should modify any piety that advocates for forced conversions or eradication of other religions. How could we be so scathing in our judgment of another faith, when we could so easily have been its adherents but for the accidents of birth, geography, and history? Yet Tutu's Christian spirituality has never wavered.

Tutu advocates for Christians to be more mindful that God is greater than we imagine God to be. We should move from a narrow-minded Christianity to a God-centered understanding of the nature of religions. In my conversations with Tutu, he conveyed to me that the mosque should exist side by side with the synagogue, the temple, and the church. His fear was that, without this, communities would destroy themselves and tear apart our networks of social relationships, all due to religious and political differences. Because of the age of technology, we are all being thrown together and must respect rather than disregard one another.

In God's original intention, creation was never meant to be red in tooth and claw. Tutu conveyed this to me in our conversations. According to Tutu, we must of course remember what religious discourse seeks out to do. For Tutu, religion is not a phenomenological description of how things were; after all, no one was around when God first brought everything into being. The purpose of the early Genesis stories is to describe profound religious verities that could not be told as effectively in any other way. For this reason, Tutu has a fondness for the Old Testament. In Tutu's theology, he knows from science that there never was such a time of pristine harmony, but we are informed what God intended for creation; we are being told some remarkable truths about God, about ourselves, and about the universe we inhabit. But something went wrong.

Instead of food and nutrients, the earth brought forth thistles and the broken relationship between humanity and the animal world. This broken relationship was depicted in the shattering words that humankind would seek to crush the serpent's head and the serpent would want to bruise humankind's heel. Something has indeed gone desperately wrong, because this is surely not how we were meant to live, separated into hostile, competing, abrasive camps, without much compassion for one another, living by the law of the jungle, eat or be eaten, and survival of the fittest.[1]

The biblical prophets were scathing in their condemnation of religious observances that had no salutary effects on how people behaved in the marketplace, in the court of law, and in their everyday life. Such a religion they universally rejected as an abomination and totally unacceptable to God. The prophets knew nothing, it seemed, about the dichotomies that are so greatly loved in our day: sacred and secular, profane and holy, material and spiritual. The prophets would have marveled at—indeed they would have been puzzled by—the parrot cry "don't mix religion with politics."[2] In Tutu's sermons it was always interesting that some in political power in the Bible, like King David in Israel, had a special concern for the weak and the oppressed; it was possible for politics to resist predation of the strong and unprincipled ethics. The correct mixture of religion and politics displays how to work for justice. We learn from Tutu that we must oppose injustice and oppression as religious people, even at the cost of personal freedom or life itself. If this understanding is part of the Christian church's DNA, then the nature of religion should not be at odds with itself. We need the humility to know that both are true: the church without society is hopeless, as is society without the church.

In Christian spirituality, it should be characteristic of true and pure contemplation that God's love transcends human biases. God's love forms human bias in such a way as to be filled with zeal and the desire to gather to God those who will love God with equal abandon.[3] According to Evelyn Underhill, love is the test that enables us to distinguish between genuine mystic ecstasy and pathological states of trance. True mystical experience is known by its fruits of love. The real mystic is not a selfish visionary. Desmond Tutu's life fits this diagnosis and encourages us all to analyze how such a life makes this world and the next life a better place. Tutu's life grows in vigor as he draws nearer and nearer to the sources of true life, and his goal is reached only when we all participate in the creative energies of God. Here Underhill concludes by writing, "Then only is our life a whole when contemplation and work dwell in us side by side, and we are perfectly in both of them at once."[4]

The aim of the mystic's life is to achieve union with God. Having examined the way in which Tutu tried to reach this goal, we are now in a position to see how Tutu's spiritual life was vital to his political life. Tutu's spiritual life also helps us see that he could never really retire; after all, how can anyone retire from God? Sometimes the mystic union with God is taken to be a form of human and divine merging; sometimes it is seen as ecstatic experience; and sometimes it is interpreted as a close personal relationship. Various forms of mysticism derive from a variety of religious traditions. This applies even to the various forms of Christian mysticism, because Christianity springs from divergent sources. From the Greeks, Christian mysticism derives the tendency toward merging from Plato and Plotinus, who possibly received it from Hinduism via the Orphic mysteries. From Judaism, Christian mysticism honors bodily particularity and how finite humanity engages God's transcendence. Irving Singer states, "As the offspring of such contrary parents, Christianity turns into a series of syntheses, each mixing more or less the same elements but in a different composition."[5]

The result is that Christian mysticism is not only a continuum of itself; it has relatives in other religions and worldviews. In the end, what makes them relatives is the consummation of religious love. In other words, God's love unites them. Tutu's spiritual life displays the extent to which his spiritual and political life provides substantial understanding of peace that is not just the absence of violence. Peace has a substance unto itself. It is the unification between the Divine and human being. This unity does not mean that God somehow ceases being God or that human beings cease being created by God; rather, it means the definition of mysticism, that both beings remain themselves in union. In Christian mysticism, Bernard states we learn to see the union of God and humanity differently: "As dwelling in each other in a very different way, because their wills and their substances are distinct and different; that is, their substances are not intermingled, yet their wills are in agreement; and this union is for them a communion of wills and an agreement in charity. Happy is this union if you experience it, but compared with the other [God's unity in the Trinity], it is no union at all."[6]

Bernard helps us avoid pantheism, distinguishing between divine and human union and the unity of God. The definition of mysticism is in the insight that the dividing line between two conceptualizations is often too indistinct to detect. Here in Christian mysticism we gain the answer to the question, How can Tutu retire from God? In Christian mysticism he cannot. In Tutu's life with God, Tutu has learned how to see the fine distinctions of conceptualization through "personhood," which for him becomes the key relational concept, in the sense that one can be a person only in relation to other persons.

Personhood produces pure love. After all, Christians believe God is love (1 John 4:8). In her autobiography, Teresa of Avila describes this experience graphically as follows: "While seeking God in this way, the soul becomes conscious that it is fainting almost completely away, in a kind of swoon, with an exceedingly great and sweet delight. It gradually ceases to breathe and all its bodily strength begins to fail it; it cannot even move its hand without great pain; its eyes involuntarily close, or, if they remain open, they can hardly see."[7] Teresa of Avila reminds Christian mystics that there must be a word of caution; that is, one should not seek these ecstatic experiences, but should seek only the relationality of God. The goal of Tutu, Bernard, Julian of Norwich, and Teresa of Avila is not merely to have visions and ecstasies. Such phenomena only help toward the journey of increasing union with God. If one becomes fixated upon them, they become impediments, because they replace the goal of continuous union with God. Visions and ecstatic experience should never be an end in themselves. Jantzen helps me make sense of the methodology of this book on the spiritual life of Tutu. Jantzen concludes, "it would be folly to suppose that union with God, the summit of Christian experience, could occur unless one were also serious about purification and illumination, and indeed were making progress in these areas."[8]

Furthermore, this kind of mystical experience excludes all narcissistic solipsism, since it is by definition the experience of living in a loving relationship with God.

Does a human being have to agree with the wishes and will of the other, or merely to identify with the other's interests? How does the union sought by others differ from that between the mystic and God? Tutu's spiritual life is full of these questions, and as long as this planet exists, we will have to return to them again and again. For the present, we can conclude that Tutu's spiritual life is about the pursuit of loving union sought after in a tactile world. Tutu's whole life and character is transformed in so doing in the likeness of God's love. For the mystic, this life-transforming personal relationship is what constitutes ultimate bliss. In some respects, however, achieving it entails suffering. In many ways we have examined Tutu's life associated with such suffering.

Perhaps Tutu's greatest strength is in his ability to long for unseen realities. Nelson Mandela and others walked out of prison free men and women because they shared similar longings. Tutu stands out because it was his seeming vocation as bishop to long primarily for God. He knew that in doing so as others had understood it, he could not also long to be a good neighbor in this world. In other words, Tutu knew that many were against him being spiritual and political at the same time. So to pursue both as one and the same was a delusional longing in the midst of an apartheid state in which several versions of God were worshipped. But this longing to love God most of all, in this way, was what he was ordained to do and be. Tutu's longings utilized practical nonviolent weapons to topple such a regime. In large part, Tutu's spirituality got the world involved. As he would recall, because of sanctions, exiles returned home; because of sanctions, South Africa remains on the threshold of exciting possibilities. Tutu states, "We are all, black and white, going to taste democracy for the first time, we are going to have the first democratic elections in our South Africa."

Tutu knew when he prayed in church that it was hallowed by the fervor of past generations. Such a church is quite different if it has not been prayed in. Tutu needed the anchor of the spirituality that a two-thousand-year-old church provided. Spirits were lifted when the Convention for a Democratic South Africa assembled, and fell when the awful massacres of Boipatong intervened and the negotiation process was thrown into disarray. Spirits swung from euphoria to despair and back again as the National Peace Accord was signed and South Africa tottered on the brink of catastrophe with the assassination of Chris Hani. Then the Multiparty Negotiation Forum happened, but some pulled out, jeopardizing a delicate process.

During this storm of history, a great deal of the violence was due to the bloody rivalry in South Africa and the world. Since South Africa took a long time to know a culture of tolerance, there could not help but be a tempest that made all cultures and races seasick. The apartheid South African government taught a lesson too eagerly learned, that those who disagreed with you were your enemies. Many who opposed apartheid were detained without trial, banned, and consigned to a twilight existence as prisoners. It was so painful that simply being in the company of more than one person could be construed to be an unlawful gathering. You could go to prison for attending weddings and funerals in your own family. You could not go on a picnic, or to a concert or on holiday.

So most South Africans under apartheid learned that your opponent was your enemy and that the best kind of enemy was the dead kind. A great deal of the violence was fomented by what was described as a well-trained "third force," security forces loyal to the government. It is not unreasonable to suppose that there were people in these forces who could turn the violence on and off at their whim. The critical question is whether the security forces would remain loyal to the government. Tutu suspected that most whites, and that includes the Afrikaners, wanted to live normal, secure, and prosperous lives. That can be possible only under a government recognized by the world and acknowledged by the majority of its citizens as legitimate and democratic. Yet Tutu's spirituality keeps him hopeful that South Africa has a bright future. South Africa, richly endowed with human and natural resources, will be the engine that drives the economies of the subcontinent, perhaps making some amends for the devastation its earlier policy of destabilization caused to our neighboring states. Tutu concludes that South Africa "will become a launching pad to propel the subcontinent, and indeed the entire African continent, into the twenty-first century. We are on the threshold of exhilarating possibilities and when apartheid and its horrendous legacy are finally done with, South Africans will look on in amazement and awe and ask, 'Why were we so stupid for so long?'"[9]

BECOMING MORE CONTEMPLATIVE

What will heaven be like? Tutu has always been fascinated by this question. Social psychologists say that this question becomes more acute as one gets older and seeks meaning in one's life. For example, in 2001, on the seventh anniversary of South Africa's first democratic election, Tutu told his interviewer this could be his last interview in London. He talked about his view of heaven. "I wonder," stated Tutu, "whether they have rum and Coke in Heaven? Maybe it's too mundane a pleasure, but I hope so—as a sundowner. Except, of course, the sun never goes down there. Oh, man, this heaven is going to take some getting used to."[10] Tutu provides us the wisdom to know how to find heaven. The wisdom is this: despite our longing for a place like heaven that meets and surpasses our needs, we often find the contradiction that we do not behave as if we really want to go there. For most of us on this planet, our needs do not quite match what we want. The mystical writer of Revelation conveys Tutu's insight this way: "I saw no temple in the city, for its temple is the Lord God the Almighty and the Lamb. And the city has no need of sun or moon to shine on it, for the glory of God is its light" (Rev. 21:22, 23). Here we gain the insight that John of Patmos, the writer of Revelation, had a preconceived desire for a temple that was not met in heaven.[11]

When Tutu was first diagnosed with cancer in 1997, he encountered this disconnect between want and need.[12] His schedule would have to change. His pace would decrease. His retirement would come earlier. Also, images of sunsets and sunrises would no longer help to describe heaven. What will heaven be like? Tutu learned to answer the question like John of Patmos, with the simple answer, God. This is a difficult answer, because it implies that God will have to be enough to satisfy our needs and desires. On the surface this seems ironic, since most religious people would understand such desire as central to life. And yet under the surface, irony becomes contradiction as God becomes self.

For Tutu, Scripture leads us to believe that heaven will be our completion, that we will have no need of anything. This should make us rejoice and take great delight in the knowledge that we will live in such a way that we will be complete, in need of nothing. We should rejoice, but often we are afraid to rejoice, because we know deep down that heaven will be more than our desires can contain. As Tutu's humor exemplifies—"Will there be rum and Coke in heaven?" The value of Christian mysticism is that it trains desire to be symmetrical with need, not in a dictatorial fashion in which a despot seeks allegiance to a hegemonic regime, but in the way in which we truly discover true desire, even true fulfillment. Instead of childish images of what delights us, we learn fulfillment of desire both for my need and your need. Individual and communal desires are no more in conflict.

If I asked you in secret—all of you who read this book—what it is that you truly desire the most, what would complete you and satiate your desires, I imagine I would have as many answers as there are readers. Despite our diversity, however, there should be at least one common desire. In the United States where I live, a Western country that aspires to be egalitarian, it is difficult to find who would agree with my approach to heaven. This is counterintuitive, because one would think most Western people socialized in an individualistic worldview would think heaven to be a good idea, because it would allow everyone to pursue personal happiness. I argue, however, that personal happiness is an oxymoron. "Personal happiness" is akin to "limited freedom"; the adjective cancels out the noun. So my counterintuitive problem of heaven, in which the vast majority of Christians in the Western world believe, leaves me with a confused audience who thinks heaven is a good idea for personal fulfillment, but can't really imagine communal or universal fulfillment.

When I use the pronoun "we" for Christian identity (at least in the Western world), it is unclear who that entails. I have this problem largely because of an individualistic Christianity. It is almost as if Christian identity can no longer be claimed in common. Maybe you have been trained to be suspicious of those who claim to be Christians, perhaps rightfully so. After all, just look at the atrocities that have been done in the name of Christianity (war, genocide, crusades, slavery, holocaust, discrimination, etc.). By looking for heaven with common ground, I imagine a Christianity in which Protestants, Orthodox, Catholics, evangelicals, fundamentalists, and liberals help the world, rather than making matters worse. In all of the ways that I fail to provide this common vision, I hold out a baton to those with greater minds and hearts than my own to move all of us beyond contentious presumptions and worldviews. By addressing the question of how a communal understanding of heaven got lost, I hope to bring the reader up to speed on an ancient conversation and help you to understand what is at stake in talk of heaven.

The framing of the problem of heaven often goes unnoticed in the Western world, which is so focused upon personal salvation or affinity groups. I am afraid the concept of heaven will continue to be conceived solely for individualistic and personal ends. As my work on Tutu's spiritual biography comes to an end, I hope that the exemplary life examined here is relevant to a general audience of religious pluralism or to new students of religion. I am even so bold as to think this spiritual biography should be of interest to agnostics and atheists who seek to be truthful and live with integrity in a world that often contradicts the presence of God. As "we" delved into issues of Christian mysticism in this book, my desire was such that the threefold mystical way of purgation, illumination, and union would frame Tutu's life in such a way that the reader could follow a progression, even a maturation, grounded in more than the typical binaries of politics or the esoteric language that often haunts religion. My hope for the reader here is that if we read it closely, Tutu's life helps us all wade through murky waters together, eventually finding some common understanding.

Although heaven will be different for each of us, I aim in this book to inspire common language for unity in the end, language that does not lead to a crusade or the exclusion of a person or group. Without common language, there is no organization of our wants and needs. When asked, What will heaven be like? we cannot answer in our typical ways of who is in and who is out. Too much is at stake within our ecosystem of being human together on a planet to continue practicing exclusion. Jesus gives us a better answer to What will heaven be like?: "I am going away, and I am coming to you" (John 14:28). The ultimate answer to what heaven is like is this strange movement of God—going away and coming to. The confluence of heaven and earth is embodied in Jesus. If you want to know what heaven is like, you and I will have to know what God is like, through this strange movement of incarnation. For Western individualists, we may not like this answer, because it may mean finding a communal solution rather than a personal one. After all, Christians believe heaven is simply God's communal presence—a communion so sweet that heaven laughs, applauds, and rejoices when those who are lost are found. Jesus tells us as much: "I tell you, there will be more joy in heaven over one sinner who repents than over ninety-nine righteous persons who need no repentance" (Luke 15:7).

Those who live in the global North are far more socially isolated today than in any other time in history. More and more people say they have no one in whom to confide, according to a comprehensive evaluation of the decline of social ties in the United States. A growing number of persons say they have no one with whom to work out personal troubles. What I am afraid of is that not many people really know how to want a communal heaven, one in which we all will be healed. In fact, few of us realize how spiritually sick all of us are. There are a few, however, who do know. The writer of Revelation helps us see the communal God in more detail:

> Then the angel showed me the river of the water of life, bright as crystal, flowing from the throne of God and of the Lamb through the middle of the street of the city. On either side of the river is the tree of life with its twelve kinds of fruit, producing its fruit each month; and the leaves of the tree are for the healing of the nations. Nothing accursed will be found there any more. But the throne of God and of the Lamb will be in it, and his servants will worship him; they will see his face, and his name will be on their foreheads. And there will be no more night; they need no light of lamp or sun, for the Lord God will be their light, and they will reign forever and ever. (Rev. 22:1–5)

When we see heaven in common, we cannot help but act here and now to effect systemic change. So when a church suffers, God relies on us to be the salt of the earth, for if we fail in being benign to the systems of the world, in some sense God also fails. God, while remaining God, is mysteriously contingent and vulnerable to and with creation. For God created us in God's image, but what is God's image? That is, What does it look like?

From the perspective of Tutu's theology of Ubuntu, God's image is such that it illumines how personhood forms through interpersonal encounter. In other words, persons need other persons to be persons. Most characteristic of God is that God is somehow three and one, unity in diversity, and community in one nature. In this light of God's image, Christianity is no opiate to society. Tutu has fought valiantly to correct the delusions of God's image as sociological projections of oppressive societies. In other words, Tutu's vital work against the theology of apartheid was in his role to destroy the idols of civil religion that existed to buttress the suffering of so many diverse peoples, suffering like that of a Virginia mother who gave up a three-year court fight to regain custody of her five-year-old son, because she was finally ruled "unfit" to be a mother because she is a lesbian.[13]

Tutu was fond of saying that everyone's destiny is inextricably bound together. Of course their contexts are different. Of course power runs amok differently against people of color and gay and lesbian people. Of course there are contradictions, even within supposedly inclusive contexts. Although this is changing in the attitudes of Western Christians, most notable are the contradictory requests going to God about gays and lesbians in the church. It is not hard to hear the contradictions; just flip the TV remote control or attend church conventions. The contradiction sounds like this: Love the sinner, and hate the sin. Implicit to the debate concerning the full participation of gays and lesbians in the church is the notion that a person who does an act is not as important as the action itself. With this division between character and action, we inevitably fall into contradictions between orientation and sexual acts; however, crucial to my thoughts is the relationship between individual desires for heaven and communal desires for heaven. Being made in the image of God who is Trinity, we cannot separate communal desire and individual desire. Trinitarian relationship helps us see that the kind of person who does an act is just as important as the act itself.

All of this leads me to believe that by focusing on heaven, we interestingly enough have better discernment for how to live here on earth—not as "stoned out" Christians who can offer the world little except prayers and songs, but as catalysts for governments to write constitutions like South Africa's. Christians can become catalysts for public repentance to never harm another human being, as with the TRC. Christian faith need not lead to delusional conclusions. Focus on the common relationship of us all in heaven helps us find synthesis in the contradictions, even more, to find this synthesis in the relationship of the catholic (the universal) church who is commissioned to move alongside suffering communities so as to facilitate participation in the salvation of the world.[14] To reiterate, what I am afraid of is that our answer to what heaven is leaves out what should be our common answer: uninhibited presence with God. If we don't understand heaven as a common destination, as God's presence in which all are invited positively into God's love, then we may be more a part of the problem than the solution. So how do we know when we are delusional?

HOW DO WE KNOW WHEN WE ARE DREAMING?

Dante begins *Paradiso* by admitting his inadequacy to define such a topic as heaven. If I am not careful, this book on Tutu's spiritual life may seem like an attempt to woo the reader with a seemingly idealistic picture of Tutu. But such intention sets me up for failure. My life with Tutu is what shapes such a positive image of Tutu's life. Such primary knowledge of Tutu hopefully will mitigate some skepticism as to how Tutu is a Christian mystic. Obviously, I am not writing this biography in the genre of the European Enlightenment's obsession with critique and so-called objectivity. I write this book with eyes wide open to his powerful spiritual life, which became Tutu's reservoir from which to gain energy to take on the civil religion of apartheid. So here I unashamedly present an exemplary life. Tutu's life is exemplary even more because it is not naturally inclined to remember revenge and resentment. Disciplines in Christian mysticism help him pass beyond what makes human beings finite creatures and into the possibilities of a new heaven and new earth. Dante helps me explain: "I was in the heaven that most receives [God's] light and I saw things which he that descends from it has not the knowledge or the power to tell again; for our intellect, drawing near to its desire, sinks so deep that memory cannot follow it. Nevertheless, so much of the holy kingdom as I was able to treasure in my mind shall now be matter of my song" (*Par.* I, 4–9).[15] As we draw near to this book's conclusion, my intention in looking at Tutu's spiritual life is indeed that the reader may too learn a desire to pass beyond the individual experience into a reorientation of what life on earth can mean. Here, Tutu's spiritual life reminds us all of the mystical paradox that no one is born to die, and that even the reality of death may not hold us to meaninglessness. Tutu's life reorients us to the realities of heaven rather than its delusions.

When it comes to seeking an understanding of heaven, many watch and pray for God's kingdom to "come on earth as in heaven," but do not feel a call to struggle and act on earth. These people believe that even if the prophetic vision and hope for heaven is not an illusion, not an unrealistic dream, there still is little we can do about heaven on earth, except trust that God will fulfill God's promise. For Tutu, utopian vision is essential to understanding strategies against racism and other negative forms of human determinism. In the beatific vision of living uninhibited with God, creation will be so transformed that we will celebrate that which is different in each other, because the logic of heaven will be such that our neighbors' differences will complement our own uniqueness. This means for Tutu that heaven will involve communal participation in such a way that we learn to appreciate and love the unique difference of the other. As Tutu concludes, "I will want to show that apartheid, separate development, parallel democracy or whatever this racist ideology is currently called, is evil totally and without remainder. . . . [Apartheid] more shatteringly denies the central act of reconciliation which the New Testament declares was achieved by God in His Son our Lord Jesus Christ."[16]

This spiritual deconstruction of the primacy of race does not mean that racial identity is insignificant; on the contrary, in Tutu's theological claims, race matters, but in the qualification of being thankful to God for God's wonderful ways of creation through difference. Therefore Tutu rejoices "that God has created me black and I rejoice that He has seen fit to create others as colored, Indian, White etc."[17] Tutu's spirituality of liberation derives from his emphasis upon interdependence and reconciliation in the South African context of apartheid. This spirituality follows from Tutu's Anglican ecclesiology and his nonviolent theological concept of Ubuntu. Tutu's spirituality illumines a different kind of liberation model of theology, one that challenges secular tendencies espoused in black and African theologies. Tutu qualifies his theological model in this way, challenging this trend in black and African theologies because, as he states,

> we are so angry at the things we don't like about ourselves, we project them onto those who may be somewhat like ourselves and become destructive of one another. I thought I was going to have to help to exorcise this demon of self-loathing and self-hate. For you see, friends, one of the most awful things about the system of apartheid, which appears to be on its last legs, is not so much the pain that it causes its victims, though that for sure is one of the evil things about it. It is not that it is just evil, which it surely is, but it is that it ultimately makes a child of God doubt that he or she is a child of God. And to that extent the system is blasphemous.[18]

So one cannot easily separate spirituality and politics in Tutu's life. Although resistance to the dualism of politics and spirituality can be seen in different degrees, Tutu's spiritual life contains as a frame of reference the ultimate *polis* (political place) in the life of God. Christian spirituality for Tutu means that interpersonal reality cannot be separated from political action. For Tutu, interpersonal spirituality is the framework within which Tutu has both envisioned and acted toward heaven on earth or earth in heaven. It becomes a mistake to separate the ideal of God's presence with us (heaven) from our reality toward God (earth).

Because both heaven and earth are interpersonally connected, Tutu perceives that those who are considered enemies are inextricably bound together and will eventually need to untangle the knot. One recent case in point is the coronavirus pandemic. South Africa has been one of the hardest hit nations in Africa. In apocalyptic fashion, Tutu has stated that the coronavirus pandemic has brought racial inequalities into stark relief, doing the country "a ghastly favor by exposing the unsustainable foundations on which it is built . . . that must be urgently fixed."[19] The current archbishop of Cape Town, Thabo Makgoba, added in a sermon, "I am desperately worried that the coronavirus is described as a European problem by some of the media. As we know, viruses do not have passports, they don't know borders, they don't respect race or colour."[20]

Tutu's Christian spirituality has remained consistent throughout apartheid and even pandemics. His ongoing role as confessor and spiritual guide during difficult times demonstrates his life as a saint, a distinction I pray the Anglican communion will eventually give him. It is a distinction that apartheid could neither extinguish nor diminish. Even amidst a deadly pandemic like COVID-19, Tutu believes that it doesn't matter where we come from or what language we speak—we are all created for each other. COVID-19 reminds us of how interdependent we are. In Tutu's spirituality, we don't just wear masks, or take any action, for ourselves alone; we act to protect our neighbor. "Please wear your masks," is the plea of Tutu and Mama Leah, spoken from their retirement home.[21]

It is difficult to close a book on Desmond Tutu. I pray many generations to come will mine the treasures of this saintly life. When all is said and done, Tutu's life invites all of us to never detach the spiritual life from our real life. Our prayers must be real and tactile, and move us to action. As is appropriate for a book on the spiritual life of Tutu, we close with him in just such a prayer:

> Thank you, God, for the spirit of unity and togetherness. Pour out your blessings on our leaders and their followers, to uphold the letter and spirit of this peace accord and beat our swords into plowshares.
>
> Send us forth to be instruments of your peace. Amen.[22]

Desmond Tutu congratulates children at the Rekgonne-Bapo Special School near Rustenburg on October 3, 2006. Courtesy of African News Agency (ANA) Archives.

Afterword
ARCHBISHOP DESMOND TUTU

It continues to be a challenge to review one's own life and how others perceive that same life. I think the crux of the challenge is in the refracted light that reflects the dynamic spectrum of how so many perceive different perspectives. I indeed appreciate Michael's perception of me here; and I realize that although he may paint a portrait of me in too fine a light, nevertheless his focus on the spiritual life is invaluable, not only for my life but for yours as well. As I have wrestled with death and dying, I realize more and more how the spiritual, physical, intellectual, and communal life are all interrelated. You cannot understand one without the other. Michael's contribution here is to say this to all of us, in a world that is often prone to avoiding what is spiritual. Life is the intersection of interrelation.

As Michael indicates here at the end of the book, I have retired from public life. This does not mean, however, that God is through with me. Perhaps, some of my work remains as seeds that will blossom in the future. I hope that my work in South Africa and over the world will be seen in all of its light; and like Michael, I hope that my spiritual work will not be seen in any lesser light. The premise of Michael's work here is that I am a Christian mystic in the sense of the mystical stages of purgation, illumination, and union. Am I a Christian mystic? I leave that for the eye of the beholder. I certainly have been trained by deep and holy people. I do my best to say my prayers and participate in communion with God on a daily basis. I indeed know what purgation is, as I struggled against apartheid and grew up in a hostile world. I also know about illumination, through the breakthroughs in my life to lead a process for my country to be conscious of what was done in the name of apartheid. And as I approach my latter years, I long for union with God and God's creation. If this is a Christian mystic, so be it that I am one as well.

When I am no longer on this planet in the physical form, I pray that I would have made a contribution in forming both a more mature consciousness and conscience for those who say they believe in God. We cannot say that we believe in God if we hate each other—much less say we love God and do the same. In order to believe in God, the consciousness and conscience of love must be present. So, I may have taken a leading role in South Africa to fight against apartheid. I may have been in an historic position such as archbishop of Southern Africa. I may have won a Nobel Peace Prize. I may have led the Truth and Reconciliation Commission in South Africa. And I may have become a global elder. If I have done all of these things, however, without love, then I have done nothing.

God is love. Spiritually, there is not much more to say than this. I depend on this acknowledgment with my life as I now face my latter years. I have said before that I believe in the sanctity of life, and that death is a part of life. I can believe this to be more of a paradox than a contradiction, because of my faith that God is love. Like my prayer for us all, I hope that when the time comes to die, that God's love known as compassion will allow not only me but you as well to pass on to the next phase of life's journey. Herein is the value of Michael Battle's work on my life—to hold up a mirror with this book and invite the reader to also mature through the mystical stages of God's love.

I have also learned that God has a sense of humor. You would think that I as a person could just die in peace, but here I go yet again in protest—even in my latter years of facing death—still being a rabble-rouser to get South Africa to legalize assisted death procedures. I have lived with prostate cancer for decades and have been in and out of the hospitals on numerous occasions. When I say I support assisted death, I mean I support its responsible use in dying well. Living well and dying well must be symmetrical. Let it be on record that I pray that politicians, lawmakers, and religious leaders have the courage to support the terminally ill in dying well—to depart this life with dignity and love.

In closing, I endorse Michael's work here. He has followed me like a duck that imprints upon its parent for many years now. He has already written several books on my theology. And I feel that what he says here will be important for those who merely situated my life in politics to see more of what I was trying to do on this planet. I have no false piety in thinking I am no role model. I know others like Michael are influenced by me. And I know that in God's sense of humor of encouraging me, even in facing my own death to fight for the right to die, that all of my work will not be done in vain. I hope when all is said and done, I will be remembered as one of God's beloved children just like you.

I do not want to be remembered as a political prop in photo ops or some kind of cartoon figure larger than life. When God meets me directly, God will not address me as archbishop or Nobel laureate. God will address me like the father in the parable of the Prodigal Son who set off to meet his son. But while the son was still far off, his father saw him and was filled with compassion. The father did not even speak. He ran and put his arms around his son and kissed him. So you, his daughters and sons, expect this from God who is love.

Chronology

1652 Europeans (Dutch East India Company) arrive at the Cape of Good Hope.
1658 Importation of slaves
1773 Frontier Wars (European vs. Xhosa)
1795 British settlement
1800 European population 20,000
1807 Abolition of slave trade in British Empire
1828 British make English official language in SA.
1836 The Great Trek: More than 10,000 Afrikaners move throughout Southern Africa
1838 Boers defeat the Zulu at the Battle of Blood River and interpret victory as God's will.
1867 Discovery of diamonds
1879 Zulu Wars
1884 Discovery of gold
1894 Gandhi arrives
1898 South African Native Congress forms.
1899 Anglo-Boer War
1910 Union of South Africa formed without official representation of African people
1911 Legislation imposed against strikes by Africans
1912 The emergence of the South African Native National Congress, later to be known as the African National Congress
1913 The Native Land Act, in which 7.3 percent of South African land is designated for black people
1919 The Industrial and Commercial Workers' Union (ICU) forms. ANC leads anti-pass campaign. 700 arrests in Johannesburg.
1921 The Communist Party of South Africa (CPSA) founded
1923 Mohandas Gandhi emerges as the key political leader in the Indian community with his Satyagraha movement.
1927 Prohibition of Mixed Marriages Act and the Immorality Act stating sex or marriage between Whites and "non-whites" is illegal
1931 Oct. 7, Desmond Mpilo Tutu born in Klerksdorp (a goldmining town), 70 miles west of Johannesburg
1936 Any vestige of black voting privilege abolished
1938 Tutu at St. Ansgar's, a Swedish mission school
1943 Tutu family moves to Munsieville in Krugersdorp and then to Sophiatown. Alexandra bus boycott. Trevor Huddleston sails from Liverpool, England, toward assignment in Sophiatown. African Mineworkers Union strike involving 73,557 workers. The term "apartheid" first used.

1944 Tutu attends Western Native Township High School; the high school was later called Madibane.

1945 Tutu contracts tuberculosis and stays in hospital for twenty months. Trevor Huddleston befriends him, brings Tutu books to read. Tutu becomes an acolyte at Huddleston's church in Munsieville. Begins his secondary school at Western High, a governmental school in the old Western Native Township, near Sophiatown.

1948 National Party victory in parliamentary elections: Afrikaners gain control of the government and grow in desire for complete independence from Britain and strengthening of apartheid. Anglican Church makes statement to the effect that discrimination on the grounds of race alone is inconsistent with the Christian principles. The Methodist Church also states that no person of any race should be deprived of constitutional rights or privileges merely on the grounds of race.[1]

1950 Tutu passes the Joint Matriculation Board examination. Tutu graduates with honors from Madibane and enrolls at Bantu Normal College. Group Areas Act passed; Hendrik Verwoerd is made Minister for Native Affairs and promotes tribalism and authority of chiefdoms. Suppression of Communism Act makes Communist Party unlawful. Population Registration Act, by which persons are racially classified as White, Colored, Indian, and Native. Eventually colored were subdivided into seven categories: Cape Colored, Cape Malay, Griqua, Indian, Chinese, Other Asiatic, Other Colored. Africans were divided into eight groups according to language. Whites remained one category containing English, Afrikaners, Portuguese, Greek, Japanese, Hungarians, and Jewish.

1951 Tutu at Bantu Normal College for teacher training

1952 The Defiance Campaign, rise in ANC membership from 7,000 to 100,000

1953 Bantu Education Act passed

1954 Tutu achieves teacher's diploma; starts teaching at Madibane.

1955 Tutu marries Leah Nomalizo Shenxane on July 2. Tutu gains BA from the University of South Africa; teaches at Munsieville High School, where his father was still the headmaster. Sophiatown is destroyed. 10,000 children stay out of school to protest the Bantu Education Act. Freedom Charter adopted by 3,000, forming the basis of ANC policy: That South Africa belongs to all of its people and that "every man and woman shall have the right to vote for and stand as candidate for all bodies which make laws."

1956 The Treason Trial (1956–61). Thousands of African women protest pass laws.

1958 Hendrik Verwoerd becomes prime minister. Implementation of Bantu Education Act makes Tutu give up teaching and enter seminary at St. Peter's College, Rosettenville.

1959 Verwoerd passes the act which sets up eight national "Homelands." Universities are segregated.

1960 ANC and PAC banned. Tutu gains Licentiate of Theology, ordained a deacon, begins work in Benoni. Sharpeville massacre (March 21) occurs during a peaceful demonstration against pass law legislation, led by Robert Sobukwe, organizer of the Pan Africanist Congress. Sixty-nine unarmed people are killed. Albert Luthuli (1898–1967) awarded Nobel Peace Prize.

1961 Tutu ordained a priest. White South Africa proclaims itself a republic, cutting formal ties with the British Commonwealth; ANC decides to utilize selective acts of force.

1962 Tutu studies theology at King's College, London, England. Mandela arrested and sentenced to five years in prison.

1963 Government imposes ninety-day detention without trial. Rivonia Trial. Mandela is sentenced to life in prison on Robben Island under the Suppression of Communism Act.

1965 Tutu achieves Bachelor of Divinity degree. Government imposes 180-day detention without trial.
1966 Tutu achieves Master of Theology degree and Honors in London.
1967 Tutu back in South Africa teaching at St. Peter's College, Alice, in the Eastern
Cape; teaches at Federal Theological Seminary in South Africa.
1968 The SACC makes a strong statement against separate development, that it is
based on the domination of one group over all others, and it depends on the
maintenance of white supremacy; thus it is rooted in and dependent on a policy
of sin.
1969 Steve Biko's Black Consciousness Movement in place
1970 Tutu, lecturer at the University of Roma in Lesotho
1972 Tutu, associate director of the Theological Education Fund, moves back to
London.
1973 Presbyterian Church makes statement: "We believe in God, the Son, who became
man, died and rose in triumph, reconciling all the world to God, breaking down
every wall that divides men, every barrier of religion, race, culture or class, to create
one united humanity. He is the one Lord who has authority over all. He summons
both the individual and society, both Church and the State, to reconciliation,
unity, justice and freedom."[2]
1974 Mozambique and Angola achieve independence from Portugal.
1975 Tutu, first black dean of Johannesburg. Government imposes education taught
in Afrikaans in black schools. World Council of Churches holds 5th Assembly in
Nairobi, Kenya.
1976 Tutu consecrated bishop of Lesotho (July); Soweto uprising (June 16).
1977 Tutu preaches at Steve Biko's funeral, after Steve Biko, leader of the black consciousness movement and founder of the South African Students Organization,
dies while in police custody; virtually all black organizations are banned.
1978 Tutu becomes general secretary of the South African Council of Churches. P. W.
Botha becomes Prime Minister.
1979 Forced removal of entire ethnic communities. Tutu first publicly supports economic sanctions against South Africa on Danish television. Tutu's honorary
degree from Harvard University. Laws passed allowing blacks to join unions for
the first time, union membership grows by 200 percent between 1980 and 1983.
The Congress of South African Students (COSAS) forms.
1980 Tutu meets with Botha. Tutu's passport is confiscated and retrieved; he visits
USA, meets John Paul II in Rome.
1981 Eloff Commission investigates Tutu and SACC.
1982 Anglican Church makes statement, "Whereas Apartheid by exalting a biological
attribute to a universal principle thereby denies that what gives persons infinite
value is the fact that they are created in God's image; whereas Apartheid further
denies a central teaching of the Christian faith, namely, that God was in Christ
reconciling the world to himself since it teaches the irreconcilability of certain
races; whereas it further has involved an unacceptable cost in human suffering; this
synod resolves that Apartheid is totally un-Christian, evil, and a heresy." Methodist Church: "Apartheid is not simply a socio-political policy, but a sinful contradiction of the gospel which cannot be justified on biblical or theological grounds
and is, therefore, an ideology which the Methodist Church rejects as heresy."[3]
1983 Tutu at WCC 6th Assembly in Vancouver. The public launching of the United
Democratic Front, a nationwide antiapartheid coalition
1984 Tutu is Visiting Professor at General Theological Seminary, New York. Tutu
meets and tries to persuade President Ronald Reagan to end policy of "constructive engagement" and "quiet diplomacy." On December 10, Tutu is awarded the

Nobel Peace Prize; Nobel Prize money of $190,000 establishes Tutu scholarship fund for blacks to study in USA.

1985   On February 3, Tutu becomes bishop of Johannesburg. There is a state of emergency. UDF is banned. Tutu (July) does funeral of four men killed by police in township of Duduza in the Transvaal; after another funeral in Duduza a crowd beat and burned a woman to death. The nation's largest black trade unions merge to form the Congress of South African Trade Unions (COSATU).

1986   In September, Tutu becomes archbishop of Cape Town (Church of the Province of Southern Africa). Botha imposes second nation-wide state of emergency. Pass laws and Immorality Act repealed; some restaurants and hotels allowed to serve blacks and whites. Winnie Mandela speaks out publicly against apartheid despite government orders restricting her speech.

1987   The Lusaka Statement issued. There is a general strike by 3 million workers and students coinciding with May 6 general election.

1988   February 29, Tutu arrested during a march opposing the government banning of 17 anti-apartheid groups

1989   The ruling National Party announces a new five-year racial reform program that stresses a willingness to negotiate with any group "committed to peace." The Mass Democratic Movement (MDM), an alliance of antiapartheid organizations formed around the UDF and the Congress of South African Trade Unions (COSATU), launches a defiance campaign—a vivid reminder of the 1952 defiance campaign. The MDM leadership proclaims this organization to be a peaceful program of nonviolent mass action, directed against apartheid laws and addressing the immediate needs. Tutu, Boesak, and Chikane are spokespersons.

1990   February 2, F. W. de Klerk lifts ban on black political organizations. February 11, Nelson Mandela is released from prison.

1992   July, South Africa participates in Olympics for the first time since 1960.

1993   October, Nelson Mandela and F. W. de Klerk win Nobel Peace Prize. July 25, St. James Massacre, 11 killed, 54 injured. I visit St. James Church in Kenilworth with Tutu (July 27).

1994   April 27 and 28, first democratic elections; May 10, inauguration of Nelson Mandela

1995   Tutu agrees to head the Truth and Reconciliation Commission and suffers from prostate cancer.

1996   On June 22, I attend festivities of Tutu's retirement as archbishop. Truth and Reconciliation Commission chaired by Tutu begins hearings on human rights crimes committed by former government and liberation movements during apartheid era.

1997   Truth and Reconciliation Commission report deems apartheid a crime against humanity and finds the ANC accountable for human rights abuses.

1998   ANC wins general elections, Thabo Mbeki takes over as president. Tutu establishes the Desmond Tutu Peace Trust. Tutu tells archbishop of Canterbury that he was ashamed to be Anglican when the church failed to fully include LGBT community.

1999   Tutu writes *No Future without Forgiveness*, in which he argues that true reconciliation does not come easily nor by merely denying the past.

2000   The Tutu Peace Center is launched in Cape Town. Tutu is awarded the Jamnalal Bajaj Award for Promoting Gandhian Values outside India.

2001   Tutu's speech advocating peace in response to September 11, 2001, at the Nobel Centennial Symposia, held on 8 December 2001 in Oslo, Norway.[4] Also in same year, Tutu visits Belfast to assist with truth and reconciliation in Northern Ireland.

2002   Tutu speaks out in the Israeli-Palestinian conflict as he became increasingly frustrated following the collapse of the 2000 Camp David summit. In 2002 he creates a great stir in his widely publicized speech denouncing Israeli policy regarding the Palestinians and calling for sanctions against Israel. The stir is in how Tutu compares the Israeli-Palestinian situation with that in South Africa. Tutu states that "one reason we succeeded in South Africa that is missing in the Middle East is quality of leadership—leaders willing to make unpopular compromises, to go against their own constituencies, because they have the wisdom to see that would ultimately make peace possible."[5]

2003 Tutu speaks out in campaign to combat the HIV/AIDS pandemic, in June 2003 stating, "Apartheid tried to destroy our people and apartheid failed. If we don't act against HIV-AIDS, it may succeed, for it is already decimating our population."[6]

2004 Tutu appears in *Honor Bound to Defend Freedom*, an Off-Broadway play in New York City critical of the US detention of prisoners at Guantánamo Bay.[7]

2005 Presented with the International Gandhi Peace Prize. On the April 2005 election of Pope Benedict XVI—known for conservative views on issues of gender and sexuality—Tutu announces that the Roman Catholic Church was now unlikely to change its opposition to the use of condoms amidst the fight against HIV/AIDS, nor its opposition to the ordination of women priests.

2006 To help combat child trafficking, Tutu launches a global campaign, organized by Plan International, to ensure that all children are registered at birth.[8] Plan International is an independent development and humanitarian organization that works in 71 countries across the world, in Africa, the Americas, and Asia to advance children's rights and equality for girls.

2007 Featured in *Vanity Fair*'s Africa Issue profiled by Brad Pitt.

2008 Travels to Gaza on a UN mission, to investigate the killing of 21 Palestinian civilians, by Israeli shelling, in November 2006. A judge throws out a corruption case against ruling ANC party chief Jacob Zuma, opening the way for him to stand as the country's president in 2009. President Mbeki resigns over allegations that he interfered in the corruption case against Mr. Zuma. ANC deputy leader Kgalema Motlanthe is chosen by parliament as president.

2009 Receives the Presidential Medal of Freedom from Barack Obama. Receives Spiritual Leadership award from Humanity's Team at Freedom Park in Pretoria, South Africa. Parliament elects Jacob Zuma as president.

2010 (July 22) Tutu announces his decision to retire from public life.

2011 October, Tutu lashes out at the South African government after the Dalai Lama is denied a visa to attend his birthday party, saying he would "pray for the downfall of the ANC."

2012 September, Tutu expresses his outrage at "failing politicians in South Africa." Tutu is awarded $1 million by the Mo Ibrahim Foundation for his lifelong commitment to speaking the truth to power. Police open fire on workers at a platinum mine in Marikana, killing at least 34 people, and leaving at least 78 injured and arresting more than 200 others. Prosecutors drop murder charges in September against 270 miners after a public outcry, and the government sets up a judicial commission of inquiry.

2013 Nelson Mandela dies, aged 95. Tributes to "The Father of the Nation" flood in from throughout the world. Tutu wins the Templeton Prize for advancing "spiritual progress." Tutu supports the Office for the United Nations High Commissioner for Human Rights, a world first global public education campaign for LGBTQ.

2014 In an interview with Ann Curry, Tutu refers to the oppression of gays as the "new apartheid." At the 2014 General Assembly of the Presbyterian Church in Detroit, June 14–21, 2014, Tutu calls on delegates to vote in favor of "divestment from companies that assist 'apartheid' Israel's occupation of the Palestinian people." Tutu also in this year announces his support of legalized assisted dying, stating that life shouldn't be preserved "at any cost" and that the criminalization of assisted dying deprived the terminally ill of their "human right to dignity."[9]

2015   October 7, Archbishop Emeritus Tutu celebrates his 84th birthday at home while recovering after several hospital visits. Tutu is reported as responding well to "minor investigative surgery." August 7, Tutu launches a petition calling on British prime minister David Cameron and the secretary general of the United Nations, Ban Ki-Moon, to respond urgently to climate change by setting a renewable energy target of 100 percent by 2050. August 27, the Desmond and Leah Tutu Foundation gives a media update after Tutu was readmitted to hospital for "a fresh course of antibiotics."

2016   April 22, Archbishop Emeritus Desmond Tutu and his wife, Leah, receive the Award for Peace with Justice for their contribution to social justice. June 8, Desmond Tutu nominates Marwan Barghouthi, a Palestinian political activist, for the 2017 Nobel Peace Prize. July 10, a church service held at St Mary's Cathedral in Braamfontein to commemorate Tutu's 40 years in Episcopal service is attended by hundreds of people. July, Tutu pens a letter to a newborn baby girl after her father wrote to him saying that he was wanting to compile a collection of letters to his newborn daughter, Juliet. In the letter in which Tutu refers to Juliet as "little sister," he writes candidly that as she is starting her life, he is reaching the end of his. He ends the letter saying, "You and I and everyone else were born with the same purpose: for love, for goodness and for one another." August 25, Tutu hospitalized for "a recurring infection." September 7, Tutu undergoes surgery on the 30th anniversary of his being ordained archbishop of the Anglican Church of South Africa. Social media hoax on Tutu death untrue.

2017   Tutu opens the New Zeitz MOCAA Museum in Cape Town, the largest museum dedicated to the continent's contemporary art. An "Arch for an Arch" monument in honor of Tutu on his 86th birthday erected between St. George's Cathedral and Parliament in Cape Town.

2018   President Zuma resigns under pressure from the governing ANC over corruption charges, which chooses veteran trade unionist and businessman Cyril Ramaphosa as his successor. Tutu resigns as Oxfam ambassador due to allegations that senior staff members of Oxfam in crisis zones paid for sex among those meant to serve. Tutu and Ndungane call during Rowan Smith funeral for recognition of gays and lesbians. Tutu in hospital Sept. 27 for tests. Tutu's writings exhibition. In Hollywood movie *The Forgiven*, Forest Whitaker plays Archbishop Desmond Tutu.

2020   Tutu continues to teach interdependent proactivity to combat and mitigate the COVID-19 pandemic.

Notes

Preface

1. Desmond Tutu, *No Future without Forgiveness* (New York: Doubleday, 1999), 157, quoting from Mary McAleese, *Unreconciled Being: Love in Chaos* (New York: Continuum Publishing, 1999).
2. John Allen interview at Bishopscourt, Desmond Tutu Center Travel Seminar, General Theological Seminary, Cape Town, South Africa, Jan. 16, 2017.
3. As an Anglican archbishop, Tutu was in charge of Southern Africa, i.e., Mozambique, Swaziland, Lesotho, Namibia, the Island of St. Helena, and the Republic of South Africa.
4. I use the term "black" throughout to include South African people of African, colored, and Indian descent.
5. John Allen interview at Bishopscourt.
6. During colonialism, the Dutch East India Company introduced racial segregation in South Africa. In 1975 the British maintained such segregation as they took over the Cape of Good Hope. The concept of race was written into law during the apartheid period, which began in 1948. In the Population Registration Act No. 30 of 1950, South Africans were divided into three main racial groups: Whites, Natives (blacks), Indians and colored people (people of mixed race).
7. Tutu, *No Future without Forgiveness*, 109.
8. Vladimir Lossky, *The Mystical Theology of the Eastern Church* (Crestwood, NY: St. Vladimir's Seminary Press, 1976), 8.
9. Tutu, *No Future without Forgiveness*, 82.
10. "Desmond Tutu to Retire from Public Life," Episcopal News Service, July 22, 2010.

Introduction

1. Subsequently throughout this book such identity will be referred to as "black," along with other black identities around the world. In turn I will also refer to those of European descent as "white."
2. *Pseudo-Dionysius the Complete Works*, trans. Colm Luibheid (New York: Paulist, 1987), 137.
3. Introduction by Paul Brett, in Tutu, "Church and Prophecy in South Africa Today," in *Essex Papers in Theology and Society* (Centre for the Study of Theology in the University of Essex, 1991), 1–3.

4. See Desmond Tutu, *No Future without Forgiveness* (New York: Doubleday, 1999).
5. Tutu, address, "The Centrality of the Spiritual," General Theological Seminary, New York, undated.
6. For such an approach, I recommend John Allen, *Rabble-Rouser for Peace: The Authorized Biography of Desmond Tutu* (London: Rider Books, 2006).
7. "Desmond Tutu to Retire from Public Life," Episcopal News Service, July 22, 2010.
8. Allen, *Rabble-Rouser*, 395.
9. Allen, *Rabble-Rouser*, 394. Also see my work on the concept of Ubuntu: Michael Battle, *Reconciliation: The Ubuntu Theology of Desmond Tutu*, revised and updated (Cleveland: Pilgrim, 1997, 2009); and Michael Battle, *Ubuntu: I in You and You in Me* (New York: Seabury, 2009).
10. Allen, *Rabble-Rouser*, 396.
11. Shirley du Boulay's biography, *Tutu: Voice of the Voiceless* (London: Hodder & Stoughton, 1998), does an adequate presentation of Tutu's rise as leader in South Africa, especially in his leadership capacities as head of the Theological Fund for the World Council of Churches, as general secretary of the South African Council of Churches, as bishop of Lesotho, and as dean and bishop of Johannesburg. She does not, however, provide a theological framework for Tutu, nor does she display Tutu's impact as archbishop, both of which I seek to do.
12. Evelyn Underhill, *Mysticism: A Study in the Nature and Development of Man's Spiritual Consciousness* (Cleveland and New York: World, 1965), xiv, 73, 81, 170.
13. See Bernard McGinn's section "Theological Approaches to Mysticism," in his *The Foundations of Mysticism*, vol. 1 (New York: Crossroad, 1992), 266ff.
14. For more information on this Christian monk who influenced Tutu, see Piers McGrandle, *Trevor Huddleston, Turbulent Priest* (London: Continuum, 2004).
15. Dionysius's Mystical Teaching, in *The Cloud of Unknowing and Other Works*, trans. Clifton Wolters (New York: Penguin Books, 1987), 209–10.
16. Tutu, "The Preacher as Prophet," St. Luke's Orchards, January 27, 1983.
17. Tutu, address, "Speaking within the South African Context," Natal Youth Congress, March [recorded as Feb.] 30, 1987.
18. Parker Palmer, *The Courage to Teach: Exploring the Inner Landscape of a Teacher's Life* (San Francisco: Jossey-Bass, 1998), 21.
19. Battle, *Reconciliation*; *The Wisdom of Desmond Tutu* (Oxford: Lion, 1999, and Louisville, KY: Westminster John Knox, 2000); *Ubuntu*; *Heaven on Earth: God's Call to Community in the Book of Revelation* (Louisville, KY: Westminster John Knox, 2017).
20. Professor Kristen Leslie, assistant professor of pastoral theology at Yale Divinity School at the time, was the first to challenge my assumptions of mutuality. Her argument was that in her pastoral care classes she was not about the creation of mutuality and needed boundaries. The second response came from Dean Joretta Marshall, Eden Theological Seminary, as she distinguished between "mutual respect" and "mutuality," namely, that the former was a more helpful category in the unequal relationship between teacher and student. Dean Marshall provided this discussion in her session: "Self in Community: Embodying Teaching and Ethics."
21. Frederick Buechner, *Wishful Thinking: A Seeker's ABC* (San Francisco: HarperSanFrancisco, 1993), 119.
22. This also seems to be the presupposition in secular theories of education in which the authentic teacher should make words and behavior congruent. See S. Brookfield, *The Skillful Teacher* (San Francisco: Jossey-Bass, 1990).

23. Robert Pear, "Falwell Denounces Tutu as a 'Phony,'" *New York Times*, Aug. 21, 1985.

24. The following educational theorists contributed deeply to the integration of service learning into the academy: John Dewey, Jean Piaget, David Kolb, and Paulo Freire. See C. W. Kinsley anda K. McPherson, eds., *Enriching the Curriculum through Service Learning* (Alexandria, VA: Association for Supervision and Curriculum Development, 1995); J. Galura, R. Metland, R. Ross, M. J. Callan, and R. Smith, eds., *Praxis III: Voices in Dialogue* (Ann Arbor: University of Michigan Office of Community Service Learning Press, 1995); and Paulo Freire, *Pedagogy of the Oppressed* (New York: Seabury, 1970).

25. Tutu, handwritten address to 100th Anniversary of the Methodist Conference, in South Africa, undated.

Part 1: Purgation

1. Tutu, "Miracle Must Work or We're for the Birds," in *Star Sun*, Sept. 22, 1991.

Chapter 1: Diving in Troubled Water

1. Tutu's undated handwritten speeches, "Perspectives in Black and White." Tutu illustrates further with this story: "A little boy excitedly pointed to a flight of geese and shouted, 'Mummy, Mummy, look at all those *gooses*.' 'My darling,' Mummy replied, 'we don't call them *gooses*. They are geese.' Then the little darling, nothing daunted, retorted, 'Well they still look like *goose* to me.'"

2. So much so that Mahatma Gandhi first developed his nonviolent system of satyagraha in South Africa and had his spiritual conversion in doing so. See Arvind Sharma, *Gandhi: A Spiritual Biography* (New Haven, CT: Yale University Press, 2013), 58.

3. For Paul's experience of purgation and illumination, see Acts 9:1–22.

4. Tutu, "Some Memories of My Life," June 28, 1990, draft to be published in King's College London's *In Touch* magazine featuring a famous alumnus.

5. I owe this insight of Tutu's mother and her fierce love for him to John Allen, Interview at Fire and Ice Hotel Cape Town, Desmond Tutu Center Travel Seminar, Aug. 13, 2017.

6. Tutu, undated text, "Christmas."

7. Tutu, handwritten address to 100th Anniversary of the Methodist Conference, in South Africa, undated.

8. Tutu, "The Reluctant Prophet," *Church Times*, Aug. 10, 1984, 9.

9. Tutu, "South Africa's Blacks: Aliens in Their Own Land," Nov. 26, 1984, in *Ethics in the Present Tense: Readings from Christianity and Crisis 1966–1991*, ed. Leon Howell and Vivian Lindermayer (New York: Friendship Press, 1991), 130–32.

10. Tutu, "Human Rights in South Africa," *Monitor*, SACC Library Resource Center, undated.

11. Tutu, "Human Rights in South Africa," undated.

12. "The Archbishop, the Church and the Nation," in *Monitor: The Journal of the Human Rights Trust* (Port Elizabeth: Monitor Publications, June 1991), 4.

13. Tutu, "An Appreciation of the Rt. Revd Trevor Huddleston, CR," in *Trevor Huddleston: Essays on His Life and Work*, ed. Deborah Duncan Honoré (Oxford: Oxford University Press, 1988), 4.

14. Tutu, "Some Memories of My Life."

15. Tutu, "An Appreciation," 2.

16. Tutu, "An Appreciation," 2.

17. Interview with Trevor Huddleston, John Ezard, "A Cry for His Unloved Country," *Guardian Weekly*, July 9–15, 1993.
18. Tutu, address, "The Centrality of the Spiritual," General Theological Seminary, New York, undated.
19. Tutu, address, "Where Is Now Thy God?," Trinity Institute, New York, Jan. 8, 1989.
20. Tutu, undated.
21. Tutu, undated.
22. Tutu, undated.
23. Tutu, "My Search for God," St. Mary's Jubilee Lenten Talks, St. Alban's, Ferreirastown, Apr. 5, 1979.
24. Allister Sparks, *The Mind of South Africa* (New York: Ballantine Books, 1990), 188–89.
25. Tutu, "Some Memories of My Life."
26. Tutu, "Some Memories of My Life."
27. Tutu, undated.
28. Tutu, "My Search for God."
29. Tutu, "My Search for God."
30. Tutu, "My Search for God."
31. Tutu, "Where Is Now Thy God?"
32. Tutu, handwritten sermon, "Centenary Celebration of SSJD," at the Cathedral of the Holy Nativity, May 10, 1987, in Pietermaritzburg, South Africa.
33. Tutu, "Centenary Celebration of SSJD."
34. Tutu, "Some Memories of My Life."
35. Tutu, "Some Memories of My Life."
36. It is interesting to note here that Mahatma Gandhi concludes the same that his study in London before going to South Africa was vital in his formation of satyagraha (nonviolent resistance). See Mahatma Gandhi, *The Collected Works of Mahatma Gandhi* (New Dehli: The Publications Division, Navajivan Trust, Ahmedabad, 1961), chap. 39.
37. Tutu, address, "The Nature and Value of Theology," undated.
38. Tutu, draft for G. S. Wilmore and James Cone, *Black Theology—A Documentary History, 1966–1979* (New York: Orbis, 1979), 657.
39. For a more sustained time line, see appendix for Chronology and outline of Tutu in South African context.
40. Tutu, undated address, "A Vision for Humanity."
41. It is fascinating that popular Christian spirituality still does not explicitly honor an African as founder of Christian monasticism.
42. See Kevin Baker, "Nothing in All Creation Is Hidden: Why America Needs Truth and Reconciliation after Trump," *New Republic*, May 17, 2018.
43. Tutu, "The Vineyard of Naboth and Duncan Village," East London, Oct. 31, 1981.
44. Dietrich Bonhoeffer would be another.
45. Desmond Tutu, "Towards Koinonia in Faith, Life and Witness," in *Translating the Word, Transforming the World, An Ecumenical Reader*, ed. Amele Adamavi-Aho Edue, Marion Grau, Atola Longkumer (Geneva: WCC Publications, 2018), 14.

Chapter 2: Tutu and Christian Mysticism

1. See the Anglican mystic Evelyn Underhill, *The Essentials of Mysticism and Other Essays* (London: Dent, 1920), 12; and Etienne Gilson, *The Mystical Theology of St. Bernard* (London: Sheed & Ward, 1940), chap. 2.

2. Underhill, *Essentials*, 14.
3. Tutu's handwritten sermons, "The Angels," St. Michaels', Observatory, 1986.
4. Bernard of Clairvaux, *On the Song of Songs*, 4 vols. (Kalamazoo, MI: Cistercian, 1971–80), Sermon 3. Also see his *The Twelve Steps of Humility and Pride, and On Loving God* (London: Hodder & Stoughton, 1985).
5. "The Spiritual life of Desmond Tutu," Interview by Anna Karin Hammar, Church of Sweden, with Lavinia Crawford-Browne, his personal assistant for more than twenty years, in Cape Town, Aug. 7, 2015. https://www.youtube.com/watch?v=Z97szLc8_YI&list=PLWS96mv0ETpzEbAi_BqmFWUpsymTAxL4W&t=186s&index=2.
6. "The Spiritual life of Desmond Tutu," interview.
7. Wyatt Mason, "The Artist's Life: How the Myth of the Hedonistic Artist Lost Its Allure," *New York Times Style Magazine*, Nov. 28, 2018.
8. Mason, "The Artist's Life."
9. Mason, "The Artist's Life."
10. Regarding "transfiguration," in 1993 I asked Tutu what theological book he would like to write. He told me it would be about the concept of transfiguration.
11. Tutu, sermon, "The Marks of the Church," undated.
12. I first experienced Tutu in 1986 as a senior undergraduate at Duke University when he spoke at Duke Chapel.
13. Description of Tutu on church bulletin at St. George's Cathedral, Services for Holy Week and Easter, 1984, together with Tutu's handwritten sermons for the services.
14. Archbishop Desmond and Mrs. Leah Tutu welcomed me to live with them at Bishopscourt, 1993–94. Archbishop Tutu also ordained me to the priesthood on my birthday, Dec. 12, 1993.
15. Tutu, handwritten sermon, "St. Mark's Centenary," Mar. 15, 1987.
16. Over 60,000 South Africans were removed from their homes by force for the advantage of white South Africans to control the land. On Feb. 11, 1966, the apartheid government declared Cape Town's neighborhood of District Six as a whites-only area under the Group Areas Act of 1950. In effect becoming refugees in their own country, these people were relocated to the Cape Flats, over twenty-five kilometers away.
17. Michael Battle, *Reconciliation: The Ubuntu Theology of Desmond Tutu* (Cleveland: Pilgrim, 1997); *The Wisdom of Desmond Tutu* (Oxford: Lion, 1999, and Louisville, KY: Westminster John Knox, 2000); *Ubuntu: I in You and You in Me* (New York: Seabury, 2009); and *Heaven on Earth: A Call to Community in the Book of Revelation* (Louisville, KY: Westminster John Knox, 2017).
18. Aylward Shorter, *African Christian Spirituality* (n.p.: Geoffrey Chapman, 1978).
19. Tutu thinks like this in his essay "The Nature and Value of Theology," in which Tutu shows that the doctrine of the Trinity assures us that we are not destined to an eternity of isolation.
20. Tutu illustrates the necessity of selflessness in the following way: just as one who only receives, finds death, so the Dead Sea exists as it only receives its current. See Tutu, handwritten sermon, St. George's Cathedral, Aug. 21, 1986; 1 Cor. 4:7 seems to be the text of sermon: "For who sees anything different in you? What have you that you did not receive? If then you received it, why do you boast as if it were not a gift?"
21. Matt. 22:37–40.
22. See Battle, *Heaven on Earth*.
23. Tutu, handwritten undated address #5.
24. Tutu, "A Christian Vision of the Future of South Africa," in *Christianity amidst Apartheid*, ed. Martin Prozesky (New York: St. Martin's, 1990).

25. Tutu, address "The Nature and Value of Theology," undated. Also see my treatment of Tutu's Ubuntu in *Ubuntu: I in You and You in Me.*
26. Tutu, "Human Rights in South Africa," in *Monitor*, SACC Library Resource Center, undated.
27. Tutu, quoted in *Prayers for Peace, An Anthology of Readings and Prayers Selected by Archbishop Robert Runcie and Cardinal Basil Hume* (London: SPCK, 1987), 41.
28. Tutu, handwritten sermon, Sunday School Teachers' Eucharist, St. George's Cathedral, Feb. 2, 1987.
29. Tutu, handwritten sermons, at St. Philip's, Washington, DC, Christmas III, 1984.
30. Tutu, "The Marks of the Church."
31. E. W. F. Tomlin, *Simone Weil* (New Haven, CT: Yale University Press, 1954), 55–56.
32. Tomlin, *Simone Weil*, 49.
33. Tutu, "Foreword," to a play on the life of Steve Biko.
34. Simone Weil, *Waiting on God* (New York: Putnam, 1951), 69.
35. Weil, *Waiting on God*, 69.
36. Tutu's handwritten sermons, "The Angels," St. Michaels', Observatory, 1986.
37. Tutu, handwritten address, July 1987, Memorial to Pakamile Mabija, who died in detention in Kimberley, South Africa.
38. Weil, *Gravity and Grace* (New York: Putnam, 1952), 4.
39. Tutu, "Credo," in *Living Philosophies: The Reflections of Some Eminent Men and Women of Our Time*, ed. Clifton Fadiman (New York: Doubleday, 1990), 234.
40. Tutu, "South Africa's Blacks: Aliens in Their Own Land," *Christianity and Crisis*, Nov. 26, 1984, 135.
41. Emmanuel K. Tsesigye, *Common Ground: Christianity, African Religion and Philosophy* (New York: Peter Lang, 1987), 84.
42. Tutu, handwritten undated speeches and address, "The Church and Mission."

Chapter 3: Purging Scales from Eyes

1. See Augustine, *The City of God*, trans. Marcus Dods, introduction by Thomas Merton (New York: Modern Library, 1950).
2. Tutu, handwritten undated address, "Robert Kennedy."
3. Bernie Sanders, quoted in Marc Tracy, "Prospective Democratic Presidential Candidates Put Their Ideas on Audition," *New York Times*, May 16, 2018.
4. Tutu, Address, "South Africa on the Way to 2000 A.D.," Mar. 31, 1980.
5. Tutu, "A Christian Vision of the Future of South Africa." Draft essay to be published in *Christianity in South Africa*, submitted to Martin Prozesky, University of Natal, July 31, 1989.
6. "The Equal Opportunity Foundation—A Beacon of Hope," in *Weekly Mail and Guardian*, Oct. 22–28, 1993.
7. "The Equal Opportunity Foundation."
8. Tutu, handwritten undated address, "USA Policy towards South Africa: The Perplexities of a Black South African."
9. Tutu, "God's Strength in Human Weakness," in *Your Kingdom Come, Papers and Resolutions of the Twelfth National Conference of the South African Council of Churches, Hammanskraal, May 5–8, 1980.*
10. Francis Wilson and Mamphela Ramphele, *Uprooting Poverty: The South African Challenge* (Cape Town: David Philip, 1989), 16ff.
11. Tutu, Address in Uppsala at their jubilee year, 1993.
12. Tutu, Address, Heading: "Matthew chapter 5 verse 13."

13. Tutu, in "Towards Koinonia in Faith, Life and Witness," World Council of Churches Faith and Order Conference, Santiago de Compostela, Spain, Aug. 3, 1993, 1.
14. Tutu, handwritten address in Soweto upon return from Moscow, June 1988.
15. Tutu, handwritten address, "Christian Witness in South Africa," Drawbridge Lecture, St. Paul's Cathedral, London, England, Nov. 19, 1984.
16. Tutu, in "Towards Koinonia in Faith, Life and Witness," 2.
17. Tutu, "God's Strength in Human Weakness."
18. Sheena Duncan, "Riekert Commission Report," *Black Sash* 21, no. 1 (Aug. 1979).
19. Tutu, "God's Strength in Human Weakness."
20. "Robert Draper Book: GOP's Anti-Obama Campaign Started Night of Inauguration," *Huffington Post*, Aug. 10, 2014.
21. Tutu, "Fundamental Change," undated. Also see Tutu, "Frankenstein Cannot Be Reformed," handwritten address, "Options Available," Mar. 26, 1987.
22. Tutu, "Fundamental Change," undated.
23. Tutu, "Fundamental Change," undated.
24. D. F. Malan, quoted in F. A. van Jaarsveld, "The Afrikaner's Idea of His Calling and Mission in South African History," *Journal of Theology for Southern Africa* (June 1, 1977): 22.
25. Van Jaarsveld, "Afrikaner's Idea," 17.
26. John Burns, "Pass Laws, Aspect of Apartheid Blacks Hate Most, Bring Despair and Pent-up Fury," *New York Times*, May 24, 1978.
27. Tutu, "Fundamental Change," undated.
28. Tutu, Addresses and Speeches, "What Jesus Means to Me," Durban University, August 6–7, 1981.
29. Charles Villa-Vicencio, "An All-Pervading Heresy," in *Apartheid Is a Heresy*, ed. John de Gruchy and Charles Villa-Vicencio (Grand Rapids: Eerdmans, 1983), 67.
30. Tutu, handwritten sermon (re: William Wilberforce), undated (during archbishopric).
31. Tutu, Speeches and Addresses, "The Challenges of God's Mission," United Methodists, Louisville, Kentucky, March 12, 1987.
32. Tutu, handwritten sermon, St. Luke's, Greton, June 15, 1986.
33. Tutu, "Just Another Day of Township Horror," *The Argus*, May 25, 1993.
34. Tutu, handwritten address, "For Justice and Peace," undated.
35. "End Violence Now, Say Black Leaders," *The Argus*, Dec. 1, 1993.
36. Tutu, address, "Whither South Africa," South African Institute of Race Relations (SAIRR) public meeting, Woodstock, Town Hall, Oct. 17, 1985.
37. "Reflections on Gandhi," in *The Penguin Essays of George Orwell* (Harmondsworth: Penguin, 1984), 470, quoted in Steven Mufson, *Fighting Years: Black Resistance and the Struggle for a New South Africa* (Boston: Beacon, 1990), 101; also note Hannah Arendt, *On Revolution* (New York: Penguin Books, 1963).
38. See Stephen R. Davis, *The ANC's War against Apartheid: Umkhonto we Sizwe and the Liberation of South Africa* (Bloomington: Indiana University Press, 2018).
39. Tutu, quoted in Mufson, *Fighting Years*, 102–3.
40. Nobel Committee, quoted in Mufson, *Fighting Years*, 103.
41. Mufson, *Fighting Years*, 98.
42. Mufson, *Fighting Years*, 99.
43. Mufson, *Fighting Years*, 99.

44. Tutu, address, "Brothers and Sisters Together," for Trans Africa, April 29, 1981.
45. Mufson, *Fighting Years*, 103.
46. UDF leaders, quoted in Mufson, *Fighting Years*, 101.
47. Ashley Jardina, "White Identity Politics Isn't Just about White Supremacy. It's Much Bigger," *Washington Post*, Aug. 16, 2017.
48. Jardina, "White Identity Politics."
49. Tutu, press statement, Apr. 2, 1986.
50. Tutu, quoted in Mufson, *Fighting Years*, 82.
51. Tutu, quoted in Mufson, *Fighting Years*, 82.
52. Tutu, quoted in David Beresford, "Fisher of Men, Seeker of Truth," *Mail & Guardian* (South African weekly newspaper), Johannesburg, Dec. 19, 1997.
53. Tutu, quoted in Beresford, "Fisher of Men."
54. Tutu, "Grace Upon Grace," in *Journal for Preachers* 15, no. 1 (Advent 1991): 20.

Chapter 4: A Boiling Nation

1. Tutu, address, undated, heading: "Strict Embargo," while general secretary of SACC.
2. Anthony Marx, *Lessons of Struggle: Internal South African Opposition, 1960–1990* (New York: Oxford University Press, 1992).
3. (1) Nederduitse Gereformeerde Kerk—Dutch Reformed Church (NGK), (2) Nederduitsch Hervormde Kerk (NHK), and (3) Gereformeerde Kerk.
4. (1) NGK, (2) the NG Sendingkerk—Dutch Reformed Mission Church, (3) the NG Kerk in Afrika, and (4) the Reformed Church in Africa-Indian.
5. (1) NG Sendingkerk, (2) NG Kerk in Afrika, (3) the Reformed Church in Africa, (4) the Evangelical Presbyterian Church, (5) the Reformed Presbyterian Church, (6) the Presbyterian Church of Southern Africa, and (7) the United Congregational Church of Southern Africa.
6. (1) Anglican, (2) the United Congregational Church (UCC), (3) the Methodist Church, and (4) the Presbyterian Church of Southern Africa.
7. See Chris Loff, "The History of a Heresy," in *Apartheid Is a Heresy*, ed. John de Gruchy and Charles Villa-Vicencio (Grand Rapids: Eerdmans, 1983), 22. Loff succinctly discusses the Afrikaner Church dilemma with two major synods of 1829 (fighting against racist tendencies) and 1857 (completely capitulating to an apartheid church).
8. Peter Storey, "Press Statement by SACC President," Sept. 11, 1981. Tutu also had to contend with a judicial commission "to investigate the financial affairs and other matters relating to the Council." Tutu, "Press Statement—For Khotso," Nov. 26, 1981.
9. Beyers Naudé, quoted in Jani Allan, "The Rebel with a Cause—Easing in the Turning Tide," *Sunday Times*, June 12, 2016.
10. Tutu, quoted in "Beyers Naudé's Struggle of Faith," *The Independent*, Sept. 7, 2004.
11. Beyers Naudé, "Report of the General Secretary—National Conference of the South African Council of Churches," June 24–28, 1985, in *Ecunews*, news service of the South African Council of Churches, Aug. 1985, 13.
12. Steven Mufson, *Fighting Years* (Boston: Beacon, 1990), 102.
13. "Chapter 3.3 Non-Violence," in *Kairos Document—Challenge to the Church* (Braamfontein: Skotaville, 1986). See https://kairossouthernafrica.wordpress.com/2011/05/08/the-south-africa-kairos-document-1985.
14. "Chapter 3.3 Non-Violence," in *Kairos Document*. See https://kairossouthernafrica.wordpress.com/2011/05/08/the-south-africa-kairos-document-1985. Also quoted in Mufson, *Fighting Years*, 102.

15. Tutu, "God-given Dignity and the Quest for Liberation," paper to the National Conference of the SACC, July 1973, reprinted from *Ecunews*, Aug. 4, 1976, in *African Perspectives on South Africa: A Collection of Speeches, Articles & Documents*, ed. Hendrik W. van der Merwe, Nancy C. J. Charton, D. A. Kotzé, and Åke Magnusson (Cape Town: David Philip, 1978), 325.

16. Tutu, "God-given Dignity," 326.

17. Tutu, "Press Statement—For Khotso," Nov. 26, 1981.

18. Tutu, "Towards Koinonia in Faith, Life and Witness," World Council of Churches Faith and Order Conference, Santiago de Compostela, Spain, Aug. 3, 1993, 10–11.

19. See Michael Battle, *Reconciliation: The Ubuntu Theology of Desmond Tutu* (Cleveland: Pilgrim, 1997).

20. *The Living Church*, May 8, 1983, Easter 6, 8.

21. John Allen, *Rabble-Rouser for Peace: The Authorised Biography of Desmond Tutu* (London: Simon & Schuster, 2006). In particular, see Allen's display of Tutu's days as head of the SACC in the chapter "Jazz Conductor."

22. Tutu, handwritten address to the Presidium Executive Committee of the 67th General Convention of the Episcopal Church, New Orleans, USA, Sept. 5–15, 1983.

23. Tutu, handwritten address to the Presidium Executive Committee of the 67th General Convention of the Episcopal Church, New Orleans, USA, Sept. 5–15, 1983.

24. Tutu, handwritten sermon on Rev. 7:9–11, Mar. 21, 1983, Khotso House, Johannesburg.

25. Tutu, "General Secretary's Report to National Conference of the SACC," 1983.

26. Tutu, draft of "Welcome and Introduction," in the *International Review of Mission*, Jan. 1994, entirely devoted to the Central Committee of the World Council of Churches, meeting in South Africa, Jan. 1994.

27. Tutu, handwritten undated address, 1980s, after Tutu's USA trip in which celebrities like Harry Belafonte, Sydney Poitier, Bill Cosby, Coretta Scott King met him, Tutu states, "Jane Fonda arranged a huge meeting at her house of entertainers who came from all over. The stars of *The Color Purple*, artist on Sun City Record, Richard Pryor, Pat Boone, Norman Lear, Diana Ross, and Stevie Wonder sent a taped message. We met Muhammed Ali. Entertained by Jewish leaders and were given a beautiful gift. Church leaders—Cardinal O'Connor took part in installation of Presiding Bishop Edmond Browning in Washington Cathedral. Whether some people in South Africa like or not, it seems I have some standing in the world and few people appear to like me and what I am doing. Jerry Falwell got himself into a lot of trouble trying to discredit us and he turned out to be one of our best pros as the result of over one million Americans signed a petition repudiating him which I received near the SA Embassy in Washington from leaders of Free SA movement." Tutu appeared on some leading TV shows, e.g., *Today Show, Phil Donahue, Nightline, The Larry King Show*, which also raised his profile. Tutu states, "The fundraising has always been successful beyond our wildest dreams. We have had donations or pledges amounting to over $500,000. This excludes scholarships and donations to the Bishop Tutu Refugee Scholarship Fund which I founded in 1984 for our refugees. In Harford we got scholarships to universities worth over $200,000 plus cash donations of $50,000 so that the total we nearly collected was one million dollars. Most of this we will share between the SACC and the Diocese of Johannesburg. . . . I have not sought any of this status out. And I intend to use it as I have always done for the good of my country for I am truly patriotic and am concerned for all South Africans black

and white. I am ashamed of nothing I have done or said. . . . My ultimate loyalty is to no man or human authority. . . . I have said before I support the ANC in its objective (nonracial, democratic, just society) not its methods. I have said many times over I reject all violence as evil; however, I hold a position in the church that there can be a time when it would be justifiable to overthrow an unjust government by violence, otherwise Christians would not have fought against Hitler and his Nazism."

28. Irwin Abrams, *The Nobel Peace Prize and the Laureates: An Illustrated Biographical History, 1901–1987* (Boston: G. K. Hall, 1988), 242.
29. Liane Rozzell, "A Gesture of Honor," in *Sojourners*, Dec. 1984, 5.
30. "A Fitting Climax to the Struggle to End Apartheid, Says 'Thrilled' Tutu," in *Weekend Argus*, Oct. 16–17, 1993, 6.
31. Anton Harber, "A Third Nobel Nudge (Will We Get the Hint?)," *Weekly Mail & Guardian*, Oct. 22–28, 1993.
32. Tutu, in *The Words of Peace: Selections from the Speeches of the Winners of the Nobel Peace Prize*, ed. Irwin Abrams (New York: Newmarket, 1990), 63.
33. Philip Russell, in *Seek*, a newsletter of the Church of the Province of Southern Africa (CPSA), now the Anglican Church of Southern Africa.
34. Tutu, handwritten address, "Christian Witness in South Africa," Drawbridge Lecture, St. Paul's Cathedral, London, England, Nov. 19, 1984.
35. Tutu, in *The Words of Peace*, 43.
36. Tutu, *The Words of Peace*, 44.
37. Tutu, handwritten address, undated (1980s).
38. Tutu, handwritten address, undated (1980s).
39. Tutu, "Stewart Memorial Lecture," undated.
40. Tutu, Isaiah 40 text, address "Memorial Service for Three ANC Condemned Men," Khotso House, June 9, 1983.
41. Tutu, Isaiah 40 text, address "Memorial Service."
42. On Wednesday, Feb. 3, 1982, a six-person Commission of Inquiry into South African security legislation, under Justice P. I. Rabie, presented its report and recommendations that a Ministry of Law and Order be established with two separate components of Police, and a Directorate of Internal Security.
43. For more discussion on how the white South African government hurt itself, see Stephen Davis, *Apartheid's Rebels: Inside South Africa's Hidden War* (New Haven: Yale University Press, 1987), 201ff.
44. Tutu, "Oxford Union Address—South Africa: Why I Am Hopeful," Feb. 23, 1994.
45. Which Tutu defines as "the obscurantist tactics of senior police. And the allegations by a supreme court judge that police were carrying out well planned murder. . . . It is good that the State President somewhat reluctantly it seemed, has appointed a judge to preside over a reopened inquest, though it is quite unsatisfactory that a magistrate with a dubious record has been asked to look into police conduct relating to the Trust Feed scandal" (Tutu, "Cape Town Diocesan Council Charge," St. Oswald's Church, Milnerton, May 23, 1992).
46. Tutu, in Hennie Serfontein, "God Has a Plan." *Vryeweekblad*, Sept. 4–10, 1992.
47. Serfontein, "God Has a Plan." Tutu was even thinking of de Klerk for the Nobel Peace Prize in 1990, "If [Mandela and de Klerk] get negotiations underway I undertake to nominate them for the joint award of the Nobel Peace Prize." Tutu, "Synod of the Diocese of Cape Town Charge," October 17–20, 1990.
48. Tutu, "Oxford Union Address."
49. "Tutu Says Local Press Is White-Oriented," in *Weekend Argus*, May 8–9, 1993, 13.

Chapter 5: The Purge of Relationships

1. Tutu, handwritten address, "The Church and Human Rights in South Africa," University of South Africa, Centre for Human Rights, May 18, 1992.

2. Albert John Luthuli, *Let My People Go* (New York: McGraw-Hill, 1962), 114. Luthuli won the Nobel Peace Prize in 1961.

3. Stephen Davis, *Apartheid's Rebels: Inside South Africa's Hidden War* (New Haven: Yale University Press, 1987), 203.

4. Tutu, "Hope against Despair," in *A Book of Hope* (Cape Town: David Philip, 1992), 19.

5. Tutu, "Hope against Despair," 19.

6. See Dennis Cruywagen, *The Spiritual Mandela: Faith and Religion in the Life of South Africa's Great Statesman* (Capetown: Penguin Random House South Africa, 2016).

7. Archbishop Desmond and Mrs. Leah Tutu welcomed me to live with them at Bishopscourt, 1993–94. Archbishop Tutu also ordained me to the priesthood on my birthday, Dec. 12, 1993.

8. Tutu, handwritten address, "The Bible and Human Rights," Madrid, Spain, 1991.

9. Tutu, remarks at St. George's Cathedral, Cape Town, on Apr. 14, 1993, for Chris Hani's memorial service.

10. Some quotes from my notes on the scene and some from John Yeld, "Tutu's Message to 'God's Rainbow People,'" *The Argus*, Apr. 15, 1993.

11. Tutu, transcript of sermon at the funeral of Chris Hani on Apr. 19, 1993, Bishopscourt update.

12. Ross Dunn, "A Loud, Strong Voice for Peace," *Age*, Melbourne, Oct. 4, 1993.

13. Tutu, "Oxford Union Address—South Africa: Why I Am Hopeful," Feb. 23, 1994.

14. Tutu, "Oxford Union Address."

15. "Tutu Arranges Watershed Talks," *The Argus*, June 7, 1993.

16. Dunn, "A Loud, Strong Voice."

17. "Tutu Pleads for Calm in Face of Attacks by 'Ghastly' Men," *The Argus*, Apr. 25, 1994.

18. Tutu, "Oxford Union Address."

19. "Tutu Warns 'Political' Priests," *Cape Times*, Apr. 14, 1994. Also, for Tutu's contention with priests who want to get involved with politics, see Tutu, "Preamble" (address, "Apartheid and Christianity," Sept. 24, 1982), 6f., about difference between authoritative and authoritarian.

20. "Tutu Condemns 'Racist Tactics,'" *Cape Times*, Apr. 18, 1994.

21. Tutu, "The Theologian and the Gospel of Freedom," in *The Trial of Faith: Theology and the Church Today*, ed. Peter Eaton (West Sussex, England: Churchman, 1988), 53.

22. Tutu, address, "Installation of John Gardener as Principal of Bishops," Oct. 21, 1988.

23. Tutu, in "Africa's Turbulent Priest," *Varsity* no. 406 (Mar. 4, 1994), Oxford, England.

24. Anthony Langenhoven, quoted in "Priest 'Unrepentant,'" *Cape Times*, Apr. 15, 1994.

25. "Catholic Church Sees a Future in Apartheid's Sunset," *Natal Witness*, Oct. 9, 1991.

26. Rowan Smith, quoted in Carmel Rickard, "Top ANC Candidates Face Church Censure," *Sunday Times*, Jan. 30, 1994.

27. Gaye Davis, "Tutu Backs Church Ban on Priestly Politics," *The Weekly Mail*, received in Rhodes University Library, July 17, 1990.

28. Boesak quoted in Ulrich Duchrow, *Conflict over the Ecumenical Movement: Confessing Christ Today in the Universal Church* (Geneva: World Council of Churches, 1981), 1.
29. Allan Boesak, quoted in Charles D. Flaendorp et al., *Festschrift in Honor of Allan Boesak: A Life in Black Liberation Theology* (Stellenbosch: SUN Media, an imprint of RapidAccess Publishing, 2016), 98.
30. Allan Boesak, *Black and Reformed: Apartheid, Liberation, and the Calvinist Tradition* (Maryknoll, NY: Orbis Books, 1984), 38.
31. Boesak, *Black and Reformed*, 38.
32. Tutu, address, "A Little Crystal Ball Gazing," Cape Town Press Club, May 15, 1981.
33. Tutu, "A Little Crystal Ball."
34. *Good Hope*, a newsletter publication from the Anglican Diocese of Cape Town, Apr. 1994.
35. Tutu, "It Has Happened at Last," unpublished end piece for book to mark election and end of apartheid for *The Guardian*, London.
36. Tutu, "The South African Elections," *Der Zeit*, May 1, 1994.
37. Tutu, "This Is Now My Country," *The Argus*, May 3, 1994.

Part 2: Illumination

1. https://www.instagram.com/p/BlR01lsHfOm/?utm_source=ig_embed&utm_campaign=embed_loading_state_control; "Trevor Noah Defends 'Africa Won the World Cup' Joke," *BBC News*, July 19, 2018, https://www.bbc.com/news/world-africa-44885923.

Chapter 6: Confessor as Tutu's Ordering Identity

1. Tutu, "The Vineyard of Naboth and Duncan Village," East London, Oct. 31, 1981.
2. Tutu, "Towards Koinonia in Faith, Life and Witness," World Council of Churches Faith and Order Conference, Santiago de Compostela, Spain, Aug. 3, 1993, 6.
3. *Pseudo-Dionysius the Complete Works*, trans. Colm Luibheid (New York: Paulist, 1987), 50.
4. It must be noted here that Anglicanism also spread with the violence of the British Empire.
5. Bernard of Clairvaux, *The Twelve Steps of Humility and Pride, and On Loving God* (London: Hodder & Stoughton, 1985), chap. 7.
6. Bernard of Clairvaux, *On the Song of Songs*, 4 vols. (Kalamazoo, MI: Cistercian, 1971–80), Sermon 7. See also Sermon 83.
7. Bernard of Clairvaux, *Song of Songs*, Sermon 7.
8. Bernard of Clairvaux, *Song of Songs*, Sermon 3.
9. See Desmond Tutu, *No Future without Forgiveness* (New York: Doubleday, 1999).
10. See Michael Battle, *Reconciliation: The Ubuntu Theology of Desmond Tutu* (Cleveland: Pilgrim, 1996); and *The Wisdom of Desmond Tutu* (Oxford, England: Lion, 1998).
11. Source unknown and seems to parallel a desert saying of Abba Lot and Abba Joseph in Benedicta Ward, trans., *The Desert Fathers: Sayings of the Early Christian Monks* (London: Penguin Books, 2003), 12.8.
12. Tinyiko Sam Maluleke, "Can Lions and Rabbits Reconcile? The South African TRC as an Instrument for Peace-Building," *Ecumenical Review* 53, no. 2 (Apr. 2001): 191.

13. I paraphrase Maluleke's version of the story here. Maluleke also acknowledges other versions of the story. See Njabulo Ndebele, "Of Lions and Rabbits: Thoughts on Democracy and Reconciliation," in Wilmot James and Linda Van der Vijver, eds., *After the TRC: Reflections on Truth and Reconciliation* (Cape Town: David Philip, 2000), 143–62.

14. Maluleke, "Lions and Rabbits," 191.

15. Maluleke, "Lions and Rabbits," 192.

16. Nelson Mandela, *Long Walk to Freedom* (London: Little, Brown, 1996), 182f.

17. Maluleke, "Lions and Rabbits," 192.

18. Maluleke, "Lions and Rabbits," 192–93.

19. Maluluke, "Lions and Rabbits," 193.

20. Daan Bronkhorst, *Truth and Reconciliation: Obstacles and Opportunities for Human Rights* (Amsterdam: Amnesty International, 1995), 85–89.

21. Maluleke, "Lions and Rabbits," 194.

22. David K. Shipler, *Arab and Jew: Wounded Spirits in a Promised Land* (London: Penguin, 1986), 15.

23. Set for Dec. 1993. Meanwhile the TRC suggested a prolongation of this period up to May 10, 1994, which is the day President Mandela took office. This extension would provide the inclusion of acts of violence committed prior to the first general elections held on Apr. 27, 1994.

24. *Truth and Reconciliation Commission of South Africa Report*, vol. 1 (Cape Town: CTP Books, 1998), 55.

25. Tutu, *No Future without Forgiveness*, esp. chap. 2, "Nuremberg or National Amnesia? A Third Way," 13–20.

26. Tutu, *No Future without Forgiveness*, 20–33.

27. See both *Truth Talk, The Official Newsletter of the Truth and Reconciliation Commission*, vol. 2, no. 1 (Mar. 1997); and more recent discussions about reparations in Ra'eesa Pather, "Ramaphosa under Pressure to Support Reparations for Apartheid Victims," *Mail & Guardian*, Dec. 17, 2018.

28. "The Mandate," in *Truth and Reconciliation Commission of South Africa Report*, vol. 1, 49.

29. Pather, "Ramaphosa under Pressure." Also see the article "South Africa Takes a Step Closer to Land Expropriation–But Opponents Say It Can't Afford It, after the Coronavirus," *BusinessTech*, July 1, 2020, https://businesstech.co.za/news/property/412357/south-africa-takes-a-step-closer-to-land-expropriation-but-opponents-say-it-cant-afford-it-after-the-coronavirus/.

30. *Truth Talk* 1, no. 1 (Nov. 1996).

31. Tutu, *No Future without Forgiveness*, 272.

32. Tutu, "Address," in *Truth Talk* 1, no. 1 (Nov. 1996).

33. To illustrate Tutu's passion for universal atonement, Professor Liz Bounds told me that several divinity students in Tutu's class at the Candler School of Theology at Emory University had great difficulty accepting Tutu's universal salvation.

34. David Beresford, "Fisher of Men, Seeker of Truth," *Mail & Guardian*, Johannesburg, Dec. 19, 1997.

35. The other chair of the TRC was Alex Boraine.

36. Beresford, "Fisher of Men, Seeker of Truth."

37. Beresford, "Fisher of Men, Seeker of Truth."

38. See *Truth and Reconciliation Commission of South Africa Report*.

39. "SA Violence: Ours Are Birthing Pains—Tutu," *Daily Nation*, Nairobi, Kenya, Oct. 9, 1993.

40. Allister Sparks, *Tomorrow Is Another Country: The Inside Story of South Africa's Negotiated Revolution* (Cape Town: Tafelberg, 1994), 204.

41. Maluleke, "Lions and Rabbits," 195.

42. "Africa's Turbulent Priest," *Varsity*, no. 406, Oxford, England, Mar. 4, 1994, 8.
43. Tutu, "Church and Prophecy in South Africa Today," *Essex Papers in Theology and Society* (Centre for the Study of Theology in the University of Essex, 1991), 14.
44. Jonathan Jansen, "The Big Read: Leah Tutu True Grit behind the Glory," *The Sunday Times*, South Africa, Oct. 25, 2013.
45. Jansen, "The Big Read."
46. Jansen, "The Big Read."
47. John Allen, *Rabble-Rouser for Peace: The Authorized Biography of Desmond Tutu* (London: Rider, 2006), 144.
48. James Loder, *The Transforming Moment: Understanding Convictional Experiences* (San Francisco: Harper & Row, 1981), 96–121.
49. Loder, *The Transforming Moment*, 103.
50. Tutu, address, "Liberating Truth and Questioning Minds," University of Cape Town, Sept. 22, 1983.
51. Tutu, Bishop's Charge: "The God Who Takes Risks," Diocese of Cape Town, Clergy Synod, St. Savior's Church, Claremont, June 3–4, 1991.
52. Tutu, sermon, printed after Oct. 7, 1989.
53. For other examples of biographical accounts of how African ecclesiastical figures impacted their contexts, see *Rise Up and Walk: The Autobiography of Bishop Abel Tendekai Muzorewa*, ed. Norman E. Thomas (Nashville: Abingdon, 1978).
54. This question was raised during a session at the 1999 Parliament of Religions, Cape Technicon.
55. Tutu, "Birmingham Cathedral Address," 1.
56. Tutu, sermons, "Blessed Are the Meek for They Shall Inherit the Earth," BBC Lenten Series, Feb. 16, 1988.
57. See Simon Maimela, "Hammering Swords into Ploughshares," in *Hammering Swords into Ploughshares: Essays in Honor of Archbishop Mpilo Desmond Tutu*, ed. Buti Tlhagale and Itu Meleng Mosala (Grand Rapids: Eerdmans, 1986), 42.
58. Michael Worsnip, *Between the Two Fires: The Anglican Church and Apartheid 1948–1957* (Pietermarizburg: University of Natal Press, 1991), 13.
59. Ms. M. McComb, Claremont, "Tutu's Stand on Violence Hypocritical," *Weekend Argus*, Aug. 14–15, 1993.
60. T. Dunbar Moodie, *The Rise of Afrikanerdom: Power, Apartheid, and the Afrikaner Civil Religion* (Berkeley: University of California Press, 1975).
61. Mahmood Mamdani, "A Diminshed Truth," in James and Van der Vijver, eds., *After the TRC*, 58–61.
62. Max Du Preez, "Foreword," in Wendy Orr, *From Biko to Basson* (Cape Town: Contra, 2000).
63. Colin Bundy, "The Beast of the Past: History and the TRC," in James and Van der Vijver, *After the TRC*, 13.
64. *TRC Report* 1, no. 2, 18.
65. Albie Sachs, "His Name Was Henry," in James and Van der Vijver, *After the TRC*, 98.
66. Maluleke, "Lions and Rabbits," 196.
67. Anthea Jeffrey, *The Truth about the Truth Commission* (Johannesburg: South African Institute for Race Relations, 1999).
68. Van Zyl Frederick Slabbert, "Truth without Reconciliation, Reconciliation without Truth," in James and Van des Vijver, *After the TRC*, 62–72.
69. Maluleke, "Lions and Rabbits," 196.
70. Tutu, *No Future without Forgiveness*.
71. Maluleke, "Lions and Rabbits," 197.

72. Albie Sachs, in Maluleke, "Lions and Rabbits," 197–98, citing Tutu, *No Future without Forgiveness*, 98.
73. Mark Gevisser, "The Ultimate Test of Faith," in *Mail and Guardian*, Apr. 18, 1996, 12.
74. Tutu, "Preface," in Anne Coomes, *Festo Kivengere: A Biography* (Eastbourne, UK: Monarch, 1990), 9.
75. Some examples are Albert Luthuli, Trevor Huddleston, Allan Boesak, Beyers Naudé, Peter Storey, Frank Chikane, John de Gruchy, Charles Villa-Vicencio.
76. This has been an incessant dualism peculiar to the Western world.
77. Tutu, handwritten undated address for Congressional Subcommittee on Africa.

Chapter 7: Mystical Illumination of Community and Suffering

1. Rebecca Davis, "Ramaphosa Stays Mum on Nene as He Delivers Tutu Lecture with Forceful Focus on Land," *Daily Maverick*, Oct. 8, 2018. I rely here on Edwin Arrison's reporting of this event and his source here of Rebecca Davis's article.
2. Andisiwe Makinana, "Ramaphosa: Returning the Land Will 'Restore the Dignity of Our People,'" *Sunday Times*, Oct. 8, 2018.
3. Davis, "Ramaphosa Stays Mum."
4. Extract from Wilhelm Verwoerd, *Verwoerd: My Journey through Family Betrayals* (Cape Town: Tafelberg Publishers, 2019), 235–37.
5. Verwoerd, *Verwoerd: My Journey*, 235–37.
6. Tutu, "Birmingham Cathedral Address," 3.
7. Vladimir Lossky, *Orthodox Theology* (Crestwood, NY: St. Vladimir's Press, 1989), 42.
8. See Catherine La Cugna, *God for Us: The Trinity and the Christian Life* (San Francisco: HarperSanFrancisco, 1991). She provides good theological insight into being a person in relation to others. Also see Harry Williams, *The True Wilderness* (London: Constable Press, 1972), which Tutu refers to in "The Nature and Value of Theology" as showing that the doctrine of the Trinity assures us that we are not destined to an eternity of isolation.
9. Tutu goes on to give an illustration about the necessity of giving for life, just as one who only receives, finds death, just like the Dead Sea, in which nothing can survive as it only receives its current. Tutu, in handwritten sermon, St. George's Cathedral, Aug. 21, 1986, where 1 Cor. 4:7 seems to be the text: "For who sees anything different in you? What have you that you did not receive? If then you received it, why do you boast as if it were not a gift?"
10. Tutu, "A Christian Vision of the Future of South Africa."
11. Tutu, address, "The Nature and Value of Theology," undated.
12. Tutu, "Human Rights in South Africa," in *Monitor*, SACC Library Resource Center, undated.
13. Tutu, quoted in *Prayers for Peace, An Anthology of Readings and Prayers Selected by Archbishop Robert Runcie and Cardinal Basil Hume* (London: SPCK, 1987), 41.
14. Tutu, handwritten sermon, Sunday School Teachers' Eucharist, St. George's Cathedral, Feb. 2, 1987.
15. Tutu, "The Nature and Value of Theology."
16. Tutu, Heading: Matthew chapter 5 verse 13, USA?
17. See Michael Battle, *Heaven on Earth: God's Call to Community in the Book of Revelation* (Louisville. KY: Westminster John Knox, 2017).
18. Tutu, undated sermon, "The Marks of the Church."
19. Tutu, address I heard at the University of Stellenbosch with Kader Asmal.

20. Here Simone Weil's distinction between pain (suffering that can be alleviated) and affliction (suffering that leaves a permanent scar) is insightful. See Simone Weil, *Waiting on God* (New York: Putnam, 1951), 69.

21. This is only one example of the depths of affliction faced in South African society. I was deeply struck by this affliction when I attended a TRC hearing in which a young man, unable to walk, wept bitterly on the witness stand (TRC Hearing, Worcester, South Africa, June 21, 1999).

22. Nelson Mandela, in Preface of the Framework of the Reconstruction and Development Program Document; https://omalley.nelsonmandela.org/omalley/index .php/site/q/03lv02039/04lv02103/05lv02120/06lv02126.htm.

23. *Truth and Reconciliation Commission of South Africa Report*, vol. 1 (Cape Town: CTP Books, 1998), 5.

24. "The Horror . . . ," *Mail & Guardian*, Aug. 8–14, 1997. I saw one of the productions of *Ubu and the Truth Commission*, in July 1997 at the Grahamstown Festival. This review article comments upon the production in Johannesburg at the Market Theater, Aug. 14–30, 1997.

25. Jan Munnik, in "Police 'Cover Up' Torture Claims," *Mail & Guardian*, Aug. 8–14, 1997.

26. Tutu, sermon, printed after Oct. 7, 1989.

27. Tutu provides the following humorous account of Adam's search for a wife in "Birmingham Cathedral Address" and "Why We Must Oppose Apartheid."

28. Tutu, "Birmingham Cathedral Address," 3.

29. Tutu, address, "Love Reveals My Neighbor, My Responsibility," Dec. 16, 1981.

30. Ifeanyi A. Menkiti, "Person and Community in African Traditional Thought," in R. A. Wright, ed., *African Philosophy* (New York: University Press of America, 1971), 166.

31. Tutu's handwritten sermons, "Genesis Chapter 3," St. Mary's, Blechingly, Surrey, Oct. 6, 1985.

32. Jean-Paul Sartre, "Existentialism Is a Humanism," in Nino Languilli, ed., *The Existentialism Tradition: Selected Writings*, trans. Philip Mairet (New York: Doubleday Anchor, 1971), 399.

33. *Facing the Truth with Bill Moyers*, DVD 1999. Bill Moyers and Gail Pellett speak with apartheid victims and participants during the TRC hearings.

34. As newly visible and often-virulent groups of white nationalists have invoked genetic research to claim racial superiority, some geneticists have suggested that the field was not doing enough to counter the claims. See Amy Harmon, "Geneticists Criticize Use of Science by White Nationalists to Justify 'Racial Purity,'" *New York Times*, Oct. 19, 2018.

35. See Jacey Fortin, "James H. Cone, a Founder of Black Liberation Theology, Dies at 79," *New York Times*, Apr. 29, 2018. Cone was a central figure in the development of black liberation theology and a professor at Union Theological Seminary.

36. Tutu may describe this also as transfiguration, a concept he told me in 1993 that he would find interest in developing further into a book.

37. I also wrote about Tutu's theology of such vision in Battle, *Heaven on Earth*, 165–66.

38. Simone Weil, "Reflections on the Right Use of School Studies with a View to the Love of God," in *Simone Weil Reader*, ed. George A. Panichas (New York: McKay, 1977), 44.

39. Simone Weil, *Oppression and Liberty*, trans. Arthur Wills and John Petrie (Amherst: University of Massachusetts Press, 1958), 108.

40. Simone Weil, *Notebooks*, 2 vols., trans. Arthur Wills (London: Routledge, 1956), 507.

41. Tutu, "My Credo," in *Living Philosophies: The Reflections of Some Eminent Men and Women of Our Time*, ed. Clifton Fadiman (New York: Doubleday, 1990).

    For Tutu quotes hereafter see Michael Battle, *Reconciliation: The Ubuntu Theology of Desmond Tutu* (Cleveland: Pilgrim, 1996), appendix.

42. E. W. F. Tomlin, *Simone Weil* (New Haven, CT: Yale University Press, 1954), 60.
43. Simone Weil, *Gravity and Grace* (New York: Putnam, 1952), 13.
44. Simone Weil, *Waiting on God* (New York: Putnam, 1951), 77.
45. Tutu, sermons, Bible Study for St Alban's Clergy, Lambeth, 1988.
46. Tutu, "My Credo," 232.
47. Tutu, sermons, Bible study for St Alban's Clergy, Lambeth, 1988.
48. Tutu, handwritten notes, undated.
49. John 3:9, 12.
50. See Battle, *Reconciliation*.
51. Tutu, "Towards Koinonia in Faith, Life and Witness," 8–9.
52. One may see how Tutu operates from restorative justice through his work as chair of the Truth and Reconciliation Commission in South Africa (1994–97).
53. Tutu, "My Credo," 232–33.
54. Weil, *Gravity and Grace*, 33; cf. also 150: "Unobtrusiveness, the infinitesimal character of pure good."
55. Weil's view here is especially crucial to how Tutu viewed his work with the Truth and Reconciliation Commission, whose objective was the complete exposure of past political crimes so as never to repeat them again.
56. See Weil's "Condition Premiere d'un Travail Non Servile," in *La Condition ouvrière*, 261–73 (1951). Published October 16, 2002 by Gallimard Education.
57. Weil, *Gravity and Grace*, 153.
58. See John Milbank, *Theology and Social Theory: Beyond Secular Reason* (Oxford: Basil Blackwell, 1991).
59. Weil, *Gravity and Grace*, 153.
60. Weil, *The Need for Roots* (Boston: Beacon, 1952), 49.
61. Weil, *Gravity and Grace*, 145.
62. Tomlin, *Simone Weil*, 56–57.
63. Weil, *The Need for Roots*, 49.
64. Weil, *The Need for Roots*, 49.
65. Tutu, "Suffering Witness."
66. Tutu, "Genesis Chapter 3."
67. Simone Weil's thought is especially interesting in her concept of affliction, *malheur* in French, because she believes that the human creature has the opportunity to "un-create" a fallen existence. This *malheur* is the only thing besides beauty with the capacity to convert one's attention toward God. In effect, "Affliction, when it is consented to and accepted and loved, is truly a baptism." See *The Simone Weil Reader*, 439–68. Augustine Shutte states that he provides "detailed application of Weil's ideas to the South African Situation," especially her ideas of uprootedness. See Augustine Shutte, *Philosophy for Africa* (Rondebosch, South Africa: UCT Press, 1993).
68. Gregory of Nyssa referred to in Vladimir Lossky, *The Mystical Theology of the Eastern Church* (Crestwood, NY: St. Vladimir's Press, 1976), 197.
69. Tutu, "Birmingham Cathedral Address," 2.
70. Maggie Ross, *The Fountain and the Furnace: The Way of Tears and Fire* (New York: Paulist Press, 1987), 79. This book is categorized by Ross in the following way, "I realize now, only at the end of writing this book, that I have undertaken a survey of spiritual theology in which the idea of kenosis is absolutely central, and in which tears play the crucial role." Ross, 3.

71. Tutu, address, "Where is Now Thy God?" Trinity Institute, New York, Jan. 8, 1989.
72. Tutu, address, "The Spirit of the Lord Is upon Me," Trinity Institute, New York, 1989. See also Ross, *Fountain and Furnace*, 201.
73. Tutu, address, "The Spirit of the Lord Is upon Me," Trinity Institute, New York, 1989.
74. Tutu, sermon, printed after Oct. 7, 1989.
75. Tutu, address, Statement of Bishop Desmond Tutu at South African Council of Churches General Conference on the Death of Jenny Curtis and her Daughter, June 29, 1984.
76. Tutu, sermon, "The Holy Spirit and South Africa Today," St Alban's Cathedral, Oct. 29, 1983.
77. Tutu, undated dddress, "Suffering and Witness."
78. Tutu, undated address, "Suffering and Witness."
79. Tutu, undated address, "Suffering and Witness."

Chapter 8: Tutu's Racial Identity

1. Tutu, *The Rainbow People of God* (New York: Doubleday, 1994.
2. Gail Gerhart, *Black Power in South Africa: The Evolution of an Ideology* (Berkeley and Los Angeles: University of California, 1978), 21.
3. Gerhart, *Black Power*, 24.
4. Leonard Thompson, *A History of South Africa* (New Haven, CT: Yale University Press, 1990), 154–87.
5. This also became known as the South African Native National Convention.
6. See all of the African groups in attendance: André Odendall, *Black Protest Politics in South Africa to 1912* (Totowa, NJ: Barnes & Noble, 1984), 168.
7. Native Affairs Commission, quoted in Gerhart, *Black Power*, 23.
8. Hopkins provides this apt description of Tutu's theology as relational black theology. See Dwight N. Hopkins, *Black Theology USA and South Africa: Politics, Culture, and Liberation* (Maryknoll, NY: Orbis, 1989), 138f.
9. Tutu, *Hope and Suffering* (Grand Rapids: Eerdmans, 1984), 66–67.
10. "Greetings from Bishop Tutu to the Soweto Students, June 16, 1977," *Pro Veritate*, June 1977, 6, quoted in Peter Walshe, *Church Versus State in South Africa* (New York: Orbis, 1983), 214.
11. See my book, Michael Battle, *The Black Church in America: African American Christian Spirituality* (Oxford: Blackwell, 2006).
12. Edward A. Gargan, "Pretoria Rescinds Pass-Law Control on Blacks' Moves," *New York Times*, Apr. 19, 1986.
13. Tutu, quoted in Gargan, "Pretoria Rescinds."
14. See André Odendaal's historical essay, "Resistance, Reform, and Repression in South Africa in the 1980s," in *Beyond the Barricades* (New York: Aperture Foundation, and the Center for Documentary Studies at Duke University, 1989), 137.
15. Quoted in Allister Sparks, *The Mind of South Africa* (New York: Ballantine Books, 1990), 67.
16. Fr. Buti Tlhagale, Introduction in *Hope and Suffering*, 21.
17. Tutu, quoted in Allister Sparks, *Tomorrow Is Another Country: The Inside Story of South Africa's Negotiated Revolution* (Cape Town: Tafelberg, 1994), 289.
18. Tutu, quoted in Sparks, *Tomorrow*, 298.
19. Tutu, *Hope and Suffering*, 38.
20. "Desmond M.B. Tutu, Dean of St Mary's Cathedral, Johannesburg, to the Hon. Prime Minister Mr John B. Vorster, 8 May 1976," *South African Outlook*, July 1976, 102–4, quoted in Walshe, *Church Versus State in South Africa*, 204.

21. Tutu, "Greetings to the Soweto Students," in Walshe, *Church versus State*, 213.
22. Sheridan Johns and R. Hunt Davis Jr., eds., *Mandela, Tambo, and the African National Congress: The Struggle against Apartheid, 1948–1990, a Documentary Survey* (New York: Oxford University Press, 1991), 98.
23. Johns and Davis, *Mandela, Tambo, and the African National Congress*, 194.
24. Tutu, quoted in Sparks, *Tomorrow*, 292.
25. Johns and Davis, *Mandela, Tambo, and the African National Congress*, 196.
26. P. W. Botha, quoted in *Journal of Theology for Southern Africa* no. 63 (June 1988): 78, quoted in Sparks, *Tomorrow*, 279–80.
27. *Journal of Theology for Southern Africa* no. 63 (June 1988): 82–83, quoted in Sparks, *Tomorrow*, 280.
28. Tutu, quoted in Sparks, *Tomorrow*, 291.
29. Bonganjalo C. Goba, from a Mar. 2, 1987, interview, quoted in Dwight N. Hopkins, *Black Theology*, 29. Bonganjalo C. Goba, a minister in the United Congregational Church in South Africa, served as president of the Albert Luthuli College of the Federal Theological Seminary and worked with Steve Biko and the Black Consciousness Movement in the 1960s and 1970s.
30. Gerhart, *Black Power*, 201.
31. Hopkins, *Black Theology*, 97.
32. Odendaal, *Black Protest*, 194.
33. Peter Walshe, *The Rise of African Nationalism in South Africa: The African National Congress, 1912–1952* (Berkeley and Los Angeles: University of California Press, 1971), 7–15, 158–69.
34. Walshe, *Rise of African Nationalism*, 7.
35. Odendaal, *Black Protest*, 4.
36. Odendaal, *Black Protest*, 21.
37. See Lamin Sanneh, *Translating the Message: The Missionary Impact on Culture* (Maryknoll, NY: Orbis, 1990).
38. Lamin Sanneh, "Christian Mission in the Pluralist Milieu: The African Experience," *International Review of Mission* 74 (1985): 200.
39. Sanneh, "Christian Mission," 202.
40. Gerhart, *Black Power*, 39.
41. Vincent Donovan, "The Naked Gospel: Stamping Out Ready-to-Wear Christianity," *U.S. Catholic* 46, no. 6 (1981): 26, quoted in Sanneh, "Christian Mission in the Pluralist Milieu," 432.
42. Gerhart, *Black Power*, 42.
43. Gerhart, *Black Power*, 73.
44. See Tutu's handwritten sermons, "Genesis Chapter 3," St Mary's, Blechingly, Surrey, Oct. 6, 1985 (Tutu was at this church in 1965–66 as a part-time curate).

Chapter 9: Leaving Church

1. Barbara Brown Taylor, *Christian Century* 116, no. 18 (June 16–23, 1999): 655. Also see her book, Barbara Brown Taylor, *Leaving Church: A Memoir of Faith* (San Francisco: HarperSanFrancisco, 2006).
2. The concept of Ubuntu remains the core of Tutu's ethic and relates to the development of Anglicanism in South Africa as a "minority" religion in that Anglicanism became "successful" only to the extent that the European hierarchy of the Church of the Province of Southern Africa was willing to indigenize its leadership and direction.
3. For more demographics during apartheid, see Peter Walshe, *Church Versus State in South Africa: The Case of the Christian Institute* (Maryknoll, NY: Orbis, 1983).

4. Albert Luthuli, *Let My People Go* (Maryknoll, NY: Orbis, 1983), 19.

5. For detailed analysis of the Cottesloe Consultation, see Walshe, *Church Versus State*, 10–19.

6. SACC, *A Message to the People of South Africa* 7 (1968).

7. Peter Walshe, "The Evolution of Liberation Theology in South Africa," in *Journal of Law and Religion* 5, no. 2 (1987): 300–303.

8. Early examples of this Black Theology, including papers by Sabelo Ntwasa, Manas Buthelezi, Steve Biko, Nyameko Pityana, and Bonganjalo Goba, can be found in Basil Moore, ed., *Black Theology: The South African Voice* (London: C. Hurst, 1973).

9. See the early works of Allan Boesak: *Farewell to Innocence: A Social-Ethical Study of Black Theology and Black Power* (Maryknoll, NY: Orbis, 1977); *The Finger of God: Sermons on Faith and Responsibility* (Maryknoll, NY: Orbis, 1982); *Black and Reformed: Apartheid, Liberation, and the Calvinist Tradition* (Maryknoll, NY: Orbis Books, 1984); and *If This Is Treason, I Am Guilty* (Trenton, NJ: African World Press, 1987).

10. Albert Nolan, *Taking Sides* (n.p.: Catholic Institute for International Relations, 1984), 9.

11. Mangosuthu Buthelezi, "Memorandum for Discussion with the Archbishop of Canterbury," Cape Town, Jan. 22, 1993.

12. Buthelezi, "An Appeal to the Primates of the Anglican Communion," Cape Town, Jan. 22, 1993. Buthelezi's relationship with Tutu has been ambivalent, as shown by Buthelezi's overt display of irritation toward the delivery of a prayer by Tutu in 1991. See "The Isolation of Chief Buthelezi," *Sunday Times*, Sept. 22, 1991. Also see "Buthelezi Critical of Church," in *Communion 93*, a publication of the CPSA on the occasion of the joint meeting of the Primates of the Anglican Communion and the Anglican Consultative Council, Jan. 1993.

13. "The Isolation of Chief Buthelezi," *Sunday Times*, Sept. 22, 1991.

14. Tutu, "Viability," in *Relevant Theology for Africa: Report on a Consultation of the Missiological Institute at Lutheran Theological College, Mapumulo, Natal, September 12–21, 1972*, ed. Hans-Jurgen Becken (Durban: Lutheran Publishing House, 1973), 39.

15. Tutu, undated speech, "The Evolution of Apartheid," 1985–86.

16. For a good investigation of this, see Charles Villa-Vicencio, *Civil Disobedience and Beyond: Law, Resistance, and Religion in South Africa* (Grand Rapids: Eerdmans, 1990).

17. Tutu, "Postscript: To Be Human Is to Be Free," in *Christianity and Democracy in Global Context*, ed. John Witte Jr. (Boulder, CO: Westview, 1993), 314.

18. Tutu, quoted in Shirley du Boulay, *Tutu: Voice of the Voiceless* (London: Hodder & Stoughton, 1988), 44.

19. Tutu, *God Is Not a Christian: And Other Provocations* (San Francisco: HarperOne, 2011).

20. Tutu, *God Is Not a Christian*, 5.

21. The Dalai Lama and Desmond Tutu, *The Book of Joy: Lasting Happiness in a Changing World* (New York: Avery Imprint of Penguin Random House, 2016).

Part 3: Union

1. Tutu, in "The Views of Society," *RSA-Beleidsoorsig/Policy Review*, Nov.–Dec. 1993.

Chapter 10: Tutu's Unifying Role

1. *Book of Common Prayer* (New York: Seabury, 1979), 258.
2. Tutu, *Apartheid Is a Heresy*, ed. John de Gruchy and Charles Villa-Vicencio (Grand Rapids: Eerdmans, 1983), 40.
3. Bernard of Clairvaux, *On the Song of Songs*, 4 vols. (Kalamazoo, MI: Cistercian, 1971–80), Sermon 3.
4. Evelyn Underhill, *The Essentials of Mysticism and Other Essays* (London: Dent, 1920), 22.
5. Etienne Gilson, *The Mystical Theology of St. Bernard* (London: Sheed & Ward, 1940), 105.
6. Martin Buber, *I and Thou* (New York: Scribner's, 1958), 8–9.
7. Bernard of Clairvaux, *Song of Songs*, Sermon 32.
8. Bernard of Clairvaux, *Song of Songs*, Sermon 32.
9. Friedrich Heiler, *Prayer: A Study in the History and Psychology of Religion* (New York: Oxford University Press, 1932), 215.
10. John de Gruchy, *The Church Struggle in South Africa* (Minneapolis: Fortress Press, 2005), 100.
11. "Africa's Turbulent Priest," *Varsity* no. 406, Oxford, England (Mar. 4, 1994): 8.
12. "Africa's Turbulent Priest," *Varsity*, 8.
13. Tutu, "Towards Koinonia in Faith, Life and Witness," in *Translating the Word, Transforming the World, An Ecumenical Reader*, ed. Amele Adamavi-Aho Edue, Marion Grau, and Atola Longkumer (Geneva: WCC Publications, 2018), 14.
14. Tutu, address, "South Africa on the Way to 2000 A.D.," Mar. 31, 1980.
15. Tutu, "South Africa's Blacks: Aliens in Their Own Land," *Christianity and Crisis*, Nov. 26, 1984, 133.
16. For a more detailed study of the arms trade in South Africa, see Terry Crawford-Browne, *Eyes on the Money* (Cape Town: Umuzi, an imprint of Random House Struik, 2007); Terry Crawford-Browne, "The Challenge to Disarm," a paper delivered at the consultation on "South Africa in Regional and Global Context: Being the Church Today," Vanderbijlpark, Mar. 19–23, 1995, 115–22; Terry Crawford-Browne, "No Farewell to Arms," *Sojourners* 24 (1995): 13.
17. U.S. Department of State, "Background Notes: South Africa," Washington, DC, May 1985.
18. *Have You Heard from Johannesburg? Apartheid and the Club of the West*, partial transcript, Jan. 2006, online version, Clarity Films, http://www.newsreel.org/transcripts/Have-You-Heard-From-Johannesburg-transcript.html.
19. See Eleanor Greene, *Bishop Desmond Tutu: Apartheid in South Africa* (New York: International Merchandising Corp., 1990), 32–33.
20. Tutu, "The United States and South Africa: Human Rights and American Policy," *Columbia Human Rights Law Review* 17, no. 1 (Fall 1985): 5–6.
21. Tutu, "South Africa's Blacks," 133.
22. Michael Schluter, "A Passion for Justice," *Third Way* 17, no. 4 (May 1994): 16. The editor of *Third Way* approached me in England in August 1993 for the possibility of my arranging this interview with John Allen, Tutu's media secretary, and Tutu later granted.
23. Tutu, handwritten undated address, "Disinvestment and All That."
24. Tutu, handwritten undated, Text #2.
25. "Happy Tutu Calls for Investment," *Evening Post*, Nov. 18, 1993.
26. "The Archbishop, the Church and the Nation," in *Monitor: The Journal of the Human Rights Trust*, June 1991 (Port Elizabeth: Monitor Publications), 7.
27. Tutu, "Towards Koinonia in Faith, Life and Witness," World Council of Churches Faith and Order Conference, Santiago de Compostela, Spain, Aug. 3, 1993, 6.

28. For a more comprehensive look at the impact of Truth and Reconciliation Commissions around the world, see Priscilla B. Hayner, *Unspeakable Truths: Transitional Justice and the Challenge of Truth Commissions* (Taylor & Francis, 2010).

29. See Janette Ballard, producer, BBC London. On Mar. 4–6, 2006, the BBC aired *Facing the Truth*, a three-part television series about victims and perpetrators in the conflict of Northern Ireland. Also see Sean Coughlan, "The Go-Between," *BBC News Magazine*, February 27, 2006.

30. M. K. Gandhi, quoted in *Truthseeker*, M. K. Gandhi Institute of Nonviolence, 9, no. 1 (Feb.–Mar. 2002): 7.

31. Tutu, "Violent Storm Will Lead to Calm," Tutu's Message of Peace on front page of *Cape Times*, Sept. 2, 1993.

32. It is interesting that Augustine said that justice was nothing but robbery on a large scale. Conditions of just war are also in *Summa Theologica* of Aquinas: Legitimate authority by due and solemn warning, self-defense, restoration of justice, punishment for justice, a just cause (end result will justify evil means).

33. Tutu, addresses, "Violence and the Church," June 1987.

34. Jean Bethke Elshtain, "A Just War?," *Boston Globe*, Oct. 6, 2002.

35. Bishop Pierre W. Whalon, "Confronting Iraq II: A Moral Justification for Going to War," *New York Times*, Opinion, Nov. 14, 2002. Episcopal Bishop Pierre Whalon is in charge of the Convocation of American Churches in Europe.

36. John Allen (Tutu's media secretary), "Re-entry of the 'Meddlesome Priest,'" *Sunday Tribune*, June 28, 1992.

37. Allen, "Re-entry."

38. Allen, "Re-entry."

39. Toby Helm, "Anti-apartheid Hero Attacks Former Prime Minister over 'Double Standards on War Crimes,'" *The Guardian*, Sept. 2, 2012.

40. Tutu, "Why I Had No Choice but to Spurn Tony Blair: I Couldn't Sit with Someone Who Justified the Invasion of Iraq with a Lie," *The Guardian*, Sept. 1, 2012.

41. Tutu, "Why I Had No Choice."

42. https://www.iraqbodycount.org/database/.

43. https://dod.defense.gov/News/Casualty-Status/.

44. Tutu, "Why I Had No Choice."

45. Tutu, "Why I Had No Choice."

46. Tutu, "Why I Had No Choice."

47. Tutu, "Violence and the Church."

48. Tutu, "Freedom Fighters or Terrorists?," in *Theology & Violence: The South African Debate*, ed. Charles Villa-Vicencio (Johannesburg: Skotaville, 1987), 77; Tutu, "Violence and the Church."

49. Tutu, "Foreword," in *A Gift of Peace*, ed. John Hartom and Lisa Blackburn, Imagine Render, Michigan Art Education Association.

50. Five criteria of Just War:

    1. **There must be a just cause.** Augustine believed there could only be a defensive war, but it could be aggressive if the aim was to restore what was taken unjustly. Luther was an Augustinian. For Calvin, war was a means to ensure peace and social stability, but if a ruler brought chaos, then rebellion against such a ruler was in order by a magistrate. Lastly, just cause includes the protection of the innocent, restoration of rights, and reestablishment of just order.

    2. **There must be a just end.** What is the likelihood of "success" of the war? Barth believed that where the community or person believes before God that the ultimate goal of war needs to be fought, the cost cannot be regarded as a decisive factor. Of course, blacks and whites would read costs and end differently. Simply put, this criterion means that a just end involves having peace

and justice as a goal, rather than mere vengeance or satisfaction of the lust of power.

3. **Just means ought to be used.** Restraint of weapons, minimizing of suffering and death and the atrocities of war are in order. This is the most difficult criteria to put into practice.

4. **War must be a last resort.**

5. **War must be declared by a legitimate authority.** Yet Augustine, Aquinas, Luther, and Calvin agree that the time comes when the tyrant should no longer be obeyed; if the will of God, the tyrant should be removed. But Charles Villa-Vicencio asks the important question, who is responsible for this removal?

51. Tutu, "Violence and the Church."

52. Tutu, draft of Foreword for 1993 Children of War Peace Calendar, War Resisters League, Mar. 13, 1992.

53. Tutu, "Freedom Fighters or Terrorists?," 73–74.

54. Stanley Hauerwas, "The End of Just War: Why Christian Realism Requires Non-violence," *ABC Religion & Ethics*, Apr. 26, 2016. https://www.abc.net.au/religion /the-end-of-just-war-why-christian-realism-requires-nonviolence/10097052.

55. Tutu, "Violence and the Church."

56. Tutu, "Freedom Fighters or Terrorists?," 76.

57. Tutu, "Postscript: To Be Human Is to Be Free," in *Christianity and Democracy in Global Context*, ed. John Witte Jr. (Boulder, CO: Westview, 1993), 314.

58. *Weekly Mail* article, quoted in Villa-Vicencio, *Civil Disobedience and Beyond: Law, Resistance, and Religion in South Africa* (Grand Rapids: Eerdmans, 1990), 99.

59. Tutu, undated speech, "Preamble" at Whit's University; Tutu, undated speeches, "The Evolution of Apartheid," 1985–86; Tutu, undated handwritten address, "Why We Must Oppose Apartheid," Grahamstown.

60. Tutu, Undated Handwritten Speeches and Addresses, "Koinonia II."

61. Tutu, "Violence and the Church."

62. Catherine Ingram, *In the Footsteps of Gandhi: Conversations with Spiritual Social Activists* (Berkeley: Parallax Press, 1990), 279.

63. Tutu, "Violence and the Church."

64. Tutu, handwritten undated address, "Conscientious Objection," before court martial.

65. Tutu, "Freedom Fighters or Terrorists?," 72.

66. Tutu, "God's Strength in Human Weakness," in *Your Kingdom Come, Papers and Resolutions of the Twelfth National Conference of the South African Council of Churches, Hammanskraal, May 5–8, 1980.*

67. Tutu, "Violence and the Church."

Chapter 11: Unifying Role of Confessor

1. Tutu, "God's Strength in Human Weakness," in *Your Kingdom Come, Papers and Resolutions of the Twelfth National Conference of the South African Council of Churches, Hammanskraal, May 5–8, 1980.*

2. Tutu, "Towards Koinonia in Faith, Life and Witness," World Council of Churches Faith and Order Conference, Santiago de Compostela, Spain, Aug. 3, 1993, 3.

3. Tutu, "Towards Koinonia," 4.

4. Tutu, "Towards Koinonia," 4.

5. Tutu, "Towards Koinonia," 4–5.

6. Tutu, "Towards Koinonia," 12.

7. For Emile Durkheim, 1858–1917, individualism in Western society is undeniable and culminates in his notion of the "cult of the individual" that transfers a false sense of a composite solidarity in society.

8. Tutu, in https://news.un.org/en/story/2013/07/445552-un-unveils-free-equal
   -campaign-promote-lesbian-gay-bisexual-transgender-rights.
9. LGBTQ are the initials for lesbian, gay, bisexual, transgender, and queer. Other
   distinctions are LGBTI (lesbian, gay, bisexual, transgendered, and intersexed).
   These initials are adopted by the majority of sexuality and gender identity-based
   communities. They are intended to emphasize a diversity of sexuality and gender
   identity-based cultures.
10. Tutu, undated address, "Suffering and Witness."
11. Zimbabwean Church Council Condemns Homosexuality (ACNS).
12. Zimbabwean Church Council Condemns Homosexuality (ACNS).
13. Tutu, in "Archbishop Tutu 'would not worship a homophobic God,'" *BBC
    News*, July 26, 2013, https://www.bbc.com/news/world-africa-23464694.
14. Also see Tutu's video on YouTube in which he says apartheid and homophobia
    are on the same scale. https://www.youtube.com/watch?v=a2PEfZvthxg.
15. Tutu, address, "Doing Theology in a Divided Society," Contextual Theology
    Hammanskraal, May 19, 1983.
16. Weil, *Gravity and Grace* (New York: Putnam, 1952), 129.
17. E. W. F. Tomlin, *Simone Weil* (New Haven, CT: Yale University Press, 1954), 50.
18. Tutu, handwritten notes, undated.
19. Tutu, "My Credo," in *Living Philosophies: The Reflections of Some Eminent Men
    and Women of Our Time*, ed. Clifton Fadiman (New York: Doubleday, 1990),
    236.
20. Simone Weil, *Gravity and Grace*, trans. Arthur Wills (Lincoln: The University of
    Nebraska Press, 1997), 94.
21. Tomlin, *Simone Weil*, 60.
22. Tutu, "Birmingham Cathedral Address," 3.
23. Tutu, "Birmingham Cathedral Address," 49.
24. Tutu, handwritten address (at top has Preachers Licensing, St. George's Cathe-
    dral, Nov. 22, 1988? marked out).
25. Tutu, "South Africa's Blacks: Aliens in Their Own Land," *Christianity and Crisis*
    (Nov. 26, 1984), 133–34.
26. Tutu, "South Africa's Blacks," 133–34.
27. https://www.bbc.com/news/world-africa-36462240.
28. https://www.theguardian.com/world/2016/jun/09/mpho-tutu-van-furth-its
    -painful-to-step-down-from-my-priestly-ministry.
29. Mpho Tutu, in https://www.theguardian.com/world/2016/jun/09/mpho-tutu
    -van-furth-its-painful-to-step-down-from-my-priestly-ministry.
30. Mpho Tutu, in Justine Lang, "Mpho Tutu: Choosing between the Church and
    Being Gay," June 9, 2016, BBC News. https://www.bbc.co.uk/news/world
    -africa-36462240.
31. Lang, "Choosing."
32. Lang, "Choosing."
33. See the Minutes of the 1989 Provincial Synod of the CPSA (Agendum 25),
    38–40, and the Synod Ditaba (June 5, 1989).
34. Louise Kretzschmar, "The Relevance of Feminist Theology within the South
    African Context," in Denise Ackermann, Jonathan A. Draper, and Emma Mash-
    inini, eds., *Women Hold Up Half the Sky: Women in the Church in Southern Africa*
    (Pietermaritzburg, South Africa: Cluster Publications, 1991), 106–21.
35. Wilma Jacobsen, "Women and Vocation: The 'If' Question," in Ackermann et
    al., *Women Hold Up Half*. Also see Hilda Bernstein, *For Their Triumphs and for
    Their Tears: Women in Apartheid South Africa* (Cambridge, MA: International
    Defense & Aid Fund, 1975).
36. Interview with John Allen, Tutu Travel Seminar in Cape Town, Aug. 13, 2017.

37. Tutu quoted in Michael Craske, "There Are No Outsiders: Desmond Tutu," Anglican Communion News Service, Feb. 27, 2004; https://www.anglicannews .org/news/2004/02/there-are-no-outsiders-desmond-tutu.aspx.
38. Tutu, quoted in Craske, "There Are No Outsiders."
39. For an important compilation of South African women theologians see "Being Woman, Being Human," in Ackermann et al., *Women Hold Up Half.*
40. Also see, Mary Daly's analysis in *Beyond God the Father: Toward a Philosophy of Women's Liberation* (Boston: Beacon, 1973), 13.
41. Ackermann et al., *Women Hold Up Half,* 98.
42. Ackermann et al., *Women Hold Up Half,* 100.
43. Tutu, handwritten sermons, at St. Philip's, Washington, DC, Christmas III, 1984.
44. Tutu, handwritten sermons, at St. Philip's, Washington, DC, Christmas III, 1984.
45. John Milton, *Paradise Lost: A Poem in Twelve Books*, 2nd ed. (London: S. Simmons); retrieved Jan. 8, 2017, via Internet Archive, 5:860.
46. Tutu, "Preface," in *To Reap a Whirlwind?*, a collection of essays in a book scientifically describing what it means to be born into an apartheid society, when Tutu was bishop of Johannesburg, Mar. 20, 1986.
47. Ross Dunn, "A Loud, Strong Voice for Peace," *Age*, Melbourne, Oct. 4, 1993.
48. Tutu, "Introduction," in *Icarus* 2 (Spring 1991) (New York: Rosen Publishing Group).
49. Tutu, "Postscript: To Be Human Is to Be Free," in *Christianity and Democracy in Global Context*, ed. John Witte Jr. (Boulder, CO: Westview, 1993), 317.
50. Tutu, "Alternatives to Apartheid," *The Gilbert Murray Memorial Lecture* (Oxford: Oxfam, 1990), 15.
51. Kairos Document—Challenge to the Church (Braamfontein: Skotaville, 1986).
52. See *Book of Confessions*, study edition, revised (Louisville, KY: Westminster John Knox, 2017). This now includes the Confession of Belhar.
53. https://www.latimes.com/archives/la-xpm-1989-03-14-me-500-story.html.
54. John D. Battersby, "Main White Church in South Africa Says Apartheid Is Sinful," *New York Times*, Mar. 11, 1989.
55. Battersby, "Main White Church."

Chapter 12: Confessor and Absolution

1. John de Gruchy, *Apartheid Is a Heresy*, ed. John de Gruchy and Charles Villa-Vicencio (Grand Rapids: Eerdmans, 1983), 82.
2. For such criteria of Christian heresy, see J. W. C. Wand, *The Four Great Heresies* (London: A. R. Mowbray, 1961). Also see G. C. Berkouwer, *The Church* (Grand Rapids: Eerdmans, 1976).
3. *The Cloud of Unknowing and Other Works*, trans. Clifton Wolters (New York: Penguin Books, 1987), 198–99.
4. *The Cloud of Unknowing*, 212.
5. Tutu, quoted in review of Rex Brico, *Taizé, Brother Roger and His Community*, in *Journal of Theology for Southern Africa* 36 (1980).
6. "James H. Cone, a Founder of Black Liberation Theology, Is Dead at 79," *New York Times*, Apr. 30, 2018, New York edition, A18.
7. Tutu, "Black and African Theologies: Soul-Mates or Antagonists?," in *Black Theology: A Documentary History, 1966–1979*, ed. G. Wilmore and J. Cone (New York: Orbis, 1981).
8. It is important to say here, however, that Cone in his later years of theology also began to emphasize the spiritual life.

9. Tutu, "Whither African Theology?," in Edward Fasholé-Luke et al., *Christianity in Independent Africa* (London: Rex Collings, 1978).

10. Athanasius, *The Life of Antony and the Letter to Marcellinus*, The Classics of Western Spirituality, trans. and intro. by Robert Gregg (New York: Paulist Press, 1980), 30.

11. Maggie Ross, *The Fountain and the Furnace: The Way of Tears and Fire* (New York: Paulist, 1987), 23.

12. Tutu, handwritten sermon, text Mark 2:13–17, Durbanville, Christmas 6, 1987.

13. Athanasius, *Life of Antony*, 31.

14. Tutu, "Postscript: To Be Human Is to Be Free," in *Christianity and Democracy in Global Context*, ed. John Witte Jr. (Boulder, CO: Westview, 1993), 318.

15. Amina Chaudary, "Interview with Desmond Tutu, Archbishop of Cape Town," *Muslim World* 100 (Jan. 1, 2010).

16. Chaudary, "Interview with Desmond Tutu."

17. Tutu, "Spirituality: Christian and African," in *Resistance and Hope: South African Essays in Honour of Beyers Naudé*, ed. Charles Villa-Vicencio and John de Gruchy (Cape Town: David Philips, 1985), 163.

18. Tutu, address, "On Being the Church in the World," Cape Town, Oct. 13, 1981.

19. Tutu, *No Future without Forgiveness* (New York: Doubleday, 1999).

20. Michael Battle, *Ubuntu: I in You and You in Me* (New York: Seabury, 2009).

Chapter 13: Sage Years

1. https://www.theguardian.com/world/2010/jul/22/archbishop-desmond-tutu-retires.

2. https://www.theguardian.com/world/2010/jul/22/archbishop-desmond-tutu-retires.

3. Tutu, "Human Rights in South Africa," SACC Library Resource Center, undated.

4. Tutu, *No Future without Forgiveness* (New York: Doubleday, 1999), 285.

5. John Allen, interview at Fire and Ice Hotel, Cape Town, Desmond Tutu Center Travel Seminar, Aug. 13, 2017.

6. Tutu, The Inaugural Desmond Tutu Peace Lecture, Funda Centre Diepkloof—Soweto, published by the World Conference on Religion and Peace South African Chapter, Sept. 14, 1985.

7. Gerrie Lubbe, president, SA chapter, World Conference on Religion and Peace, Sept. 14, 1985, Johannesburg.

8. https://theelders.org/about.

9. https://www.theelders.org/who-we-are.

10. https://theelders.org/about.

11. Tutu, "Church Leaders' Meeting, Koinonia."

12. Tutu, handwritten address, "Jesus and the Justice of the Kingdom of God," undated.

13. Tutu, "General Secretary's Report to National Conference of the SACC," 1983.

14. Tutu, "Towards Koinonia in Faith, Life and Witness," World Council of Churches Faith and Order Conference, Santiago de Compostela, Spain, Aug. 3, 1993, 3.

15. Tutu, handwritten sermon, "Christmas 7," St. George's Cathedral, Grahamstown, 1987.

16. Gen. 1:28.

17. https://www.nytimes.com/1993/02/09/world/nobel-laureates-rallying-to-burmese-s-cause.html.

18. Tutu, "Burma as South Africa," in *Far Eastern Economic Review* 156, no. 37 (Sept. 16, 1993): 23.

19. Tutu, quoted in Naaman Zhou and Michael Safi, "Desmond Tutu Condemns Aung San Suu Kyi: 'Silence Is Too High a Price,'" *The Guardian*, Sept. 8, 2017. https://www.theguardian.com/world/2017/sep/08/desmond-tutu-condemns -aung-san-suu-kyi-price-of-your-silence-is-too-steep.

20. Aung San Suu Kyi, quoted in Rebecca Ratcliffe, "Who Are the Rohingya and What Is Happening in Myanmar?," *The Guardian*, Sept. 5, 2017. https://www.theguardian.com/global-development/2017/sep/06/who-are-the-rohingya-and-what-is-happening-in-myanmar.

21. Tutu, quoted in https://twitter.com/TheDesmondTutu/status/905835225 518931970; Zhou and Safi, "Tutu Condemns."

22. Tutu, quoted in Alison Flood, "Dalai Lama and Desmond Tutu Collaborate on Book of Joy," *The Guardian*, Apr. 15, 2015.

23. Kgalema Motlanthe, quoted in David Smith, "Desmond Tutu Uses 80th Birthday to Berate ANC over Dalai Lama Visa Snub," *The Guardian*, Oct. 7, 2011.

24. Willie, a so-called colored man from South Africa, photographer from *The Argus*, told me in 1993 this vision by "beautiful" Navaho Indian man who told this to Willie upon arriving in the United States. After sharing this reflection, the Navaho man said to Willie, "Go and enjoy my country."

Conclusion: How Can Tutu Retire from God?

1. For Tutu on the Old Testament see, "Some African Insights and the Old Testament," in *Relevant Theology for Africa: Report on a Consultation of the Missiological Institute at Lutheran Theological College, Mapumulo, Natal, September 12–21, 1972*, ed. Hans-Jurgen Becken (Durban: Lutheran Publishing House, 1973); and Tutu, "South African Insights and the Old Testament," *Journal of Theology for Southern Africa* 1 (Dec. 1972).

2. Tutu, quoted in Chris Shannahan, "Desmond Tutu Was Right: As the UK General Election Campaign Heats Up, Who Says Politics and Religion Don't Mix?," *Open Democracy*, May 29, 2017. https://www.opendemocracy.net/en /transformation/desmond-tutu-was-right/.

3. Bernard of Clairvaux, *On the Song of Songs*, 4 vols. (Kalamazoo, MI: Cistercian, 1971–80), Sermons 57, 58. Thomas Merton explains this point as follows: "Indeed, the mystical marriage must bring forth children to the Spouse, that is, souls to the mystical life. But since the faculties cannot give themselves to the work of preaching and the care of souls when they are completely absorbed in the fruition of the highest graces of union, there must remain even in the mystical marriage some alternation between the pure love of God in himself and love of God through our fellow men" (*Thomas Merton on St. Bernard*, ed. Jean Leclerq [Kalamazoo, MI: Cistercian, 1980], 218). This way of relating love of God to neighborly love is very similar to that defended by Augustine.

4. Evelyn Underhill, *The Essentials of Mysticism and Other Essays* (London: Dent, 1920), 23, For an interesting analysis of the relation between mysticism and ethics, see Grace M. Jantzen, "Ethics and Mysticism: Friends or Foes?," *Nederlands Theologisch Tijdschrift* 39 (1985): 314–26.

5. Irving Singer, *Nature of Love 1* (Chicago: University of Chicago Press, 1984), 220.

6. Bernard of Clairvaux, *Song of Songs,* Sermon 71.

7. Teresa of Avila, *The Book of Her Life*, chap. 18, "Works," 108.

8. Jantzen, "Ethics and Mysticism," 307.

9. Tutu, "1994 Darwin Lecture Series, Change in Southern Africa," Cambridge University, Feb. 25, 1994.

10. Tutu, quoted in electronic *Telegraph*, www.telegraph.co.uk, Apr. 27, 2001.

Today, Archbishop Tutu has found an equilibrium of wellness and continues to work on the international scene.

11. See my commentary on the Revelation. Michael Battle, *Heaven on Earth: God's Call to Community in the Book of Revelation* (Louisville, KY: Westminster John Knox, 2017).

12. https://www.apnews.com/6790b4b52dd71b6c0e4a5c83a94e6143.

13. "Gay Rights: What's the Agenda?," *USA Weekend*, Feb. 28–Mar. 2, 1997.

14. Tutu, undated address, "Suffering and Witness."

15. All quotes from Dante are found in Dante Alighieri, *The Divine Comedy*, trans. John Sinclair (New York: Oxford University Press, 1961).

16. Tutu, address, "Apartheid and Christianity," Sept. 24, 1982. This is a powerful speech given by Tutu.

17. Tutu, address, "Blacks and Liberation," South African Indian Congress, Mar. 29, 1982.

18. Tutu, "Grace upon Grace," *Journal for Preachers* 15, no. 1 (Advent 1991): 20–21.

19. Mogomotsi Magome and Andrew Meldrum, "South Africa's Inequalities Exposed by Virus, Says Leader," *AP News*, April 27, 2020, https://apnews.com/article/55028ce4285870c6cd19bd4c3ffa2f2e.

20. Anli Serfontein, "Coronavirus Is Not a European Problem, Says Archbishop of Cape Town," *Church Times*, March 20, 2020, https://www.churchtimes.co.uk/articles/2020/20-march/news/world/coronavirus-is-not-a-european-problem-says-archbishop-of-cape-town.

21. "Shining Lights—Arch & Leah Tutu!" Desmond and Leah Tutu Legacy Foundation, accessed November 25, 2020, https://www.tutu.org.za/stories/shining-lights-arch-leah-tutu/; see also Episcopal News Service, "Tutu, Southern Africa Bishops Issue Unprecedented Joint Statement on Coronavirus," March 17, 2020, https://www.episcopalnewsservice.org/2020/03/17/tutu-southern-africa-Bishops-Issue-Unprecedented-Joint-Statement-on-Coronavirus-2/.

22. Tutu, "God Bless South Africa," *Vrye Weekblach*, Sept. 20–26, 1991. Tutu's Prayer at closing of National Peace Convention.

Chronology

1. Bernard Spong et al., *Come Celebrate* (Johannesburg: South African Council of Churches, 1993), 18f. Also see archives of official documents in library of SACC, Johannesburg.

2. SACC document, SACC archives, 17.

3. SACC, 17.

4. Desmond Tutu—Nobel Symposia. Nobel Media AB 2019. Apr. 4, 2019. https://www.nobelprize.org/prizes/peace/1984/tutu/symposia/.

5. John Allen, *Rabble-Rouser for Peace: The Authorized Biography of Desmond Tutu* (London: Rider, 2006), 388.

6. Steven Gish, *Desmond Tutu: A Biography* (Westport, CT: Greenwood Press, 2004), 166.

7. Jeremy Cooke, "Tutu in Anti-Guantanamo Theatre," BBC News, Oct. 2, 2004. Archived from the original on May 25, 2018, retrieved Jan. 23, 2008.

8. "Tutu Calls for Child Registration," BBC News, Feb. 22, 2005. Archived from the original on Oct. 7, 2013, retrieved Jan. 23, 2008.

9. "Desmond Tutu: A Dignified Death Is Our Right—I Am in Favor of Assisted Dying," *The Guardian*, July 12, 2014. Archived from the original on Jan. 5, 2018, retrieved May 14, 2017.

Selected Bibliography

Ackermann, Denise. "The Role of Women in the Church—Certain Practical Theological Perspectives." In *Sexism and Feminism in Theological Perspective*, edited by W. Vorster, 61–83. Pretoria: UNISA, 1984.

———. "Women, Violence and Theology." In *Theology and Violence: The South African Debate*, edited by Charles Villa-Vicencio, 255–70. Johannesburg: Skotaville, 1987.

Allen, John. *Rabble-Rouser for Peace: The Authorized Biography of Desmond Tutu.* London: Rider, 2006.

Balcomb, Tony. *Third Way Theology: Reconciliation, Revolution and Reform in the South African Church during the 1980s.* Pietermantzburg: Cluster, 1993.

Battle, Michael. "The Ubuntu Theology of Desmond Tutu." In *Archbishop Tutu: Prophetic Witness in South Africa*, edited by Leonard Hulley, Louise Kretzschmar, and Luke Lungile Pato, 93–105. Cape Town: Human & Rousseau, 1996.

———. *Reconciliation: The Ubuntu Theology of Desmond Tutu.* Cleveland: Pilgrim, 1997.

Baum, Gregory, and Harold Wells, eds. *The Reconciliation of Peoples: Challenge to the Churches.* Maryknoll, NY: Orbis, 1997.

Biko, Nkosmathi. "Amnesty and Denial." In Villa-Vicencio and Verwoerd, *Looking Back, Reaching Forward*, 193–98.

Boraine, Alex, Janet Levy, and Ronet Scheffer, eds. *Dealing with the Past: Truth and Reconciliation in South Africa.* Cape Town: Idasa, 1993.

Botha, Nico, Klippies Kritzinger, and Tinyiko Maluleke. "Crucial Issues for Christian Mission—A Missiological Analysis of Contemporary South Africa." *International Review of Mission* 81, no. 328 (Jan. 1994): 21–36.

Botman, Russel, and Robin M. Petersen, eds. *To Remember and to Heal: Theological and Psychological Reflections on Truth and Reconciliation.* Cape Town: Human & Rousseau, 1996.

Chidester, David. *Shots in the Streets: Violence and Religion in South Africa.* Oxford: Oxford University Press, 1992.

Connor, Bernard F. *The Difficult Traverse: From Amnesty to Reconciliation.* Pietermantzburg: Cluster, 1998.

De Gruchy, John W. "Guilt, Amnesty and National Reconstruction: Karl Jaspers' *Die Schuldfrage* and the South African Debate." *Journal of Theology for Southern Africa* no. 83 (June 1993): 3–13.

Dowdall, Terry. "Psychological Aspects of the Truth and Reconciliation Commission." In Botman and Petersen, *To Remember and to Heal*, 27–36.

Frost, Brian. *Struggling to Forgive: Nelson Mandela and South Africa's Search for Reconciliation.* London: HarperCollins, 1998.

Harper, Charles. *Impunity, An Ethical Perspective: Six Case Studies from Latin America.* Geneva: WCC, 1996.

Hay, Mark. *Ukubuyisana: Reconciliation in South Africa.* Pietermantzburg: Cluster, 1998.

Jacques, Genevieve. *Beyond Impunity: An Ecumenical Approach to Truth, Justice and Reconciliation.* Geneva: WCC, 2000.

James, Wilmot, and Linda Van der Vijver, eds. *After the TRC: Reflections on Truth and Reconciliation in South Africa.* Cape Town: David Philip, 2000.

Krog, Antjie. *Country of My Skull.* Cape Town: Random House, 1998.

Magona, Smdiwe. *Mother to Mother.* Cape Town: David Philip, 1998.

Maluleke, Tinyiko S. "Black Theology Lives on a Permanent Crisis." *Journal of Black Theology in South Africa* 9, no. 1 (1995): 1–30.

———. "Black and African Theologies in the New World Order: A Time to Drink from Our Own Wells." *Journal of Theology for Southern Africa* no. 96 (Nov. 1996): 3–19.

———. "Do I, with My Excellent PhD, Still Need Affirmative Action? The Contribution of Black Theology to the Debate." *Missionaha* 24, no. 3 (Nov. 1996): 303–21.

———. Book review of Botman and Petersen, *To Remember and to Heal: Theological and Psychological Reflections on Truth and Reconciliation. Missionaha* 25, no. 1 (Apr. 1997): 136–38.

———. "The 'Smoke-Screens' Called Black and African Theologies: The Challenge of African Women Theology." *Journal of Constructive Theology* 3, no. 2 (Dec. 1997).

———. "Christianity in a Distressed Africa: A Time to Own and Own Up." *Missionaha* 26, no. 3 (Dec. 1998): 324–40.

———. "The Truth and Reconciliation Discourse: A Black Theological Evaluation." In *Facing the Truth: South African Faith Communities and the Truth Commission,* edited by J. Cochrane, J. de Gruchy, and S. Martin, 101–13. Cape Town: David Philip, 1999.

———. "The South African Truth and Reconciliation Discourse." In *Democracy and Reconciliation: A Challenge for African Christianity,* edited by L. Magesa and Zeblon Nthambun, 215–41. Nairobi: Acton, 1999.

———. "Sechs Thesen zum Sudafrikanischen Experiment der Versöhnung und innergesellschaftlichen Vergebung (social forgiveness)." *Ökumenische Rundschau* no. 4 (Oct. 2000): 457–63.

———. "The Rediscovery of the Agency of Africans." *Journal of Theology for Southern Africa* no. 108 (Nov. 2000): 19–37.

———. "The Quest for Muted Black Voices in History: Some Pertinent Issues in (South) African Mission Historiography." *Missionaha* 28, no. 1 (Apr. 2000): 41–61.

Mbeki, Thabo. *Africa, The Time Has Come.* Tafelberg: Mafube, 1998.

McCullum, Hugh. *The Angels Have Left Us: The Rwanda Tragedy and the Churches.* Geneva: WCC, 1994.

Mkhize, Hlengiwe. "Truth and Justice for Peace: Healing the Memories of the Apartheid Experience—Lessons from the Truth and Reconciliation Commission in South Africa." Paper read at an international seminar on building peace from the roots, Zurich, Switzerland, Oct. 27–31, 1997.

Mofokeng, Takatso. "Reconciliation and Liberation." In *Cry Justice,* edited by J. de Gruchy. London: Collins Liturgical Publications, 1986.

Mosala, Itumeleng. "The Meaning of Reconciliation." *Journal of Theology for Southern Africa* no. 59 (June 1987): 19–25.

———. "Jesus in the Parables: Class and Gender Readings." *Journal of Black Theology in South Africa* 8, no. 2 (Nov. 1994): 142–47.

———. "Spirituality and Struggle: African and Black Theologies." In *Many Cultures, One Nation: Festschrift for Beyers Naudé*, edited by Charles Villa-Vicencio and Carl Niehaus. Cape Town: Human & Rousseau, 1995.

Muller-Fahrenhholz, Geiko. *The Art of Forgiveness: Theological Reflections on Healing and Reconciliation.* Geneva: WCC, 1996.

Nuttal, Sarah, and Carli Coetzee. *Negotiating the Past: The Making of Memory in South Africa.* Cape Town: Oxford University Press, 1998.

On, Wendy. *From Biko to Basson.* Cape Town: Contra Press, 2000.

Pauw, Jacques. *Into the Heart of Darkness: Confessions of Apartheid's Assassins.* Johannesburg: Jonathan Ball, 1997.

Petersen, Robin M. "The Politics of Grace and the Truth and Reconciliation Commission." In Botman and Petersen, *To Remember and to Heal,* 57–64.

Pityana, Barney, and Charles Villa-Vicencio, eds. *Being Church in South Africa Today.* Johannesburg: SACC, 1995.

Ross, Fiona. "Existing in Secret Places: Women's Testimony in the First Five Weeks of Public Hearings of the Truth and Reconciliation Commission." Unpublished paper read at University of Cape Town conference on "Faultiness," July 1996.

Ross, Maggie. *The Fountain and the Furnace: The Way of Tears and Fire.* New York: Paulist Press, 1987.

SACC. *Confessing Guilt in South Africa: The Responsibility of the Churches and Individual Christians.* Johannesburg: SACC, 1989.

Shriver, Donald W. *An Ethic for Enemies: Forgiveness in Politics.* Oxford: Oxford University Press, 1995.

Smit, Dirkie J. "The Truth and Reconciliation Commission: Tentative Religious and Theological Perspectives." *Journal of Theology for Southern Africa* no. 90 (Mar. 1995): 31.

———. "Confession-Guilt-Truth-and-Forgiveness in the Christian Tradition." In Botman and Petersen, *To Remember and to Heal,* 96–117.

Soyinka, Wole. *The Burden of Memory, The Muse of Forgiveness.* Oxford: Oxford University Press, 1999.

Statutes of the Republic of South Africa. *Constitutional Law 1995 Promotion of National Reconciliation Act No 34 1995* 801.

Storey, Peter. "Until Our Whole Nation Feels the Victim's Pain and Atones for Past Evils, Every Sacrifice Will Have Been in Vain." *Sunday Independent,* Apr. 21, 1996, 4.

"The TRC Puzzle Starts to Fall into Place." *Truth Talk,* the official newsletter of the Truth and Reconciliation Commission 1, no. 1 (Nov. 1996): 2, 7.

Tutu, Desmond. *An African Prayer Book.* New York: Doubleday, 1995.

———. "African Theology and Black Theology: The Quest for Authenticity and the Struggle for Liberation." In *African Challenge*, edited by Kenneth Best. Nairobi: Trans Africa Publishers, 1973.

———. "Afterword." In *Christianity amidst Apartheid: Selected Perspectives on the Church in South Africa*, edited by Martin Prozesky. New York: St. Martin's Press, 1990.

———. "Apartheid: An Evil System." In *The Anti-Apartheid Reader*, edited by David Mermelstein. New York: Grove, 1987.

———. "An Appreciation of the Rt. Revd Trevor Huddleston, CR." In *Trevor Huddleston: Essays on His Life and Work*, edited by D. D. Honoré. Oxford: Oxford University Press, 1988.

———. Article to honour M. M. Thomas's 75th birthday, a collection of essays focusing on the reformulation of a new theological methodology from different perspectives shaped by James Cone by Orbis Books, New York. Tutu is to write on Spirituality. In Tutu's 2 June 1988 letter he said he would do his best to send something by the end of 1988.

———. "Barmen and Apartheid." *Journal of Theology for Southern Africa* no. 47 (June 1984).

———. "The Basic Paradigm Must Be the Family." In *A Democrative Vision for South Africa: Political Realism and Christian Responsibility*, edited by Klaus Nürnberger. Pietermaritzburg: Encounter Publications, 1991.

———. "The Best for Our Family." *The Living Pulpit* 2, no. 1 (1993): 25.

———. "The Bias of God." *The Month: A Review of Christian Thought and World Affairs*, November 1989.

———. "Black and African Theologies: Soul-Mates or Antagonists?" In *Black Theology: A Documentary History, 1966–1979*, edited by G. Wilmore and J. Cone. New York: Orbis, 1981.

———. "Black Theology." *Frontier* 17, no. 2 (1974): 73–76.

———. "Black Theology/African Theology—Soul Mates or Antagonists?" *Journal of Religious Thought* 32, no. 2 (1975).

———. "Blacks and Liberation." South African Indian Congress, Mar. 29, 1982.

———. "The Blasphemy That Is Apartheid." *Africa Report* 28, no. 4 (1983): 4–6.

———. "Burma as South Africa." *Far Eastern Economic Review* 156, no. 37 (Sept. 1993).

———, and Mpho Tutu. *The Book of Forgiving: The Fourfold Path for Healing Ourselves and Our World*. London: William Collins Publishing, 2014.

———. "Called to Unity and Fellowship." In *The Church and the Alternative Society: Papers and Resolutions of the Eleventh Conference of the SACC*, edited by M. Nash. Johannesburg: SACC, 1979.

———. "Catholics in Apartheid Society." *International Bulletin of Missionary Research* 8, no. 2 (1984): 78–79.

———. "The Centrality of the Spiritual." Undated address, General Theological Seminary, New York.

———, et al. "The Christian and the X." With Bishop Charles Albertyn, Bishop Geoffrey Quinlan, Bishop Edward Mackenzie, and Bishop Merwyn Castle, flier put out by Diocesan Organisers for Voters Education (DOVE), Cape Town, 1993.

——— "A Christian Vision of the Future of South Africa." Essay submitted to be published in *Christianity in South Africa*. Submitted to Prof. Martin Prozesky, University of Natal, July 31, 1989.

———. "Christmas Letter 1." 1985–1986.

———. "The Church and Human Rights in South Africa." Handwritten address, University of South Africa, Centre for Human Rights, May 18, 1992.

———. "Church and Nation in the Perspective of Black Theology." *Journal of Theology for Southern Africa* no. 15 (1976).

———. "Church and Prophecy in South Africa Today." In *Essex Papers in Theology and Society* (Center for the Study of Theology in the University of Essex, 1991).

———. "Clarifying the Word! A Sermon by Desmond Tutu." Jim Wallis interview. In *Crucible of Fire: The Church Confronts Apartheid*, edited by Jim Wallis and Joyce Hollyday. Maryknoll, NY: Orbis, 1989.

———. "Cold Comfort Confronted." *Theology* 76, no. 636 (1973): 328–30.

———. *Crying in the Wilderness*. Grand Rapids: Eerdmans, 1982.

———. "Deeper into God—Spirituality for the Struggle." Jim Wallis interview. In *Crucible of Fire: The Church Confronts Apartheid*, edited by Jim Wallis and Joyce Hollyday. Maryknoll, NY: Orbis, 1989.

———. "The Divine Intention." Presentation by Bishop D. Tutu, general secretary of the South African Council of Churches to the Eloff Commission of Enquiry on Sept. 1, 1982. Braamfontein: SACC Publications, 1982.

———. Draft of Article mailed to *Woord en Daad* (*Word and Action*), June 24, 1991.

———. "The Education of Free Men." In *Apartheid in Crisis*, edited by Mark A. Uhlig. New York: Vintage Books, 1986.

———. Essay on Justice to be published in *Living Pulpit*, sent on July 17, 1992.

———. "Faith." In *The New World Order*, edited by Sundeep Waslekar. New Delhi: Konark Publishers, 1991.

———. "Fleshly Love." *The Other Side* 40, no. 4 (2004): 16–17.

———. "Foreword." In Anthony Heard, *The Cape of Storms: A Personal History of the Crisis in South Africa*. Fayetteville: University of Arkansas Press, 1990.

———. "Foreword." Draft for 1993 Children of War Peace Calendar, War Resisters League, Mar. 13, 1992.

———. "Foreword." In *Dramatic Play: The Life of Steve Biko*.

———. "Foreword." In *A Gift of Peace*, edited by John Hartom and Lisa Blackburn. Imagine Render, Michigan Art Education Association.

———. "Foreword." In *The Green Bible: Understand the Bible's Powerful Message for the Earth*. New York: HarperCollins, 2008.

———. "Foreword." In *I Was Lonelyness: The Complete Graphic Works of John Muafangejo*. Cape Town: Struik Winchester, 1992.

———. "Foreword." Letter draft of foreword for *I Will See You in Heaven Where Animals Don't Bite*, by Michael Seed. Westminster, London: St. Paul Publications, September 17, 1990.

———. "Foreword." For *Independent Churches and Movements in Southern Africa*, edited by G. C. Oosthuizen and H. J. Becken, faxed Apr. 28, 1994.

———. "Foreword." In *Nelson Mandela: The Man and the Movement*, by Mary Benson. New York: W. W. Norton, 1986.

———. "Foreword." In *The Politics of Love: Choosing the Christian Way in a Changing South Africa*, by Michael Cassidy. London: Hodder & Stoughton, 1991.

———. "Foreword." In *The Politics of Peace*, by Brian Frost. London: Darton, Longman & Todd, 1991.

———. "Foreword." In *Poor Man, Rich Man: The Priorities of Jesus and the Agenda of the Church*, by Peter Lee. London: Hodder & Stoughton, 1986.

———. "Foreword." In *Sing Freedom! Songs of South African Life*, edited by Margaret Hamilton. London: Novello, 1993.

———. "Foreword." In *South Africa the Cordoned Heart*, edited by Omar Badsha. Cape Town: The Gallery Press, 1986.

———. "Foreword." In *Soweto: Portrait of a City*, photography by Peter Magubane, text by Avid Bristow and Stan Motjuwadi. Cape Town: Struik Publishers, 1990.

———. "Foreword." In *Turning Points in Religious Studies: Essays in Honour of Geoffrey Parrinder*, edited by Ursula King. Edinburgh: T. & T. Clark, 1990.

———. "Foreword." In *World Winds: Meditations from the Blessed of the Earth*, edited by Earl and Pat Hostetter Martin. Scottdale, PA: Herald Press, 1991.

———. "Foreword." In *The Worshipping Church in Africa*, a special issue of *Black Sacred Music: A Journal of Theomusicology* 7, no. 2 (Fall 1993). Durham, NC: Duke University Press, 1993.

———. "Franciscan Vocation." Submitted with July 30, 1991, letter for the American Province of the Society of St. Francis Provincial Publication *The Little Chronicle*.

———. "Freedom Fighters or Terrorists?" In *Theology & Violence: The South African Debate*, edited by Charles Villa-Vicencio. Johannesburg: Skotaville Publishers, 1987.

———. "Fulfilling the Dream." *The Catholic Worker* 53 (1986): 1.

———. *Geen Vrede Met Apartheid, Nobelprijsrede 1984 en andere Texten. Uitverij Jan Mest, Werkgroep.* Amsterdam: Kairos, 1985.

———. "God and Nation in the Perspective of Black Theology." *Journal for Theology for Southern Africa* 15 (1976).

———. "God—Black or White?" *Ministry* 11, no. 4 (1971).

———. "God-Given Dignity and the Quest for Liberation." Paper to the National Conference of the SACC, July 1973. Reprinted from *Ecunews*, Aug. 4, 1976, in *African Perspectives on South Africa: A Collection of Speeches, Articles and Documents*, edited by Hendrik W. van der Merwe, Nancy C. J. Charton, D. A. Kotzé, and Åke Magnusson, 325. Cape Town: David Philip Publisher, 1978.

———. "God-Given Dignity and the Quest for Liberation in the Light of the South African Dilemma." In *Liberation: Papers and Resolutions for the Eighth National Conference of the SACC*, edited by D. Thomas. Johannesburg: SACC, 1976.

———. *God Has a Dream: A Vision of Hope for Our Time*. London: Rider, 2005.

———. "God Intervening in Human Affairs." *Missionalia* 5, no. 2 (1977).

———. *God Is Not a Christian: And Other Provocations*. New York: HarperOne, 2011.

———. "The God of Surprises." In *A Democratic Vision for South Africa: Political Realism and Christian Responsibility*, edited by Klaus Nürenberger. Pietemaritzburg: Encounter Publications, 1991.

———. "God of the Oppressed." *Journal of Theology for Southern Africa* 31 (1980): 73–74.

———. "God's Dream." In *Waging Peace II: Vision and Hope for the 21st Century*, edited by David Krieger and Frank Kelly. Chicago: The Nobel Press, 1992.

———. "God's Love." *Tradition and Unity: Sermons Published in Honour of Robert Runcie*, edited by Dan Cohn-Sherbok. London: Bellew Publishing, 1991.

———. "God's Strength in Human Weakness." In *Your Kingdom Come, Papers and Resolutions of the Twelfth National Conference of the South African Council of Churches, Hammanskraal, May 5–8, 1980.*

———. "Grace upon Grace." *Journal for Preachers* 15, no. 1 (Advent 1991).

———. "Greetings." In *The Future of Liberation Theology: Essays in Honor of Gustavo Gutiérrez*, edited by Marc H. Ellis and Otto Maduro. Maryknoll, NY: Orbis, 1989.

———. "Greetings from Bishop Tutu to the Soweto Students, June 16, 1977." *Pro Veritate*, June 1977.

———. "Hope against Despair." In *A Book of Hope*. Cape Town: David Philip Publishers, 1992.

———. *Hope and Suffering*. Grand Rapids: Eerdmans, 1984.

———. "Hope That South Africa May Be on Path to Reconciliation." In *Chronicle Zimbabwe*, May 13, 1993.

———. "How Can You Say You Love God Whom You Have Not Seen When You Hate Your Brother Whom You Have Seen? *Engage/Social Action* 13 (1985): 18–19.

———. "Human Rights in South Africa." In *Monitor*, SACC Library Resource Center, undated.

———. *In God's Hands: The Archbishop of Canterbury's Lent Book 2015*. London: Bloomsbury, 2014.

———. Interview. Warick Beutler interviews Tutu for Parliament of the Commonwealth of Australia, Department of the Parliamentary Library, May 2, 1984.

———. Interview. "The Blood of the Lamb." *Leadership: For Reconciliation and Reconstruction* 12, no. 3 (1993).

———. Interview. "The Church in Africa: Interview with Archbishop Desmond Tutu." In Charles Villa-Vicencio, *Challenge: Church and People* no. 12 (Feb. 1993).

———. Interview. "A Conversation with Desmond Tutu." *St. Louis Post Dispatch*, July 25, 1993.

———. Interview. "Racism. We Need a Prophet," James S. Murray interview, *The Australian*, May 10, 1984.

———. Interview. In *Dispensations: The Future of South Africa as South Africans See It*, by Richard John Neuhaus. Grand Rapids: Eerdmans, 1986.

———. Interview. *The Guardian*, London, Aug. 11, 1986.

———. Interview. In *In the Footsteps of Gandhi: Conversations with Spiritual Social Activists*, by Catherine Ingram. Berkeley: Parallax Press, 1990.

———. Interview. In *The Rise of Christian Conscience: The Emergence of a Dramatic Renewal Movement in the Church Today*, edited by Jim Wallis. San Francisco: Harper & Row, 1987.

———. "Into a Glorious Future." *Sojourners*, Feb. 1985.

———. "Introduction." *Icarus* 2, Spring 1991.

———. "Introduction." In *Marx-Money-Christ: An Illustrated Introduction into Capitalism, Marxism and African Socialism—Examined in the Light of the Gospel*, edited by O. Himer. Gweru, Zimbabwe: Mambo Press, 1982.

———. "Introduction." In *We Are Anglicans: An Introduction to the Church of the Province of Southern Africa*, edited by Michael McCoy. Marshalltown: CPSA, 1993.

———. "It Has Happened at Last." Endpiece for book to mark election and end of apartheid. *The Guardian*, London.

———. "Jesus before Christianity: The Gospel of Liberation." *Journal of Theology for Southern Africa* 19 (1977): 68–69.

———. "The Jesus I Love." In *Star Sun*, Aug. 20, 1992.

———. "Lament from Africa." In *Praying for Peace: Reflections on the Gulf Crisis*, edited by Michael Hare Duke. London: Fount Paperbacks, 1991.

———. Letter, March 8, 1982, to Helen Muller in response to teach "The Old Testament" at the Academy for Christian Living.

———. Letter. Handwritten draft of letter to the Rev. Canon Malusi Mpumlwana and Mpho Tutu. In *Made for Goodness: And Why This Makes All the Difference*. New York: HarperOne, 2010.

———. "Mass Action—for a Better Sense of Values." *NCW News*, Jan. 1993.

———. "Mission in the 1980s." *Occasional Bulletin of Missionary Research* 4, no. 1 (1980): 12–13.

———. "Mission in the 1990s." *International Bulletin of Missionary Research* 14, no.1.

———. "Momentous Choice, Without Us." *Los Angeles Times*, Mar. 20, 1992.

———. "My Credo." In *Living Philosophies: The Reflections of Some Eminent Men and Women of Our Time*, edited by Clifton Fadiman. New York: Doubleday, 1990.

———. "The New World Order." Paper in absentia. The International Foundation for Socio-Economic and Political Studies, Moscow Conference, July 14–15, 1992.

———. *No Future without Forgiveness*. New York: Doubleday, 1999.

———. "Not Alone: A Story for the Future of Rhodesia." *Theology* 76, no. 636 (1973): 328–30.

———. "On Behalf of Millions: A Sermon of Thanksgiving." *Sojourners*, Feb. 1985.

———. "On Being the Church in the World," Address, Cape Town, Oct. 13, 1981.

———. "Opening Worship." In *The Road to Rustenburg*, edited by Louw Alberts and Frank Chikane. Cape Town: Struik Christian Books, 1991.

———. "The Options Which Face South Africa: Real Political Power Sharing or a Bloodbath." In *Divided or United Power: Views on the New Constitutional Dispensation by Prominent South African Political Leaders*, edited by J. A. du Pisani. Johannesburg: Lex Patria Publishers, 1986.

———. "Pastoral Letter to Anglicans in South Africa." Lent 1994.

———. "Persecution of Christians under Apartheid." In *Martyrdom Today*, edited by Johannes-Baptist Metz and Edward Schillebeeckx. Edinburgh: T. & T. Clark and New York: Seabury, 1983.

———. "The Plight of the Resettled and Other Rural Poor: The Stand of the Church." In *Up Against the Fences: Poverty, Passes and Privilege in South Africa*, edited by Hermann Giliomee and Lawrence Schlemmer. Cape Town: David Philip, 1985.

———. "Postscript: To Be Human Is to Be Free." In *Christianity and Democracy in Global Context*, edited by John Witte Jr. Boulder, CO: Westview, 1993.

———. "A Prayer for Peace." In *Prayers for Peace: An Anthology of Readings and Prayers*, compiled by Robert Runcie and Basil Hume. London: SPCK, 1987.

———. "Preface." For a booklet in support of a Global Peace Service. Published by the Swedish Ecumenical Council, Aug. 30, 1991.

———. "Preface." In *Festo Kivengere: A Biography*, by Anne Coomes. Eastbourne, E. Sussex: Monarch Publications, 1990.

———. "Preface." In John Hartom and Lisa Blackburn, *Imagine/Reader: Gift of Peace*. Michigan Art Education Association, 1990.

———. "Press Statement—For Khotso," Nov. 26, 1981.

———. "The Processes of Reconciliation and the Demand of Obedience." *Transformation* 3, no. 2 (1986): 3–8.

———. Quoted in review of Rex Brico, *Taizé, Brother Roger and His Community. Journal of Theology for Southern Africa* 36 (Sept. 1980): 80.

———. *The Rainbow People of God: The Making of a Peaceful Revolution.* Edited by John Allen. New York: Doubleday, 1994.

———. The Rainbow People of God: The Ministry of Desmond Tutu as Anglican Archbishop of Cape Town. First Manuscript: Speeches, sermons, writings, off-the-cuff remarks and interviews reflecting South Africa's path from the depths of oppression to the euphoria and confusion of transition. Draft of John Allen, ed.

———. "The Religious Understanding of Peace." First Desmond Tutu Peace Lecture by Bishop Desmond Tutu. Krugersdorp: WCRP-SA, 1985.

———. Reply, Nov. 7, 1991, to Publication Request. In *Fondest Hopes/Deepest Concerns: Lessons from the 20th Century*, edited by Neal Sperling, unpublished.

———. "Restoring Justice." *The Tablet* 258, no. 8525 (2004): 13–14.

———. Review of J. H. Cone and G. S. Wilmore, eds., *Black Theology: A Documentary History, Vol. I, 1966–1979.* Maryknoll, NY: Orbis, 1981. *Journal of Theology for Southern Africa* no. 46 (1984).

———. Review of James Cone, *God of the Oppressed. Journal of Theology for Southern Africa* no. 31 (June 1980).

———. "Review of J. Mbiti, *The Prayers of African Religion*." *Journal of Theology for Southern Africa* 17 (1976).

———. "Sanctions vs. Apartheid." Adapted from Commencement Address at Hunter College, New York. *New York Times*, June 16, 1986.

———. Selected Prayers. In *Prayers, Praises, and Thanksgivings*. Compiled by Sandol Stoddard, art by Rachel Isadora. New York: Dial Books, 1992.

———. Selected Quotes. In *Freedom Is Coming: Songs of Protest and Praise from South Africa*. Uppsala: Utryk, 1984.

———. Selected Quotes. In *The Meaning of Life: Reflections in Words and Pictures on Why We Are Here*, edited by David Friend. Chicago: The Time Inc. Magazine, 1991.

———. Selected Quotes. In *Tips from the Top: Wise and Witty Words from Well-Known South African Personalities*, compiled by Oliver M. Souchan. Cape Town: Don Nelson, 1988.

———. Selected Quotes. In "Vision of the Future: An Anthology of Writings and Speeches of Nelson Mandela, Winnie Mandela, Allan Boesak, Desmond Tutu." *Third World Quarterly* 9, no. 2 (Apr. 1987).

———. Selected Quotes. In *The Words of Peace: Selections from the Speeches of the Winners of the Nobel Peace Prize*, edited by Irwin Abrams. New York: Newmarket, 1990.

———. Sermon. St. George's Cathedral, Pentecost 18, 1987.

———. Sermon. Handwritten. "Quiet Day: Why Be Silent?" Text: Mark 6:30ff. Durbanville, January 2, 1987.

———. Sermon. Handwritten, Text Mark 2:13–17, Durbanville, Christmas 6, 1987.

———. "Some African Insights and the Old Testament." In *Relevant Theology for Africa: Report on a Consultation of the Missiological Institute at Lutheran Theological College, Mapumulo, Natal, September 12–21, 1972*, edited by Hans-Jurgen Becken. Durban: Lutheran Publishing House, 1973.

———. "Some Memories of My Life." Draft of June 28, 1990, to be published in King's College London's *In Touch* magazine featuring famous alumni.

———. "South Africa: A World Apart: An Urgent Message from Bishop Desmond Tutu to Presbyterian Women." *Concern*, Oct. 1984.

———. "The South African Council of Churches on Namibia." *International IDOC Bulletin* 1982, no. 7 (1982): 18–21.

———. "The South African Elections." *Der Zeit*, May 1, 1994.

———. "South African Insights and the Old Testament." *Journal of Theology for Southern Africa* 1 (Dec. 1972).

———. "South African Violence: Ours Are Birthing Pains—Tutu." *Daily Nation*, Nairobi, Kenya, Oct. 9, 1993, 16.

———. "South Africa's Blacks: Aliens in Their Own Land." *Christianity and Crisis*, Nov. 26, 1984.

———. "Spirituality: Christian and African." In *Resistance and Hope: South African Essays in Honour of Beyers Naudé*, edited by Charles Villa-Vicencio and John de Gruchy. Cape Town: David Philips, 1985.

———. "The State of South Africa." Interview, in *Monitor: The Journal of the Human Rights Trust*, June 1991.

———. "The State of South Africa." *Africa Forum* 2, no. 1 (1992).

———. "Stop the Rot Everybody." *City Press*, Mar. 14, 1993.

———. "Tearing People Apart." *South African Outlook*, Oct. 1980.

———. "The Theologian and the Gospel of Freedom." In *The Trial of Faith: Theology and the Church Today*, edited by Peter Eaton. West Essex: Churchman Publishers, 1988.

———. "The Theology of Liberation in Africa." In *African Theology en Route, Pan African Conference of Third World Theologians, Accra, Ghana*, edited by Kofi Appiah-Kubi and Sergio Torres. Maryknoll, NY: Orbis, 1979.

———. "This Is Now My Country." *The Argus*, May 3, 1994.

———. "Towards Post-Apartheid South Africa." In *Religion and Politics in Southern Africa*, edited by Carl Fredrik Hallencreutz and Mai Palmberg. Uppsala: The Scandinavian Institute of African Studies, Seminar Proceedings, Nov. 24, 1991.

———. "Troubled but Not Destroyed." Unpublished presidential address, All Africa Conference of Churches, seventh general assembly, Addis Ababa, Oct. 1997.

———. "Ubuntu." *Catholic Worker* 69, no. 2 (2002): 5.

———. "The United States and South Africa: Human Rights and American Policy." *Columbia Human Rights Law Review* 17, no. 1 (Fall 1985).

————. "Viability." In *Relevant Theology for Africa: Report on a Consultation of the Missiological Institute at Lutheran Theological College, Mapumulo, Natal, September 12–21, 1972,* edited by Hans-Jurgen Becken. Durban: Lutheran Publishing House, 1973.

————. "A View from South Africa." In *Robert Runcie: A Portrait by His Friends,* edited by David L. Edwards. London: Fount Paperbacks, 1990.

————. "Violent Storm Will Lead to Calm." Tutu's Message of Peace on front page of *Cape Times,* Sept. 2, 1993.

————. "Wall of Fire." *Trinity Seminary Review* 7, no. 1 (1985): 17–24.

————. "The WCC's Major Contributions—A Testimony." In *Commemorating Amsterdam 1948: 40 Years of the World Council of Churches.* Geneva: WCC, 1988.

————. "Welcome and Introduction." Draft for WCC Central Committee Meeting in Johannesburg. In *International Review of Mission,* Jan. 1994.

————. "Whither African Theology?" In *Christianity in Independent Africa,* edited by Edward Fasholé-Luke et al. London: Rex Collings, 1978.

————. "Whither Theological Education? An African Perspective." *Theological Education* (South Africa), Summer 1973.

————. *The Words of Desmond Tutu.* Selected by Naomi Tutu. New York: Newmarket Press, 1989.

"Tutu Arranges Watershed Talks." *The Argus,* June 7, 1993.

"Tutu Condemns 'Racist Tactics.'" *Cape Times,* April 18, 1994.

"Tutu: A Mandate from God." Tribute, Sept. 1988.

"Tutu, Mandela Clash over Parliament's Pay." *News & Observer,* Sept. 28, 1994.

"Tutu Pleads for Calm in Face of Attacks by 'Ghastly' Men." *The Argus,* April 25, 1994.

"Tutu Says Local Press Is White-Oriented." *Weekend Argus,* May 8/9, 1993.

"Tutu Warns 'Political' Priests." *Cape Times,* Apr. 14, 1994.

Villa-Vicencio, Charles. "On Taking Responsibility." In Botman and Petersen, *To Remember and to Heal,* 131–39.

————. "Reconciling Our People." *Sunday Times,* Feb. 23, 1997, 26.

Villa-Vicencio, Charles, and Wilhelm Verwoerd, eds. *Looking Back, Reaching Forward: Reflections on the Truth and Reconciliation Commission of South Africa.* Cape Town: University of Cape Town Press, 2000.

Volf, Miroslav. *Exclusion and Embrace: A Theological Exploration of Identity, Otherness, and Reconciliation.* Nashville: Abingdon, 1996.

West, Gerald. "Don't Stand on My Story: The Truth and Reconciliation Commission, Intellectuals, Genre, and Identity." *Journal of Theology for Southern Africa* no. 98 (July 1997): 3–12.

West, Gerald, and Jim Cochrane. "War, Remembrance and Reconstruction." *Journal of Theology for Southern Africa* no. 84 (1993): 25–40.

White, S., and R. Tiongco. *Doing Theology and Development: Meeting the Challenge of Poverty.* Edinburgh: Saint Andrew Press, 1997.

Index

Page numbers in italics refer to photos.